Laptop Music POWER!

THE COMPREHENSIVE GUIDE

John von Seggern

THOMSON
COURSE TECHNOLOGY
Professional ■ Technical ■ Reference

ISBN: 1-59200-822-4

Library of Congress Catalog Card Number: 2005924925

Printed in Canada

05 06 07 08 09 WC 10 9 8 7 6 5 4 3 2 1

THOMSON

COURSE TECHNOLOGY

Professional ■ Technical ■ Reference

Thomson Course Technology PTR, a division of Thomson Course Technology
25 Thomson Place
Boston, MA 02210
http://www.courseptr.com

Publisher and General Manager, Thomson Course Technology PTR:
Stacy L. Hiquet

Associate Director of Marketing:
Sarah O'Donnell

Manager of Editorial Services:
Heather Talbot

Marketing Manager:
Kristin Eisenzopf

Senior Editor and Acquisitions Editor:
Mark Garvey

Marketing Coordinator:
Jordan Casey

Developmental Editor:
Orren Merton

Project Editor:
Brian Proffitt

Technical Reviewer:
Steve Nalepa

Thomson Course Technology PTR Editorial Services Coordinator:
Elizabeth Furbish

Copyeditor:
Brian Proffitt

Interior Layout Tech:
Digital Publishing Solutions

Cover Designers:
Mike Tanamachi and Nancy Goulet

Indexer:
Katherine Stimson

Proofreader:
Carla Spoon

This book is dedicated to: my family (who have always wanted me to write a book about something!); Susan Mainzer, my constant inspiration; my DJ partner Stephen Ives; and my friends in the Cali laptop underground, constantly pushing the boundaries of music technology.

Acknowledgments

Special thanks to all those performers whose ideas and techniques are described in this book. I would also like to thank everyone I have learned from and studied with in the last few years as I have pursued the strange path of a computer musician: Stephen Ives, Dr. René T.A. Lysloff at the University of California–Riverside, Dr. Paul Attinello at the University of Hong Kong, and all my teachers at M-Audio: Calvin Banks, Roland Weihmayer, Alex Tinsley, Jess Macintyre, Chad Carrier, Jamii Leighton, Steve Nalepa, Craig Perkins, Raul Resendiz, and many others.

Thanks also to Aubrey Tang for her patience and support during these years.

Also special thanks to my editors at Course Technology for having the interest in this project in the first place and for their work in helping make this book a reality: Mark Garvey, Orren Merton, and Brian Proffitt.

About the Author

John von Seggern has worked in the international music industry for the past fifteen years as a bassist, computer DJ, producer, remixer, researcher, writer, and commentator. John has lived and worked in Tokyo, Hong Kong, and now Los Angeles, where he is currently employed by leading computer music technology company M-Audio (http://www.m-audio.com). John has been performing music live with computers since 1999 and has DJed techno electro jazz mixes on his laptop at numerous clubs and festivals in Asia and the US, often with some incarnation of his Hong Kong-based band Digital Cutup Lounge (http://www.digitalcutuplounge.com).

John is closely involved with the underground electronic music scene in California, performing frequently at clubs, parties, and events with his trusty Apple G4 iBook running Ableton Live 4.1. John also promotes and organizes multimedia digital art events in LA with Sariah Storm

(Native Instruments) and Steve Nalepa (M-Audio) as part of the Terpsichore Group (http://www.terpsichoregroup.org).

John holds two Master's degrees, in Music and Ethnomusicology, from the University of Hong Kong and the University of California-Riverside, and his approach in this book is closely informed by his anthropological training as an ethnomusicologist. In 2000, John's musical explorations led him to graduate school to investigate the intersections between music and rapidly accelerating advances in information technology. John is particularly interested in digital audio technologies and the power they give us to record, copy, mutate, and combine sounds, as well as to redistribute the results around the globe via the Internet.

Much of this book is written from John's own perspective as a professional musician (bassist, DJ, producer), watching first-hand as the use of computers has become more and more common in every corner of the global music industry.

TABLE OF Contents

Introduction

This book is meant to be both an introduction to using computers in live music performance, as well as an advanced practical guide to this growing area of modern music. More and more musicians and bands working in a wide variety of different musical styles are using computers and software as part of their live performance rigs these days, but there is little information available comparing the various possible hardware and software setups, the musical advantages and disadvantages of each, and how to get started using computers to perform your own music live. This book is meant to fill that gap.

It also features numerous interviews with contemporary performers who are using computers in genres ranging from experimental underground electronica to big-budget rock and pop, explaining how they use computers to perform their music and their exact equipment setups. In trying to give a taste of the widespread changes computers are bringing to live music performance, I have included many other voices besides my own in these pages, many of them active laptop performers in the California electronic music underground.

Although the primary focus of the book is on the *practical* side of how to use computers to perform live, I am also very interested in the deep changes that computers and the Internet are bringing to the process of music creation and how this is affecting our relationship with music more generally. In addition to my own reflections on these topics, scattered throughout the book, I also tried to explore this topic with the artists I interviewed.

1 Using Computers Live!

Computers in Today's Live Music Scene

In 1999, when I first started using a laptop computer to play live on DJ gigs in Hong Kong, it was rare to see someone using a computer in a concert or nightclub setting. As I began to play more frequently at clubs, DJ bars, art galleries, and dance parties, members of the audience frequently approached the DJ booth in disbelief and asked if we were really using computers to play the music and why. The first couple of times our newly formed computer band, Digital Cutup Lounge, played, even I was thinking that it was a bit strange (and somehow very geeky) to be on stage fiddling around with my Mac laptop while an audience watched.

One patron entered a small DJ bar where we were playing very late one night. The man walked straight up to my partner Stephen as he was playing some downtempo tracks on his beat-up PC laptop, and stopped directly in front of him. Seemingly intoxicated and looking bewildered, the man studied my partner for quite a long time as Stephen cued up and played a succession of tracks with his PC and a pair of DJ headphones (see Figure. 1.1). Finally the man couldn't stand it any longer and loudly blurted out, "WHAT THE &$!# ARE YOU DOING WITH THAT COMPUTER??!!"

These days, however, more and more performers are using computers live in a variety of musical contexts. Sometimes the computers are behind the scenes, such as the Mac G5s that Mike McKnight uses to run the pre-recorded music sequences that power Madonna's live concerts, while in other cases the computer takes center stage as an instrument, as in this recent televised European performance by Beijing-based laptop duo fm3 (see Figure 1.2).

It is increasingly common for the computer to play a variety of different musical roles as well. In addition to being used as a replacement for turntables or a hard disk recorder, more and more often we see the computer being used as a synthesizer module (running a software application), an effects processing unit (using processing software such as Native Instruments' Guitar Rig), or a mixing console. The possibilities are limited only by the software being used.

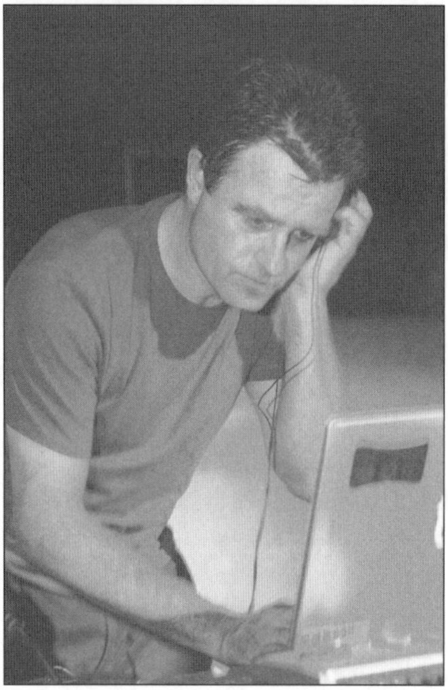

Figure 1.1 My partner Stephen Ives DJing with his PC laptop.

Figure 1.2 Zhang Jian and Christiaan Virant of fm3 performing live in Utrecht, Holland.

This book will introduce you to a variety of ways that a computer can be used live as a musical performance tool. However, before diving into the nuts-and-bolts descriptions of various live computer music setups and how to use them, let's have a quick look at just a few of the diverse performance situations where we might hear a computer being used live.

Underground Electronic Music in Los Angeles: Scenes from a Revolution

The portability of laptop music setups means that events can be held nearly anywhere that can hold a sound system. Here in California, a relative glut of private spaces has led to a wide variety of alternative venues being used for computer music performances. I have attended electronic music gigs here in warehouses, lofts, hangars, private clubs, downtown alleyways, and the middle of the Mojave Desert.

Live at the Blue Bongo with ELM Conceptions

Park your car on the street in front of a large Japanese Buddhist temple glimpsed by moonlight, and you have arrived at the Blue Bongo club in downtown Los Angeles (see Figure 1.3). It's 1 a.m. and the surrounding neighborhood of loft-style apartments and industrial buildings appears completely deserted. As you walk down the dark street and approach the club, you can see a few smokers talking on the corner in front of the main entrance and throbbing low waves of rhythm become distinctly audible.

How to describe this music to someone who's never heard it before? Rapid-fire shifting changing beats and breaks coupled with ultra-low subbass lines that seem to shake the entire building, periodically interrupted by pixelated explosions of postdigital noise. This must be the place: Another ELM Conceptions (http://www.elmconceptions.com) underground electronic music event in Los Angeles, this time featuring Phoenecia, Jega, Otto von Schirach, RD and Trichome of ELM, and Sariah Storm.

Figure 1.3 Little Pedro's Blue Bongo, downtown Los Angeles.

SARIAH STORM (Terpsichore Group, Los Angeles)

There are some signature things about ELM events that are the shining elements in crowning them some of the innovators of the experimental UNDERGROUND here in LA. First, it is the completely pitch black room—in my experience, the darker the better—pulsating with sound. I don't say music, I don't say beats. I say sound because that word encompasses the broad range of frequencies the artists showcased at these parties emit; pure, extraordinary sound. Next, you have the line of laptops on the stage, usually with one or two faces glowing in the artificial light beaming from the screen of a titanium laptop with a partially-eaten apple on its cover.

There's usually some extremely geeky visual architectures happening on a lit screen hanging above the stage. The lit screen is like a beacon in the darkness to somehow help you find the door without tripping on top of the many people rocking on the dance floor.

Steadying yourself by grabbing at one of the pillars around the edge of the dance floor for support, you look up at the main stage to see a pair of performers using laptop computers, triggering all the sonic mayhem by pointing and clicking on unseen software interfaces.

These are the organizers of tonight's event, computer DJs RD and Trichome of ELM Conceptions. Both of these well-known names in the California electronic underground started out as turntable DJs spinning vinyl, later switching to computers as the technologies improved. Now they use a pair of Mac laptops almost exclusively for their live sets. (We'll meet RD again in Chapter 8 on digital DJing.)

Not that long ago, computer performances in dance clubs were rare, limited mainly to the live electronic bands that used a computer to control racks of outboard gear. In the last few years, it has become more and more common to see the person in the DJ booth using a laptop computer to pump out the beats instead of records or CDs. A mini-industry has sprung up to meet the needs of mobile computer musicians, with companies such as M-Audio, Evolution, Echo, Hercules, and Edirol making interfaces and accessories specifically with laptop musicians and DJs in mind.

A very active scene of live computer music performers has developed here in Los Angeles in the last several years, working in electronic music genres such as techno, IDM, electro, and breakbeat. The scene has developed a healthy degree of competitiveness, with various local performers continually experimenting with different hardware and software approaches in their quest for new sounds, grooves, and textures. There are numerous live computer music events, and many local artists are releasing their own recordings on labels in the US and overseas (primarily in Europe). LA-based indie computer musicians with recent or upcoming recordings include Ken Gibson (eight frozen modules, [a]pendics.shuffle), Deru, RD, edIT, Dntel, Phthalocyanine, and Daedalus, among others. I interviewed many of these artists in the course of writing this book, and their thoughts about the future of music and technology are interspersed throughout.

The following chapters of this book explore many of these new performance techniques. I explain how to set up your computer and software in various ways for different styles of music and different musical approaches, with practical examples of live setups drawn from some well-known international performers as well as from some of my friends from the LA underground.

Outlaw Computing in the Mojave

Sariah Storm is my collaborator in the Terpsichore Group (http://www.terpsichoregroup.org) and one of LA's most innovative digital DJs. I pick her up at her house in Pasadena and we drive up to the desert together on a Saturday evening, I pick her up at her house in Pasadena and we go from there. We've got everything we need for the party: Extra warm clothes and blankets in case we go to sleep in the car later, flashlights and batteries, snacks and drinks. And of course, Sariah's laptop and other digital DJ gear (see Figure 1.4), her MIDI controller (an Evolution X Session), and audio interface (an M-Audio FireWire Audiophile). She is scheduled to play an IDM/experimental DJ set at around 2 a.m. when the party should be in full swing.

Figure 1.4 Sariah Storm DJing with laptop.

When we arrive, I park the car in the midst of a few dozen others and the two of us walk back towards the source of the music. As we reach the crowd and see some of our friends, the music changes and a new track comes on. "Wait a minute, I know this one," I say to Sariah, but where had I heard it before?

Then I remember—three years earlier, when I was still living in Hong Kong, I was browsing for information about new music on the Net one day and downloaded some sample MP3s from review site Epitonic.com (http://www.epitonic.com). I found a couple futuristic electro tracks from an artist named Dream Electric that I really liked and I started playing them in my DJ sets.

The music I was hearing now in the desert was one of those same tracks—and it turned out that the young computer artist spinning it was the original producer himself, Dream Electric, seen here in Figure 1.5. I had finally caught up with the creator in person, in the middle of the California desert, after playing his tracks so many times at nightclubs, art galleries, and festivals in Hong Kong.

Figure 1.5 Dream Electric.

I walk over behind his computer setup so I can take a closer look at what he is actually doing. He's using Native Instruments' popular DJ software Traktor, mixing a selection of his original tracks. He's not using a MIDI controller at all, but simply cueing up tracks with the trackpad on his Toshiba laptop, and running the sound out of his M-Audio Quattro audio interface straight to the PA mixer.

I later interviewed Dream Electric at an electronic music house party at his home back in LA and asked him more about his live setup. Since I had seen him play in the desert that night, he had had a number of power-related problems with his Toshiba machine and switched to using one of the new iMac G5s instead. (These are larger and heavier than even the biggest laptop, but because of their all-in-one design, they are still relatively portable compared to most desktop systems.) He was still using Traktor, but had also added an Evolution X Session MIDI controller to his live setup for better hands-on control of his DJ mixing. His musical approach remained consistent that night however, simply DJing a selection of his original electro and breaks with Traktor.

In my later interviews with other laptop music performers, I found that this was one of the most common approaches to performing a set of original electronic music. Many of the performers I spoke to felt that the time they had spent carefully arranging their tracks in their home studios would be wasted if they tried to take a more improvisational approach to performing live, and strongly preferred to DJ a set of their own finished tracks at their live gigs.

Live at Coachella 2005

I attended the 2005 Coachella Music and Arts Festival, held each spring at the Indio Polo Grounds in the Southern California desert, about a two-and-a-half-hour drive east of Los Angeles. The Coachella festival, one of the biggest music festivals in North America, is well known for showcasing some of the most innovative of today's musical artists. Coachella's programmers especially focus on rock, hiphop, and electronic music. At this year's festival, I was very interested to see how many of the top electronic and hiphop performers were using a compact laptop computer setup to perform live, and how well these performers were received by the festival audience. A few of the outstanding laptop performers I heard included Four Tet, M.I.A. and Diplo, and Matthew Dear, and each performed in a distinctly different style.

Four Tet

I had seen UK digital music experimentalist Four Tet perform live at the LA Knitting Factory a couple years before, and expected to hear another beautiful melodic set of chopped-up acoustic instrument samples and drum loops this time.

However, Kieran Hebden surprised me by rocking the tent with a far-out experimental live performance in which he twisted and tweaked various bits of material from his albums in some radical directions, using two laptops at once. The tempo sped up and slowed down drastically, sounds mutated and morphed into new shapes and forms, and the whole performance was completely improvisational and unpredictable. The crowd seemed to love it, though, especially when he went off for awhile on a flight of experimental fancy and then brought a slamming beat back in at just the right moment to rock the dance floor.

M.I.A./Diplo

Of all the artists at Coachella this year whose live performance involved a computer in some capacity, none drew a bigger crowd or a more enthusiastic reaction than Sri Lankan émigré rapper/singer Maya Arulpragasam, or M.I.A. as she is better known.

Maya has become quite well known in the past year for her Internet-only mixtape *Piracy Funds Terrorism, Vol. 1.*, as well as for her debut album *Arular*, both produced with American producer/DJ Diplo. The pair has made waves on the international music scene for their uniquely cosmopolitan global hiphop, which incorporates musical influences from Maya's native Sri Lanka as well as Jamaican dance hall and Brazilian *baile* funk rhythms courtesy of Diplo.

M.I.A. devastated the overflow Coachella crowd with a set of beats and rhymes from her album, backed by nothing but a single backup singer/rapper and Diplo mixing up the *baile* funk and dancehall beats on a Mac PowerBook G4 in the desert heat.

Matthew Dear

Young techno star Matthew Dear played an outstanding set at Coachella as well, showcasing his distinctive brand of funky glitchy noise techno with a set mixed on a PC laptop.

Dear's set of stripped-down beats and experimental noise was well received by the Sunday afternoon crowd and made an interesting contrast with the Chemical Brothers' mega-blowout the night before. Whereas the Chems were dwarfed on stage by their massive live performance rig, including a large mixing console and racks of outboard audio gear, Dear managed to get by just fine with nothing but a single computer, and in many ways, I found his set more interesting and enjoyable. (Then again, there's no accounting for taste....)

Programming Mega-Pop Concerts

Of course it is not only techno freaks in the California desert who are using computers and software for live music performance. The world's biggest pop artists have been using computers in some capacity for years to augment their live backing bands in concert and provide audiences with a concert experience that more closely resembles what they have already heard on the artists' own CDs.

Sequencing on Tour in Asia with Jacky Cheung and Andy Lau

When I was playing bass guitar on tour with various Asian pop artists in the mid-late '90s, we nearly always had a sequencer/programmer with us to control various sound effects, sampled loops, electronic percussion, and synthesizer parts from the original recordings. Before the use of laptop computers became widespread, a live programmer typically used a dedicated MIDI hardware sequencer such as one of Roland's MicroComposer series. This required taking an entire MIDI hardware setup along on tour, with the sequencer as well, or else using standard synths and modules, and renting the needed equipment locally for each concert. My first big pop tour was with Hong Kong star Jacky Cheung in 1995 (see Figure 1.6). At that time, programmer Fabio Carli used a Roland MC-500 sequencer to control an Akai S3000 sampler and a Roland JV-1080 synthesizer for most of the sequenced sounds, carrying only the disks for the MC-500 and the sampler himself, and renting these commonly-used hardware modules locally in each city we played.

Figure 1.6 The author with Hong Kong pop artist Jacky Cheung in London's Wembley Arena.

Working on singer/actor Andy Lau's concert tour in 1996-97, however, programmers Peter Kam and Joey Lo began using a tiny Macintosh laptop running Mark of the Unicorn's Performer MIDI sequencing software to control all of the outboard synths and samplers. Although some of the other programmers in Hong Kong still swore by the Roland MicroComposers for their rock-solid reliability and road-worthiness, Peter and Joey preferred running Performer on the Mac because it was much easier for them to see what they were doing on the Mac's large screen than on the MicroComposer's tiny digital readout. They could also easily edit and change the arrangements in Performer during rehearsal or even at a last-minute sound check if necessary, and even jump back and forth to different points in the arrangement during the live performance if the singer made a mistake, came in too soon, or jumped to the bridge instead of the chorus.

Using Computers on Madonna's Re-Invention Tour

These days, the world's biggest pop artists use multiple computers to control a variety of outboard gear that powers their live shows. In many cases, the master music sequence will also send MIDI sequencing data to the video and lighting techs as well, keeping every element of the performance in perfect sync with the action on stage.

Mike McKnight, programmer and synthesist on Madonna's Re-Invention tour, described his gear setup and working methods in an interview on the Mark of the Unicorn Web site from September 2004. (The original interview can be found at http://www.motu.com/newsitems/atnewsitem.2004-09-01.8308068605.) Mike has been the programmer on many of Madonna's major concert tours and in this interview, he describes the mix of software and hardware that he used for the performances on the Re-Invention tour:

- Three Apple Macintosh G5 tower computers running Digital Performer to run the main sequences for the entire show one runs the sequence and the other two are there for backup in case of a crash
- Two MOTU 1296 audio interfaces and four MOTU HD192 audio interfaces connected to the G5s
- Three MOTU Micro Express MIDI interfaces, one for each G5
- One MOTU MIDI Timepiece AV that serves as the master for the G5s and enables seamless switching between the 3 G5 rigs if necessary
- A custom-made 72 in/24 out switcher to switch between the audio for the three G5s
- A Brainstorm Distripilyzer to send time code to the video and lighting controllers
- One Apple Macintosh G4 laptop running Digital Performer hosting various virtual synths
- One MOTU 828mkII interface connected to the G4 laptop
- An additional MOTU MIDI Timepiece AV connected to the G4 laptop

Mike describes how he controlled Madonna's entire show running Digital Performer on the G5 Macs. Once he started the main sequence at the beginning of the show, the video and lights were activated and the sequence ran 45 minutes non-stop. Then there were seven or eight individual songs in the middle of the show, then another 30-minute-long non-stop sequence to close the show.

In addition to the extra backing tracks augmenting the live musicians, Mike actually had everybody's part for the entire show recorded in digital audio within Digital Performer running on his G5 setup. If the guitarist happened to get sick one night and couldn't do the show, Mike could just un-mute the guitar tracks when playing back the sequences in Performer and the parts would still be there during the concert.

Although not all parts were used simultaneously, even after trying to consolidate and compact the separate tracks, Mike still had 250 separate audio and MIDI tracks running in his main show sequence. Each of the three G5s ran a duplicate of the same main show sequence, to ensure that the show would not come crashing to an unexpected halt in the middle because of a computer error or hard disk crash. In the event of a crash on the main system, Mike could smoothly switch over to one of his backups with the audience hopefully none the wiser, although in practice he rarely had these kinds of computer problems with his setup.

However, this multiple-backup system also gave Mike more flexibility to compensate for the inevitable spontaneous changes that happen in live performance: "Madonna will sometimes forget that the whole show is on a strict timecode time line. She'll get excited and start talking to the crowd, and she won't come in singing when we're all expecting. When that happens, I instantly switch to my B system, get the A system back on track, and then switch back to the A system, while on my headset telling the video and lighting guys, 'Hey guys, time code is jumping back four bars, get ready!' When Madonna decides to add four bars to the intro, then we add four bars to the intro. That's just the way it has to be with a superstar. And this system gives me the flexibility to do these things on the fly, while at the same time feeding time code to the entire rest of the show."

Jason Halbert: Laptop Music Director for Kelly Clarkson

Jason Halbert (see Figure 1.7) is another Los Angeles laptop music performer, just like Dream Electric, and his working methods are in some respects very similar: He performs running Ableton Live on a laptop computer (an Apple G4 PowerBook), with an audio interface (an M-Audio FireWire 410) and MIDI controller (an Oxygen8 keyboard, also from M-Audio) attached. Yet he inhabits a rather different musical world than my friends in the LA underground.

Figure 1.7 Jason Halbert performs at NAMM 2005.

JASON HALBERT (Los Angeles)

Grammy-nominated producer and platinum-selling recording artist Jason Halbert's career has spanned from Nashville to London to Los Angeles. After landing in Los Angeles to serve as Music Director for Backstreet Boy Nick Carter's solo project, Jason was brought in by "American Idol" judge Randy Jackson to act as music director and keyboardist for Grammy-nominated Kelly Clarkson, Clay Aiken, Ruben Studdard, Justin Guarini, and more. His television appearances encompass The Tonight Show with Jay Leno, Saturday Night Live, Good Morning America, The Ellen DeGeneres Show, The Sharon Osbourne Show, The View, American Music Awards, Billboard Music Awards, Radio Music Awards, and Teen Choice Awards.
(From Halbert's online bio at http://www.m-audio.com/artists/en_us/JasonHalbert.html.)

As mentioned in his biography sidebar, Halbert has been the musical director and keyboardist for a number of top 40 pop music artists. However, in recent years he often leads the band with his laptop rather than a keyboard.

With Clarkson and other artists, Halbert uses Ableton's Live software to perform. Like Madonna's programmer Mike McKnight, Halbert runs a master audio sequence on his laptop computer that contains the full tracks of the songs, every part in the arrangement. He can mute or un-mute any or all of the sequenced tracks as needed, depending on how many live musicians are in the band for that particular performance. While Clarkson typically performs live with a full band, and Halbert only plays the extra tracks that the musicians are unable to play (such as percussion tracks or sound effects), he can play the entire arrangement from his computer if necessary.

At a recent mini-performance at the M-Audio booth at the NAMM (National Association of Music Merchants) show in Anaheim, California in January 2005, Clarkson sang a few songs backed only by Halbert, a guitarist, and a bassist. (You can watch a video of this performance online at http://www.m-audio.com/index.php?do=media.jason_kelly, in which Halbert gives a very clear description of how his live rig works.) For this performance, Halbert muted just the guitar and bass parts in his Live arrangement, leaving the musicians to play those parts live while the drums, synthesizers, and other sequenced parts played from his Mac.

Before it became possible to play the entire audio sequence of a pop arrangement from software running on a single laptop computer, pop music programmers would often use a hard disk recorder system to play back prerecorded backing tracks. Just like Mike McKnight with Madonna, though, Halbert uses audio sequencing software and a computer to provide the background vocals and other sequenced parts for Kelly Clarkson's live performances.

JASON HALBERT USES LIVE

To prepare for the live gigs, all the producers on the album sent Halbert their master sessions so he could make basic copies of all the individual files and import them into Live. Then he took Live into the rehearsal studio, where he taught the musicians their parts by soloing out tracks, pulling out the unnecessary ones, and finally arranging the song in linear mode. In the end, Halbert was left running eight channels of audio

> alongside the band, including two tracks of stereo loops, background vocals, keyboard samples, and more—essentially using Live like a hard disc recorder.

Halbert uses Live because it gives him a lot more flexibility in live performance than a prerecorded sequence: "Another great thing about Live is there's no lag time or latency if you're in a televised situation where a vocalist misses a cue and comes in a bar early on a chorus or something like that. If we were locked into hard disc recorders, then we would be stuck; we would have to re-tape. With Live, if I go to the next bar and just click on it, it waits in real time and then drops it in right on the beat."

(Quotes in this section taken from an interview with Jason Halbert on the M-Audio Web site http://www.m-audio.com/index.php?do=media.new&ID=8562b02e0407e733866420892a9497e4.)

Now that we've seen just a few of the many surprising places where a computer might turn up in the modern music scene, from the California desert to underground dance parties to massive pop concerts, let's move on to Chapter 2, a brief survey of the recent history of the music technologies used by the current generation of computer musicians.

2 The (Recent) History of Computers in Live Music Performance

Although the main focus of this book is on the practical aspects of how to use a computer and software in live music performance, first let's take a brief look at how we got where we are now. In this chapter, I will talk about how computers were used live in the '80s and '90s before the current trend towards laptop music performance started. I will also step back for a minute to consider the larger picture of the changes that computers have brought to the contemporary music world.

If you're not interested in a history lesson and you want to jump straight to the practical part of the book, you can go ahead and skip to the next chapter. If you can bear with me for a few pages though, let's consider the recent developments in music technology that have made possible the computer music performance scene of today.

Live Computer Music Starts in the '80s

As with many other innovations in music technology, the use of computers in live performance was first explored by composers and researchers at university music departments and institutes for research on computer/electronic music such as IRCAM in Paris, the *Institut de Recherche et Coordination Acoustique/Musique*. (For more on IRCAM, check their excellent Web site at http://www.ircam.fr.)

The first use of computers in the creation of music began as far back as the 1950s with the early work of Max Mathews, then an engineer at the Bell Telephone Laboratories in New Jersey, who began experimenting with programming mainframe computers to generate and manipulate sound. Mathews developed the first computer program capable of working with and editing sound in 1957, called MUSIC4. However, making music with this program and its successors in the early years was an extremely painstaking and time-consuming process, and completely unsuited for live performance.

> **RECORDING BLEEPS AND BLOOPS**
>
> Composing computer music used to mean laboring for months on a mainframe to produce a seemingly random assemblage of bleeps and bloops that would be taped and replayed in performance.
> (From http://www.wired.com/wired/archive/1.05/binary.beat.html?topic=music_sound&topic_set=newmedia.)

This was pretty much the situation for the next two and a half decades. From the '50s through the '70s, would-be computer music creators needed to have access to a hugely expensive mainframe computer and software system to write computer music. There were only a small number of universities and institutes around the world that had such systems at all, with IRCAM, the Columbia University Computer Music Center, Stanford University's CCRMA (Center for Computer Research in Music and Acoustics), and UC-Berkeley's CNMAT (Center for New Music and Audio Technologies) among the leading facilities.

Although there were isolated experiments in using computers live in this period, because of cost, lack of access, and other factors it wasn't until the 1980s that computers started to be used more widely in live performance in the academic music world. There were two crucial innovations in this period: The advent of cheaper and smaller computers (in particular the Apple Macintosh, first introduced in 1984) and the creation of the MIDI (Musical Instrument Digital Interface) protocol in 1983—the result of cooperation between a group of American and Japanese musical instrument manufacturers.

MIDI provided a standardized protocol by which computers and electronic musical instruments could communicate with each other, setting the stage for the incredible musical innovations to follow in the '80s and '90s. A single person could now control an entire room full of electronic gear from a single small computer system, using the various synthesizers and other MIDI devices like the instruments in an orchestra.

The MIDI standard also allowed for musical performances to be recorded as digital data, usually on a MIDI keyboard instrument, and then played back later. Instead of recording the sound of the performance as digital audio data (this would come later), MIDI recorded the musical aspects of the performance such as the notes played, their exact temporal sequence, how hard the notes were struck on the keyboard (the velocity), and so on. This also allowed for easy editing and rearranging of the music—any aspect of the recorded performance could be isolated and changed in the digital realm.

Following the introduction of the MIDI standard, numerous software programs were developed to work with MIDI data on the computer. The most significant of these early efforts is probably MAX (now often known as MAX/MSP), an object-oriented music programming environment that in many ways is more like a musical programming language than the kind of graphic interface-driven software we are more familiar with today. MAX was developed at IRCAM by programmer Miller Puckette and later further developed by David Zicarelli. It is now distributed and supported by San Francisco-based software company Cycling74 (http://www.cycling74.com), which continues to develop and extend the capabilities of the original software.

As an object-oriented language, MAX allows the user to create an entire virtual studio of custom-designed software objects that perform various musical functions. It also provides significant facility for interactive performance: Input from a live human performer can be received by the computer/software configuration, and then incorporated into the ongoing musical flow in a variety of complex ways. The computer can modify the audio input and output it again, or react to the input as a signal that triggers other musical events.

Although MIDI was designed as much for use in the studio as for live performance, it opened the door to all the innovations in live computer music that followed. Inexpensive computers and software and the MIDI protocol that enabled them to communicate with outboard hardware, such as synthesizers and samplers, were the two crucial innovations that enabled the further development of electronic and computer music performance as we know them today.

Live Sequencing in the '90s

As we saw in Chapter 1, computers have been used for live sequencing in pop and dance music since at least the early 1990s. Pop artists have long used hardware sequencers, and later computers, running MIDI sequencing software to control a variety of outboard gear including synthesizers, samplers, and drum machines. This equipment would augment the sound of their live backing band, providing sound effects, electronic drums, percussion, and synthesizer textures.

Some dance artists in the early '90s took a similar approach as well, using hardware and software MIDI sequencers for their live shows, controlling racks of studio gear and manipulating and mixing the output live. Live electronic bands such as Orbital, the Crystal Method, Electric Skychurch, and Skylab2000 became big draws on the '90s rave circuit because of their relatively improvisational approach to performing. While most dance acts either DJed live or simply played back pre-recorded material with little variation at live shows, these innovative acts worked out methods of using MIDI sequences and outboard gear to play a more truly "live" show, with no performance the same twice.

Digital Audio and Software-Based Performance in the Late '90s

The next wave of innovation in computer-based music performance technology came in the late 1990s with the move to live audio sequencing and software-based performing. A combination of technological factors came together in the late 1990s, which enabled the computer itself to take over the functions of all the outboard gear formerly attached to it.

One important development here was the replacement of hardware synthesizers, samplers, sequencers, effects, and mixers by software emulations, enabling a radical reduction in the amount of equipment necessary for a live performance. Some contemporary laptop performers are using setups quite similar conceptually to the sequencer with outboard audio and MIDI hardware rigs that were common in the early '90s (and are still used by some live electronic acts today). These days, however, each of the various hardware pieces has been replaced by a software counterpart. One of today's most popular software production tools, Propellerhead's Reason software, owes its commercial success in part to the accuracy of its simulation of a complete hardware studio, containing a mixer, synthesizer modules, samplers, drum machines, and effects. If we press the Tab key in Reason to flip the interface backwards, we can even see a colorful array of patch cables dangling between each of the various "hardware" modules we have connected (see Figure 2.1).

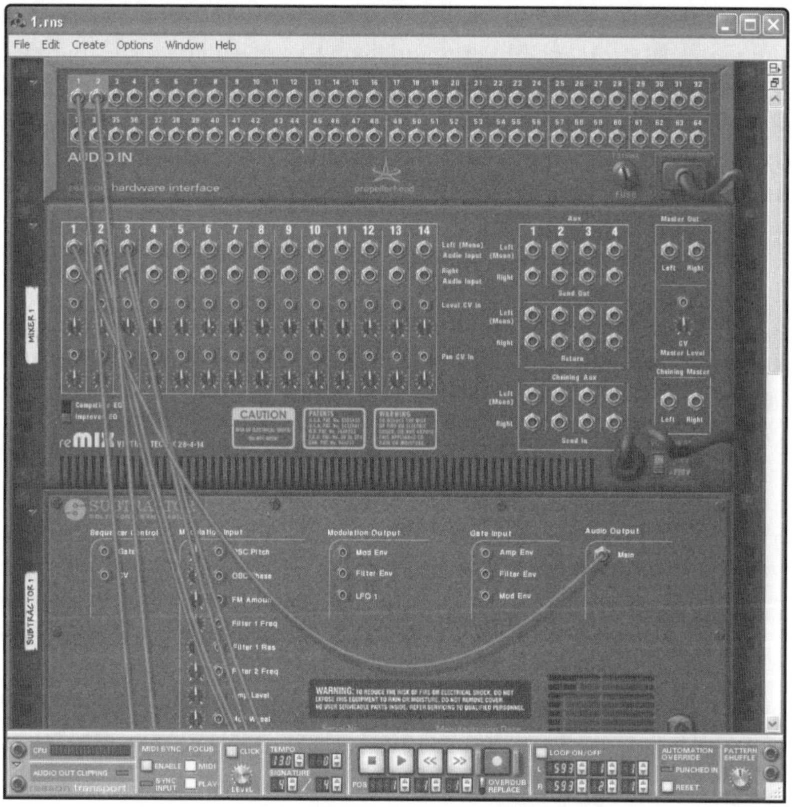

Figure 2.1 The back of Reason's "virtual console."

The other crucial technological developments that paved the way for the current crop of laptop-based performers were the general advances in computer speed, power, and hard disk storage capacity that enabled the recording and storage of digital audio on a computer. This made it possible to record and play back actual audio data from a computer system, rather than just MIDI data. Live audio sequencing and remixing then became a musical possibility, giving rise to a whole new set of possible performance paradigms.

These days, the new generation of laptop performers are able to perform with only a laptop computer, with perhaps a MIDI controller of some kind attached to control the devices on-screen, and a small portable audio interface that offers superior sound quality to the built-in sound hardware of a Mac or PC laptop.

The succeeding chapters of this book will describe various laptop-based performance setups in greater detail, together with practical tips and advanced techniques for getting the most out of a given setup. Before moving on, I will recap the recent development of these technologies by describing how I got started myself as a laptop performer/DJ.

I started performing live with my laptop computer early in 1999, when these developments in music technology were coming together to make live audio sequencing and processing with a computer a viable live performance option. I spent a lot of time in 1999-2000 exploring many different software approaches. Since new performance-oriented software for Mac and PC were being released regularly, it took quite some time before I could find software applications that could give me the results I desired. The different approaches I first tried out in the Chinese dance music scene around this time outline the recent history of these technologies, as the software and ideas rapidly circulated around the world via the Internet.

The Internet was the final piece of the puzzle, accelerating the exchange of software and ideas for playing live with a computer and making them available worldwide. Once the Internet had advanced to a certain point and we all had broadband Net connections, we could keep up with what was going on just as well as anyone else around the world.

Desperately Seeking Software in Hong Kong: Digital Cutup Lounge

I started my first laptop band, Digital Cutup Lounge (see Figure 2.2), in Hong Kong in August 1999. My partner Stephen Ives and I had gotten together previously a few times to work on tracks in our home studios, but DCL was our first attempt to establish a live project. We wanted to start a live electronic band to play at some of the many dance events in the very active Hong Kong club scene of the late '90s, but neither of us had much experience DJing with the traditional two-turntables-and-a-mixer setup typically used by dance artists, nor were we interested in breaking down our studios and bringing large racks of heavy equipment to each performance, as had been the norm among earlier electronic bands.

Figure 2.2 Digital Cutup Lounge: Stephen Ives (left) and the author (right).

Prior to starting this project with Stephen, I had played a couple club gigs with my Ztar MIDI controller (http://www.starrlabs.com) and a bank of synthesizers, improvising with house/techno DJ Teng Boon and electronic percussionist Neil Irwin, but the difficulty of transporting, setting up, and tearing down such a large and complex equipment setup had discouraged me from performing electronic music more frequently.

Stephen and I wanted to find a more compact live setup that would be easily transportable, still sound great, and provide us with a wide range of artistic options. As we were already using computer-based studios to produce tracks at home, we immediately thought of using laptop computers for live performances.

I had already tried a few different ways of playing live with my Mac PowerBook on some gigs with a local percussion ensemble earlier that year, using Mark of the Unicorn's Digital Performer software to mix together a selection of synchronized loops and sounds and adjusting digital effects in real time using DP's software mixer. However, while this works great for some performers (see Chapter 6 for more on live computers artists who use digital audio workstations or DAWs like Digital Performer to do live audio sequencing), I was looking for a more improvisational approach and using DP seemed too limiting to me for live use. I had to make too many musical decisions in advance to set everything up.

At around the same time, I was getting interested in the growing online music scene and the explosion of MP3 files available from obscure and unsigned artists on the Web, and this started me thinking about the possibility of using MP3 files for DJing on a computer and mixing together digital audio files live. I began searching for DJ software on the Internet, only to find that the few programs available at that time were very limited in their capabilities, and that there was almost no DJ software available for the Mac OS. After posting requests for information on a number of DJ-related newsgroups, however, I got an email from a house DJ in Chicago informing me that the company responsible for the popular Macintosh MP3 player MacAmp was working on a new product for DJs, MacAmp DJ (see Figure 2.3), which was still in the testing phase of its development. He subsequently emailed me a copy of this (never released) program which, while incomplete and still lacking many features, was stable enough to be used live.

MacAmpDJ was not a full-fledged DJ application, and even some of the few controls it did offer didn't work consistently. However, even this simple app was enough for me to start doing gigs. At the very least, I could play a succession of tracks, mix from one to another with the crossfader, and use the onscreen EQ for some control over the sound.

At first I used the built-in sound output of my Mac with MacAmpDJ, but soon I started thinking about how to get a better quality audio output from my G3 PowerBook. However, while there were many pro-quality PCI audio cards to put in a desktop computer system, in 1999 there were few options available that offered better sound quality for laptop systems. Looking around the Net, the best solution I could find was the VXPocket PCMCIA audio card from French company Digigram (see Figure 2.4). This card had a pair of XLR ins and outs as well as S/PDIF digital I/O, and while it was designed more for use by journalists and broadcasters than musicians, it worked well for me for several years in various laptop systems and sounded great.

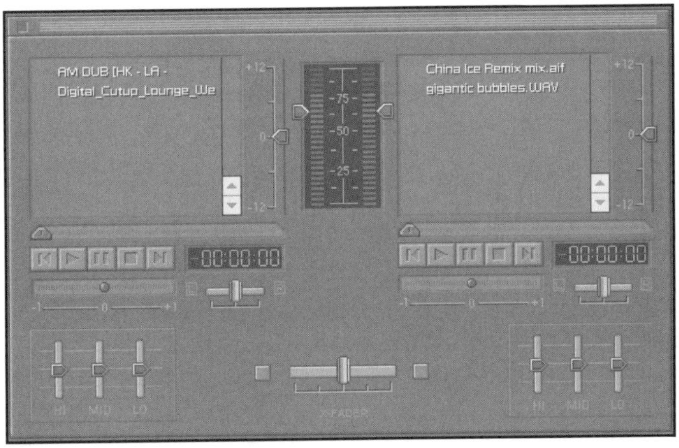

Figure 2.3 MacAmpDJ.

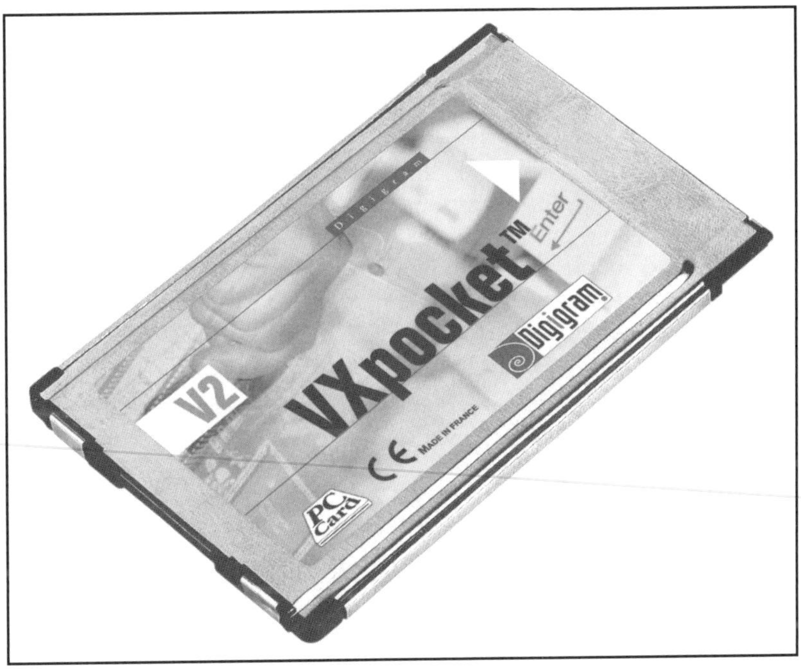

Figure 2.4 Digigram VXPocket PCMCIA audio interface.

After a few days of experimenting with MacAmp DJ on my PowerBook, I called Stephen and told him what I had been doing, and found that he had already found a similar software application for his PC called Virtual Turntables, shown in Figure 2.5.

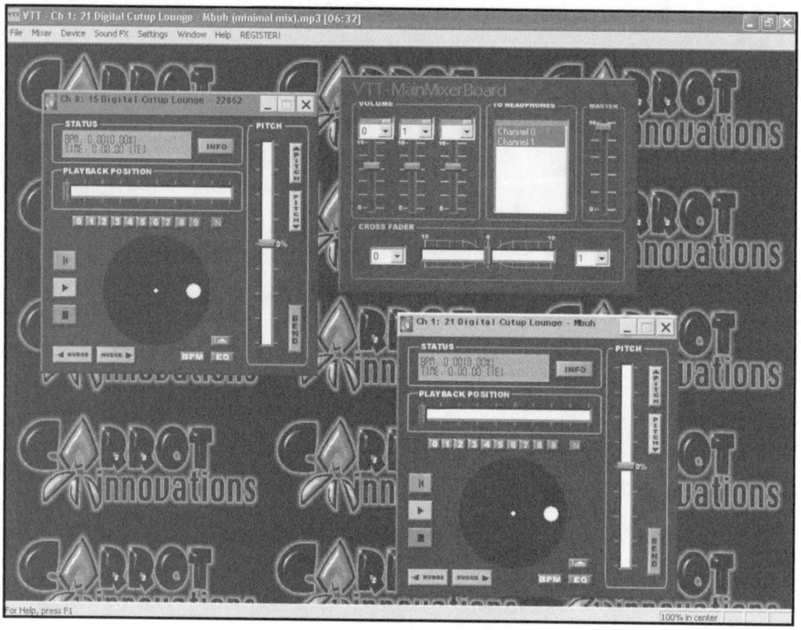

Figure 2.5 Virtual Turntables.

I took my Mac to his studio for an impromptu jam session and we spent an enjoyable evening mixing together a load of triphop, dub, recordings of William S. Burroughs, radio static noise, and an assortment of other audio bits and pieces. We decided to start a new project and do some live performances at a couple clubs in Hong Kong, DJing audio files on our laptops and making an improvised mix together with a couple of local jazz musicians.

We did a number of gigs like this, playing a mix of downtempo, triphop, and drum'n'bass for the most part. After some months, though, we became interested in dance floor club gigs and wanted to play more four-on-the-floor techno beats. Neither MacAmp DJ or Virtual Turntables was much good for beatmatching a live dance set, so we continued to look online for new software releases, purchasing a number of such programs from developers in the US, France, Germany, and Chile. Nothing really did what we wanted until we found Atomixmp3, from Atomix Productions in France, shown in Figure 2.6.

Atomix was the first program we found that could reliably determine the tempo of dance tracks on the fly and enable them to be mixed in real-time. Although its mixing controls were fairly basic, just a couple volume faders and a crossfader, it was stable and reliable enough to be used for major gigs with worrying too much about a system crash. The beatmatching feature was good enough to do a professional-sounding mix with a bit of practice. The tempo detection feature only worked well with 4/4 dance music (house and techno) for the most part, but since we were mostly interested in playing techno at that point, we didn't really see that as a problem.

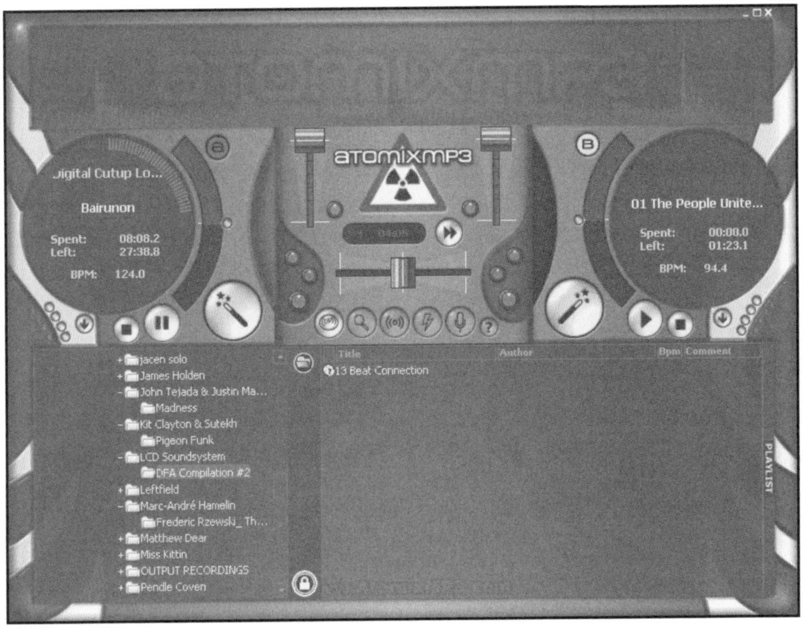

Figure 2.6 Atomixmp3.

Atomix would only run on Windows, though, so I had to abandon my beloved Mac and use a Windows PC for a while. (Two PCs later, I am now back to using a Mac for live gigs, the 12" G4 iBook that I'm writing this book on, but more on that in Chapter 3.) I picked up an inexpensive IBM ThinkPad running a 500MHz Celeron processor and Windows 98SE, and outfitted it with two of the new USB audio interfaces Stephen had started using, Roland UA-30s (see Figure 2.7).

Atomixmp3 was the software tool at the center of the first really workable DJ setup that I had managed to put together, and I used it on countless DJ gigs in Asia and California. I could send the output from each of the two virtual decks in Atomixmp3 to one of the UA-30s, and from the UA-30 into an external DJ mixer for cueing, EQing, and mixing. (Stephen and I used the industry standard Pioneer DJM-500.) With the computer only playing back and syncing the tracks and not providing any more advanced functions in software, even my relatively slow 500MHz Celeron ThinkPad with 128MB of RAM was perfectly able to run Atomix on gigs with few performance problems, even when I started using mostly WAV files ripped from the original CDs for DJing rather than MP3 files (which are much smaller) because of their superior sound quality.

At the same time as Stephen and I were trying to work out the kinks in our digital DJ concepts, looking for better DJ software that would enable us to better execute our ideas, another musician friend of ours was wrestling with similar technical issues as he tried to put together a software-based setup that would let him pursue a different musical approach. Let's take a

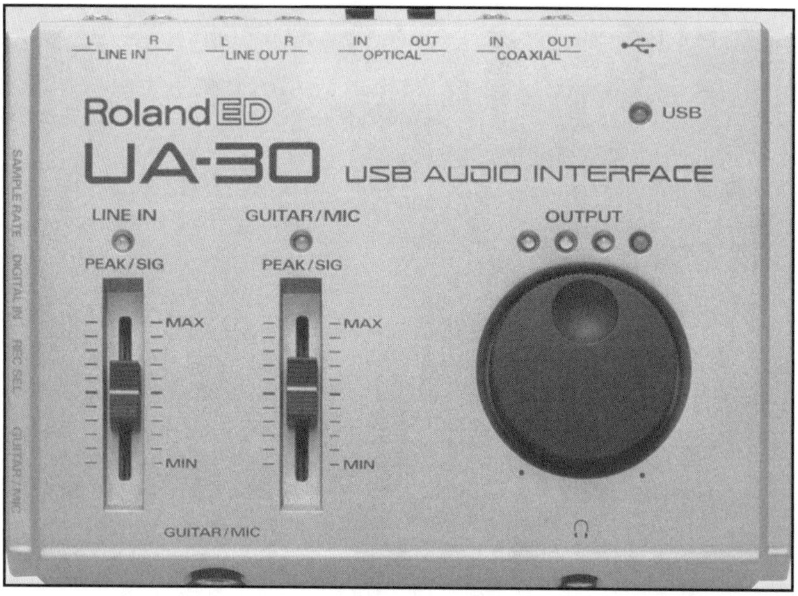

Figure 2.7 The Roland UA-30 USB audio interface.

look at how he solved some of these problems with the music software technology available at the time.

Covert Computer Music Operations in Beijing: Christiaan Virant

Christiaan Virant (also sometimes known under his minimal techno alias STAFFER3) is an American computer musician who has lived in Beijing, China since 1998. His band fm3, with Chinese laptop experimenter Zhang Jian (see Figure 2.8), has toured Europe extensively in the past couple years playing their trademark blend of 'very quiet' ambient electronic music with East Asian influences and have released recordings through a number of small European labels.

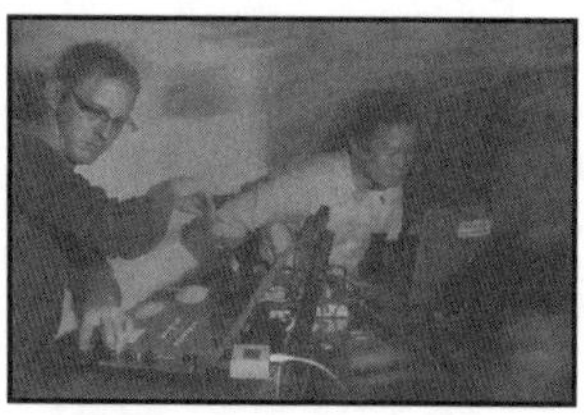

Figure 2.8 Fm3 performing live in Chengdu, China.

Christiaan originally got interested in digital music and laptop-based performance at about the same time I did—around 1999—but when he first started playing he was much more into a dance floor approach than I. Christiaan tried using a number of different software programs as he tried to find something that would let him freely mix together a set of techno loops, beats and grooves, pads and basslines, aiming at creating a hour-long set that was never the same twice.

As we will see later, Ableton Live has now become the software of choice for musicians who prefer this loop-based style of playing, but Live 1.0 wasn't released until November 2001, so in 1999 Christiaan was just looking around the Net trying to find something he could use.

> **CHRISTIAAN VIRANT**
>
> Early operations (detailed in Annex VS-45-A394) relied on covert tech support from an Australian contractor and accessed via codeword AUDIOMULCH channels. STAFFER3 used AUDIOMULCH version beta for low-level electro explorations in Beijing and Shanghai circa 2000.

Christiaan played his first live techno gigs in early 2000, playing solo with a Toshiba Satellite PC laptop running the interactive music studio software AudioMulch (http://www.audiomulch.com), which features real-time sound synthesis, on-the-fly music composition functions, and audio processing capabilities. AudioMulch is a fully modular system and provides users with the possibility of creating all kinds of customizable configurations (see Figure 2.9).

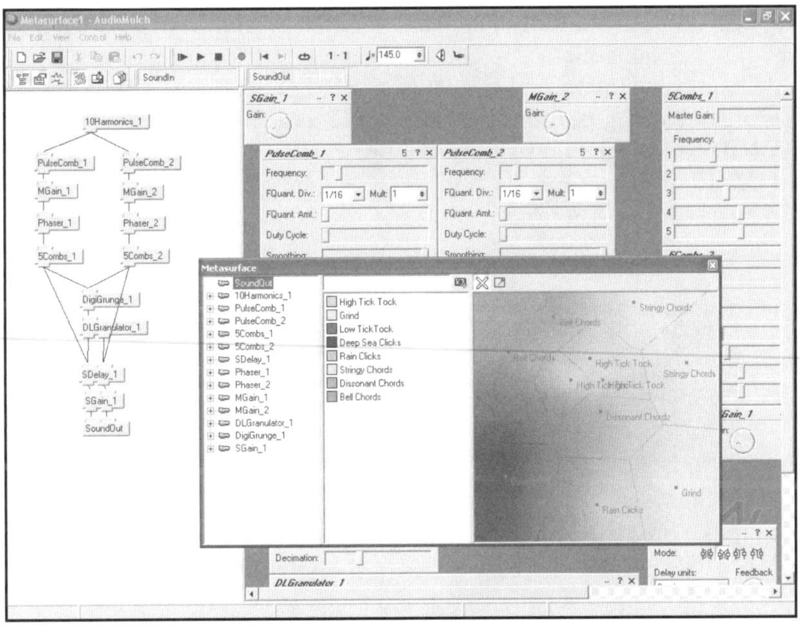

Figure 2.9 AudioMulch.

As mentioned above, Christiaan was looking for the ability to mix together minimal techno drum rhythms and other loops on the fly to play a live club set. To do this, he created his own AudioMulch setup that enabled him to draw from a library of drum loops and rhythms he had either created himself or clipped from other sources, mixing them in new combinations while playing live. Although this was a solid concept for doing live techno, Christiaan found the creative possibilities of AudioMulch somewhat limited for his purposes: I only allowed him to use a maximum of ten loops at a time before stopping the music and restarting with a new set of material.

Later that year, STAFFER3 began using Propellerhead Software's Reason program (released in December 2000) to play live, which later became the main weapon in his computer music arsenal.

CHRISTIAAN VIRANT

STAFFER3 went back underground shortly after the successful acquisition of integrated club command and control system Reason in late 2000. Designed primarily for headquarters-level collection and analysis of encrypted sonic data, a few modifications can convert the code into a weapons-grade beatbomb perfectly suited to real-time dance floor dominance.

As Christiaan cryptically refers to here, Reason was originally designed mainly for studio use; however, he created his own virtual studio configuration within Reason, adapted to the style of live performance that most interested him, mixing together and filtering drum and percussion samples in various combinations. He could achieve subtle layering effects by playing a number of sample loops simultaneously via multiple instances of Reason's Dr. Rex loop player module while carefully varying parameters such as EQ and volume using a Kenton Control Freak 8-channel MIDI mixer (shown below in Figure 2.10) and two early USB audio interfaces, a Roland UA-30, and an Opcode Sonic Port. Each of these interfaces had only one stereo output, so he needed to use two of them, one for the main output and one for DJ-style headphone cueing.

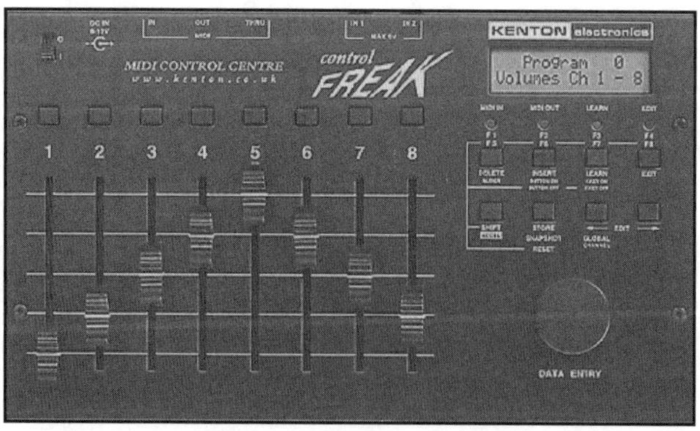

Figure 2.10 Kenton Control Freak MIDI controller.

While this approach worked quite well for Christiaan for a while, in the long run it proved to have some problems. He was using Reason in a role it wasn't really designed for, as a live sequencer and loop mixer. He was able to make it work, but the awkwardness of having to work with all the Dr Rex players onscreen eventually led him to try different solutions as new audio software continued to appear on the market.

As you can see, as recently as five or six years ago there were few options available for DJing or loop mixing on a computer, which are the two most common requirements of contemporary performers. Musicians like Christiaan and myself played with whatever cobbled-together hardware and software setup we could manage to get working, trying to find a way that we could make the computers do what we wanted at our live gigs!

I interviewed Christiaan in February 2005 via email about his current working methods. I wanted to know how his setup and approach had changed since I had last talked to him. I also wanted to find out more about his background as a musician and how that affected his ideas about computer music performance.

Q: Did you play an instrument or DJ before you began using computers live? Can you briefly describe your experience?

A: I'm classically trained in piano and violin. But when I hit 15, all that went out the window and I turned into a guitar-playing punk. This was in about 1983 or so. I had a number of different bands with friends playing hardcore thrash and then psychedelic punk and we would do simple multi-track recordings by bouncing tracks from one cassette deck to another.

Sometime in '83 or '84, a friend turned me on to Kraftwerk and I started doing more experimental tape compositions using reel-to-reel. I picked up an Apple II and started using it to make electronic tunes but back then, I never used the computer on stage. By 1986, I was a big fan of repetitive serialist music and drone stuff. Most of my compositions from then are heavily influenced by early Philip Glass minimalism.

Then I went to China and got completely cut off from everything that was happening in the West. I didn't really come out of the bubble until the late '90s when I started up a punk band in Beijing that quickly evolved into a post-rock kind of thing with a bit of electronic influence. Nothing was really happening in the Beijing electronic scene back then, so shortly after the punk band dissolved, I picked up a cheap Toshiba laptop and started a band that was focused on live computer performance.

Q: When did you start using computers in live performance? How/why did you get into it?

A: I founded my band, fm3, in Beijing in early 2000. From the very beginning it aimed at live, improv computer performance. Our first live set was in May 2000 at an underground Beijing punk bar. It was the first time a laptop was used on stage in China as a performance instrument.

When I was younger I was very interested in computer music, but back then, in the 1980s, no one really thought you could take computers on stage, so live performance was not really a consideration. But by the late '90s, the concept of live computer performance was reaching the realm of the possible. With new software, suddenly an entire recording studio could be carried on stage, and effects processing that used to take hours could be done in real time.

Q: Can you briefly describe your live setup and how you use it?

A: I currently use a PowerBook G4 with a MOTU 828 MKII FireWire sound card and a Doepfer MIDI controller. The current setup is very small, very powerful, and very portable. I've toured Europe for more than seven months with this gear and have had absolutely no problems.

My live set is extremely simple. Musically I limit myself to no more than four tracks, or four sounds working together at once. When I play live, often I try to keep it below three tracks. Naturally, the final output is decidedly minimal. So the way I use my computer and audio gear is very low-tech and very simple. I have a matrix of samples produced in the studio and then loaded into Ableton Live. These samples, about 50 of them, are mostly in the same pentatonic scale, so they can all be combined in various different ways to create different textures and rhythms.

When I play live, I don't have a particular set order worked out in advance. I use the Doepfer MIDI controller to pick different samples, and mix them together depending on my mood. Basically I run the entire show with 16 MIDI knobs and never need to touch the computer keyboard. In fact, I play with my eyes closed, so I can better concentrate on the sound and not be distracted by the computer screen.

Sometimes I even hide the computer offstage and just sit on the floor with my MIDI controller.

Occasionally, when I am playing with one of my bands in Beijing, I will play guitar and use the computer for real-time processing. But this is rare.

Q: What does the computer enable you to do live that you couldn't do without it?

A: Simple. My music would be impossible to perform live without a computer. I am still able to produce it in the studio without computers, and in fact, I use outboard effects boxes and a reel-to-reel for most of my work... But I can't imagine how I could play live without a computer. The only option would be to bring loads of tapes or CDs and mix them, but that would be a poor, less-flexible approximation of my current live set.

All of my sounds that I work with come from a whole host of Chinese classical instruments, which I play at home or in the studio and then are processed live to create the fm3 sound. Most of the Chinese instruments are "modified" to make them easier to play for me... and I have even built some of my own instruments based on the kind of sound I want created... but to be honest, my band has played entire sets with the actual instruments and it actually felt limiting.

This is because the computers provide much greater control over the final sonic output. There is simply no way to apply effects and do on-the-fly editing and looping if you are playing a "traditional" stringed instrument. I'm not interested in virtuoso performance or command over an instrument. I am interested in creating an atmosphere that impacts the listener. Without software and a fast CPU, I would be limited to creating my music in the studio and playing tapes during live performances, instead of doing it all in real-time. Although it is not my main compositional tool, the computer has become my main performance tool.

End Interview.

OK, I hear you saying—enough with the history already. As we will see, the technologies for playing music live with a computer have advanced tremendously since 1999. Let's turn to the next chapter and have a look at some of the latest hardware and software available to computer musicians today.

3 Choosing a Computer for Live Performance

Before moving on to consider specific performance setups in subsequent sections of this book, let's use the next few chapters to look at the state of the art in equipment for today's live computer musician. Of course, this is an incredibly fast-changing area, and any specific recommendations I try to make will quickly become outdated as new products continue to be released. As we look at some of the latest computer music gear available as of mid-2005, I will try to draw out some more general points to consider, such as the comparison between Mac and PC computers, USB and FireWire technology for audio interfaces, and so on.

In addition to an overview of what hardware to use for a live computer music setup, the next few chapters also contains extensive information on optimizing your computer for audio and music use. There are also some valuable troubleshooting tips for both Mac and PC platforms, distilled from my experience as a digital DJ and support tech. Computers are imperfect, and it is essential for you as a live computer musician to learn a bit about how your system works, how to maintain it, and what to do if something goes wrong—because something inevitably *will* go wrong, and you may well find yourself reinstalling your software drivers backstage just before you're supposed to go on and play for hundreds of people!

Whatever problems you may encounter, whether major or minor, the important thing is to simply figure out what is happening and how to fix it or work around the issue. It is useful to recognize that playing music live with computers is still a fairly new area of the music world, and the machines we use to play our music (PC and Macintosh laptops) were never really designed to stand up to the stresses we put them through. Not only that, but as we are constantly getting new software versions or hardware interfaces, many of us are using new and relatively untested technologies to play live. Some minor problems are bound to crop up from time to time.

Of course, your choice of what hardware to buy will largely be determined by your musical goals. If you want to use your computer primarily for DJing, you will likely choose different audio and MIDI hardware than if you are playing your computer in a live band with non-electronic instruments, and so on. However, I will give an overview of all the different types of hardware that are out there so you will have a better idea of what we're talking about once we start looking at particular types of live setups a bit later.

I repeat my disclaimer here that I am employed by M-Audio as a tech support supervisor, and I suppose I am inevitably biased in favor of our products to some extent. I have tried to be fair in my opinions and as objective as possible, but apart from any bias I might have, M-Audio is currently one of the biggest players in this quickly evolving field of music technology, so our gear would necessarily occupy a large place in any review of laptop music equipment.

First of all in our consideration of what hardware to use for computer music performance is obviously the computer itself. Your choice of computer platform is the basic choice that affects all subsequent decisions about your setup, and the computer itself is in most cases the most expensive single piece of equipment you will buy as well, so it important to choose carefully. As I have learned the hard way, if you buy a computer that is fundamentally unsuitable for live music performance for whatever reason (and I will explain some of the reasons in a moment), you may never be able to get it working well.

Mac vs. PC

In considering what computer system to buy, of course, the most fundamental decision you have to make is choosing which of the two major operating systems you want to use, Microsoft's Windows XP or Apple's Mac OS X. (Although there seems to be slow, steady progress in the field of Linux audio, at this point it is still not a serious choice for most computer musicians because of the limited availability of software and drivers.) If you choose Windows, you can choose from a variety of different PC manufacturers, or even build your own system from component parts, but of course if you want a Mac, you will be buying one from Apple.

The question of which is better, Mac or PC, has long been one of the most controversial and hotly-debated topics in the tech world. For our purposes, I think the best way to look at this is that whatever your musical goals, you can probably accomplish them with either a Mac or PC system (unless you want to use some particular music software that is only compatible with one platform or the other). However, there are definitely pros and cons of each that should be taken into consideration.

I will look more closely at both Mac and PC computers below, but first a general discussion of some of the important factors to consider in deciding which way to go on this crucial question. My discussion here of the relative merits of Mac and PC systems for live music is based upon extensive live experience with both platforms. In addition, as I interviewed all kinds of laptop performers in the course of writing this book, I asked each of them how they felt about the Mac vs. PC issue for live performance, and much of what I have to say here is based on these conversations.

Mac

Apple Macintosh computers, particularly PowerBooks (see Figure 3.1), have always been the most popular models among live electronic musicians, and the small glowing Apple logo has become a familiar stage presence at today's live venues, with multiple PowerBooks often being used to control the video, lights, and sound system as well as play the music. But is it just the mystique of the Apple brand that leads so many of today's performers to stick with the Mac, or is Apple's reputation for quality deserved?

Figure 3.1 An Apple Macintosh PowerBook G4 laptop computer.

The Apple partisans I spoke to in the course of my interviews gave various answers as to why they preferred the Mac platform, but they boiled down to the same few basic reasons, which I have outlined below.

Greater Reliability of an Integrated Hardware/Software Platform

The most fundamental reason for the intense loyalty of Apple-using laptop musicians is the Mac's greater reliability under live performance conditions. This is in part a result of the fact that the Macintosh is an integrated hardware and software platform. Unlike the Windows PC, both the operating system and the underlying hardware it runs on are designed by the same company. This integration of design results in fewer small incompatibilities, conflicts, bottlenecks, and other problems such as are endemic in the PC world.

One of the laptop musicians I interviewed commented that in this respect, the Mac is in some ways similar to a piece of outboard music gear, like a road-tested and reliable Akai sampler.

The whole unit, both software and hardware, is made by the same company and so compatibility issues simply do not arise. Hardware conflicts on a Windows PC can be hidden and only surface intermittently, as in the case of an underlying IRQ/resource conflict between your USB ports and your graphics controller that knocks your USB audio interface offline in the middle of a live performance, even though it was seemingly working fine an hour earlier during the sound check! These kinds of sporadic unpredictable problems are rarer when using a Mac. (See Chapter 5 on PC troubleshooting for more on IRQs.)

Another musician/technician interviewee remarked that at least with a Mac, you know what you're getting: An all-in-one hardware and software system comprised of parts that are all guaranteed to work together. He added that even though some might complain that Macs are slower than PCs of the same price, have less software available, have limited upgradeability, etc., still, in the end, reliability is by far the most important issue to a live performer, and he felt strongly that the Mac is the more reliable contender of the two major OS platforms.

Better Overall Design and Functionality for Media Applications

The design of the Apple Macintosh computer incorporates many tiny invisible design decisions that make it better suited to audio and multimedia work than most PCs. For example, although the USB ports and cables look the same (and are physically identical) on a Mac and a PC, the way that Apple has chosen to implement the USB standard in their hardware and software is different from how this works on a PC with Windows, and Apple's implementation works better for most media applications. Without getting too technical, this means that audio and video interfaces will often work more smoothly on a Mac, with fewer problems and less chance of conflicts with other devices in the system.

Anecdotal and Empirical Evidence

Although of course all computers and audio hardware are tested under a variety of conditions before being offered for sale, live computer music performance is an exceptionally demanding application that can push your machine to the limit. In many ways, the experience of other computer musicians is a better guide to the kind of performance you can expect than the results of a laboratory performance test such as can be found in the profusion of PC buyer's guides on the market. Live laptop musicians frequently use their machines under the most demanding conditions—such as the time I DJed with my PowerBook outdoors in 99% humidity just before a typhoon was due to roll in and the condensation was dripping down my LCD screen and running off onto the table I was using!

Many of the Apple users I interviewed mentioned the problems they saw their PC-using friends having as a major factor in their decisions to stick with the Mac. One mentioned that he had seen too many Blue Screens of Death on his friend's PC to ever trust a PC in live performance. In fact, most of the Macintosh users I spoke to mentioned this as an important reason for avoiding the PC for live use, although many of this same group did use PCs in their home studios for various reasons.

Easier to Troubleshoot

One more factor mentioned by some of the musicians I talked to was that, assuming that you know what you're doing in the first place, the Mac is easier to troubleshoot when a problem does develop. There are fewer things that commonly go wrong, and so fewer things to check by process of elimination. Working in music/computer tech support as I do and dealing with hundreds of end users' computer audio problems, I would tend to agree with this assessment. Rather than go into further detail here however, I will have more to say about this in the subsequent chapters on basic troubleshooting techniques for both Mac and PC platforms.

PC

OK, now after all of that PC-bashing, I want to turn around and stick up for the Windows platform as a viable alternative for live music-making (see Figure 3.2). I myself have been a Mac user since 1994, switched over to Windows for a few years soon after I got involved in live computer performance, and now am back to using a Mac again, so I can well understand the pros and cons of both platforms.

Figure 3.2 A Dell laptop PC.

In spite of the Mac's greater reputation for reliability for the reasons discussed above, there are still a significant number of laptop musicians that use the Windows platform instead, even when cost is not the crucial deciding factor. In fact, cost has become less and less of a factor in the decision of which platform to use for live performance as both PCs and Macs have become more and more powerful, and prices of both have continued to fall. Prices of the lower-level Macs are currently low enough to be competitive with PCs, with the 12" iBook G4 1GHz I use for gigs now costing less than the Compaq Presario model I was previously using.

However, it is still certainly true that at any given price point, you will get more computing power for your dollar by going with a Windows PC rather than a Mac, and this was a major factor cited by many of the PC users I spoke to. No matter how powerful computers become, audio software designers always seem to find new uses for the latest increases in speed and power. In practical terms, this means that on a Windows machine you will be able to run more plug-in audio effects, use more software synths, and automate more parameters of the arrangement in your digital audio sequencer simultaneously than you would be able to do with a comparably-priced Mac.

It is also true that there is a greater variety of software available for the Windows platform. More specifically for our purposes, there is more live performance oriented audio and MIDI software available for Windows. There is also much more freeware and shareware available online for Windows users on sites like the Shareware Music Machine (http://www.hitsquad.com/smm). The greater availability of software from freeware to professional production software is certainly one of the biggest advantages to working on a PC. Several of my interviewees asserted that it was possible to keep a PC-based performance system running as smoothly and reliably as a Mac, but that it simply took more work "tuning up" the system for optimum audio performance, and I do agree with this to some extent. Whereas a Mac might work fine for audio right out of the box, if you plan to use a PC for live music performance, you had better optimize it for audio use and test it extensively for reliability before you set foot in the DJ booth or on stage. (See Chapter 5 for more specific information on how to do this.) For example, reformatting the hard drive and reinstalling Windows (even on a regular basis) was a common technique used among PC musicians and DJs to ensure a smoothly running system for performance.

In addition, many of the PC users mentioned taking great care with their music computers, often dedicating them solely to music use and not using them at all for other applications. Keeping a PC off the Internet as much as possible was also often cited as an important factor in keeping a system free from performance problems.

Laptop vs. Desktop

In addition to the age-old Mac vs. PC question, another important decision you have to make when choosing a computer system is whether to use a laptop or desktop computer for your live performances.

This book is called *Laptop Music Power!* for a reason—the vast majority of computer musicians you see performing live today use laptop rather than desktop systems, primarily (obviously!) because they are more portable and convenient. Because of this, I mainly concentrate on laptop computers throughout. However, laptops suffer from significant limitations compared to desktops that can impair their performance, and if you are willing to consider transporting a desktop system to gigs instead, you will see that doing so offers major advantages.

In addition, more and more "mini" desktop systems have been coming out recently (both Mac and PC) that are both inexpensive as well as easier to transport than older systems. These might be considered as serious alternatives to laptops, particularly for those on a tight budget who are looking to maximize the computing power they can get for their money.

It is also worth saying that there are a number of advantages to having separate production and performance systems if you can afford it. I use a powerful PC system I built myself for production and use my little iBook for live performances. This combination gives me the best of both worlds—a powerful home production workstation and a reliable and easily portable Mac for live gigs—and still cost me less than a top of the line PC or Mac laptop would have by itself.

Now let's have a quick look at some of the most significant factors that differentiate laptop and desktop computer systems in terms of audio performance.

Hard Drive Speed

Hard drive speed is one of the most important factors in determining the performance of your computer music system, limiting the rate at which data can be read from the hard disk. This will directly limit the number of audio tracks or large samples that can be simultaneously streamed from your drive.

The hard disk drive that comes built into most laptops (either Mac or PC) will usually be slower than that in a typical desktop system, even if the data storage capacity is identical. For example, even Apple's latest series of G4 PowerBooks have only 5400rpm hard drives in them, while the recently released iMac G5 series desktops, which are slightly less expensive, have faster 7200rpm drives. Few laptops, either on the Mac or PC side, have drives that are faster than 5400rpm, though IBM, Toshiba, Hitachi, and some others are currently manufacturing 7200rpm drives for use in a laptop computer if you want to upgrade.

If you buy a laptop with a slow built-in drive thinking that you are going to add a faster drive later, make sure also to check with the manufacturer and confirm whether or not the hard drive can easily be swapped out of the particular model of laptop you are considering.

Overall Power and Performance Limitations

It is important to remember that there are significant differences in the design of laptop and desktop computer systems. Even if a particular laptop has the same CPU speed, RAM and hard drive capacity as a given desktop system, generally speaking its performance won't be quite as good as that of the desktop system because of various data bottlenecks or other design limitations.

Input and Output Limitations/IRQ Problems

One of the biggest limitations of a laptop as opposed to a desktop system is the type of ports available for input and output and their efficiency. On a laptop we might have USB, FireWire, and/or CardBus ports available for audio use, while most desktop systems will offer USB, FireWire, and of course, the internal PCI card bus.

In the case of a desktop system, the best solution is usually to use PCI cards for audio I/O. PCI is still the best interface standard for audio use, with the greatest bandwidth and also the most robust in terms of trouble-free performance. With other factors being equal, we would generally expect to have somewhat fewer problems with a PCI-based audio system than one using a USB or FireWire interface.

The reasons for this are somewhat complex, but in the case of PC systems, one important factor is IRQ sharing. This means that two or more devices in your computer are sharing a single IRQ "line" to communicate with the CPU. This can be a problem on either desktop or laptop PC systems, but on a desktop, it is easier to resolve. In many cases, an IRQ conflict with a PCI audio card can be fixed simply by moving the card to a different slot in the computer, but of course, this is not an option with a laptop.

Furthermore, many laptop manufacturers format their computers at the factory with a hardware allocation in which many of the input and output ports are sharing IRQs. This is fine for many general-purpose applications but for audio, it can cause many problems. In some cases, if there are many devices sharing the IRQs with the I/O ports you want to use for audio, you may need to disable some of your other devices in order to free up more system resources for audio use.

There is more information about how to deal with IRQ issues in the optimization and troubleshooting sections below. However, not all IRQ problems can be resolved; some PC laptops were just not meant for music and audio use, it seems. In this case, the usual advice applies: Buy the computer from a retailer that will accept an exchange if it turns out that the model you bought just won't work for you.

My Laptop Odyssey

Later in this chapter you will find more specific advice about choosing a computer for live music performance. However, before moving on, I want to briefly recount how I have switched from Mac to PC and back again myself over the last few years, and elucidate some of the factors in my decision of what OS to use. Hopefully this will be helpful to readers trying to decide what kind of computer to use as a platform for live performance. I want to tell this tale in some detail because it demonstrates some of the unexpected problems that can arise when trying to get a smoothly-working live performance rig together. It's not just a matter of buying a machine, installing the software, and going to the gig—you always have to be prepared for surprises.

Me and My G3

When I first started doing laptop music performances, I was using a G3 PowerBook 300MHz "Wall Street" model running Mac OS9 while my partner Stephen was running Windows 98SE on a generic Taiwanese laptop he picked up for half the price of my G3 in a street market somewhere. I loved my G3 dearly, and it was one of the most powerful laptop computers on the market when I bought it. Although my Mac was more powerful and dependable than Stephen's little ghetto-style Windows machine, I soon grew jealous of the constant stream of crazy little software apps that my friend was finding on the Internet to run on Windows, while I could find only a few programs for OS9 to use at our first gigs and none of them really did what I wanted.

I also faced another disadvantage because Windows 98SE supported the use of multiple sound cards simultaneously, while OS9 did not. As mentioned in Chapter 1, I did manage to get a high-quality sound card for my Mac, the Digigram VXPocket CardBus card, but this only had one stereo output, and so I was unable to cue on headphones—a huge handicap in DJing, making it impossible to do beatmixing or most other common DJ techniques, for that matter.

Meanwhile Stephen had bought two of Roland's UA-30 USB interfaces and was easily able to assign multiple audio outputs in a number of the programs he liked to use at our gigs. The Mac OS lacks this basic capability to use multiple audio devices. Even today, OS X will not work with this in most cases, although now there are many portable interfaces on the market with multiple outputs (like my M-Audio FireWire Audiophile), so this is less of an issue.

After waiting for months for some usable DJ software for my Mac, I was getting frustrated. I even installed Linux PPC on it at one point because I had found an interesting-looking DJ software application called GDAM that only ran in Linux (see Figure 3.3) and I wanted to try

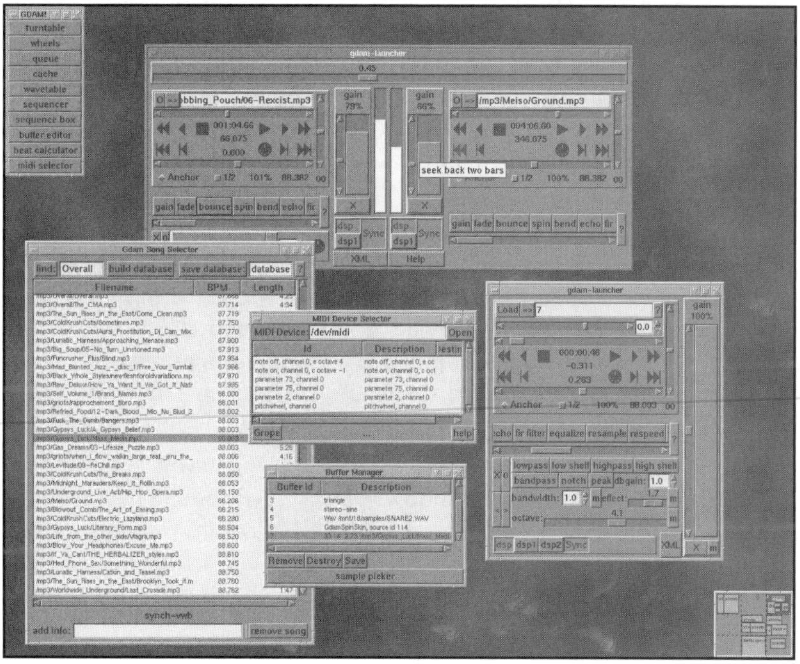

Figure 3.3 The GDAM DJ mixing software.

and use it, but I never quite got that whole setup running smoothly because of my lack of experience with Linux.

Switching to Windows: My IBM ThinkPad

Finally I got tired of watching my partner have so much fun at gigs with the latest groovy software he had downloaded from a free Web archive while I pathetically tried to mix with no headphones by clicking on tracks and edited clips in MacAMP DJ, which was a broken and unfinished application in the first place. The last straw came when the Atomixmp3 DJ application was released for Windows in late 2000 and Stephen was able to start doing completely beatmatched techno sets on his PC. Then I knew I couldn't wait any longer and it was time to switch. Although I had never used Windows before, I decided to take the plunge and managed to find an inexpensive secondhand IBM ThinkPad to play around with and see how it would work for me.

This entry-level model ThinkPad was my first PC, and in many respects it was the best PC laptop I have owned. Although it wasn't very fast or powerful by current standards, with only a 500MHz Intel Celeron CPU and 128MB of RAM, it proved to be very stable and reliable. The important thing was that it was powerful enough to do what I needed it to do: Play two different MP3 or WAV tracks simultaneously, match their tempos, and mix them together.

With two USB ports on the ThinkPad, I was able to start using a pair of Roland UA-30s for separate main and cue audio outputs. Together with a copy of Atomixmp3 1.0 and an external Pioneer DJM-500 DJ mixer, this was a fully functional digital DJ rig. I kept using this same setup, with various DJ mixers, for about two and a half years, until the LCD screen of the IBM got damaged in 2002 and I had to think about buying a new computer. At this point, I was still pretty satisfied with the combination of Atomixmp3 running on my PC, the two UA-30s, and my Pioneer mixer, so I decided to buy a new PC to replace the ThinkPad, a laptop running Windows XP.

I had few problems with my inexpensive ThinkPad running Atomixmp3, so I decided to stick with an inexpensive entry-level PC. I was still producing tracks in my project studio with a Dual G4 533MHz Mac running Digital Performer, and I liked the idea of using a relatively cheap computer at gigs. After many late nights playing at DJ bars and clubs in Hong Kong and watching severely intoxicated patrons pouring drinks over themselves and others in the midst of the frenzied weekend revelry, I preferred not to use a top-of-the-line computer system to play live.

Also, another reason for sticking with the PC platform at the time was that I really liked using Atomixmp3 as mixing software and it was Windows-only. If I switched to a Mac, I would have to start using another DJ software application: Probably Native Instruments' Traktor. I had already tried an early version of Traktor on my ThinkPad but still preferred Atomixmp3 because it had a less-cluttered interface and the beat-detection and matching utilities seemed to work just a bit better than Traktor's at that point.

However, although this seemed like a reasonable decision at the time, little did I know that this would be the beginning of a major computer nightmare for me! Although I had very few hardware problems with my G3 PowerBook or my ThinkPad when I was first DJing with computers, I soon found out a lot more about what can go wrong when using a computer system not designed for audio use for live music performance.

Bear with me while I tell the rest of this story as there is a cautionary tale in here somewhere for those thinking about buying a cheap PC system for their gigs and saving some money!

My Sony Vaio: Everything Goes Black

Looking around the market I quickly found that there were many entry-level PC laptops available in the $1000-$1500 range, so I started comparing prices and features and settled on a Sony Vaio model. I brought it home and started setting it up for DJ work; unfortunately, after only a couple hours of use, I rebooted it and the screen went black. After some calls to Sony tech support, we determined that the video board had gone bad and it was recommended that I simply return it to the retailer for exchange.

I had bought the Vaio at Fry's Electronics, a popular electronics megastore chain in California with a well-known generous return policy, so I was able to return the laptop the next day without any problem. (Tip to the reader: *Always* buy computer and electronics gear at a store where you can take it back for return or exchange if it doesn't work properly with your system, there can always be strange unforeseen incompatibilities or other problems.) I decided to get a different brand laptop in exchange, though, having had such bad luck with my first Sony.

Calling Hewlett-Packard

Next I brought home a handsome slim Hewlett-Packard laptop. I paid a bit more and got a bit better model than what the Vaio had been. Surely this time I would have better luck.

I set up the latest version of Atomixmp3 on the HP laptop and had some success at first. My new HP machine running Windows XP seemed to run this more advanced DJ software with no perceptible problems. Upon taking the machine over to a friend's for a jam session one day, however, the power abruptly switched off and the screen went black right in the middle of our session. The same thing happened to me again and again in subsequent days, although not more than once in several hours of use. It was not an insurmountable problem using the computer in the studio to produce music, but obviously on live gigs this was totally unacceptable.

Many calls to Hewlett-Packard tech support later, it was determined that my laptop was probably suffering from some kind of unusual power problem that caused it to suddenly shut off now and then for no particular reason, and it was recommended that I return the machine to the retailer. At this point I wasn't sure quite what I should do as far as getting another machine, so I returned the HP to Fry's as defective merchandise and got a full refund.

The Case of the Toshiba Satellite and the Leaky USB Ports

After some more research, I decided to try a Toshiba machine next. My friend Christiaan in Beijing had been using a Toshiba Satellite model laptop for his live gigs for quite awhile with few problems, so I got a an inexpensive Toshiba myself at a Best Buy electronics store in Los Angeles.

Unfortunately, this machine also had a strange hardware problem: When I connected both the Roland UA-30 audio interfaces to the PC and then to my DJ mixer, I found that a little bit of the sound would leak across the USB bus somehow. The effect was that if I was playing a track out the main PA and then played another track on the other software deck in order to cue it in my headphones, a bit of the sound would leak out the main PA as well. I'm not sure how this could have been happening, some kind of freak interconnection of data, but it made the Toshiba useless for live use, and I decided to return it as well.

The Compaq Presario 700: Welcome to my Nightmare

Finally, looking around Best Buy in desperation for a brand of PC I hadn't tried yet, I saw a Compaq Presario 700 laptop that looked acceptable for my needs: A 1.3GHz Athlon processor running Windows XP, 256MB RAM, and a 20GB hard drive. It looked great and worked well at first, so I was excited. I had no problems with it the first few times I ran Atomixmp3 on it at DJ gigs, so it looked like my PC problems were finally over.

Unfortunately, this machine later provided me with a long string of problems that gave me a great overview of almost everything that could go wrong with a PC. Here are some of the problems I had, and how I diagnosed and fixed them. Hopefully these descriptions will be useful in showing the kinds of things that can go wrong and how to go about dealing with them.

The first problem I had with the Compaq was episodes of overheating because of a manufacturing defect. After first, while using the Compaq machine on a number of short gigs under varying circumstances, I was having no serious problems and was pretty satisfied with its performance. However, then I played an experimental improv gig with saxophone player Andrew Pask at a small underground venue in Riverside, California and started having a very disturbing problem midway through our set: The system started to freeze up about every 10-15 minutes or so. It didn't seem connected to anything I was doing particularly; it appeared to happen randomly after the computer had been in use for some time.

Many calls to Compaq tech support later, we figured out that my laptop must have some kind of defect in the heat-dissipating structures. The freezing problem was a result of overheating, and the reason it started happening at that particular performance was that it had been quite hot that night in the venue after a long hot desert day in Riverside and the computer got hotter during our performance than it would have otherwise.

In any event, I sent it back for warranty repair and this was apparently successful, for the problem stopped happening after that. Well at least *that* problem stopped happening—there were more problems soon to come, and the next problem I had to face was the seeming incompatibility of my laptop with virtually any external audio gear I tried to use.

When I first got the Compaq machine, I was still using the two Roland UA-30 USB audio interfaces to DJ, but these weren't giving me very good performance so I was ready to upgrade. The Roland units were certainly reliable enough (in fact they still work now, although I rarely pull them out of storage), but they were only class-compliant with Windows

XP, meaning that they didn't use any special software driver but rather relied upon the built-in USB support in Windows XP to work properly.

Class-compliant audio and MIDI devices tend to be relatively stable in my experience, simply because there is one less thing to go wrong. There is no possibility of miscommunication or error between the device, the software driver, and the OS, because there is no driver in the first place. However, if a device lacks drivers and only works as a class-compliant device, then it will also lack certain features that can be crucial to us as computer musicians, such as support for low-latency ASIO drivers.

The latency issue is particularly problematic: While there are several types of software drivers used in Windows for audio devices, ASIO is by far the best, offering the lowest latency times. Lack of ASIO support is a major problem with using a computer for real-time performance, so I wanted to get a new audio interface that would at least come with ASIO drivers, as well as at least two output pairs so that I could play a track and cue the next track on headphones simultaneously without having to use two separate interfaces as I had been with the UA-30s.

About this same time, I began working at M-Audio, and had easy access to a wide variety of USB and FireWire audio interfaces to try with my PC: Both M-Audio's own products as well as assorted competitors' products that we had in the office for purposes of testing, comparison, or whatever. I began trying a long succession of these with my Compaq machine, only to discover a variety of intractable problems with virtually every device I tried.

In the case of the USB devices, I found that I was able to use any of them trouble-free for some period, somewhere between 10 minutes and an hour, but then I would inevitably experience a system freeze. It didn't seem to matter which device I tried or what software I used—it would always just freeze up at some point.

My computer lacked a built-in FireWire port, so after trying every USB device I could get my hands on, I bought a CardBus FireWire card to add a couple ports and then started trying to use various FireWire audio interfaces instead. The performance I got this way was even worse: The sound would start playing out through the FireWire interface for only about 5-10 seconds, then there would be a short crackle sound and the music I was playing would simply stop coming through. The software on the computer didn't freeze in this case, but the sound would stop, usually until the computer was rebooted.

Giving up on this approach, I dug my old CardBus soundcard out of the closet, the Digigram VXPocket, got a new Windows XP driver for it from Digigram's Web site and tried using it for my main output and the Compaq's built-in sound card for headphone cueing. This did work after a fashion, and I played quite a few DJ gigs this way, but this kind of configuration can suffer from sync and other problems and is usually not to be recommended. One major reason for this is that the built-in sound card of most computers lack ASIO support, and so will suffer from much higher latency values than a third-party interface using an ASIO driver. There are other possible problems as well.

In my case, using my DJ software (I had by now upgraded to the latest DJ software release from Atomix Productions, Virtual DJ) with this configuration gave me overall better performance than I had been getting with USB or FireWire, but when it came time for a real performance, weird stuttering and looping problems started happening: A portion of the audio playing back through the Digigram card would be looped back over and over again. Sometimes it would loop for only 5-10 times and then the track would continue playing, while other times it would loop forever and the machine would freeze. In this case, only a hard shutdown (by holding down the power button) and reboot could get the computer running again.

Having exhausted all the available possibilities for upgrading my computer's audio—USB, FireWire, and CardBus interfaces—I began troubleshooting the computer itself in greater depth, trying to optimize it in every possible way in order to get better audio performance. In fact, I had been doing this all along as I tried to get all of these different external interfaces to work, but although I did improve the performance of the machine to some degree, I never managed to make FireWire audio work properly or stop the system freezes and other problems from occurring with USB and CardBus devices. Here are some of the most important things I tried, things that every PC-based musician should probably do as well as a matter of routine. (There is more detailed information on PC optimization and troubleshooting in Chapter 5.)

- Frequently defragmenting the hard drive
- Wiping the system clean and reinstalling Windows
- Making sure I always had all the latest updates for Windows from Microsoft, as well as clean installs of the latest drivers for any external devices I was using
- Checking the IRQ arrangement and disabling other devices in my system that might have been conflicting with the input/output ports
- Using the Speedswitch XP utility (available from http://www.diefer.de/speedswitchxp) to stop Windows from running the CPU at lower speeds to save power
- Optimizing my system for audio use
- Adding more RAM to my system
- Searching on the Internet for any information posted by others who might be having similar problems
- Hours of intensive performance testing with various software packages to make sure everything was working right and wouldn't crash on me in the middle of a performance

All of these things did improve the functioning of my system considerably, but no matter what I did, no matter what hardware I tried to use, it seemed that I could never fix the basic problem: The computer would eventually freeze up and stop playback after being in use for awhile. Sometimes it happened after 30 minutes and sometimes after several hours, but it always happened eventually.

Finally, after months of trying, I was digging around in some Internet forums looking for specific error reports about the Compaq Presario 700 and I found some new postings indicating that there was a known problem with this particular laptop: It would unpredictably freeze up now and then. Eureka! I had finally discovered the root cause of all my troubles DJing with this laptop: A problem intrinsic to this model of computer itself. All the troubleshooting and optimization I had done was for nothing, as there was nothing I could have done to prevent the machine freezing up.

Mac is Back

Finally (*really* finally this time), after this online revelation I went out and bought a little Mac iBook, a 12" G4 1GHz, upgraded to 768MB RAM (see Figure 3.4). Since getting my new Mac, for only $1000 (less than I had paid for the Compaq two years earlier), I have had no real problems with hardware and software in live performance. I have performed with both Traktor as well as Ableton Live (my preferred performance software these days) on the Mac and it has never let me down.

Figure 3.4 My 12" iBook G4.

On the other hand, there is always a trade-off. My bandmate Matt Piper bought a mid-range Dell PC laptop at about the same time that I bought my Mac, and it far surpasses my iBook in raw power and speed. Matt can run a lot more simultaneous virtual instruments, audio and MIDI tracks, ReWire applications, or anything else on his Dell than I can on my iBook.

In fact, the limited power of my G4 iBook does present a constant challenge to me as I reconfigure and update my live setup for gigs, particularly now that I am designing my own custom performance setups in Ableton Live. When creating a setup in Live, I always have to bear in mind the limited processing power of my Mac and set things up so that I won't draw too heavily on the CPU at any given time. For example, I have a number of complex CPU-intensive plug-in effects set up on various tracks for live use, but I am careful never to use too many of these simultaneously. I also find that I need to set a large audio buffer size in my applications to avoid overloading the CPU, thus giving me a fairly high latency (although I do not find this to be a problem for the kinds of gigs I do).

However, my iBook worked perfectly from the first day I bought it and I have never had a problem with it. (Nor did I have many problems with the G3 PowerBook I started out with at the beginning of this little journey, although Mac OS9 was never as stable as OSX is now.) Meanwhile, I watched my friend Matt struggle to resolve all kinds of strange installation and software problems on his shiny new Dell PC after he bought it. After months of going through all the same kinds of troubleshooting procedures I had used, he finally figured out that he had gotten a virus on his system soon after he got it, but it was in a hard disk partition that never got checked by his virus checker and didn't get wiped clean during his frequent reformattings of his system partition when reinstalling Windows.

In fairness, Matt would have me tell you that his Dell has been working great for him ever since he figured out the virus issue, and he keeps his music software running smoothly by not going on the Internet and only using the computer for music and audio applications.

Live and Learn: Conclusions and Buying Advice

OK, now that I've told that story, obviously you can tell that my own experiences have colored my opinions considerably on the whole Mac vs. PC question. Clearly I have had pretty terrible luck with PCs, and perhaps if I had just bought another IBM ThinkPad to replace my first one, I might have avoided many of the problems I had and I might still be playing live with a Windows machine now. However, whether you decide to use a Mac or PC yourself, there are some general points we can draw from my story that may be useful to you.

Buying a Mac

On the Mac side, I think the most important general point to be made has to do with how much the prices of Macintosh laptops and desktops have dropped in recent years. This has also to do with the general increases in computing speed and power during this period. When I was first doing live computer music in 1999, my top-of-the-line G3 300MHz PowerBook wasn't nearly powerful enough to run Digital Performer and do all the things I wanted to do live, and it cost nearly $4,000. In 2005, I bought Apple's most inexpensive model from the lower-priced iBook line for a bit less than $1,000, and although it does limit me in some ways, it is still plenty powerful enough to mix together multiple audio tracks with enough live processing and effects for an interesting live performance.

The point here is that while in the past Macs were too expensive for many people, the situation has now changed to the point where a Mac should be a serious consideration even for the tightest budget; price shouldn't really be the main factor in your decision whether to buy a Mac or PC.

Mac Laptop Recommendations

It is useless for me to recommend particular computer models here, as the marketplace is changing constantly and new models are released all the time. In any event, there are only a few models of Mac laptops available in the first place, so there is really not that much to consider if you have already decided on a Mac laptop.

For the last several years, Apple has maintained a policy of selling two distinct laptop lines, their flagship PowerBook series as well as the less expensive iBook models. At any given time they offer three different models in each line, for a total of six distinct Apple laptop models available. Therefore, in buying an Apple laptop there are basically two decisions to make: Whether to get a PowerBook or an iBook, and whether to get the low-, middle-, or high-priced model.

Considering the question of whether to get a PowerBook or an iBook, in the past, the lowly iBook was considered largely unsuitable for music and audio use and the PowerBook was almost universally preferred among laptop musicians. More recently, however, the power and speed of all of Apple's laptops has increased to the point where even the most inexpensive

Apple laptop, the entry-level iBook, is a viable choice for live music performance. Indeed, as mentioned earlier, I am using a 1GHz iBook G4 myself and although there are limits on what it can do, when I play live, I can run 6-8 tracks of MIDI and audio in Ableton Live as well as adding some effects to the mix, and this is enough for virtually anything I would want to do in a live performance.

However, there are still some important differences in design between the two machines, and although you can buy an iBook and add RAM or a bigger hard drive for better performance, it will never give you the same performance as a PowerBook. I have listed the main advantages of Apple's current PowerBook line over their iBook series here:

- Faster CPU speeds
- More built-in RAM, and the maximum amount of RAM the system can hold is significantly larger as well
- Larger hard drives
- PowerBooks have both FireWire 400 and 800 ports while iBooks have only a single FireWire 400 port
- PowerBooks are now equipped with Apple's Sudden Motion Sensor technology to help protect the hard drive in case of a drop or fall
- An Apple Super Drive with DVD-burning capability
- PowerBooks have both DVI and S-Video ports built-in as well as dual display support
- Faster graphics hardware
- A PCMCIA CardBus slot for attaching external peripherals
- An ⅛" mini-jack stereo audio input

For more current information on the iBook vs. PowerBook comparison, check these pages on the Apple Web site:

http://www.apple.com/powerbook/specs.html

http://www.apple.com/ibook/specs.html

Although the exact differences between the current iBook and PowerBook models will change over time as Apple continues to release faster and more powerful machines, my basic recommendation here will remain the same for some time: The iBook is fine for a lot of applications (and I love my 12" iBook) but if you can afford it, you should probably go ahead and spend a few hundred dollars more for the PowerBook model. It will always give you better performance and you can always use the additional power for music production and performance. A more powerful machine will also last you longer before you need to replace it, which is another important consideration.

Portable Desktop Macs

In addition to the familiar PowerBooks and iBooks, there are also some newer Mac desktop choices that would be interesting possible alternatives for live use because they are somewhat more portable than most desktop systems of the past. For example, there is the new iMac G5, an all-in-one Mac that consists of only a large LCD flat screen mounted on an aluminum stand with a keyboard and mouse attached.

There is no large, bulky computer case with the iMac G5; instead, the entire computer is inside the flat case behind the LCD screen. I actually considered buying one of these instead of my G4 iBook, figuring that it would just barely be portable and it would be a much more powerful production workstation in my studio than the iBook when I wasn't using it on gigs. However, I was put off mainly by the heavy weight of the iMac. Even the smallest model, with a 17" screen, weighs in at 18.5 pounds, while my tiny 12" iBook weighs less than a third of that at only 4.9 pounds.

Having spent years of my life lugging around heavy bass guitars and amps to gigs (not to mention when I used to wheel my acoustic bass around on the Tokyo subway system going to jazz clubs), and being a small guy in the first place, weight and portability are very important considerations to me. I love the fact that now I can pack my entire performance rig into my M-Audio backpack and throw it over my shoulder, so the thought of carrying a 20-pound iMac around with me all the time is not very attractive.

Apple has recently released an even smaller desktop Mac that might be interesting for some live performance applications, the new mini Mac (see Figure 3.5).

Figure 3.5 The mini Mac.

The mini Mac is a reasonably powerful machine by current standards and should be sufficient for many live performance applications, with the cheapest model boasting a 1.25 G4 processor, a 40GB hard drive, and 256MB of RAM. It is miniscule compared to any other desktop system on the market, only 2 by 6.5 by 6.5 inches in size and weighing only 2.9 pounds.

Of course, one reason the Mac mini is so light is that it does not include a monitor as does the iMac, so carrying around a monitor to use with it would still be a major hassle. However, if you wanted to get really crazy, you could plug in a head-mounted display such as this i-Scape II from i-O Display Systems and use it instead of a normal monitor (see Figure 3.6).

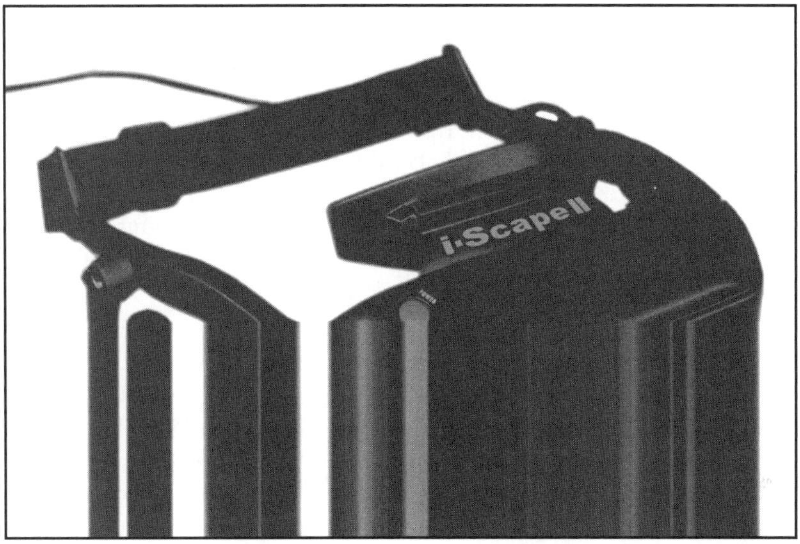

Figure 3.6 i-Scape II head-mounted display.

Together with a compact keyboard and a mouse or other control device, you could put together an incredibly portable cyber-DJ rig around a mini Mac and the whole thing would cost less, weigh less, and be more powerful than my iBook laptop. Together with a mouse or some kind of 3D cyber-glove controller, you could be the freakiest retro-techno computer DJ on the virtual block.

OK, maybe I'm getting a bit carried away here! Back to reality: Let's look at some of the factors to consider if you're buying a PC system.

Buying a PC

On the PC side, there are a number of things you can do to try and avoid the kind of difficulties I experienced.

The maddening thing about the problems I had with my Sony, Hewlett-Packard, Toshiba, and Compaq machines is that for the most part, they were caused by defects, flaws, or incompatibilities in the computer itself, not any kind of software settings that I could access and adjust, so there was nothing I could have done directly to prevent them. However, there are some things I could have done to minimize my chances of getting a defective product.

I think the most important factor was that I was buying entry-priced laptops, one of the lower-priced models from each manufacturer. My thought at the time was that I didn't need a very powerful laptop for DJing, and I was concerned that the computer might get damaged somehow on a gig anyway so I didn't want to invest a lot of money in my performing rig. However, in retrospect, I think that using entry-level PCs brought with it a higher chance of getting a machine with some defects or other minor hardware problems. For those thinking of buying a PC now, I would recommend not to get an entry-level model if possible; I think it is worthwhile to pay a bit more and get a better-quality machine.

PC Laptop Recommendations

It is impossible for me to make any particular recommendations about PC laptop computers because there are so many different models on the market, so many manufacturers and brands, and new models are constantly being released. At the moment, IBM, Dell, and Toshiba laptops seem to have the best reputation among the computer musicians I spoke to in the course of writing this book. As your stockbroker will tell you, however, past performance is no guarantee of future returns, and if you are contemplating buying a new computer, I would highly recommend doing some online research on the specific models available. Search the Net for reviews and forum postings as much as you can about the ones you are interested in and see what you turn up.

One good source of particular recommendations is the Digidesign Web site, as Digidesign does extensive testing of particular computer systems to approve them for use with Pro Tools. This does not necessarily mean that the systems they approve will be the best for all purposes, but their expert recommendations are certainly helpful in steering us towards computers that will most likely work well for audio use. Look on the Digidesign Web site for the system requirements and recommendations for Pro Tools, and you will find their list of approved computer models.

Some of the most important points to consider are the CPU speed, the hard drive speed and capacity, the RAM size and expandability, and the number of input and output ports (USB, FireWire, and CardBus card slots). The exact specs you need depend on what you want to do with the machine and which audio/MIDI hardware and software you are planning to use. If you are thinking of buying a new machine, I would strongly advise doing a bit of research about what kind of live performance rig you want to run first (i.e., finish reading this book for starters!), and make sure that the computer you choose well exceeds the minimum power and speed recommended by the manufacturers of the audio hardware and software you want to use.

The thing to remember is that it is not only the basic specs of the machine that are important. You *do* need to take these factors into account, but the overall quality of the components and efficiency of the design are also crucial in assuring you of a smoothly running performance rig. Any of the budget PC laptops I bought would have been powerful enough to do what I wanted at the time, if they hadn't each had some strange hardware problems.

The hard drive speed and RAM size are also the areas you should consider upgrading if you later find that you are frequently bumping up against the limits of your computer when you are performing; you can add another RAM stick to most laptops to increase the total memory size, or exchange the hard drive for a faster model. It is important to remember to check and find out whether or not it is possible to replace the hard drive on a particular model before you buy it.

Finally, it is important to optimize your PC for audio use if you are going to be using it in live performance, particularly if your machine is a bit older/slower than today's state of the art.

4 Music on a Mac

Optimizing Your Mac for Audio Use

There are a number of optimizations you can make to get better audio performance from your Macintosh music system, just as there are for Windows (see Chapter 5). However, most of the Mac-based computer musicians I spoke to didn't feel optimizing a Mac OS X system for audio was as crucial as it was for a Windows system. The typical OS X system will run digital audio just fine out of the box. Many of my interviewees preferred to leave the operating system well enough alone for fear of doing something that might inadvertently destabilize system reliability, which is an even more important consideration than raw power and performance for most laptop musicians.

Nonetheless, there are a number of optimizations you can perform to make your Mac system run faster and more efficiently for audio use. It is difficult to say just how much improvement in performance you can expect on your particular system from these optimization tips as there are so many different variables involved, and reported claims of improvements vary. Some magazine articles and Web sites on this topic claim performance improvements of as much as 30 percent after implementing a long list of optimizations, as measured by an objective standard such as the number of resource-intensive plug-in effects that can be used simultaneously in a DAW. However, no one I spoke to in the course of writing this book was able to get more than a modest increase in audio and music performance in actual practice from optimizing their Mac.

I have included here some of the better-known Mac OS X audio optimizations. If you want to try these, be aware that they fall basically into two categories. The first tips I have listed here involve primarily adjusting certain settings in the operating system itself; these tips should be safe for all users and should not impair your system functioning.

Some of the subsequent tips, however, involve downloading third-party applications and making deeper changes to the operation of the operating system. Although I have tried all of these tips myself on my iBook, I would recommend exercising some caution when using these. Be careful and don't change settings if you don't know what they are or what you are changing—some of these tools can significantly impair the functioning of your system. If you are interested in fine-tuning your system further, you should carefully consult the documentation for the programs I mention below.

Please note that while I refer to some hardware from M-Audio in the examples that follow, none of the specific techniques I recommend here are necessarily endorsed or recommended by my employer. This is simply a collection of practical tips and tricks that I have found to work in my personal experimentation and tinkering with live computer systems.

Turn Off Startup Items

One of the simplest (and yet potentially important) tips is to double-check your startup items list to see what applications are being loaded each time your Mac boots up. You can check this by going to Apple Menu → System Preferences → Accounts. Choose your user account, then select the tab that says "Startup Items" as shown in Figure 4.1.

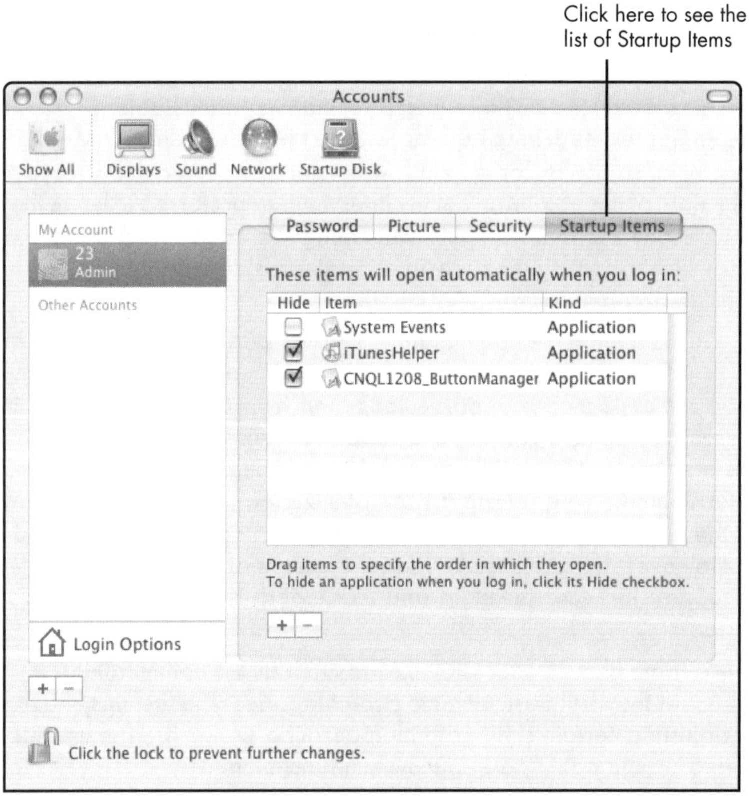

Figure 4.1 The list of Startup Items.

Here you will see the list of items that are loaded at startup. Check and make sure that there are no applications loading in the background that you don't want using up system resources while you are working on music, such as instant messaging clients or system utilities. You can delete items from this list by clicking them to select them, and then clicking the minus sign below.

Add More RAM

In Mac OS X, once programs have used all of the available RAM, they will start using free hard disk space. This will slow things down significantly. The more RAM you have, the less this function will be called upon. For this reason, it is a good idea to have as much RAM as possible in your system for optimum audio performance.

Upgrade to the Latest Version of Mac OS X

If you are using a Mac with an older OS X version, I would recommend upgrading to the latest version of the Mac OS. Apple is continually introducing improvements to improve audio performance and you will typically get the best results with Apple's latest version. This is also important to maintain compatibility with software and hardware vendors.

At the same time, before you upgrade it is also a wise idea to check the Web sites of the manufacturers of your audio hardware and software to make sure that they support the latest OS X version. There is sometimes a time lag before third-party vendors are able to release drivers and software upgrades to maintain compatibility with Apple's latest operating system upgrade.

Defragment Your Hard Drive Frequently

You should defragment your hard drives frequently using a third-party software utility that provides this function. This is particularly important when you are doing a lot of audio recording and editing work, which constantly reads and writes very large files to your hard drive. Good commercial defragmenting utilities include DiskWarrior and Norton Speed Disk.

Repair Your Disk Permissions

To keep your OS X system working smoothly, it is a good idea to repair your disk permissions fairly often as well, particularly after you have been installing or uninstalling software or device drivers on your system.

To repair the permissions on your OS X system drive, go in the Applications → Utilities folder and double-click the Disk Utility to open it.

Then select your system boot volume on the left side of the Disk Utility window, click on the First Aid tab, and then click the button towards the bottom labeled Repair Disk Permissions as shown in Figure 4.2.

This will take a few minutes but don't interrupt the process.

It is also a good idea to try repairing the permissions if you are having any kind of strange software-related problem on your Mac.

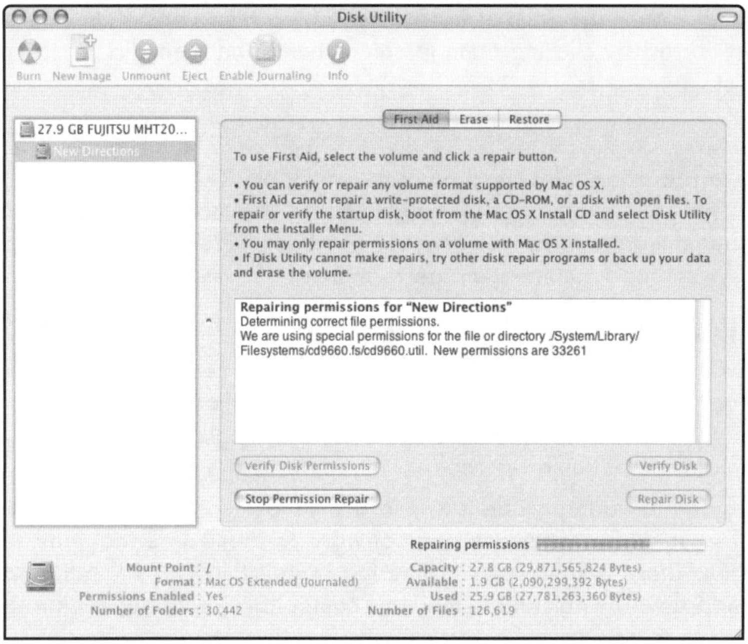

Figure 4.2 Repairing the disk permissions on your OS X system drive.

Turn Off the Animated Features in the Preferences for the OS X Dock

The animated effects built into the OS X Dock can slow down performance a bit. To turn them off, go to Apple Menu → Dock → Dock Preferences (see Figure 4.3).

On this screen, set the "Minimize using:" to "Scale Effect," and uncheck the "Animate Opening Applications" box.

Remove the Shadows Around System Windows

You can also gain a slight increase in system speed by using a utility such as Shadowkiller (http://www.unsanity.com/haxies/shadowkiller) to turn off the shadows in the OS X window and menu graphics.

Remove Unused Language Files

This is not a speed optimization tip, but you can save several hundred megabytes of hard drive space by deleting unused support files for languages that you don't need. You can do this with a free downloadable utility such as Monolingual (http://monolingual.sourceforge.net). Audio files are large and take up a lot of hard disk space and it seems like I am always running out of space on any laptop I am using, so saving even a few hundred megabytes is welcome.

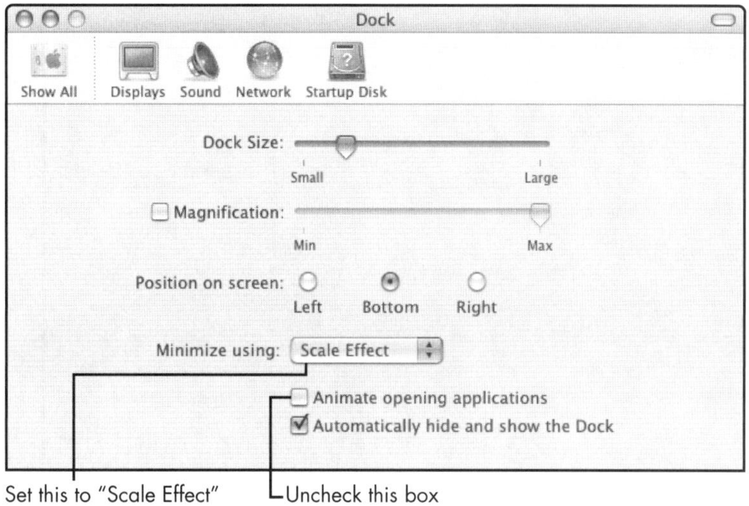

Figure 4.3 The Dock Preferences.

Check Your Mac's Hard Drives

You should check your Mac's hard drives for errors on a regular basis (at least once a month is recommended), using a utility such as Norton Utilities, Techtool Pro, or DiskGuardian.

Change Display Color Properties

Another simple optimization tip is to change the display color properties from millions to thousands. This will reduce the amount of processing power used by the video controller and free up some system resources.

To do this, simply go to Apple Menu → System Preferences → Displays. Then click the Display tab, as shown in Figure 4.4. You will want to change the Colors setting from Millions to Thousands.

Raise the Processing Priority of Your Audio Software

A more advanced technique for optimizing your Mac for audio is to use a third-party utility to adjust the processing priorities of running applications. Two excellent utilities for this purpose are Process Wizard (http://www.lachoseinteractive.net) and Nicer (http://www.resexcellence.com). Of these two, Process Wizard will give you more control over the operation of the operating system, but Nicer is probably a better choice if you have never experimented with these settings before.

Using either of these utilities, you can increase the processing priority of your audio software and potentially gain significant increases in performance. However, it is important to emphasize that if you change the wrong thing here, you can destabilize your system and possibly cause crashes and freezes. If you want to experiment with these settings, I would recommend

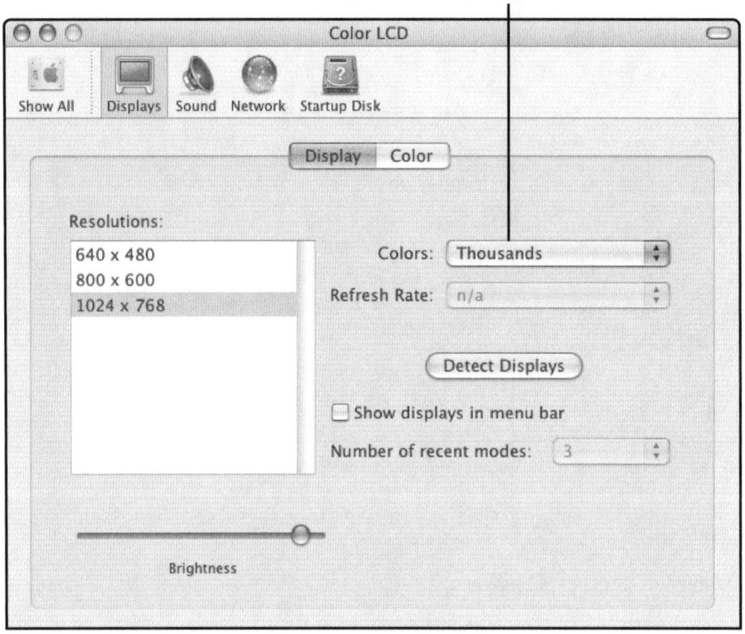

Figure 4.4 Changing the Display Colors setting.

reading the documentation with the software carefully prior to changing anything. In addition, you should thoroughly test your system for performance reliability after making any changes like this.

Make Sure Your Maintenance Scripts Get a Chance to Run

There are a series of system maintenance scripts that run automatically to keep your OS X system clean and updated. These maintenance scripts will run daily, weekly, and monthly at 3 a.m. This means that if you shut your computer down every night, they will never run, and the performance of your system will gradually degrade over time,

You can change this maintenance schedule if you want using a utility called Cronnix (http://h5197.serverkompetenz.net/cronnix/). Just make sure that whenever you schedule them for, the scripts do get a chance to run regularly. This will help prevent a variety of operating system problems. You can also use Cocktail (http://www.macosxcocktail.com) or MacJanitor (http://personalpages.tds.net/~brian_hill/macjanitor.html) to run these scripts at any time.

Basic Audio Troubleshooting for Macs

As I mentioned above, audio troubleshooting on a Mac system is easier than on a PC, which is one of the attractions of the Mac system for live music performance. There are fewer things to check when something goes wrong, and you can fix the majority of problems by following just a few simple troubleshooting procedures.

Problem: Pops, Clicks, or Noise in the Audio

One possible problem you may experience is pops, clicks, or other small artifacts in your audio stream. If you are having this issue with your system, here are some of the fixes you should try first.

Increase the Buffer Size/Latency for Your Audio Interface

Probably the most common cause of audio artifacts is having your audio buffer size set too low. In Mac OS X, you need to adjust this in the audio preferences of your application software (see Figure 4.5).

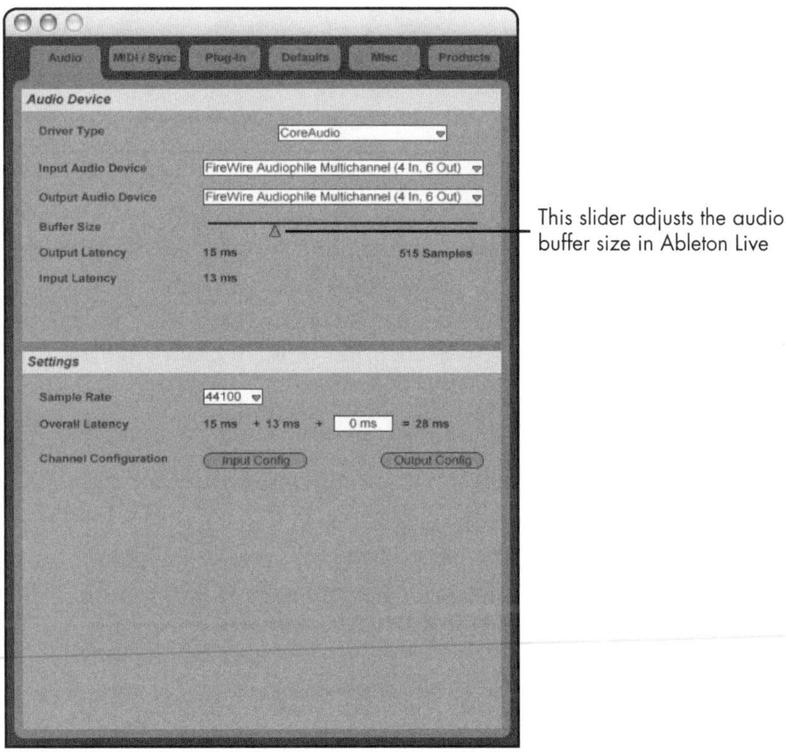

Figure 4.5 Setting the buffer size for my M-Audio FireWire 410 in Ableton Live.

The buffer size is the amount of sample data stored in the audio buffer at one time, and this is what causes latency in your computer audio system.

Please understand that there is no "correct" setting or value for the buffer size. Adjusting the buffer size is a compromise between performance and pristine audio. The best setting for you depends on a number of different factors including the speed and power of your system, the particular application you are running, and the number of simultaneous audio tracks and effects you are using.

If you have a very powerful system and/or are running a stripped-down software setup that doesn't require a lot of system resources, you may be able to get good results even with a very low buffer size setting. However, if you start to hear pops, clicks, or other digital audio artifacts, try increasing the buffer size setting bit by bit until the problems go away. Basically, you want to use the lowest setting you can without running into audio problems.

AUDIO LATENCY AND BUFFER SIZE IN MAC AUDIO

At the most basic level, latency is simply the delay during which audio is being translated from the analog to digital realm or vice versa. We can never get rid of this delay entirely, although on a powerful system with a professional sound card, the latency may be so small as to be unnoticeable. In other cases, you may find that you need to work with quite a high buffer size/latency setting in order to get clean audio input and output with your system.

Install All Mac OS X Updates and Patches from Apple

If your Mac is connected to the Internet, you can use the OS X Software Update panel to automatically receive the latest OS updates from Apple. You can find the Software Update panel in the Apple menu (see Figure 4.6).

Simply check the boxes by the updates you want to receive and click the button marked Install... to download and install them. (After the updates have been installed, you may be required to restart your computer.)

You can use the Software Update panel to receive all kinds of software updates from Apple. However, for our purposes we are primarily concerned with receiving OS updates. If you are experiencing audio problems, you should try updating to the latest version of OS X, then uninstall your device driver and reinstall with the latest version available (see the next section).

Before trying this procedure, however, you should first check with the manufacturer of your audio device to see the most recent version of the Mac OS that they are supporting with their current drivers. In some cases, there can be problems with a new OS update and it will take a little time for the manufacturer to change their drivers to reflect the changes in the operating system. If you update to the latest version of the OS first and then find out that the manufacturer's latest driver doesn't support it, your device may not work properly again until the manufacturer releases a driver update! If there is no update available, you may have to reformat your computer and reinstall the Mac OS in order to revert to an earlier version.

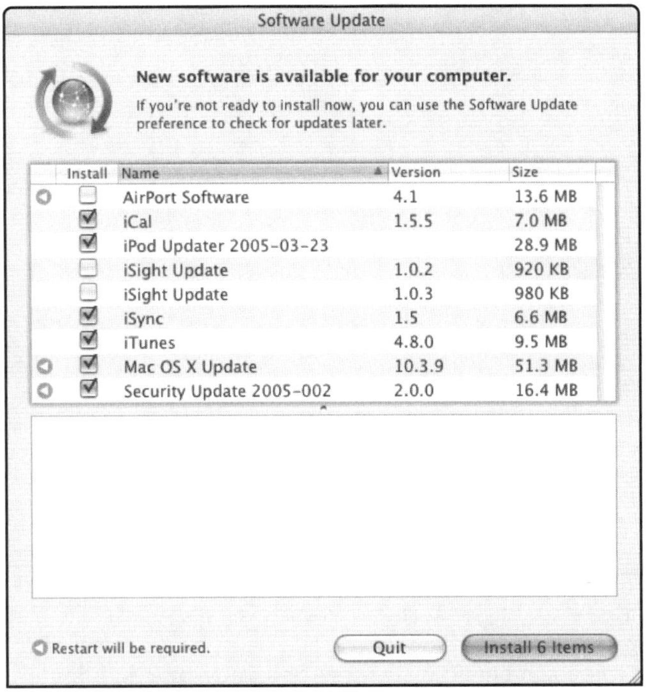

Figure 4.6 The OS X Software Update panel.

Make Sure You Are Running a Clean Installation of the Latest Drivers for Your Audio Interface or Sound Card

Try reinstalling the drivers for your audio interface. Sometimes driver files can get corrupted and this can cause all kinds of audio problems.

If you want to try reinstalling, you should first go to the manufacturer's Web site and get the latest driver update for your device.

Then make sure you uninstall the old driver first. In many cases the manufacturer will provide you with a proprietary software uninstaller (see Figure 4.7).

If your device lacks an uninstaller, or if you have already tried uninstalling and reinstalling the driver but are still having problems, you can also delete the driver files for your device by using the OS X Terminal utility. Then reinstall the driver with the latest version from the manufacturer's Web site, and then repair your disk permissions (as described above in the optimization section).

You do need to be careful and precise if you want to try this procedure. If you enter the commands incorrectly, you can erase important system files and damage the functioning of your OS installation. However, I have fixed a lot of driver problems this way and it can be a

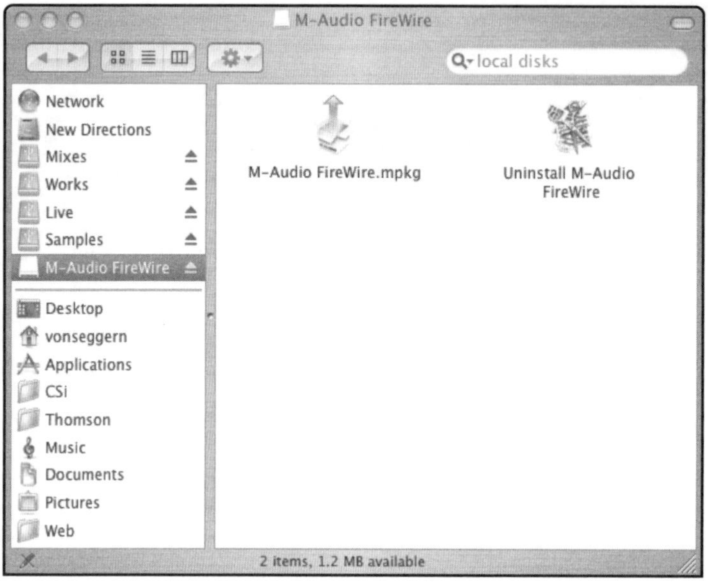

Figure 4.7 The M-Audio FireWire 410 driver uninstaller.

very useful trick to try when something is going wrong and you can't figure out why. I have also used this method to fix driver problems with other system devices, such as printers and scanners.

First of all, we need to find all of the driver files for your device so we can delete them. We can do this with a simple disk search (Apple-F), but the tricky part is knowing what to search for. Usually you can find the driver files you are looking for by doing a search for either the name of the device manufacturer or the device itself. For example, I can find all the drivers for the M-Audio devices I have installed on my system by searching for "m-audio" (see Figure 4.8a) and then running a second search for "maudio" (see Figure 4.8b).

Note here that I have more than one M-Audio driver installed on my system, and this search has found all of the related driver files. I am going to go ahead and delete all of these files from my system in order to make a fresh start with all my audio drivers. Just be aware that if you have more than one device or software package on your system from the same manufacturer, the procedure I am outlining here will delete all of the files indiscriminately.

After finding the driver files, leave this search window open and find the OS X Terminal utility on your system hard drive. Go to Applications → Utilities and double-click the Terminal icon to open it (see Figure 4.9).

At the prompt <username>$, type this command exactly as it is printed here:

sudo rm -R

Make sure that you insert a space between sudo and rm, as well as between the rm and the -R, and also after the final capital R, like this:

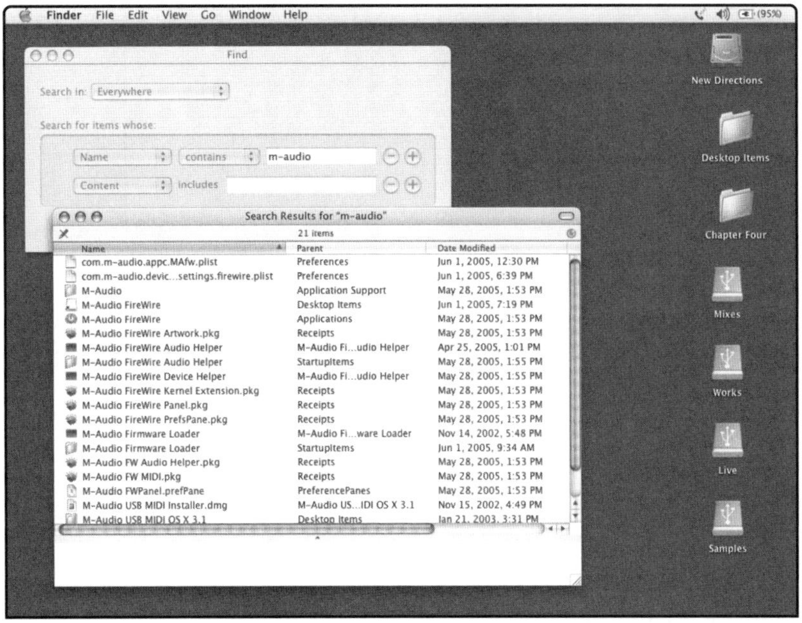

Figure 4.8a Search results for "m-audio".

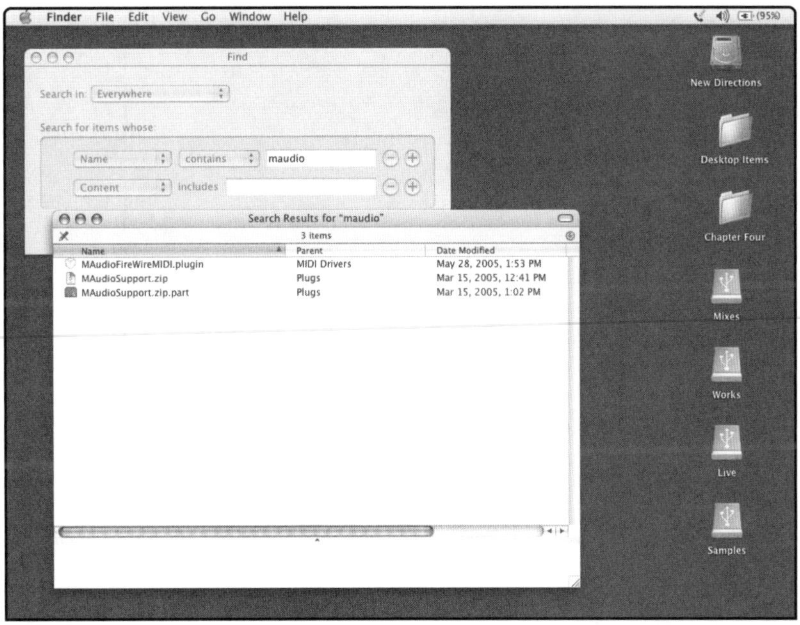

Figure 4.8b Search results for "maudio".

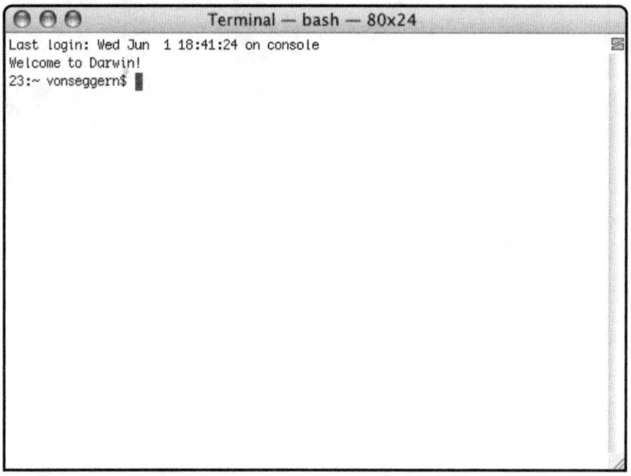

Figure 4.9 The Terminal window.

sudo_rm_-R_

The screen will now look like Figure 4.10.

Next, you need to go back to the search window we left open and select all the files shown, as shown in Figure 4.11.

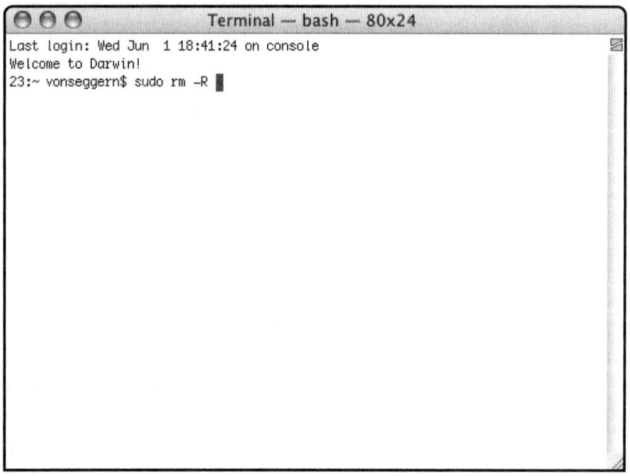

Figure 4.10 Entering the sudo command in the Terminal window.

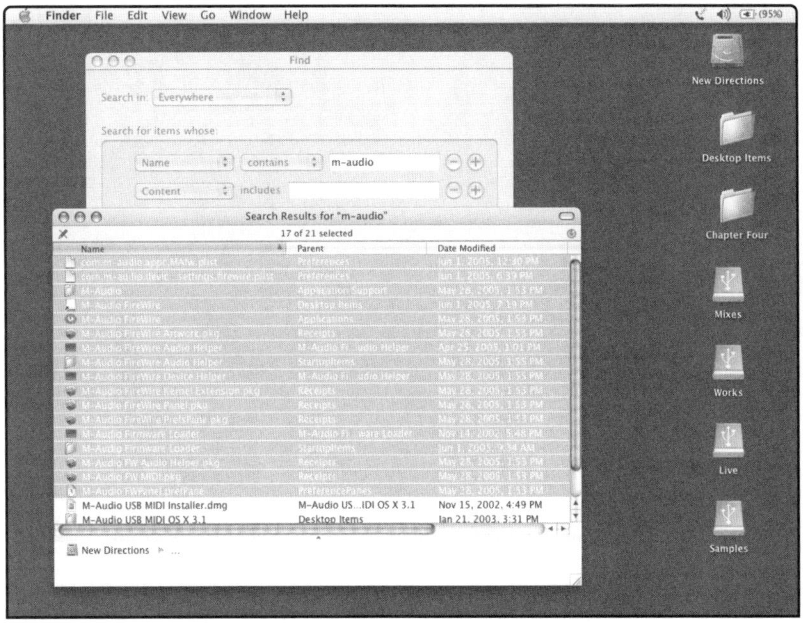

Figure 4.11 Selecting the driver files in the search window.

Now drag the selected files from the search results window into the Terminal window and drop them at the end of the command line you typed. The filenames will appear in the Terminal window as in Figure 4.12. Be careful not to move any files that you don't want to delete.

Now, click on the Terminal window and press Enter on the keyboard. You will be prompted for your OS X password. Type your password and then press Enter again. In some cases, the Terminal will ask you again if you wish to override permissions on a particular file; in this case, simply continue by typing y as in yes, and then pressing Enter to override.

When you are finished with this, you will see the <username>$ prompt again. This indicates that the operation is complete and the files have been deleted. If you want to confirm this, you can repeat the same disk search again and see if any files are found.

If You Are Using a USB or FireWire Audio Interface, Check for Possible Conflicts with Other Devices

Make sure you are not connecting through a USB hub or through the typing keyboard; if you are, try connecting the device directly to a USB port on the computer itself instead. This is particularly important if you are using a device that draws its power from the USB port in lieu of an external power adapter.

You should also try disconnecting any other USB devices (other than your keyboard and mouse) while you are working on audio or MIDI projects. If you are still having problems, try using the device on any other available USB ports on your computer.

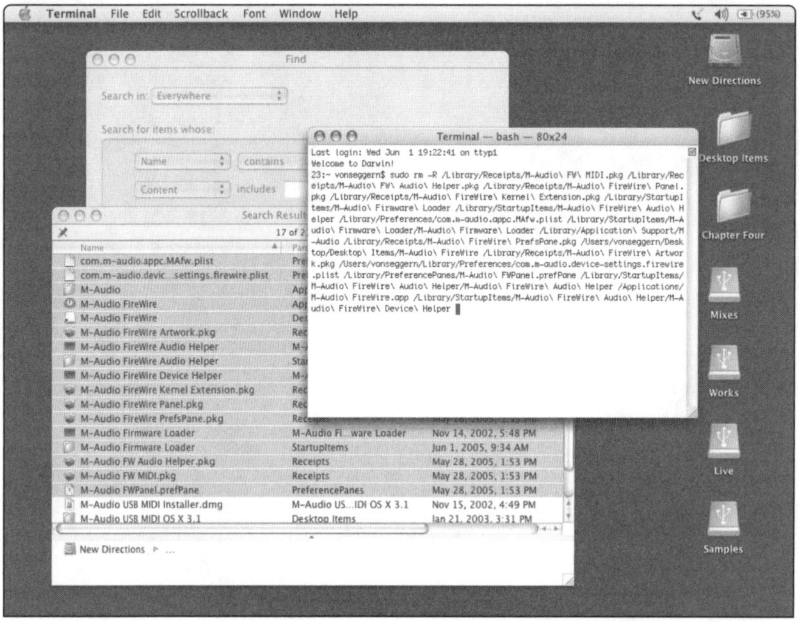

Figure 4.12 The filenames as they will appear in the Terminal window.

Similarly, in the case of a FireWire interface, try disconnecting any other FireWire devices you may have connected and see if you still have the problem. You may also need to check the Web site of your audio interface's manufacturer for any information about possible incompatibilities or known conflicts. In many cases, FireWire audio devices may require that other FireWire devices on your system be connected in a particular order or configuration. For example, with the M-Audio FireWire series, it is recommended you connect the FireWire audio device directly to the FireWire port of your computer, and then connect any additional FireWire peripheral (such as an external hard drive) to the extra FireWire port on the audio interface.

Check for Potential RAM Problems

If you are using more than one RAM module in your computer, remove all but one of them and check if the audio problem still occurs. This is a good test. It is important not to use mismatched RAM modules, and audio problems may also be caused by low-quality RAM in some cases.

Check Internet Forums and Web Sites for More Information on Your Specific Problem

Whenever you are trying to troubleshoot a computer problem, always remember that the Internet is a fantastic resource. If you can't figure out what is going on, go to your favorite search engine and look around for whatever information you can find about the issue you seem to be having. Information directly from users on Internet forums is often more up-to-date and current than the official Web site of the manufacturer itself, with more specific information about even very recently-occurring bugs.

Reformat Your Hard Drive and Reinstall the Mac OS

This is a somewhat drastic solution and is usually not necessary on a Mac unless your system has become seriously corrupted somehow. If it does become necessary to reinstall the OS, simply insert the OS installation CD-ROM that came with your system and then hold down the c key on your keyboard as you restart your Mac. The installer's on-screen instructions will tell you what to do next.

An external hard drive of some kind is also recommended to back up your data when you need to reformat. External drives connecting to your computer via USB 2.0 or FireWire are recommended for this purpose.

Problem: My Audio Interface Isn't Recognized by My System and Doesn't Appear in My System Preferences

If your audio interface is properly installed and operational, it should appear as a choice in the Sound Preference panel, as shown in Figure 4.13.

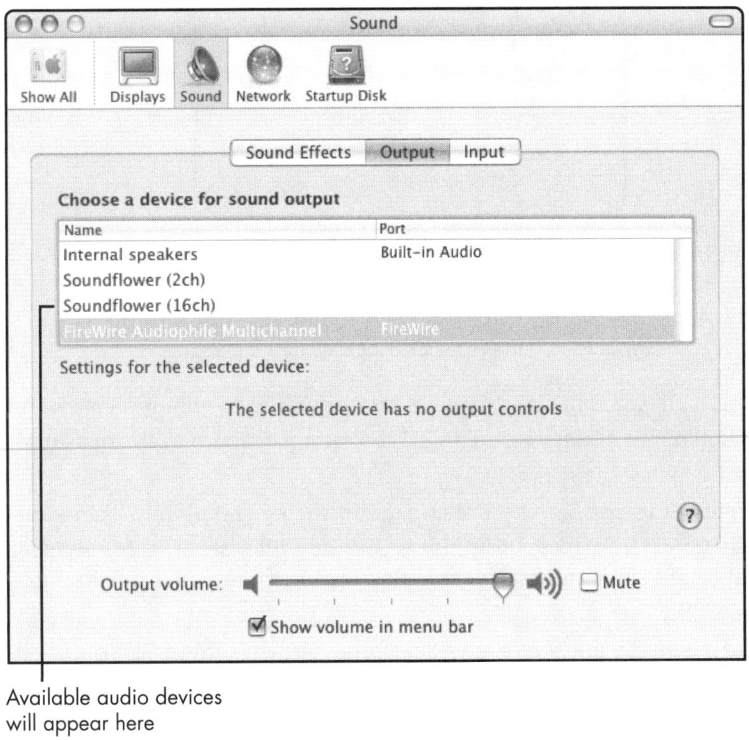

Figure 4.13 The Mac OS X Sound Preference panel, showing all audio devices currently available.

If your device is not appearing here, there may be a problem with your driver installation or with your actual audio hardware. In this case, I would recommend following the points above regarding updating the Mac OS and reinstalling your device drivers. Also try repairing your disk permissions.

In the case of USB or FireWire devices, disconnect any other devices of that type from your system. Also try changing the device cable for a new one.

For USB devices only, try unplugging and replugging the cable into the computer and see if the device is recognized.

If you have just installed the device and it is not being recognized, try restarting the Mac. Perhaps this is all that is necessary.

Problem: System Freezes When Using Audio Applications

This is a relatively uncommon problem with OS X but if it does happen, press Option- Apple-Esc on the keyboard to open the OS X Force Quit Applications dialogbox and end the application, as shown in Figure 4.14.

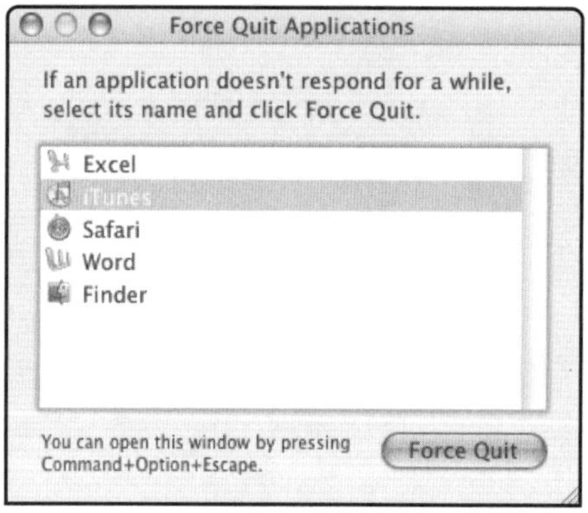

Figure 4.14 The Force Quit Applications dialogbox.

In most cases, you will not need to restart the machine to continue; simply relaunch the application and continue working. However, if the issue recurs, a system restart is always a good idea.

If the problem continues to happen, try erasing the program completely from your hard drive and then reinstalling it. It may also be useful to use the uninstall procedure outlined above using the Terminal window to delete all files related to the application from your system before reinstalling the application.

Having looked at some of the ways you can tune up your Mac for audio and keep it humming along smoothly, in the next chapter, let's look at how to do the same thing with a Windows PC.

5 Music on a Windows PC

This chapter presents a wealth of information that will help you keep your PC working smoothly at your live performances. There is information both on optimizing your PC system for audio use (very important), as well as some basic troubleshooting information in case anything goes wrong (and it will!).

Optimizing Your PC for Audio

Whether you have just gotten a new PC or you are refitting an old one for music use, it is very important to optimize your Windows machine for audio use. There are numerous settings and adjustments that can be made in Windows to get better system performance when working with music and audio. You can find lists of these on various Internet sites. In this section, I have put together my own such list of the optimization tips I have found the most helpful, together with some instructions and screenshots so you can see exactly what I'm talking about.

Please note that the instructions here are written specifically for Windows XP. If you are going to be performing live with a Windows PC, you really should be using Windows XP anyway, as it is the most stable of Microsoft's various OS releases.

Using Windows Hardware Profiles

Some of the optimizations in this section will have little noticeable effect on the performance of non-audio applications. However, in some cases, you may want to make changes in your system's hardware configuration for audio use but keep a more standard configuration for non-music applications. You can do this by using Windows' Hardware Profiles feature.

For example, your Ethernet card might be sharing an IRQ with your FireWire controller and causing audio problems with your FireWire audio interface. (See the Troubleshooting section below for more on IRQ issues.) In this case, you might choose to create two Hardware Profiles: One for audio/music use in which the Ethernet controller is disabled, and one for normal use in which the Ethernet controller is enabled so you can connect to the Internet or a local area network.

Go to Start → Control Panel and open the System control panel. Click the Hardware tab and then on the button labeled Hardware Profiles located at the bottom of the dialog box. Then you will see the Hardware Profiles dialog box (see Figure 5.1).

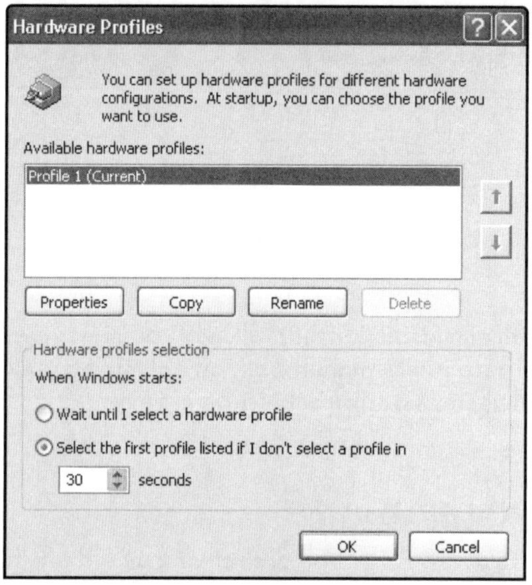

Figure 5.1 The Hardware Profiles dialog box.

If you haven't already created any additional profiles, you should see the words Profile 1 (Current) in the window, as shown here.

To make a new profile, click the Copy button and give your new profile a name such as Music or Audio.

Beneath this field are some more options that affect how Windows will choose which profile to use at start up. These options are self-explanatory.

Now click the OK button and reboot your computer. During reboot, you will see a screen allowing you to choose one of the Hardware Profiles you created.

It is advisable to perform this step first, before attempting the other optimization tips below. This allows you to keep one normal hardware profile for general use and have another particularly optimized for audio in which unneeded hardware devices are disabled in the Device Manager.

Disable Background Applications

If other applications are running in the background while you are using your music software, the audio performance may be significantly impeded. To see all applications running on your Windows XP machine, press Ctrl-Alt-Del on the keyboard to start the Windows Task Manager. You will see the current list of running applications under the Applications tab (see Figure 5.2) . The only applications you want to see open here are your music software and the drivers for your audio and/or MIDI interfaces (if you need to have the drivers open for some reason while you are using the software).

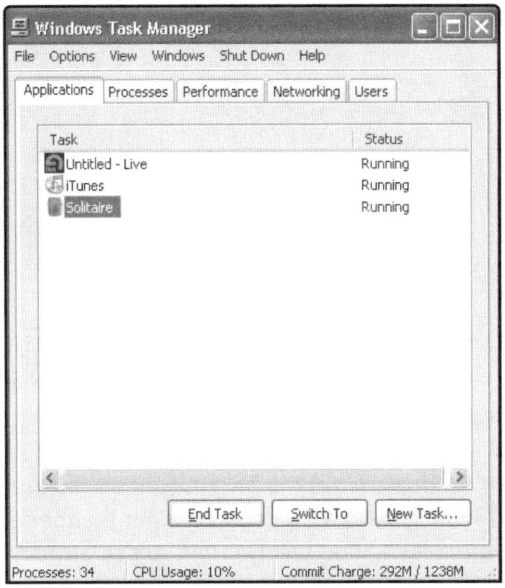

Figure 5.2 The Windows Task Manager, showing a list of currently running applications.

If you see other unneeded applications running here and consuming resources, you can stop them here by clicking End Task. Some of them will probably come back when you next restart your computer, so this solution is not much use.

For a more permanent fix, what you really need to do is to stop other applications from being launched at startup. You can do this by going to Start → Run in Windows. Type msconfig in the Open field and click OK. This opens the Windows XP System Configuration Utility (see Figure 5.3).

Then click the Startup tab. This shows all the applications and utilities that load each time you start your PC. By going down this list and checking or unchecking the items here, you can enable or disable applications loading at startup. You shouldn't just disable all of them however, some of them might be important to your system's operation or you might be using them for music.

For example, when I start my PC, the control panel for my M-Audio sound card loads in the system tray in the lower right-hand corner of the screen. I often use this to access my sound card driver and make adjustments when I am working on music in my home studio, so I leave this one enabled.

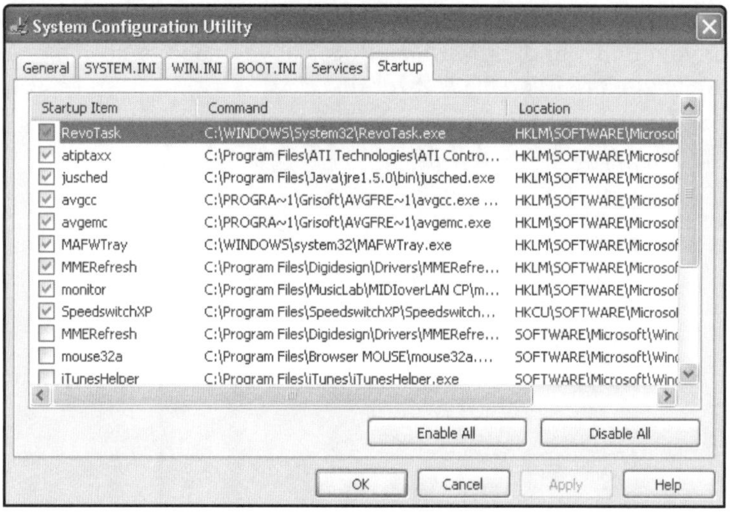

Figure 5.3 The list of startup applications in the System Configuration Utility.

Each PC will have a different list depending on what applications and drivers are installed, so I cannot advise you about exactly what you should or should not disable. However, if you look under the Command column here, you will be able to see exactly which executable file or command is being called upon. By examining this list, you can probably figure out what each item is and whether or not you need it. If you're not sure or don't recognize an item, you can play it safe and leave it enabled. Or if you disable it and later figure out that you made a mistake, you can always come back here and enable an item again.

Anti-Virus and Firewall Software

Anti-virus and firewall software are special cases here as the purpose of these programs requires that they run all the time. Thus, you would usually want these to load at startup.

However, to optimize audio performance, you may choose *not* to load these at startup. When you are actually performing, you probably won't be connected to the Internet, so you wouldn't need these programs on anyway.

If you do this, just make sure you run the anti-virus and firewall programs manually before you plug in your Internet connection again!

An alternative approach to this issue would be to carefully choose anti-virus and/or firewall software that is less resource-intensive. For example, the anti-virus applications from Norton and McAfee, while among the market leaders, are known for being rather demanding on system resources. A better alternative might be AVG Anti-Virus (http://free.grisoft.com/freeweb.php/doc/2), a free downloadable application that is less resource-intensive than many commercial offerings.

Enable DMA (Direct Memory Access) for IDE Hard Disks

Direct Memory Access allows your computer's hard drive to transfer data without having to disturb the operation of the CPU as it processes audio. Enabling DMA on your IDE hard drives will give you better overall system performance as well as increase the number of audio tracks that you are able to play simultaneously in an audio sequencing application.

If DMA mode is not enabled, you may hear various problems in your audio as it streams from the hard drive including pops and clicks, dropouts, or stuttering/repeated audio.

To check if DMA is enabled on your machine, you need to go to Start → Control Panel and open the System control panel by double-clicking it (see Figure 5.4).

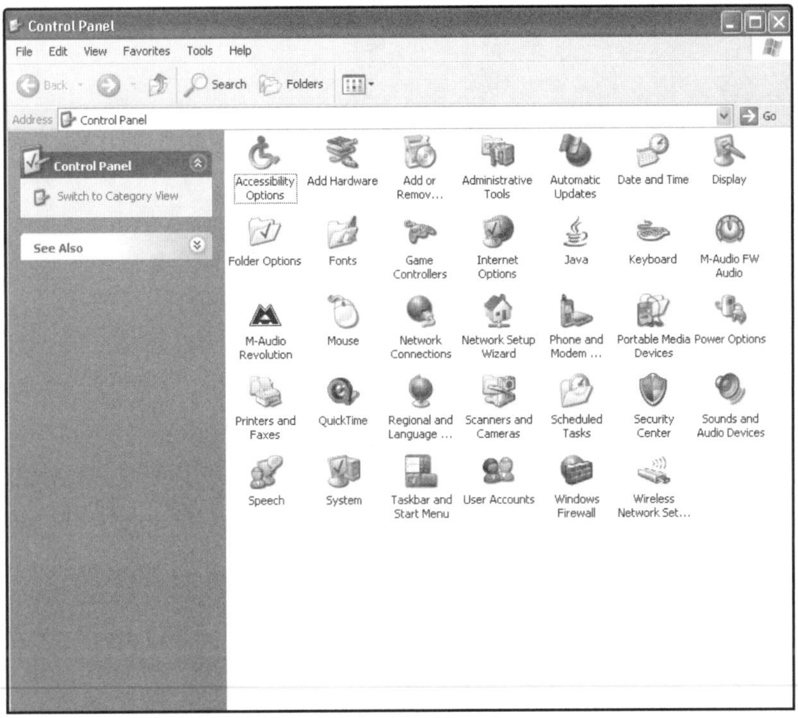

Figure 5.4 Windows Control Panel folder in Classic View.

If your Control Panel folder does not look like this, then you are probably in the Windows XP Category View instead (see Figure 5.5).

In this case, you need the click the link at the left that says Switch to Classic View, then you will see all the control panels as in Figure 5.4 above.

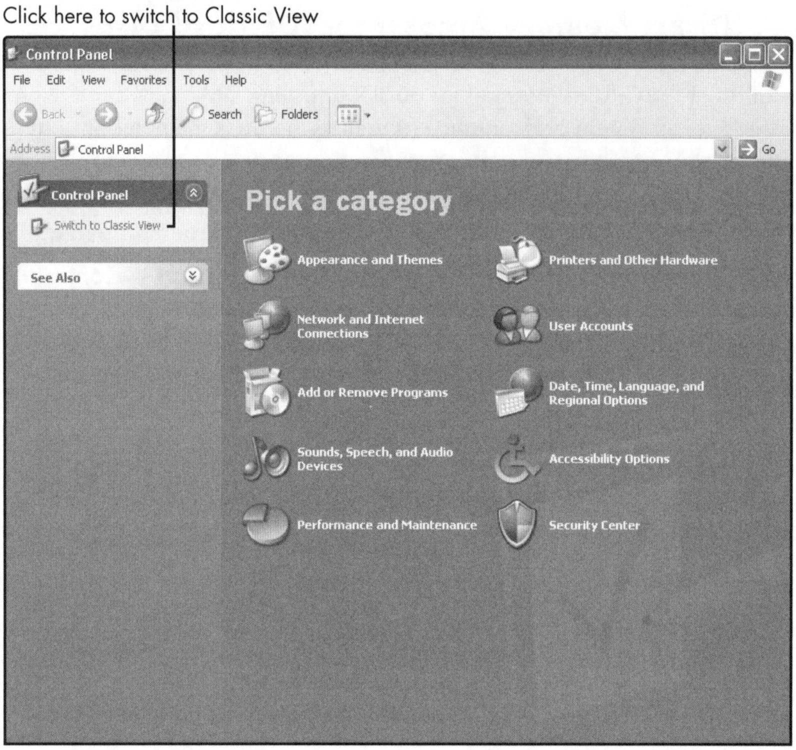

Figure 5.5 Windows Control Panel folder in Category View.

After opening the System control panel, click the Hardware tab to select it and then click the Device Manager button. This will bring up the Device Manager, showing all the hardware installed on your computer.

Click on the small + next to where you see IDE ATA/ATAPI controllers to see your IDE hard drive controllers (see Figure 5.6).

Double-click each of the Primary and Secondary IDE channels in turn to open its Properties window, then click the Advanced Settings tab to see the DMA settings, as shown in Figure 5.7.

Here you want to choose DMA if available as your selected Transfer Mode.

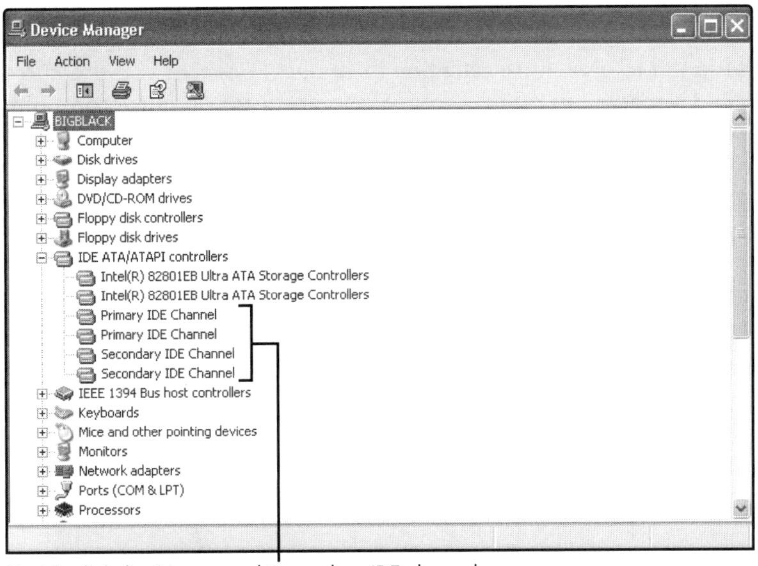

Double-click the Primary and Secondary IDE channels to open their Properties

Figure 5.6 The IDE controllers in the Device Manager.

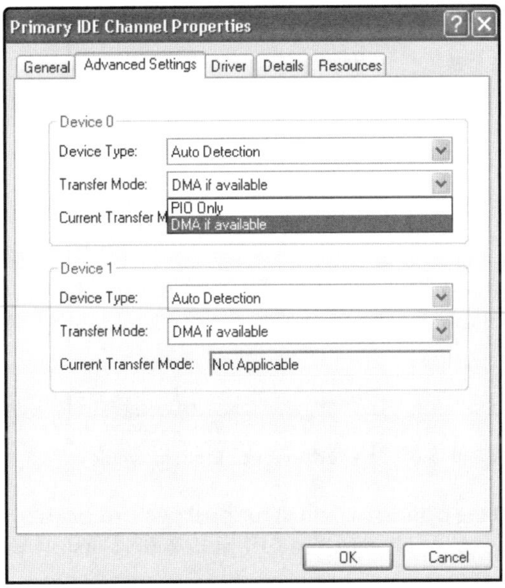

Figure 5.7 Setting the transfer mode to "DMA If Available".

Optimize Performance for Background Applications

Windows XP is designed to give more attention to applications that you are currently using by giving foreground applications more resources than services and programs running in the background. These background applications will include the driver for your sound card, for example. Thus, for audio use it is usually recommended to set Windows to optimize performance for background applications instead. (Also important: Before you do this, make sure you have already followed the instructions in the previous tip on preventing *unnecessary* applications from being loaded at startup so that there won't be a lot of unneeded applications running in the background.)

To do this, click Start → Control Panel, then double-click the System control panel to open it. Click the Advanced tab and click the Settings button, which you will see in the Performance section. Click yet another Advanced tab. The screen should now look like the one shown in Figure 5.8.

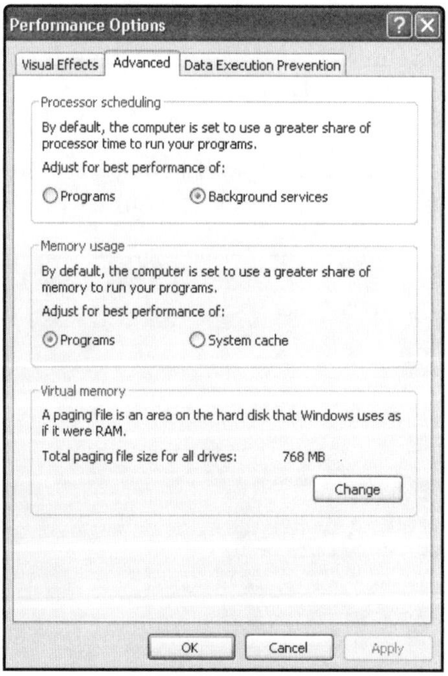

Figure 5.8 The Performance Options window.

In this tab, you want to select the option to Adjust for best performance of background services, as is shown in the figure above. Then click the OK button and restart Windows.

Reduce Graphics Acceleration

Another useful tip for optimizing your PC for audio is to reduce the hardware acceleration setting on your graphics card. This will help prevent your graphics card from taking too much of the system bandwidth away from the audio card when you need the resources for audio processing.

To change this setting, you need to select Start → Control Panel and double-click the Display control panel to open it. Then click the Settings tab. Then click the button labeled Advanced, and then click the Troubleshoot tab (see Figure 5.9).

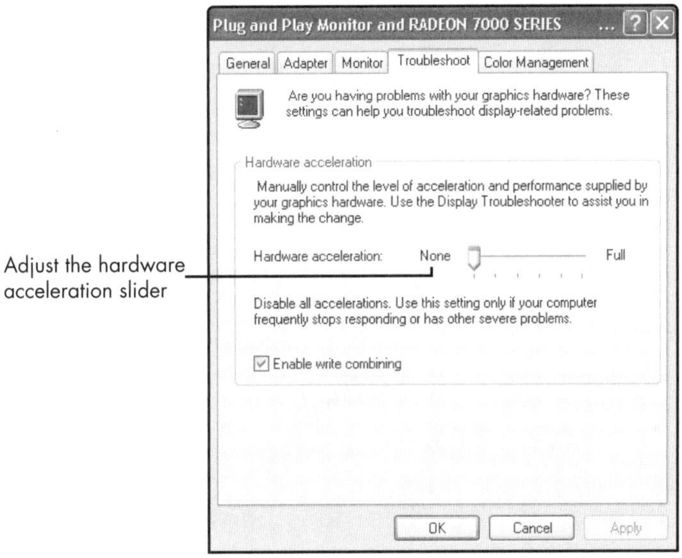

Figure 5.9 Setting the graphics hardware acceleration.

This is a screenshot from the control panel for the Diamond Radeon graphics card in my desktop PC, but yours should look similar.

Adjusting the Hardware acceleration slider here will allow you to set the level of acceleration and performance supplied by your graphics hardware. As you turn this down towards None on the left side of the window, the graphics card will use less system resources, but if you turn it down too far, you may start to notice some degradation in graphics performance.

Regularly Defragment Your Hard Drive

You should regularly defragment the hard drive on your Windows machine to avoid problems and optimize audio performance. You can do this by clicking Start, then right-click the My Computer icon and choose Explore. In the Windows Explorer window that opens up, you will see your drives appear on the right-hand side of the screen, for example C: and D:. To defragment one of them, right-click it and choose Properties. Click the tab marked Tools and choose Defragment Now... to begin the data defragmentation process (see Figure 5.10).

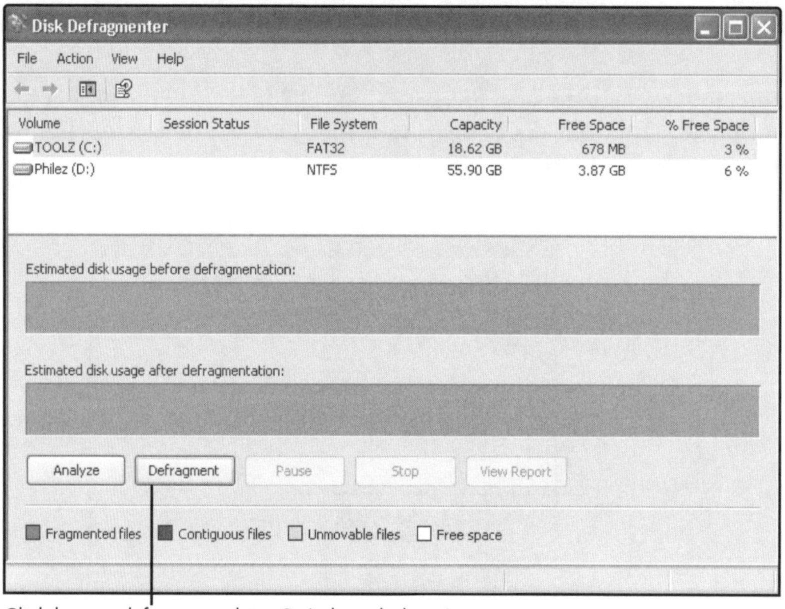

Click here to defragment drive C: (selected above)

Figure 5.10 Defragmenting drive C:.

Turn Off SpeedStep and CPU Throttling Features

SpeedStep and CPU Throttling technologies, most commonly found on laptop computers, attempt to save power and make your battery last longer by changing the speed of the processor, raising or lowering its maximum speed depending on the kinds of tasks it is performing. However, this can interfere with your digital audio processing and cause various problems including noise, dropouts, or audio distortion. For this reason, you should definitely turn this feature off when setting up your PC for music performance.

To see what speed your CPU is running at, go to Start → Control Panel and double-click the System control panel to open it. The speed of your processor will be displayed at the bottom of the first window that opens, the General tab. See Figure 5.11.

You can do this by using a small freeware program called SpeedswitchXP. This is the one that I have used on my PC laptops. You can download it from http://www.diefer.de/speedswitchxp.

SpeedswitchXP is a utility that allows you to control how or whether Windows XP will use this SpeedStep technology. It lets you adjust all of the power saving settings in Windows, which are not accessible otherwise through the Windows control panels.

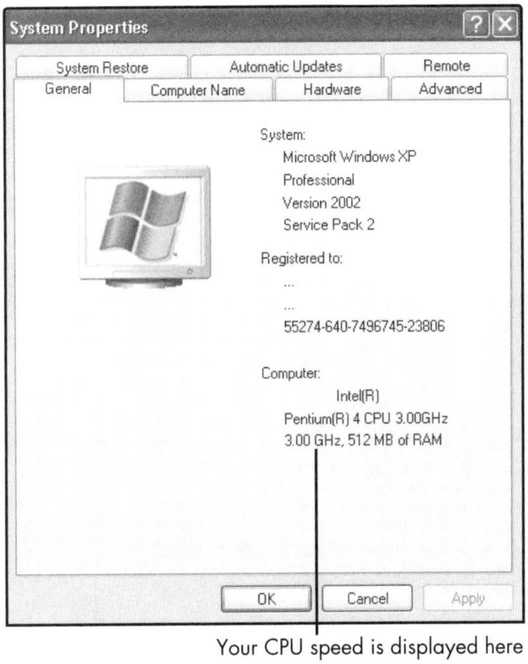

Figure 5.11 The System control panel, showing the CPU speed of the computer.

The author of SpeedswitchXP claims to have tested it with a number of different mobile CPUs and laptop computer models, and he has listed the specific results on his site. However, since the program works through Windows XP's own processor control functions, it should work on all laptop computers that feature this type of energy-saving technology.

By using this application, you are able to select a balance between performance and saving energy. For our purposes, using the computer for audio processing, you want to deactivate all energy-saving features and set the computer for maximum performance. Here's how to do this.

First, download SpeedswitchXP from the above Web site, then double-click the downloaded file and install the program.

After SpeedswitchXP is launched, it will appear as a small blue-and-green checkered flag icon in the System Tray. Double-click this small icon to access the program. Then you will see the opening screen, as shown in Figure 5.12.

For best performance, all you need to do here is go through and turn off all the modes that would enable energy saving. Make the same settings here for both the On AC column and On Battery columns:

- For CPU Speed, select Max. Performance
- For Display timeout, Disk timeout, Enter Standby, and Enter Hibernation, select Never

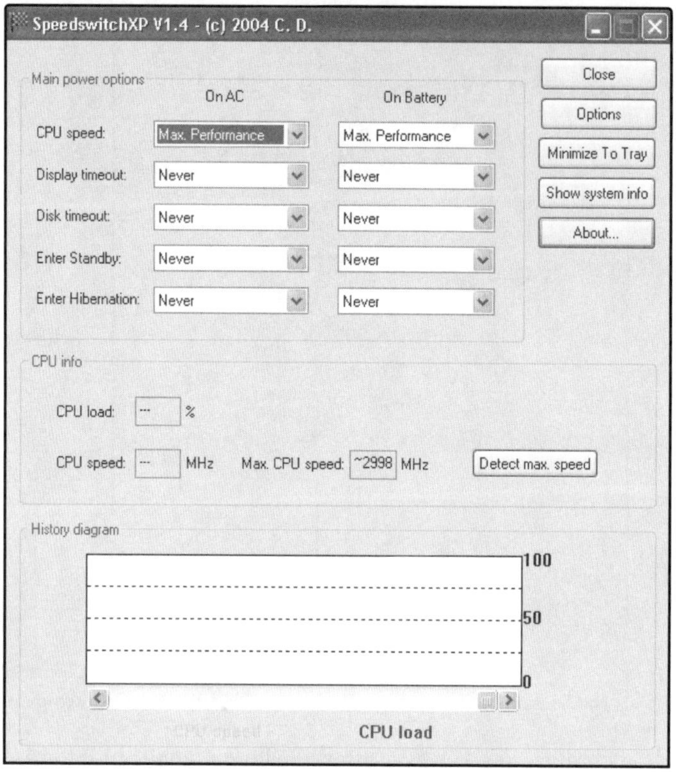

Figure 5.12 Setting the power options with SpeedswitchXP.

Adjusting the Visual Effects Modes

Another way to conserve some CPU power for use by your audio applications is to turn off unneeded graphics "bells and whistles" such as Windows' transition effects. This will help prevent potential problems such as dropouts in the audio when you open a new menu on-screen, for example.

First, you should adjust Windows handling of Visual Effects. To do this, go to Start → Control Panel and double-click the System control panel to open it. Click the Advanced tab and then click the button marked Settings in the Performance section. In the window that opens here, under the Visual Effects tab, you should select Adjust for best performance (see Figure 5.13).

Among other things, this will cause the appearance of Windows to switch back into a grittier "old-school" user interface, but it will save some system resources.

To disable the transition effects, go to Start → Control Panel, and double-click the Display control panel to open it. Choose the Appearance tab and then click the Effects button (see Figure 5.14).

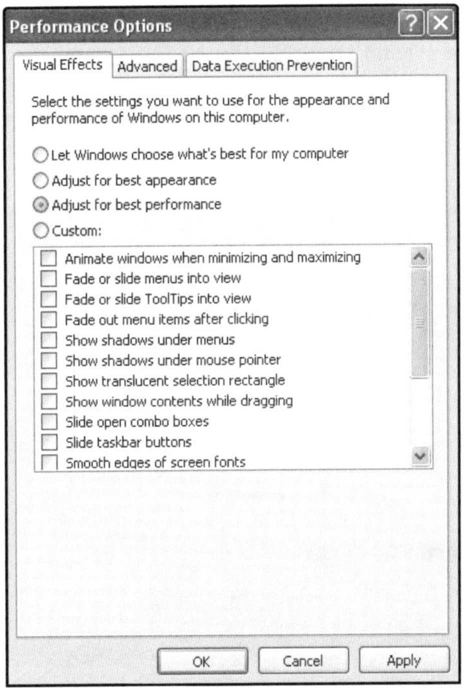

Figure 5.13 Adjusting the Visual Effects.

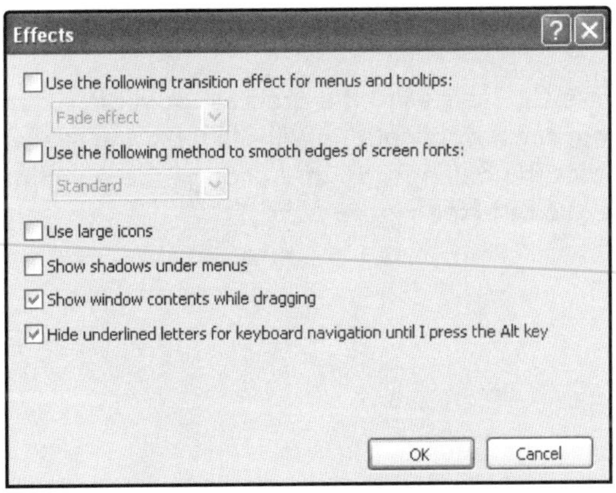

Figure 5.14 Disabling transition effects in the Display control panel.

Here you want to un-check the box that says, Use the following transition effect for menus and tool tips. You can also un-check the selection Show shadows under menus to save a few more CPU cycles. After you have un-checked these boxes, click OK to apply the settings.

While we are in the Display control panel, it is also a good idea to turn off the screen saver function in order to avoid the screen saver suddenly turning on at a live performance and causing an interruption in the audio stream. To change this setting, click the Screen Saver tab here and change the selection in the Screen saver drop-down chooser box to (None) (see Figure 5.15).

Figure 5.15 Disabling the screen saver.

If you really want to conserve CPU cycles to the greatest possible extent, you can also try a lower color resolution setting. Most applications will still look fine this way anyway. While in the Display control panel, click the Settings tab and change the selection in the Color quality drop-down box to Medium (16-bit) (see Figure 5.16).

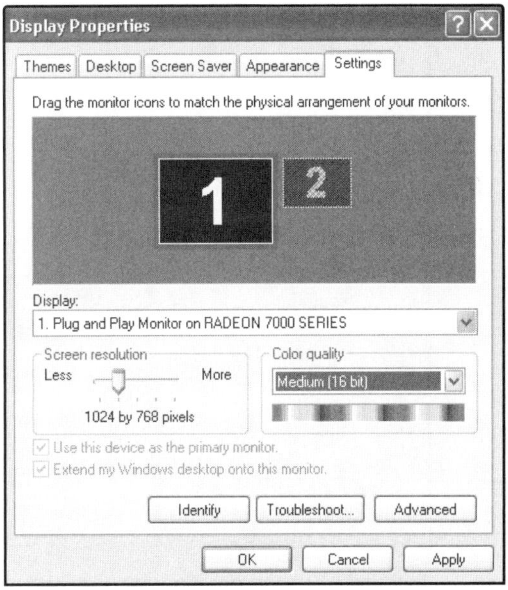

Figure 5.16 Changing the color quality.

Do Not Map Through Sound Card

This tip will also help conserve CPU power. To change this setting, go to Start → Control Panel and double-click the Sounds and Audio Devices control panel to open it. Choose the hardware tab and then highlight your sound card in the list of drivers and devices (see Figure 5.17).

Click the Properties button here, and then choose the Properties tab. Click the small + sign by the small speaker icon labeled Audio Devices and highlight your sound card, as shown in Figure 5.18.

Click yet another Properties button. In the window that opens, check the box that say, Do not map through this device (see Figure 5.19).

Then click OK to apply the changes. However, the new settings here will not take effect until the next time you restart Windows.

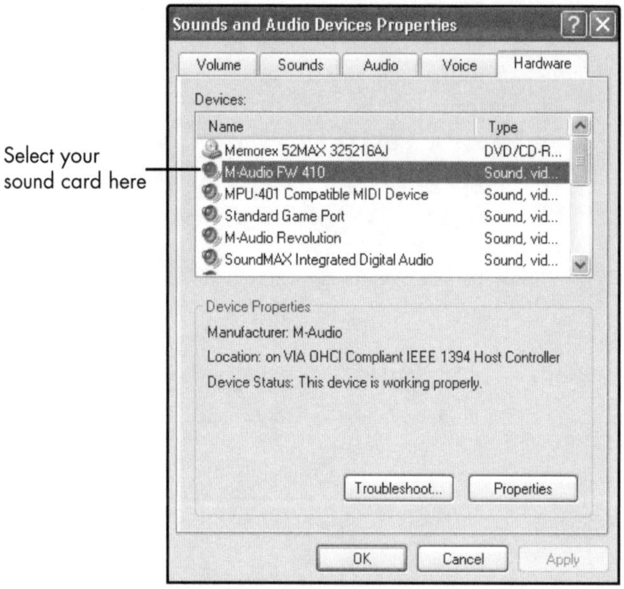

Figure 5.17 Selecting your sound card.

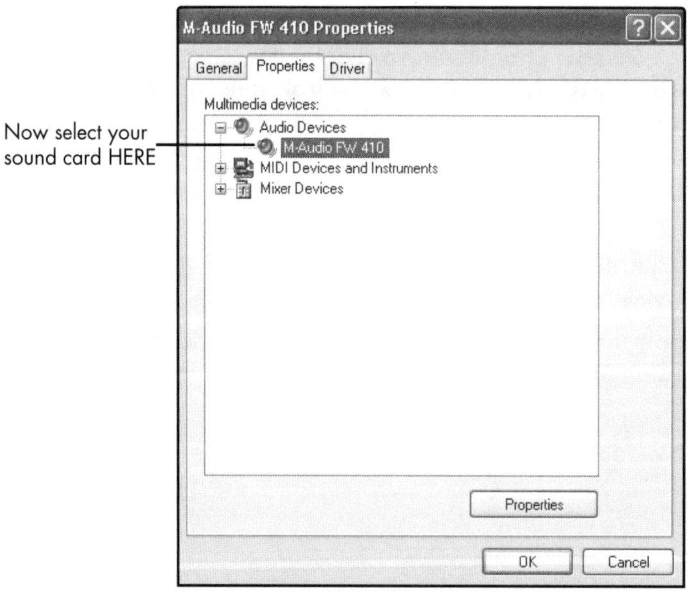

Figure 5.18 Selecting your sound card AGAIN.

Figure 5.19 "Do not map through this device".

Turn Off System Sounds

It is a good idea to turn off the Windows system sounds in order to prevent unwanted system beeps and alarms from interjecting themselves into your performance! To do this, go to Start → Control Panel, double-click the Sounds and Audio Devices control panel and select the Sounds tab (see Figure 5.20).

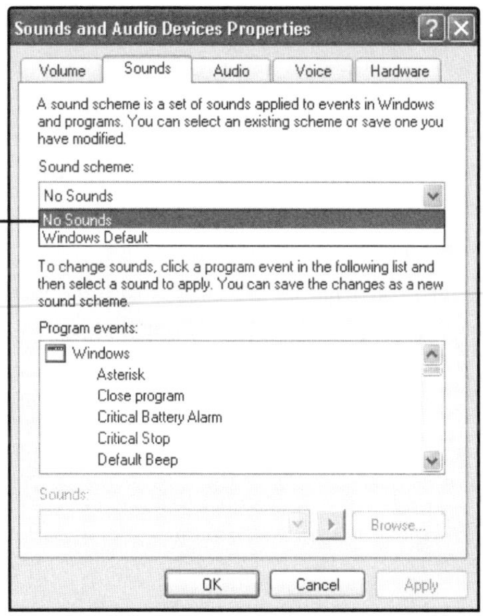

Figure 5.20 Turning off the Windows system sounds.

Here you should select No Sounds in the drop-down chooser box labeled Sound scheme.

Turn Off USB Root Hub Power Management

This optimization helps prevent problems with your USB audio and/or MIDI gear, directing Windows *not* to stop providing power to devices connected to the USB ports of the computer. (Why anyone thought that it was a good idea for Windows to behave this way in the first place is another question, but anyway...)

To stop Windows from doing this, you need to change some settings in the Device Manager.

To access the Windows Device Manager, go to Start → Run and type devmgmt.msc in the Open field (see Figure 5.21).

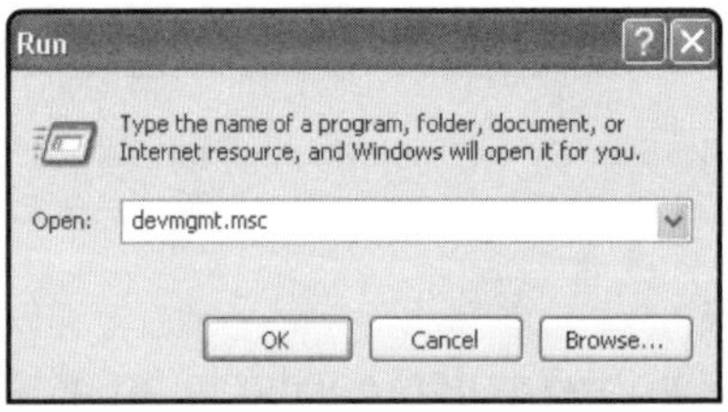

Figure 5.21 Using the Start → Run interface to run commands in Windows.

This will bring you to the Device Manager window. Now click on one of the small + signs below, just to the left of the USB icon labeled Universal Serial Bus controllers to see all of your USB root hubs and host controllers. You will have varying numbers of these depending on how many USB ports your computer has. On my PC, the screen looks like that shown in Figure 5.22.

Now, right-click on one of the icons labeled USB Root Hub and select Properties. In the USB Root Hub Properties window that opens, click on the Power Management tab. In this window, you want to un-check the box that say, Allow the computer to turn off this device to save power. See Figure 5.23.

Click OK to apply the setting.

Repeat this same procedure for each of the USB root hubs visible here.

You will have to restart your computer to make these changes effective.

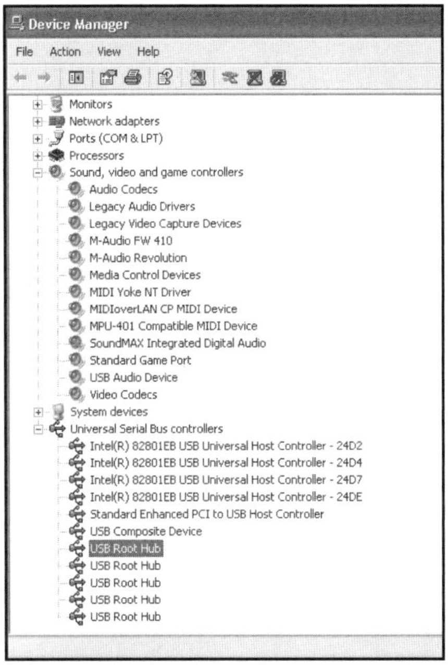

Figure 5.22 Accessing the USB root hubs in the Device Manager window.

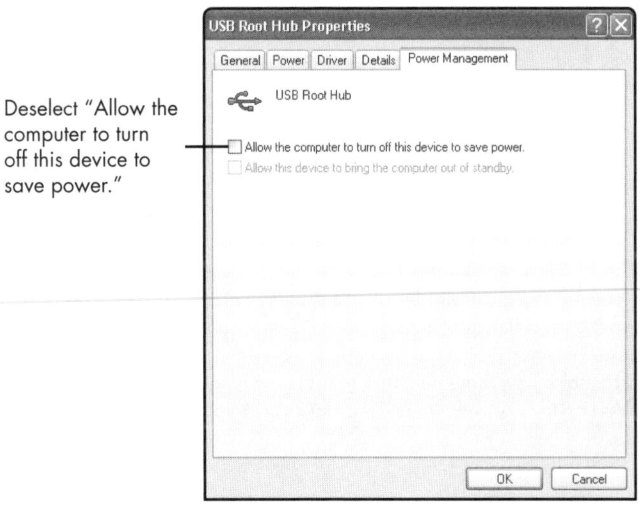

Figure 5.23 Disabling the USB root hub power management function.

Disabling Windows' Automatic Update Feature

You should turn off Windows' Automatic Update feature in order to prevent your computer from suddenly locking onto a local wireless network while you are performing and trying to update itself while you are playing your set.

To change this feature, go to Start → Control Panel and double-click the System control panel to open it. Click the Automatic Updates tab and select Turn off Automatic Updates (see Figure 5.24).

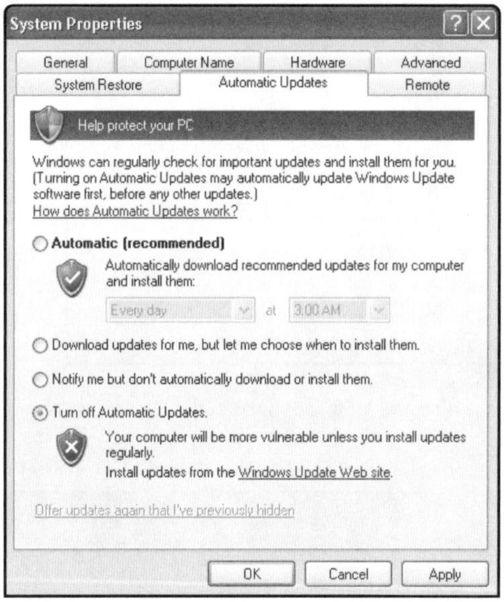

Figure 5.24 Turning off Automatic Updates.

> **WINDOWS UPDATES**
>
> Although disabling the Windows Automatic Update feature is a useful precaution for preventing problems in an audio performance, you should also be aware that many of the updates released by Microsoft are critical to maintaining the proper functioning of your PC and preventing access by hackers or intruders, particularly if you also use your PC on the Internet. If you do turn off the Automatic Update feature in Windows, you need to make sure that you check in fairly frequently at http://www.windowsupdate.com and keep your machine up-to-date with the latest patches and updates.

Disable Windows Error Reporting

You can stop Windows' automatic error reporting feature by going to Start → Control Panel, double-clicking the System control panel to open it, then clicking the Advanced tab. Click the button marked Error Reporting and click Disable error reporting. Make sure the adjacent box labeled "But notify me when critical errors occur" is still checked (see Figure 5.25).

Figure 5.25 Disabling Windows' error reporting feature.

Virtual Memory Settings

You may also get improved performance by setting the minimum and maximum virtual memory paging file sizes to be the same. To set this, go to Start → Control Panel → System → Advanced, then click the Settings button in the Performance section of the window. Then click the tab labeled Advanced, and click the button marked Change under Virtual memory. The screen should now look like Figure 5.26.

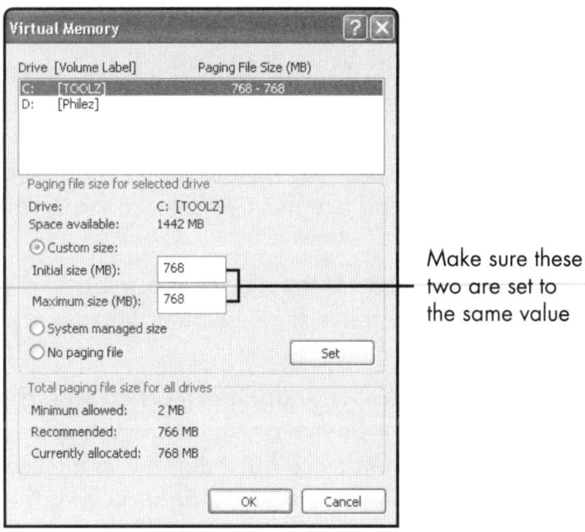

Figure 5.26 Setting the virtual memory paging file size.

Where it says Paging file size for selected drive in this window, click the Custom size button and set both the initial size and the maximum size to the recommended paging file size for your system (found in the lower part of this window). Click the button labeled Set, then OK. Click OK twice more to close all windows. (Note that these settings will not take effect until the next time you restart Windows.)

Basic Audio Troubleshooting for PCs

There are numerous potential problems with getting your audio running smoothly on a Windows PC, particularly on a laptop. Some of these are specific to the particular type of audio device you are using while others are more general problems. I have listed some of the most common problems you might have working with audio on your PC, and how best to troubleshoot them.

Problems with Devices Not Being Recognized

Q: I tried to install my audio or MIDI interface but it doesn't seem to be recognized by my system/There was a problem with the installation/I don't see the device as a choice in my applications

To check if Windows is recognizing your audio or MIDI device, look in the Device Manager. Go to Start → Run, type devmgmt.msc, and click OK. In the Device Manager window that opens, click the small + next to Sound, video and game controllers and a list of installed drivers/devices will appear (see Figure 5.27).

Check this list to see if your audio and/or MIDI interface appear. In this list from my system, we can see my two M-Audio audio interfaces as well as other built-in audio and MIDI devices and drivers.

If your device does not appear here at all, try reinstalling the driver according to the instructions below. If it is a USB or FireWire device, also try changing the cable connecting the device to the computer, check the external power supply (if any) to make sure you are using the right type, unplug any other USB or FireWire devices connected to the computer while you are doing the installation, and confirm that you are not trying to connect your device through a USB or FireWire hub.

Also make sure that the small speaker icon for the device is not marked with a yellow exclamation mark indicating some problem. If there is an exclamation point, try uninstalling and reinstalling the driver following the instructions below.

If you see any device anywhere in the Device Manager marked with a yellow exclamation mark and named something like Unknown Device or Multimedia Audio Controller, this probably indicates that the computer detects the device but it didn't find the correct driver for some reason. In this case, you can try to install the driver by right-clicking the device here in the Device Manager list and then choosing Update Driver. Then follow through the instructions here to update the driver.

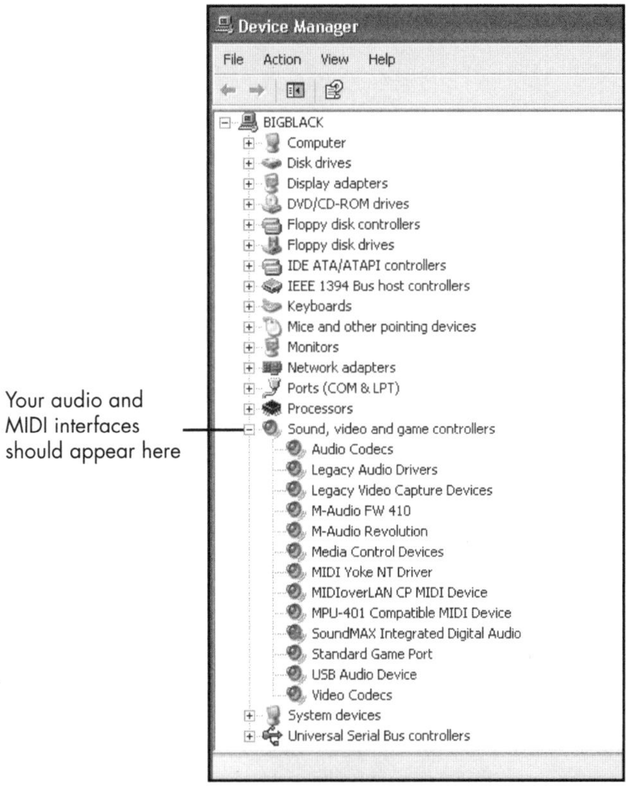

Figure 5.27 The Sound, video, and game controllers list in the Device Manager.

If you need to reinstall the driver, first clear the Windows TEMP folder. You can do this by right-clicking Start and choosing Explore, then find the folder C:/Documents and Settings/<your username>/Local Settings/Temp. Select all the files in this folder and delete them. (Don't worry, if you needed any of these, Windows would have copied them to a permanent location already.)

After doing this, check the Web site of your device's manufacturer for the latest updated driver for your device. Particularly if you first installed your interface by using an installation CD-ROM that came with the product, there are probably newer (and quite possibly better) drivers available for the device.

In most cases, you should uninstall the previous driver installation first before installing the new version. Some companies will provide an uninstaller with the driver; check for this first. If you can't find a proprietary uninstaller for your device, you can also uninstall the driver manually from the Device Manager.

You can uninstall your device drivers here by right-clicking your audio device and choosing Uninstall (see Figure 5.28).

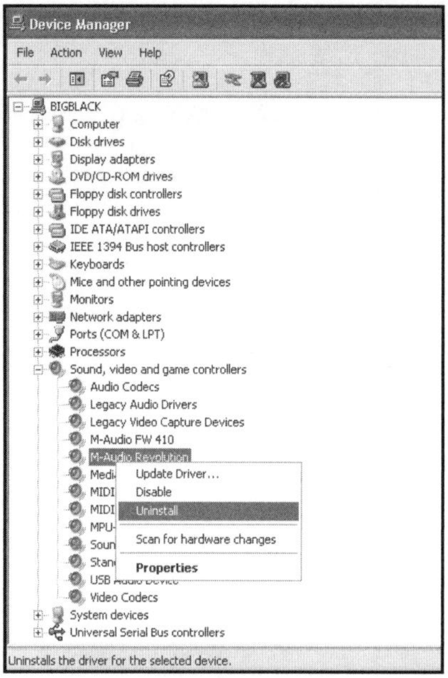

Figure 5.28 Uninstalling your device in the Device Manager.

After doing this, you should also physically unplug/detach the device from your computer.

Then reinstall with the most recent driver for your device, making sure that no other applications are running during the installation and following all on-screen instructions in the driver installer.

Specific Error Messages

Q: I am getting some specific error message from Windows during an audio or MIDI operation but I don't know what the message means.

The best solution to this problem is to copy down the *exact* text of the error message and then enter this into your favorite Internet search engine. Search for the exact text of the error message and place it between quotation marks; this will cause most search engines to search for only that exact wording, as shown in Figure 5.29.

This may seem like an obvious tip but it is often the best way to find out specific information about a Windows error message.

Figure 5.29 Googling for information about a Windows Code 10 error.

Pops and Clicks and Other Audio Problems

One of the most common problems with computer audio manifests itself as audible pops, clicks, or other small artifacts in your audio stream. There are many possible causes for this problem, but if you are having this issue with your system, here are some of the fixes you should try first:

Try Increasing the Buffer Size/Latency for Your Audio Interface

Probably the most common cause of audio artifacts is having your audio buffer size set too low. In Windows, you should adjust this in the control panel of your audio interface, *before* you open your audio application. See Figure 5.30.

In some audio applications there are also settings for this within the application itself, typically in its audio preferences.

The buffer size is the amount of sample data stored in the audio buffer at one time, and this is what causes latency in your computer audio system.

It is useful to understand that there is no "correct" setting or value for the buffer size. Adjusting the buffer size is a compromise between performance and pristine audio, and the best setting for you will be dependent on a number of different factors including the speed and power of your system, the particular application you are running, and the number of simultaneous audio tracks and effects you are using.

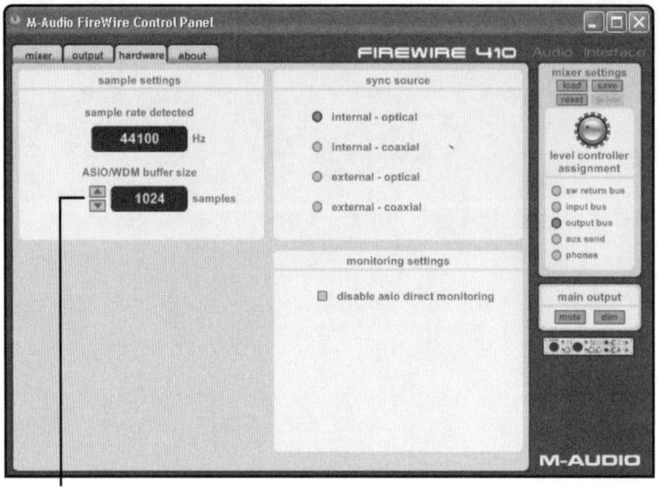

Figure 5.30 Setting the buffer size on my M-Audio FireWire 410.

If you have a very powerful system and/or are running a stripped-down software setup that doesn't require a lot of system resources, you may be able to get good results even with a very low buffer size setting. However, if you start to hear pops, clicks, or other digital audio artifacts, you can try increasing the buffer size setting bit by bit until the problems go away. Basically, you want to use the lowest setting you can without running into audio problems.

AUDIO LATENCY AND BUFFER SIZE IN PC AUDIO

Just what are these buffer size and latency settings anyway? And why IS there always that slight delay when recording or playing back audio on my PC? There are actually a number of related situations in which latency can be an issue when working with computer audio. However, at the most basic level, latency is simply the delay during which audio is being translated from the analog to digital realm or vice versa. We can never get rid of this delay entirely, although on a powerful well-set-up system with a professional sound card, the latency may be so small as to be unnoticeable. In other cases, you may find that you need to work with quite a high buffer size/latency setting in order to get clean audio input and output with your system.

Make Sure You are Running a Clean Installation of the Latest Drivers for Your Audio Interface or Sound Card

Try reinstalling the audio card drivers following the procedure in the section above on troubleshooting audio card installation problems to ensure a clean installation.

Install All Windows Updates and Service Packs

Run Internet Explorer and go to http://www.windowsupdate.com to check and make sure you have all the latest available updates from Microsoft.

In the case of a major update such as a new Windows Service Pack, it may be wiser in some cases not to install right away when the update is first released, as it may take some time for application software and device drivers to be updated by third party manufacturers to maintain compatibility with the latest Microsoft update.

In general, however, it is best simply to install the latest patches and updates from Microsoft as soon as they come out. As long as you keep your audio and other device drivers current as well, you should be OK. In addition to fixing actual problems with the OS, it is important to keep everything updated because third party manufacturers will also be using machines running the latest updated OSes to design and test their own new drivers and application updates. If you don't keep your installation of Windows updated, then your device(s) might not work correctly when you update/reinstall the device driver(s).

Check Your Installation of DirectX

You should also check and make sure you have the latest version of Microsoft's DirectX installed. You can see which version of DirectX you are currently running on your system by going to Start → Run, typing dxdiag, and clicking OK. This will open the DirectX Diagnostic Tool, shown in Figure 5.31.

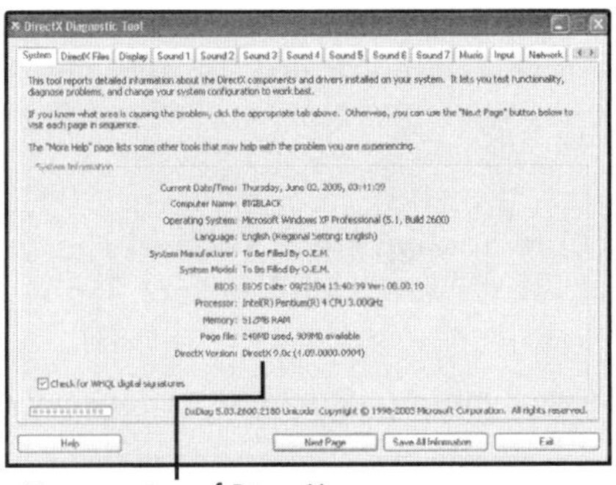

Figure 5.31 The DirectX Diagnostic Tool.

Look down at the bottom of this window to see what version of DirectX you are running. You should make sure that you have the latest version released by Microsoft. To see the current version and download updates if necessary, check this page on the Microsoft Web site http://www.microsoft.com/windows/directx/default.aspx. This can be the cause of a lot of problems if it is out of date.

Try Following All the Windows Audio Optimization Tips in this Chapter

This seems obvious, but it is worth mentioning that I have seen numerous cases of audio problems that were suddenly resolved after applying just one of the optimization tips I went over in the previous section.

If only you can find the *right* one to apply... but that's all part of the fun of computer audio!

Update Drivers for Other Hardware on Your System

In some cases, audio problems can be caused by minor conflicts or incompatibilities with other devices in your system. You can fix this by making sure you are using the latest updated drivers for all the devices you are using.

If Using a USB or FireWire Audio Interface, Check for Possible Conflicts with Other Devices

Make sure you are not connecting through a USB hub; if you are, try connecting the device directly to a USB port on the computer itself instead. This is particularly important if you are using a device that draws its power from the USB port in lieu of an external power adapter.

You should also try disconnecting any other USB devices (other than your keyboard and mouse) while you are working on audio or MIDI projects. If you are still having problems, try using the device on any other available USB ports on your computer. (Your system may ask you to reinstall the drivers for the device when you do this, but this is okay.)

Similarly, in the case of a FireWire interface, try disconnecting any other FireWire devices you may have connected and see if you still have the problem. You may also need to check the Web site of your audio interface's manufacturer for any information about possible incompatibilities or known conflicts.

Check for IRQ Conflicts

If you go through the other troubleshooting steps listed above and are still having audio problems, you should check and see if there is an Interrupt Request (IRQ) conflict with your audio or MIDI device.

Windows PCs use interrupt requests to manage communications between the CPU and various hardware devices, such as sound cards, Ethernet connections, keyboards, and so on. For example, when the Ethernet controller needs to access the CPU to process some data, it sends an interrupt request to the CPU along its designated IRQ line. The CPU then interrupts its current job to let the controller run its command.

Problems can arise because your computer has only a limited number of IRQs (16 of them, numbered 0-15), and multiple devices sharing the same IRQ can interfere with each other. This is not a big problem for many operations because most data transfers on your computer are *asynchronous,* meaning that they can stop and resume again without causing problems. However, a stream of audio data is a *synchronous* transfer, a continuous flow. If this flow of data is interrupted by communications with another device in your system, problems in your audio can result, including pops, clicks, drop-outs, application freezes, sample rate changes, or other anomalies.

To check if your audio problems are being caused by an IRQ conflict, you can look in your Device Manager. Go to Start → Run, type devmgmt.msc, and click OK. The Device Manager window will then open. Then click View in the menu bar and choose Resources by type. You will see a small display containing four silicon-chip-style icons. Click the small + sign next to the icon labeled Interrupt request (IRQ) and a list of the IRQ assignments for your system will be displayed (see Figure 5.32).

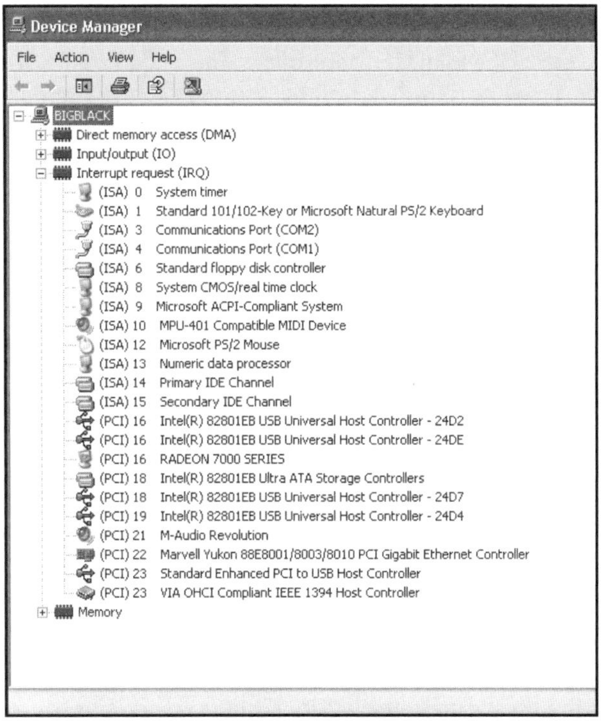

Figure 5.32 The IRQ list in the Device Manager.

In order to determine if you have a possible IRQ conflict with your audio device, you need to find which IRQ it is using. If you are using a PCI sound card in a desktop PC, it will show up here under its own name if it is properly installed in your system. (See the M-Audio PCI card installed in my desktop system in Figure 5.32.)

However, this will of course not be the case for most computer musicians as the majority are using laptop computers, which do not have PCI slots. Most laptop musicians will be using a USB, FireWire, or CardBus audio device, and these external devices will not show up directly in this list. In this case, you need to find the IRQ being used by the appropriate controller through which the device is communicating with the CPU.

Looking again at the list above, my USB ports appear here as Intel(R) 82801EB USB Universal Host Controller and my FireWire controller is labeled VIA OHCI Compliant IEEE 1394 Host Controller. If this were a laptop computer and it had a CardBus card slot in it, this would appear something like Texas Instruments PCI-1420 CardBus Controller, for example.

In general, your various controllers will show up in this list as the name of the manufacturer and perhaps some model number code, followed by USB Universal Host Controller, IEEE 1394 Host Controller, or CardBus Controller, depending on what kind of interface it is.

In some cases, there will be more than one controller of a given type present. For example, in my system we can see four of the Intel USB controllers. This indicates the presence of multiple ports, and in some cases, these ports will not all be assigned to the same IRQ. In my system, we can see that I have two USB ports on IRQ16 and IRQ18, for example. However, it is difficult to determine exactly which controller on this list is assigned to which physical port on your machine.

In any event, having found which IRQ your audio interface is using, you can look up and down the list for possible IRQ conflicts. A possible conflict would be any case in which other hardware devices are sharing an IRQ with the IRQ your audio device is using.

For example, in my system, we can see that IRQ16 is being shared by my Diamond Radeon graphics card and two of the USB controllers. This is probably the most serious conflict you can have, a conflict with the graphics card, because graphics processing is such a CPU-intensive activity. If you have a conflict between your audio interface and your graphics controller, this is virtually guaranteed to cause audio problems.

However, this particular conflict does not cause audio problems for me because I am not using a USB audio interface with this system. I am using an M-Audio FireWire 410 interface, connected to the FireWire controller in my computer. As noted above, my FireWire controller appears in this IRQ list as VIA OHCI Compliant IEEE 1394 Host Controller and we can see that it is assigned to IRQ23 and is not sharing with any other devices in my system.

But wait a minute... didn't I just say that there were only 16 IRQs numbered 0-15? (Answer: Yes, I did.) So why are the IRQs numbered up to 23 here? This is because in Windows XP, with motherboards that have an Advanced Programmable Interrupt Controller (APIC), up to 24 IRQs are now available. This is accomplished by mapping a virtual interrupt table to a single IRQ (usually IRQ 9 or 11) and letting Windows determine the priority of a device's interrupt request at the operating system level for the additional new IRQs.

While this "virtual IRQ" system allows for more devices to be connected and assigned to a Windows system, it also presents us with the potential for more problems with audio as there is potential for IRQ problems with any device on an IRQ higher than 16. In this case, my FireWire controller may still be sharing with another device in my system although it seems to be all by itself on IRQ 23. This is only a virtual IRQ, though, and there actually IS no physical IRQ 23.

So to recap: If your device or the controller it is using is sharing its IRQ with any other device, there may be an IRQ conflict occurring that is causing your audio problems. In addition, if your device or its controller is on an IRQ higher than 15, it is on a virtual IRQ and may be sharing with other devices in your system even if it does not appear to be sharing on this table.

In my case, since my FireWire controller is on IRQ23, we can see that there is a potential IRQ sharing problem here. However, it is important to emphasize that this is only a *potential* conflict, this does not mean that problems will necessarily occur. If your computer has plenty of CPU power and RAM memory, you may notice no problems. (In my case, my PC is just fine with the FireWire controller on IRQ 23 and the audio from my FireWire 410 is crystal-clear.)

If you determine that an IRQ conflict may be occurring and causing your audio problems, there are several things you can do. Unfortunately, you can *not* directly change the IRQs however you want in Windows—this is not possible.

If you are using a desktop computer system, the best way to deal with an IRQ conflict is to swap slots: Power down the computer, unplug the power cord, and move the PCI audio card (or PCI FireWire or USB expansion card) to another slot in your computer. The manual provided by your computer or motherboard's manufacturer should give some information about which PCI slots are sharing with other slots or devices, helping you to determine which slot would be most likely not to suffer conflicts.

Another option with a desktop PC is to switch Windows XP from what is called "ACPI" mode into "Standard PC" mode, which changes how the computer assigns IRQs and makes it possible to manually reassign the IRQs within Windows. However, changing to Standard PC mode is something of an ordeal and is not recommended for use with laptops anyway.

Thus, if you are on a laptop computer, your options to deal with an IRQ conflict are more limited. What's more, there is more often than not the potential for some conflict on a cramped laptop system, as most laptops will assign the USB, FireWire, and CardBus controllers to virtual IRQs above 15, and it is impossible to move them.

In this case, there are still a few things you can do to minimize the possibility of problems.

For one thing, I would recommend following the optimization tips discussed in the previous section. With enough free system resources available, your computer may be able to properly route all the audio signals in time even though your IRQ list indicates a potential conflict. In the case of my studio PC system, my powerful Pentium 4 processor never seems to have a problem routing audio through any of the ports or cards and I haven't had to worry too much about this particular issue.

Another thing you can do is to disable some of the devices in your system, particularly if you are not using them anyway. You can do this from the same IRQ list in the Device Manager. Simply right-click on any of the devices in the list and choose Disable. After you do this, the device will disappear from the IRQ list, though it will still appear in the device list. For example, in my PC system, I have disabled the onboard audio controller in my motherboard because I don't need it.

Going back up to the Device Manager's menu bar and choosing View → Devices by type brings us back to the device list. Click the small + sign next to the category labeled Sound, video and game controllers to open it and you will see a list that looks like the one in Figure 5.33.

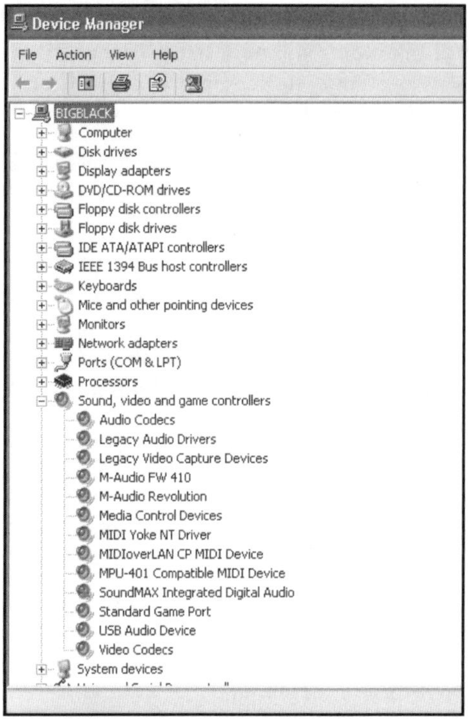

Figure 5.33 My SoundMAX Integrated Digital Audio controller is disabled.

Here you can see that the small speaker icon next to my onboard sound controller (the SoundMAX Integrated Digital Audio Controller) is marked with a small red x, indicating that it is still installed in the system but is currently disabled.

For maximum performance and to avoid potential IRQ conflicts, you can go through the IRQ list and disable any devices that you do not need to use when you are performing; for example your modem, Ethernet controller, unused interface controllers, COM ports, and so on. However, you need to exercise great care here, as many of the devices on the IRQ list are essential to the operation of your computer and your PC will not function properly if they are disabled. In particular, you should not disable any of the following devices or device types:

- System timer
- Keyboard
- System CMOS/real time clock
- ACPI-Compliant System

- Mouse
- Numeric data processor
- IDE Channels
- ATA Controllers

Unfortunately, it is possible that you will still have IRQ-related audio problems even after optimizing your system and disabling unused devices. In this case, another workaround may be to try connecting through a different type of interface on your machine. For example, if you are using USB or FireWire audio, you can install a CardBus expansion card in your laptop to give you extra USB or FireWire ports and try connecting this way instead of the computer's built-in USB or FireWire ports. If the CardBus controller in your machine is on a different IRQ than the USB/FireWire controllers, this may solve your problem.

If this doesn't help, another option is to switch to another type of interface and see if that gives better results on your system. For example, my Compaq Presario 700 simply wouldn't work with any FireWire audio device for more than a few seconds, and then some drastic resource problem caused the audio to stop playing entirely. However, I got much better results with a CardBus audio card on this machine (although I still had a few unresolvable problems, unfortunately).

If you are still having problems no matter what you try, a final drastic solution is to reformat the entire hard drive and reinstall Windows. If you do a fresh reinstall of Windows from scratch, in theory it is supposed to reinstall all your hardware and create an optimized IRQ allocation for you, and in some cases, this can resolve otherwise-insoluble IRQ conflicts that are causing audio problems.

There is a catch, though. When you buy a laptop computer with Windows XP, it typically comes not with the standard Microsoft Windows installer disks, but rather with a customized version made especially for your particular model of laptop. In most cases that I am aware of, this means that when you reinstall from these disks, it will simply copy a cloned disk image onto your hard drive instead of actually reinstalling Windows from scratch. After you reinstall from these disks, your IRQ allocation (and all other system settings) will be exactly the same as they were when you originally purchased the machine. Thus, it will probably not improve the IRQ allocation if you reinstall Windows from a set of OEM installer disks like this, although it will cure a lot of other system problems that might also be causing your audio problem.

Chipset Problems

In some cases, if you are having problems that resemble an IRQ conflict even though you have gone through the above IRQ troubleshooting procedures and it doesn't appear that you have a conflict, the problem may be your actual motherboard/chipset combination you are using. This is usually not a question of particular incompatibilities but rather general resource problems, i.e., the motherboard/chipset is unable to transmit the streaming audio data in an orderly fashion because of data bottlenecks, poor quality components, or whatever reason.

It is impossible for me to test or recommend specific motherboards here because there are so many, and in any event, if you buy a laptop computer you will be using whatever is in the computer already; you cannot change the motherboard in a laptop yourself. However, as a general rule of thumb you get what you pay for, and problems with cheap motherboards and chipsets are one of the main reasons I advised above that using entry-level PCs for audio work is *not* recommended, particularly in live performance applications.

Check to See If a BIOS Update is Available for Your Computer

Sometimes a BIOS update from your computer or motherboard's manufacturer can make all the difference in maintaining compatibility with third-party peripherals and keeping your computer audio system running smoothly.

Check for Potential RAM Problems

If you are using more than one RAM module in your computer, remove all but one of them and check if the audio problem still occurs. This is a good test. Low-quality RAM can also cause audio problems.

Check Internet Forums and Web Sites for More Information on Your Problem

Whenever you are trying to troubleshoot a computer problem, always remember that the Internet is a fantastic resource on computer problems. If you can't figure out what is going on, go to your favorite search engine and look around for whatever information you can find about the issue you seem to be having. Information directly from users on Internet forums is often more up-to-date and current than the official Web site of the manufacturer itself, with more specific information about even very recently-occurring bugs.

Reformat the Hard Drive and Reinstall Windows

Although this is a somewhat drastic solution, in fact I have known many PC-based laptop musicians who regularly reformatted their machines to keep them running at peak performance. As you install more applications and device drivers on a Windows computer and shuttle large amounts of data around, files can become corrupted, errors can creep into the Windows Registry, and other minor OS problems may be compounded over time through normal use. If you are willing to spend the time and effort, periodically reformatting and reinstalling Windows is definitely recommended to assure best performance and eliminate possible OS issues as a cause of audio problems.

An external hard drive of some kind is also recommended to back up your data when you need to reformat. External drives connecting to your computer via USB 2.0 or FireWire are recommended for this purpose.

Know When to Give Up

All PCs are different, and as I noted earlier, PCs were not designed for audio use in the first place. Although most current PC models are capable of at least some audio processing tasks, I speak from experience when I say that there are definitely some models that will not work properly with any third-party audio interface, no matter how it is connected or how the system is optimized. (Recall the case of my Compaq Presario 700 in Chapter 3.)

If your system is still giving you problems after you have followed all the optimization tips and troubleshooting tips in this book, it might be time to upgrade. Another tip for computer musicians: Remember that eBay is your friend and sell off your old computer or gear while it is still worth something.

System Freezes When Using Audio Applications

This can happen for a variety of reasons, and this is one of the most problematic issues that you can experience with your system. Obviously it is crucial to have a reliable system to use for live performances, in order to avoid a mid-set system crash that will make you look like an idiot and decrease your chances of getting any future gigs.

The most important thing you can do to prevent this problem is to do extensive performance testing in the comfort and safety of your own home studio. Set up your system *exactly* as it is going to be when you are playing live, and play for extended periods of time in order to see if anything goes wrong. If you get a system freeze or other problem, apply the optimization tips detailed in the previous section and then test it again.

It is also possible in some cases that an application or driver has become corrupted somehow and in this case, you should uninstall and then reinstall the application or driver in question to ensure that your system is functioning correctly.

Reinstalling drivers is described in greater detail above. If you need to reinstall an application program, uninstall it first from the Add or Remove Programs control panel and then reinstall by using the original disks, a backup copy, or by downloading the latest fresh installer version of the software from the software maker's Web site. Make sure you have any necessary serial numbers and/or registration codes handy so you can re-authorize the program if necessary after reinstalling it.

To uninstall a program in Windows, go to Start → Control Panel and open the Add or Remove Programs control panel. Scroll down the list to find the application you want to uninstall, select it, and choose Change/Remove to remove it (see Figure 5.34).

If reinstalling your application and drivers doesn't help, you should troubleshoot for an IRQ problem as described above in the previous section on fixing pops and clicks.

If you have already addressed the IRQ situation and you are still having the problem, you should probably try reformatting your machine and reinstalling Windows as described in the previous section.

Now that we've seen how to set up and maintain your Windows or Mac system for audio use, let's look at some of the audio and MIDI interfaces available to connect to it.

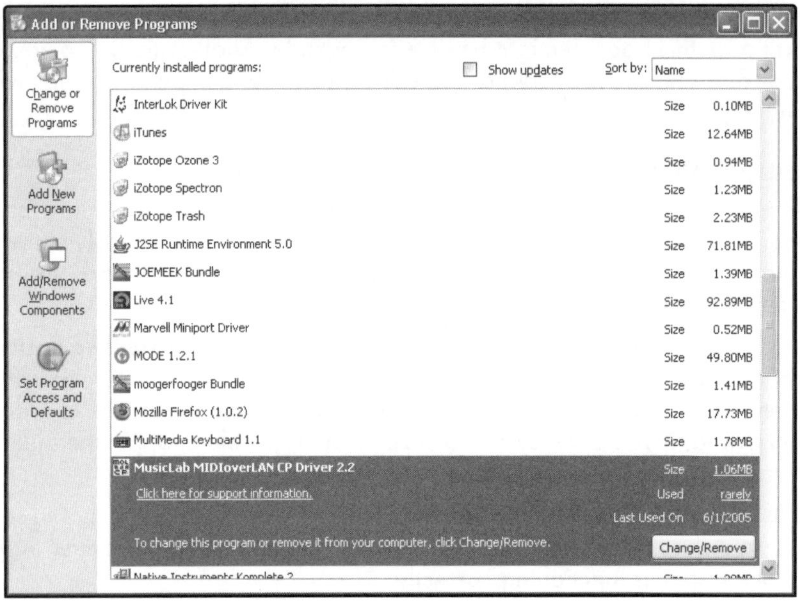

Figure 5.34 Uninstalling an application through the Add or Remove Programs control panel.

6 Choosing an Audio Interface

After making a decision about what computer to use, the next thing you need to play computer music live is an audio interface. Of course, most computers have some built-in audio capabilities, but for live music performance, you will probably want better audio quality and more input and output channels than your computer's built-in hardware offers.

Main Factors to Consider

In considering which audio interface to use for live performance, there are several main factors to consider, detailed in the next sections.

Type of Interface

There are several possible interface standards by which external devices can be connected to a Mac or PC computer, including USB, FireWire, CardBus, and, in the case of desktop computers, internal PCI card slots as well. Each has its own advantages and disadvantages.

Number of Inputs and Outputs

A fundamental point to consider is the number of audio inputs and outputs the device has, both analog and digital. You need to consider if this is enough for the style of live performance you are aiming for.

Of course, in the simplest scenario, you could always play with an interface that had only one stereo output and no particular special features, but this will limit you in a number of ways when it comes to performance. This will become clearer later in the book.

If you are planning to DJ with your computer, then you probably want to get an interface with at least two stereo output pairs and a headphone jack. This will enable you to cue up the next track on the headphones before you introduce it into the main PA mix.

If you are planning a more complex live setup, editing arrangements in real-time using a multi-track digital audio sequencer for example, then you may want to get an interface with more outputs. This will enable you to route individual tracks or groups of tracks through the outputs on your interface and then into separate channels on your mixer.

Reliability

The reliability of an interface is another crucial point to consider. If your interface sounds great but crashes every time you play, it's not much use! For this reason, I would advise searching on the Internet for consumer information or reviews before buying anything. Nothing is a better guide than the experience of others.

Also, make sure you always buy from a retailer that will allow you to return a purchase within a set period of time (usually 30 days) if it doesn't work for you. Sometimes a particular device and a particular computer just won't work well together, although nothing may be particularly wrong with either of them. In this case, you might want to just return what you bought and get a different device instead. If you have problems with a certain *type* of device (USB, FireWire, CardBus) with your machine, then it may be a good idea to try a different type and see if that works better for you.

Audio Quality

Quality is, in part, subjective but obviously very important. Probably the best way to find out how various audio interfaces stack up against each other is, again, to look for information and comparisons online. First check out the basic specs of the unit you are looking at, particularly the maximum audio bit rate (16- or 24-bit) and sample rate (ranging from CD-quality 44.1kHz all the way up to 192kHz on some of today's devices), and see how this compares to other similar devices. Then check online forums and see what current users are saying about how it sounds.

In the case of audio quality especially, it is safe to say that you generally get what you pay for. Sure you may be able to pull off your gigs with a small plastic USB audio device that cost less than $100, or even just use the built-in sound capability of your laptop (*not* a good idea, especially if you are on a PC). Just keep in mind that the sound quality is never going to measure up to something like Digidesign's 002 multi-channel FireWire interface, currently going for more than $2,000.

On the other hand, the Digi 002 is probably overkill for a laptop performer, and I would hate to carry one around to all my gigs—it's just too bulky. Audio quality is a major factor in choosing an interface, but it is not the only factor.

Headphone Volume Level and Overall Output Level

The overall output level is not as important—once you plug into your mixer you can always boost your signal there if necessary—but you should test the device with headphones and make sure that there is a good strong level coming out the headphone jack. (Also make sure that the headphones you are using are not too high-impedance for the interface; this could also cause the level to sound low in your headphones.)

Some computer audio interfaces (particularly those that are bus-powered) may lack a strong headphone signal, and this can be a problem when using the interface on live club gigs. You need to be able to hear the headphone signal loud and clear even when you are in a noisy club so you can cue the next track or sound that you are going to introduce into the mix.

Software Driver Support and Features

You should also check and see what audio driver standards a particular device supports (the main formats to know are ASIO, WDM, or MME on Windows XP and CoreAudio on Mac OS X), as well as what features for internal audio routing it may have built into its driver software. Personally, I tend to handle routing inside my audio applications and not at the driver level for the most part, but for some applications (such as direct monitoring) it is better to set things up in the sound card's mixer. You can probably find this information in most cases by going to the manufacturer's Web site and finding the documentation for the product.

Specific Interface Types and Choices

Now let's take a look at some of the different audio interfaces available today and how they might fit into a live performance rig. This is not an attempt to give a complete list or even a representative overview of all the various mobile computer audio interfaces available. Rather, I give just a few examples chosen to illustrate the types of devices available and how they might fit into a live performance setup.

Of course, by the time you buy this book, a whole new generation of devices probably will have hit the market, but hopefully these examples will still be useful to you in knowing what kinds of options are available and what you should be looking for.

USB

One easy way to connect an audio interface to your computer is by using one of the many devices on the market that connect via the USB, or Universal Serial Bus standard. All USB connections are not created equal, however. When USB was first introduced, the standard was USB 1.0, which was rapidly superceded by USB 1.1 (USB 1.1 connections are found on many computers still in use today). Later, USB 2.0 was introduced, which uses the same plugs and cables as USB 1.1 but has a much higher maximum data transfer rate: A theoretical maximum of up to 480 megabits-per-second, as opposed to only 12 mbps for the older standard.

This is one point you need to check if you are thinking of using a USB audio interface on your machine: See if you have USB 2.0 ports or just 1.1. This is a very important point because the limited bandwidth of a USB 1.1 connection will restrict you to using audio devices with at most four input and output channels. All current-model Apple computers have USB 2.0 built-in but if you are buying a PC, you should double-check.

A USB 2.0 port on your computer is designed to work with both USB 2.0 and USB 1.1 devices, and usually this works fine. However, I have seen a few cases with PCs where USB 2.0 ports didn't recognize a USB 1.1 device. Just another point to look out for if you are troubleshooting your devices.

It is also important to consider how USB devices generally measure up against other types of interfaces when deciding which you are going to use. Although USB 2.0 has a higher theoretical maximum data transfer rate than a standard FireWire 400 connection (480 megabits-per-second vs. 400mbps), this measures the speed of bursts of data transfer and is more relevant to the performance of asynchronous devices such as an external hard drive. FireWire has superior characteristics as far as the sustained data transfer rate it is capable of, which makes it more suitable for media applications such as audio and video.

This is one reason why more audio manufacturers have chosen to develop midrange mobile audio devices for FireWire than USB 2.0, although there are many USB audio devices in lower price ranges, which generally offer just a few inputs and outputs.

USB audio devices can also be quite vulnerable to conflicts with other devices connected to your computer's USB bus. If you are having drop-outs or other problems with your USB audio interface, one of the first things you should do to troubleshoot is to make sure you are connecting via a USB hub. Ideally, you want to connect your audio device directly to a USB port on the computer itself. You should also try disconnecting any other USB devices attached to the machine, such as a printer, scanner, or USB mouse.

Another potential issue with USB audio devices, just as with other interface standards, is audio problems caused by IRQ sharing problems. A surprising number of PC laptop manufacturers seem to feel that it is a good idea to pre-configure the computer so that the USB ports are sharing an IRQ with the graphics controller, and this can make the USB ports virtually unusable for audio.

Now let's take a look at a few of today's USB audio interfaces and see how they might be used for live performance.

M-Audio Audiophile USB

The M-Audio Audiophile USB (see Figure 6.1) is a good example of a simple USB interface that provides good sound quality and reliable performance.

The Audiophile USB offers a single pair of analog inputs (you can use either ¼" balanced or RCA connectors) and outputs (RCA only) as well as a headphone out, digital in/out via coaxial S/PDIF, and a single MIDI input and output, as shown in Figure 6.2.

The Audiophile USB works via the USB 1.1 protocol, not USB 2.0, so it is somewhat limited as far as the bandwidth available for audio data. It is capable of 24-bit/96kHz operation, but a USB 1.1 connection is not capable of carrying four simultaneous audio channels at this rate for stereo input and output—there is not enough bandwidth available. For this reason, selecting various options in the Audiophile USB control panel in different combinations offers the following choices, representing possible trade-offs that you can choose between audio quality and number of simultaneous ins and outs:

- 16-bit/44.1kHz–4-in/4-out
- 24-bit/44.1kHz–4-in/2-out or 2-in/4-out
- 24-bit/48kHz–4-in/2-out or 2-in/4-out
- 24-bit/96kHz–2-in or 2-out

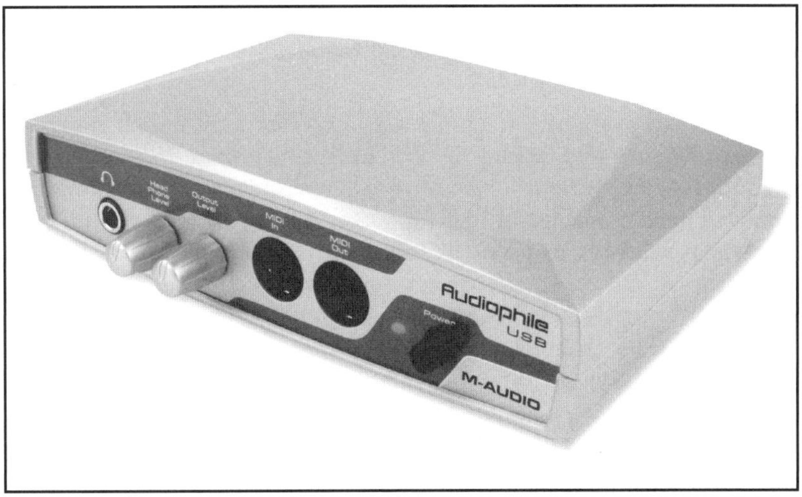

Figure 6.1 The M-Audio Audiophile USB.

Bear in mind here that the Audiophile USB has only two physical analog ins and outs (as seen in Figure 6.2), so the references to four possible ins or outs in the list above refers to two analog plus two digital channels possible for a total of four channels.

This limitation is not really a big issue for live performance, however. Even the lowest audio quality setting here, 16-bit/44.1kHz, is the same as the quality of an audio CD and is perfectly usable for live performance.

A bigger limitation is the fact that the Audiophile only has one stereo output pair. Although there is a separate headphone jack, this will only allow you to hear the signal present on the main outs. In other words, it is impossible to use the headphones to cue up new tracks or sounds on a different output bus without interrupting the playback of the main track. This

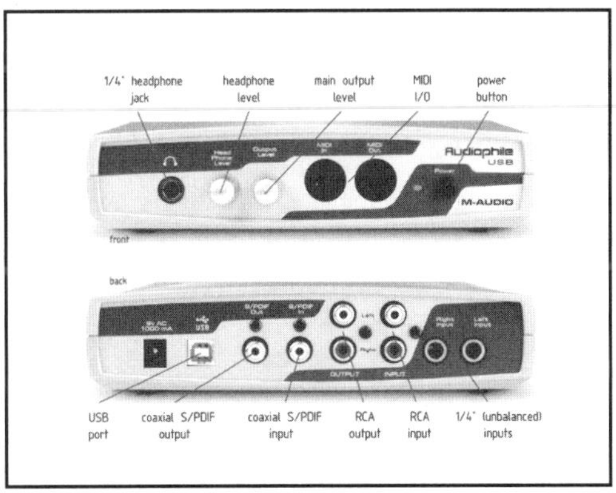

Figure 6.2 The M-Audio Audiophile USB (front and back).

means that the Audiophile would not be a good choice for digital DJing or any other live performance configuration in which you want to be able to cue new sounds before playing them.

The Audiophile is fine, however, as the main sound card for a computer being used as a software synthesizer or effects processing rig. For example, I have done a number of gigs together with keyboardist Matt Piper in which Matt was playing an M-Audio Radium 61 MIDI controller keyboard connected to his Dell PC laptop and using the software synthesizers in Propellerhead's Reason software as his main sound sources. He was using the Audiophile USB as his audio interface, and this gave him a clean stereo out to the main board, which is all he really needed. Although it only has one stereo output, it does have separate volume controls for the master and headphone outs, and this enabled Matt to mute the main output while he cued up new sounds on his software synths.

In addition, we used the MIDI port on the Audiophile to synchronize the tempo setting in Matt's software to the copies of Ableton Live we were running on two other computers. We did this by running a MIDI line from the output of the MIDI master computer to the MIDI input on Matt's Audiophile USB. Of course, you can always use a separate MIDI interface with your laptop if you want, but having a built-in MIDI port on your audio device is often more convenient.

There are a variety of other inexpensive USB audio devices on the market from a variety of manufacturers that are similar to the Audiophile USB in terms of offering just a few input and output channels; the Audiophile USB is among the higher-quality examples of this type of device. However, for more creative live performance options, you will need an interface with at least two stereo pairs of analog outputs. M-Audio used to offer such a device in the form of the well-known Quattro (see Figure 6.3), but this has since been discontinued.

Maya44 USB

One small USB audio interface that might be a good solution for DJs or other laptop performers is the MAYA44 USB by Audiotrak (see Figure 6.4).

This unit is something like the small and inexpensive Roland UA-30s that I used to use, but Audiotrak (the consumer division of ESI, a Korean electronics company) has put two stereo pairs of analog input and output on the unit via RCA plugs and added ASIO support for efficient operation with your pro audio applications. It also has S/PDIF optical digital output as well as a headphone output (these two share a combo jack).

This unit would be a very convenient solution for DJs with its pair of analog stereo outputs, but you would most likely want to use this together with an outboard mixer to mix the outputs and cue as there are no controls on the unit itself, and the headphone routing does not appear to be adjustable in hardware or software.

Numark DXM01 USB DJ Mixer

This USB DJ mixer from Numark (see Figure 6.5) is an example of another kind of computer audio device that has started showing up in the market more and more: Devices designed specifically for the needs of DJs.

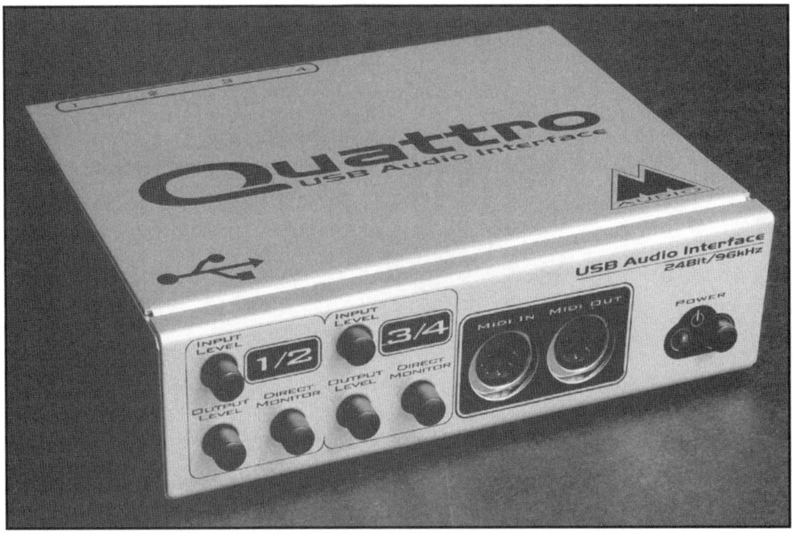

Figure 6.3 The M-Audio Quattro USB audio device.

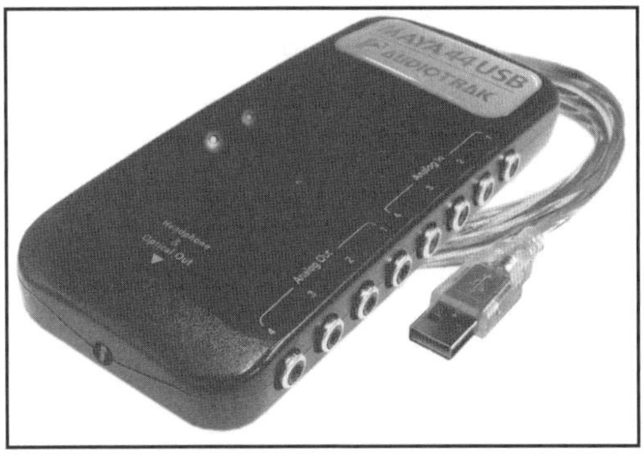

Figure 6.4 The Maya44 USB by Audiotrak.

This is an innovative combination unit in many respects, putting two USB 1.1 audio interfaces inside of a standard Numark DJ mixer. This means that you can simply connect the two USB jacks on the mixer to two USB ports on your computer and you're ready to play.

This unit seems in many ways like an ideal solution for a digital DJ. It also offers the additional advantage of zero-latency (i.e., analog) faders and EQ controls since these are not MIDI controllers routed through the computer, but actual analog controls.

However, one drawback of the unit is that Numark has not provided it with ASIO or CoreAudio drivers (for Windows and Mac, respectively) for optimal audio performance. Rather, they have made it class-compliant within Windows XP and Mac OS X. This makes the unit easy to

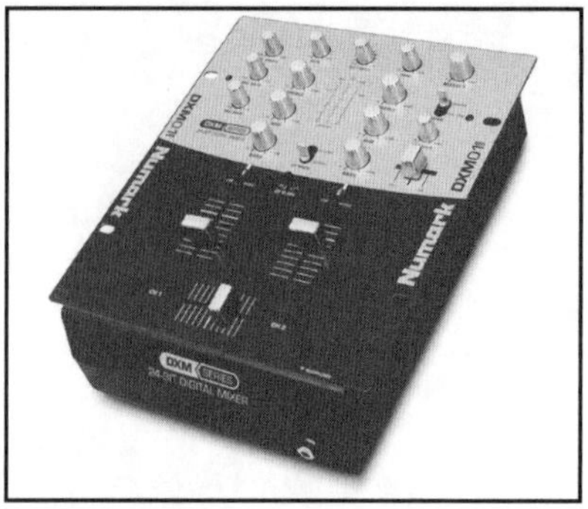

Figure 6.5 The Numark DXM01 USB DJ mixer.

work with—just plug it in and it should work. However there will be significant audio latency in the system, tens or even hundreds of milliseconds in some cases, and no way to adjust this.

This latency would not be a problem for some applications. When using the faders and knobs on the mixer itself, it would not be a problem at all because these are analog controls. Latency could be an issue with beatmatching tracks when DJing, however. In this case, you would be using some controls on the computer itself to match the tempos, but the effect of anything you did would be delayed before you would hear it because of the latency. Very high latencies might make it impossible to do beatmatching manually in a program like Traktor or Virtual DJ.

I mention this to point out the importance of checking a device's driver support before you buy it. If this Numark mixer had better software driver support for its audio interfaces it would be a better value, and the lack of ASIO or CoreAudio support might actually render it useless for some live performance applications.

Edirol UA-1000

Introduced in March 2003, Edirol claims its UA-1000 (see Figure 6.6) as the industry's first multi-channel USB 2.0 audio recording interface.

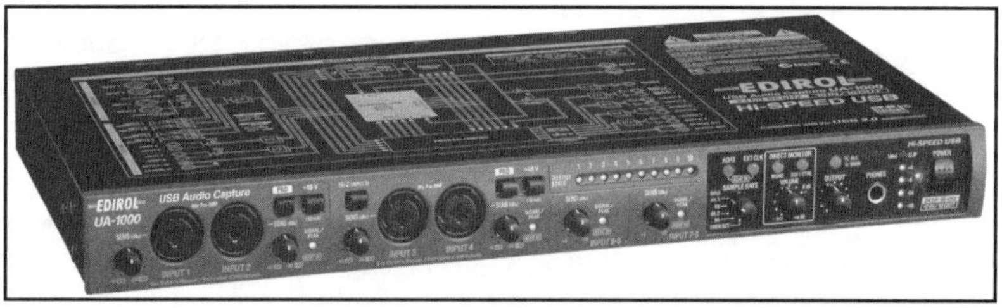

Figure 6.6 The Edirol UA-1000 USB2.0 audio interface.

According to Edirol, the USB 2.0 connection gives the UA-1000 sufficient bandwidth to offer a wide range of input and output options (see Figure 6.7) including four XLR/TRS combo inputs on the front with mic preamps and phantom power, optical and coaxial S/PDIF digital in and out, eight channels of digital ADAT lightpipe, one MIDI in and out, a BNC word clock connector, and four inserts on the rear of the unit for routing effects sends and returns.

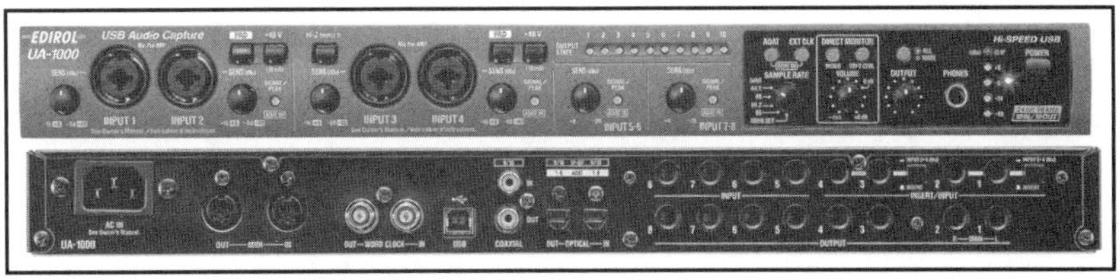

Figure 6.7 The front and back panels of the UA-1000, showing the inputs and outputs.

The UA-1000 is a good example of a more expensive class of mobile audio devices, having a relatively large number of both analog and digital inputs and outputs and two built-in mic preamps. There are a number of other similar devices in this category, although most of them use FireWire connectivity rather than USB 2.0 (such as the M-Audio FireWire 410 and 1814 models, shown below).

In some ways these larger devices seem better suited for use in mobile recording setups than in live performance, but the mic preamp channels can be very useful for performance as well. For example, when I saw laptop artist Steve Nalepa with violinist Lili Haydn at the Temple Bar in Santa Monica, he was taking a line out from Lili's violin setup and running into one of the mic input channels on his M-Audio FireWire 410, then running that through some effects in Ableton Live, and then sending the processed signal back out to the main PA. I have also seen Steve bring a mic to ambient gigs, plug it into his 410, and create beautiful unfolding sound textures by whistling into the mic and running the output through plug-in effects in Live.

The multiple outputs of a larger unit like the UA-1000 are also useful if you want to run a number of tracks in an audio sequencer out individual outputs on your interface and then into an external mixer. The advantage of this is that using an external mixer gives you direct hands-on control of parameters including the volume of each track, pan, EQ, auxiliary effects sends, and so on. I will include more information on this kind of performance approach later, in the sections concerning live performance with Ableton Live and various other digital audio sequencer programs.

FireWire

The interface technology that seems to be gaining the most ground recently with both developers and consumers is FireWire, originally developed by Apple and now supported by many PC manufacturers and makers of third-party peripherals as well. FireWire is one of the fastest input/output technologies ever developed for personal computers, with maximum data transfer rates from 400 to 800 megabits-per-second.

(To avoid confusion, it is useful to know that the FireWire 400 and 800 standards are also known as IEEE 1394a and 1394b, respectively, official electronics industry connectivity standards.)

FireWire technology is popular with computer audio manufacturers for its high sustained data transfer rate. While USB 2.0 (the main competitor to FireWire for connecting external computer peripherals) has a slightly higher data transfer rate for short bursts of information, FireWire provides better performance for applications requiring a continuous data transfer such as an audio or video stream.

With so much bandwidth available, it is possible to send a lot of audio information up and down a FireWire cable, and manufacturers have taken advantage of this by offering many different configurations of input and output on their devices, both analog and digital in the form of coaxial or optical S/PDIF or ADAT lightpipe connections. For example, up to 35 input sources can be connected to the RME Fireface 800 and recorded onto 28 separate tracks in your recording application! Of course, your CPU and hard drive may not be able to keep up with that many simultaneous recording tracks, but it does show what the FireWire interface is capable of.

A 6-pin FireWire connection can also provide power to an external audio device, and some FireWire-bus-powered devices also offer mic preamps and phantom power, such as the M-Audio FireWire 1814 or the MOTU Traveler.

At present, all Macintosh computers as well as Windows desktop models have these 6-pin powered FireWire ports, while PC laptops almost universally have a smaller 4-pin FireWire connection (called i.Link by Sony). This 4-pin connection functions the same but cannot provide power, so a FireWire device connected to a PC laptop will have to be powered via its own external power supply.

On a PC system, FireWire audio devices can suffer problems from IRQ sharing just as can USB or CardBus devices. I described the procedure for IRQ troubleshooting in the previous section; you just need to remember that if you are using an external audio device, it won't be listed in your IRQ list by name. Instead, you will be looking for something called the "IEEE 1394 Host Controller" and trying to resolve possible conflicts with this; this is the FireWire controller in your computer.

Now let's look at just a few of today's FireWire audio interfaces and how they might fit into a live performance rig.

M-Audio FireWire Audiophile

The M-Audio FireWire Audiophile (see Figure 6.8) is a relatively small FireWire audio interface designed especially for digital DJs.

The FireWire Audiophile gives you one stereo input pair and two stereo outputs, along with digital input and output via S/PDIF and 1 MIDI in and out (see Figure 6.9).

The Audiophile also has one additional feature that makes it particularly well suited for DJing. Looking at the front panel photo in the Figure 6.9, you can see that there is an A/B selector button next to the headphone jack. This allows you to toggle back and forth between the pair

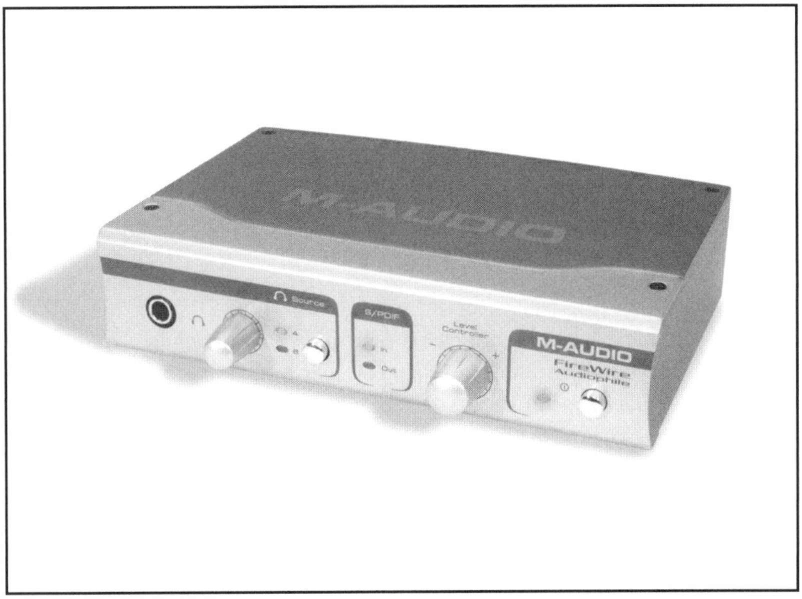

Figure 6.8 The M-Audio FireWire Audiophile.

of analog outputs you are listening to, enabling you to do DJ-style headphone cueing. Of course, many computer DJing applications will enable you to do something like in software

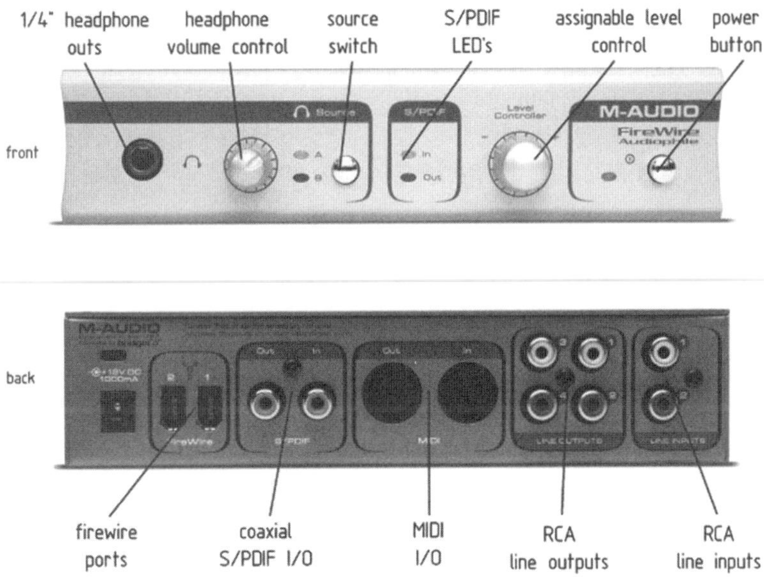

Figure 6.9 FireWire Audiophile front and back panel.

as well, but switching the output you are monitoring directly on the hardware is quick, easy, and reliable.

I have been using a FireWire Audiophile myself for gigs running Ableton Live on my Mac for the past six months or so, and this interface is just about perfect for my performance setup. It is stable and reliable, sounds great, enables me to cue on headphones, and has built-in MIDI and S/PDIF I/O for the occasions when I need those capabilities. It is also sturdy and durable as well as small and portable, and it powers off my Mac's FireWire bus, so I don't have to carry along an extra power supply for it either.

M-Audio FireWire 410

The M-Audio FireWire 410 is the big brother of the FireWire Audiophile. The two are similar in overall sound quality and performance, but the 410 has built-in mic preamps for recording as well as more input and output channels available: A total of four input channels and 10 output channels (see Figures 6.10 and 6.11).

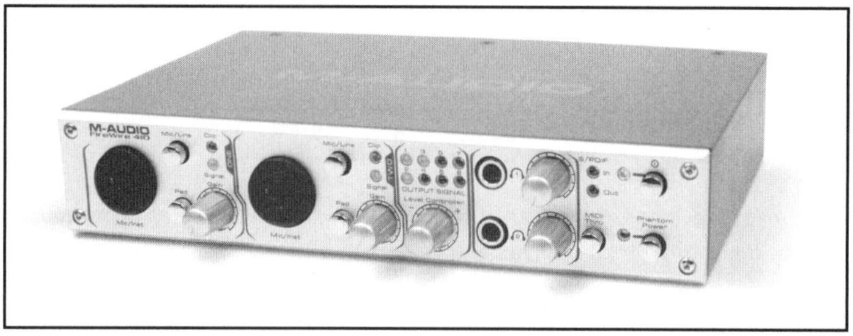

Figure 6.10 The M-Audio FireWire 410.

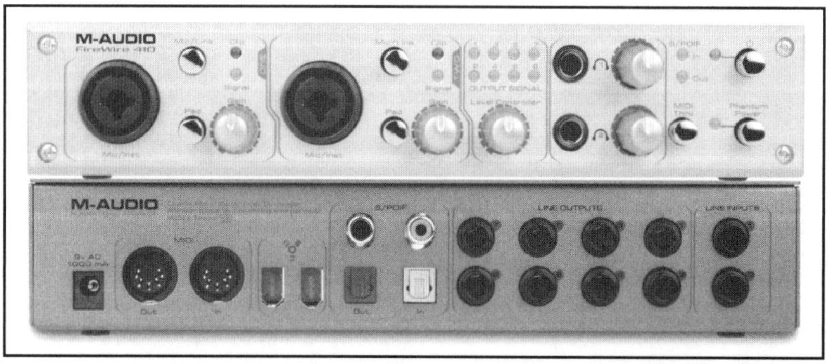

Figure 6.11 The FireWire 410 front and back panels.

The 410 is a great unit and very popular, but as I observed above in connection with the Edirol UA-1000, you don't need a unit with so many input and output channels if all you want to do live is DJ or use a sequencer program in which all the audio will be mixed inside the computer. However, if you want to run multiple channels out of the computer and mix them using an external mixing board, then a compact FireWire interface like the 410 would be a good choice. M-Audio also makes a FireWire 1814, which offers even more input and output channels.

Compared to the UA-1000, the FireWire 410 is smaller and more portable, particularly considering that (on a Mac, at least) you can power the FireWire 410 from your computer and not have to carry a separate external power supply. This is one of the advantages of FireWire connections over USB, as FireWire can carry more power to external devices as well as providing a high-speed data link.

CardBus

CardBus interfaces are a convenient option for laptop musicians, but there are only a few CardBus audio devices available for Mac and PC computers that are of interest for live use. The two major manufacturers in this area are French company Digigram, and US company Echo.

Digigram Cards

Digigram was the first major company to make high-quality CardBus audio devices, and they make a number of different interfaces offering various analog and digital input and output configurations. Some of Digigram's cards have only stereo input and output, while others have multiple input and output channels using a breakout cable (see Figure 6.12).

As I mentioned earlier, I have a Digigram VXPocket card myself, which I used in my G3 PowerBook when I first started using my computer for live gigs. At the time I bought it (1999), it was the only CardBus audio interface I could find, though it seemed to be targeted more at the journalism market than musicians.

Digigram's cards are generally to be recommended in my experience, with good audio quality and reliability. Their major drawback is that they are not particularly designed for live use by musicians, lacking any capacity to connect headphones, for example. Many of Digigram's cards connect via XLR balanced plugs on a breakout cable. This is a good-quality connection and may even prevent some noise problems in your audio output. This means that you will probably need to connect the breakout cable to an external stage mixer to use one of these cards live.

Echo Indigo DJ

The Echo Indigo DJ card is the CardBus interface best suited to use by a laptop DJ (see Figure 6.13), being specifically designed for this purpose.

The Indigo DJ has two ⅛" stereo mini-jacks on it that provide two stereo outputs. One of these can be routed to the PA system as your main output while you can plug your headphones in to the other output for cueing the next track when DJing. Simple!

It is worth noting that the Indigo DJ is a favorite among laptop performers for its small size, convenient design, and reliable performance.

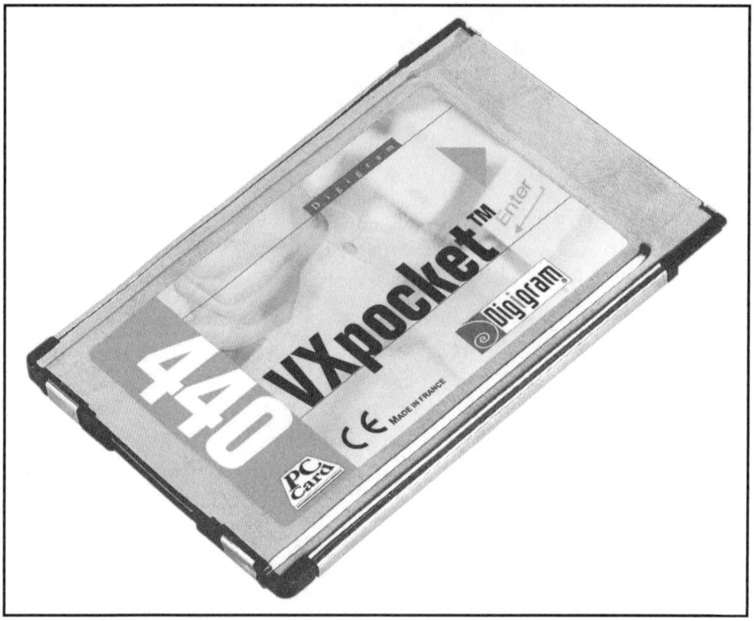

Figure 6.12 The Digigram VXPocket 440.

Figure 6.13 The Echo Indigo DJ CardBus interface.

PCI

PCI bus technology refers, of course, to the standard PCI cards that you can install inside a Mac or PC computer. Although not as flashy as FireWire, PCI is actually the most efficient of these interface technologies for audio use, having plenty of bandwidth for audio streams as well as being quite robust and stable. If you are using a desktop computer, PCI is still the best choice for most applications.

There are a wide range of PCI audio cards on the market today, from companies like M-Audio (see Figure 6.14), Echo, Digidesign, RME, MOTU, Steinberg, and Terratec.

Figure 6.14 The M-Audio Delta 1010LT card, with eight analog and two digital inputs and outputs.

Just as with the external interfaces I have described above, these various PCI cards are differentiated by their number of inputs and outputs, lack or presence of mic preamps, overall sound quality, software driver features, and so on.

I am not going to go into too much detail here about specific PCI audio cards because I am assuming that the vast majority of readers of this book will be using laptop computers. If you are considering playing live with a full desktop system and looking for a PCI sound card, you need only to look for the same features I have described above for mobile interfaces: The number of inputs/outputs, facility to do headphone cueing, and so on.

One more point specific to PCI audio cards is the lack or presence of a breakout box such as the one used by Echo Audio's Gina 3G card (see Figure 6.15).

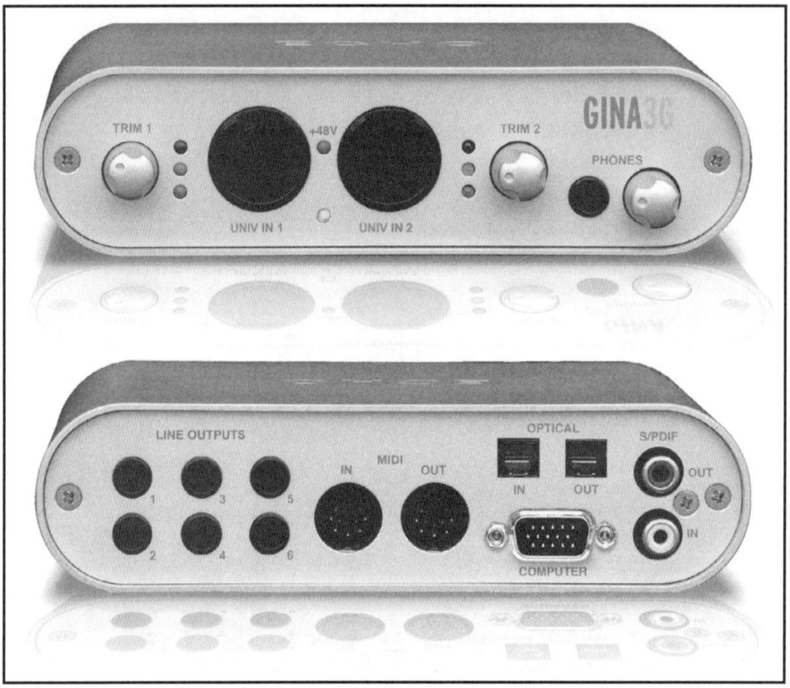

Figure 6.15 The Echo Audio Gina 3G card.

As you can see in this picture, the Gina 3G card has an external breakout box to which headphones can be attached as well as input and output cables, making this card somewhat more convenient to use on live gigs.

Then again, if you are taking an entire desktop computer system to your gigs, convenience is probably not a major concern for you, and you might as well just take along an external mixer as well as your computer to handle all your audio routing!

General Audio Troubleshooting Tips

In addition to the various software and hardware problems that are more specific to the Mac and PC problems (and which I discussed above), there are a number of general issues that can cause computer audio problems. Here are a couple important points you should keep in mind when troubleshooting:

Check Your Cables

This is a tip that seems obvious but can never be repeated enough. If you are having audio or data transfer problems, check all cables and connections. A problematic USB, FireWire, or analog audio cable could be the source of all your problems.

This problem can be especially insidious in the case of USB and FireWire cables, as your bus-powered device may still be able to receive power via the cable although it has been damaged enough to interfere with data connections. In this case, your external device may power on normally but fail to be recognized by the computer, so you may first suspect that there is a software driver problem or even a hardware problem with the device itself before realizing that it is the cable that is at fault.

In any event, carrying spare cables of all kinds to gigs is always a good idea.

Electrical Grounding Problems

When you are actually on a gig, in most cases you will want to plug your laptop's power adaptor into an AC wall socket for power. You don't want to run out of battery power in the middle of a performance!

Here's something to look out for, though: One of the most common problems for laptop performers is electrical noise that can sometimes be picked up through AC connections. Some laptop models are more prone to experience this problem than others, depending on the internal design.

Sometimes this problem manifests itself as that familiar 60-cycle ground buzz or hum that you may be familiar with if you have ever played guitar in a garage band. However, with computer audio, electrical grounding issues can also cause other audio problems such as noise, interference, hum, static, and so on.

If you are in your studio or on a gig and you think you may be experiencing a ground issue, one quick fix is to simply unplug your computer's power adapter. If your audio interface can run on bus-power via USB or FireWire without requiring a power supply, try unplugging it as well. Unplugging these power connections is a quick fix that will work for the majority of ground issues in the short term. However, if you don't want to do your whole gig on battery power or if you are having this problem in your studio at home, here are some fixes you can try.

First of all, make sure that your computer, your audio and MIDI interfaces, and the mixer or PA you are plugging into are all connected to the same ground, which in most cases would mean connecting them all to the same electrical outlet or power strip. You may get the kind of grounding problem I am talking about here if one or more of the devices are grounded to something else (for example via a different power outlet) and these devices are connected to each other.

The easiest way to deal with this issue is to use a 3-to-2-prong electrical ground lift plug in order to interrupt the ground loop that is causing the noise. This kind of ground lift commonly has a wire attached that allows it to be grounded to something else in the absence of the three-prong outlet that it is properly intended to be plugged into. Most commonly you can attach this grounding wire to the screw fastening the outlet cover to the wall and ground your plug this way.

However, you may not have the time or inclination to ground it like this on a live gig, and using it without grounding the wire will mean that your equipment is completely ungrounded.

Not all devices will work correctly with the ground lifted, and might be prone to overheat or fall prey to other electrical hazards. Most laptop computers will work fine with the ground lifted, but this may leave you vulnerable to power surges or other electrical anomalies.

My partner Stephen learned this the hard way once at a gig we did in Hong Kong. We played our laptops together with a live drummer and guitarist in a packed live club, and our first set of the night felt great. The audience was digging it and we were excited. After a short break, though, we came back on stage only to find that Stephen's PC wouldn't start up anymore, in fact it gave no sign of life whatsoever.

Later he took the machine to a repair shop and figured out what had happened. He had started using a ground lift with his computer a few months previously, since it usually seemed to have problems with ground noise, and he had never had any problems with it. However, on that particular night, there must have been an electrical surge or similar phenomenon, and with the ground lifted, there was nowhere for the surge to go and it burned out some components in the computer.

In any event, the moral of that story is: Don't use a ground lift on a regular basis with your laptop without consulting the manufacturer about whether or not this is safe with your model of computer. Having said that, it is a good idea to always keep a ground lift or two in your gig bag as a quick and dirty fix to electrical noise problems that could ruin your performance.

Another and perhaps safer way to deal with this is by using a ground loop isolator. You can get one of these at an electrical supply store. These are sometimes found in the car audio section.

7 Choosing a MIDI Controller

In most cases, you will want to use some kind of external MIDI device to control your audio software in a live performance. When you are just experimenting and doing your first gigs, you may be able to get by just using your trackpad or mouse. However, as you become more advanced, you will probably want to control more parameters simultaneously, such as volume, EQ, panning, effects, and so on, and for this you will need an external controller.

This chapter looks at the various types of controllers available and the ways you might want to use them in performance. Again, as with the previous chapter on audio interfaces, this is not meant to be an exhaustive survey of the market, and the various manufacturers' product lines change rapidly in any event. My main aim here is to give examples of different possibilities so that you can decide how you might use an external controller to augment your own live setup.

There are many different types of MIDI controllers. The one best for you will in part depend on what style of live performance to which you aspire. If your main goal is DJing with the computer, then a purpose-built DJ-style controller such as the Evolution X-Session or the Hercules DJ Console may be the best choice. If you are mixing loops in Ableton Live, then a compact mixing console-style controller like the Evolution UC-33e may suit your needs better. On the other hand, if you tend to experiment a lot and change your performance setup frequently (like me!), then the best idea might be to get a general-purpose controller with many assignable knobs like the Doepfer Drehbank.

There are also MIDI keyboards and other control surfaces to consider if you are interested in actually playing some of the parts of your music live. Most of the MIDI keyboard controllers on the market today also incorporate some knobs and faders for software control. In addition, there are numerous experimental MIDI controllers that allow you to control your software using physical gestures, the input of a video camera, or other means. I will cover some of these in this chapter.

An increasing number of MIDI controllers today also feature an integrated audio interface all in one unit, such as the Edirol PCR-1 or the M-Audio Ozonic. In some respects it is advantageous to have your audio interface integrated in your MIDI controller, if only for the sake of convenience. However, in some cases, an integrated audio/MIDI device may not have the right feature set for what you want to do, and you may be better off getting separate audio and MIDI interfaces instead.

One additional factor to consider in choosing an external controller is the overall quality of its construction, its ruggedness, and likely reliability under performance conditions. Although there are more and more MIDI and audio devices available these days aimed at live computer musicians, some of these devices are aimed more at the consumer/hobbyist market and are not really intended for professional use. These consumer-grade devices are typically less expensive because they are made of cheaper components and are also flimsier and more likely to malfunction when pushed to the limit in performance.

There is a lot of variation in quality in the devices in this chapter, and I would highly recommend trying out these devices in your local music store if possible before buying. The purpose of having a controller is to give you a physical interface with which to control the operation of your computer, so the quality and feel of the interface itself are very important. A given controller might look great on the Internet, with all the controls and features that you are looking for, but when you try it out, you might find that it is more of a toy than a real performance tool. (This is particularly likely in the case of MIDI devices aimed at the "bedroom DJ" market such as the Hercules DJ Console.)

If you are first getting interested in computer music performance, it may make sense for you to get a cheaper consumer-grade device to play around and experiment with. However, in the long run you get what you pay for, as with anything else, and if you start playing out a lot, you will probably want to upgrade your gear.

DJ-Style Controllers

First let's have a look at some controllers made specifically for computer DJs. These controllers typically feature CD-DJ-style jog wheels for cueing as well as play/stop buttons, EQ knobs, pitch controllers, and the all-important DJ crossfader to help you do DJ tricks like rapidly cutting back and forth between two tracks that are playing in sync on two different decks. I will have a lot more to say about digital DJ mixing and tricks in the Chapter 8, but first let's look at some of the MIDI hardware you can use for these tasks.

Hercules DJ Console

The Hercules DJ Console (see Figure 7.1) is a good example of these DJ-style MIDI controllers and is one of the few devices currently on the market aimed exclusively at the digital DJ market. It is both a MIDI controller and an audio interface.

As you can see in the above image, the controls of the DJ Console duplicate the buttons, knobs, and faders on a standard pair of DJ CD players connected to a DJ mixer. There are dedicated controls for adjusting the pitch, volume, and EQ of tracks as well as play, cue, rewind, and fast-forward buttons just as you would find on a standard DJ CD deck. There are a total of eight knobs, three sliders, and 28 phosphorescent buttons, as well as a mini-joystick in the center.

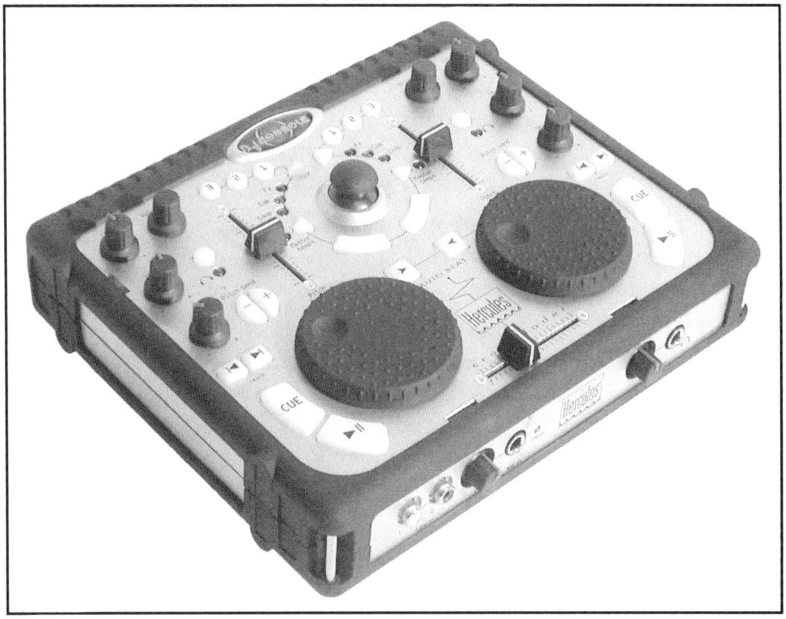

Figure 7.1 The Hercules DJ Console.

Looking at the front and back panels of the unit (see Figures 7.2a and 7.2b), we can see that it provides us with a plethora of input and output options.

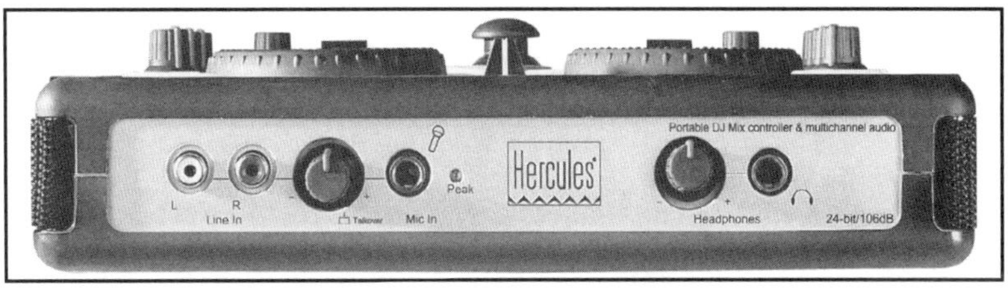

Figure 7.2a Front panel of the Hercules DJ Console.

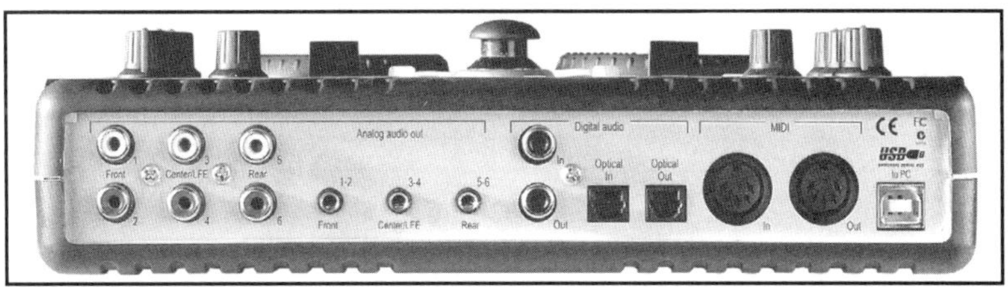

Figure 7.2b Rear panel of the Hercules DJ Console.

For input, the DJ Console offers a stereo line in via a pair of RCA-style inputs as well as a ⅛" stereo microphone input plug that could be used for talking over the music on a gig, rapping, singing, MCing, or whatever. Output options include three stereo output pairs via either three pairs of RCA-style outs or three ⅛" stereo outs. This means that not only can you play two stereo outs at once for DJing, but you can even use all the outputs at once and play your mixes back in Dolby 5.1 surround sound if you are using a surround sound PA system.

In addition to these analog input and output options, the DJ Console also offers digital S/PDIF I/O via either coaxial or optical jacks, as well as a MIDI in and MIDI out plug so you can connect external MIDI equipment. It connects directly to your computer via USB and does not require a separate MIDI interface.

At first sight, the Hercules DJ Console seems like a perfect solution for digital DJing, but after having tried one myself, I was somewhat disappointed. Its basic design and control layout make sense and its sound quality is good enough for a professional gig, but the controls themselves feel cheaply made and not really up to the standard you would expect from pro DJ gear. For this reason, I would also doubt the unit's durability and reliability if it were frequently used in actual performance situations.

However, the DJ Console is priced competitively and might be a good choice for someone who is just getting into DJing and wants to try mixing and matching some of the tracks from their MP3 collection.

Evolution X Session

Evolution's attractive X-Session controller (see Figure 7.3) has proven popular with many of today's laptop performers because of its durability, stability, compact size, and built-in DJ crossfader.

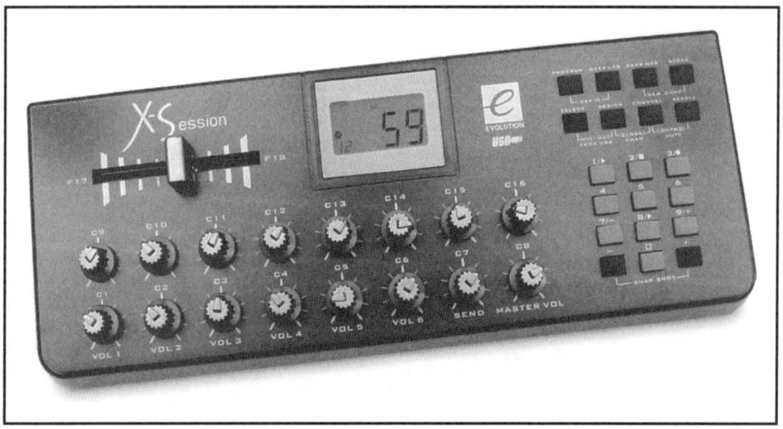

Figure 7.3 The Evolution X-Session.

Although the inclusion of the crossfader clearly indicates that this is a device designed for DJs, it is significant that the rest of the controls are generic assignable knobs and buttons instead of being modeled after a DJ CD player like the Hercules DJ Console. In addition to the crossfader, it features 16 assignable knobs as well as 10 assignable buttons to the right of the knobs. These can be used to trigger samples, effects, or other functions within your software. This gives you the flexibility to set up your controls however you want, to get quick access to the software controls that you use most frequently. You can personalize your setup as you like without necessarily having to use the same performance setup as every other DJ in the world.

With 16 knobs and 10 buttons, this compact controller still has plenty of scope for a wide range of performance setups. For example, when I DJ, I like to make a lot of subtle EQ adjustments in order to mix my tracks together more smoothly. When I was using my X-Session to control Virtual DJ on a PC laptop, I would assign six of the knobs to control three separate bands of EQ on each channel as well as three more knobs assigned to separate crossfaders for the various frequency bands, giving me a lot of control over my mix. I also assigned the buttons of the X-Session to control the bass, midrange, and treble EQ kill switches in Virtual DJ, as I like to use EQ kills a lot in my live DJ mixing.

RD of ELM Conceptions on the other hand, when using his X-Session with Traktor DJ Studio on a G4 PowerBook, prefers to map a number of the X-Session's knobs to control the various parameters of the built-in filter in Traktor and he uses these more extensively in live performance than the EQ controls.

Having generic assignable controls like this also allows you to more easily use the X-Session with a wide range of software, making it equally suitable for use with Ableton Live as with any of the digital DJ software applications.

You can even use the X-Session in the studio to control some of the basic functions of your DAW when you are working on new music. I often use my X-Session to control various parameters of my arrangements in Ableton Live.

For example, with two rows of eight knobs each, one easy and logical setup is to assign the bottom row of knobs to control your track volumes and the top row to control some other parameter on each track like an auxiliary send to an effects bus. Although you cannot access every important controller in your DAW at once with the limited number of controls on the X-Session, 16 knobs will allow you to automate your mix much more easily than if you have to use your mouse/trackpad to control every channel individually.

The X-Session is class-compliant under Windows XP and Mac OS X, so there is no need to install a software driver; just plug it into your computer's USB port and it will work.

In addition to the built-in functions of the X-Session as a MIDI controller, it is also a MIDI interface that will allow you to connect additional MIDI controllers or modules to your system via the external MIDI In and Out ports on the back of the device.

You can edit the MIDI settings of your X-Session using the buttons on the device itself or by using Evolution's Enigma software (available as a free download from their Web site) to edit the settings remotely from your Mac or PC. However, in most cases, it is easier to set up your

MIDI assignments in your application software than in the controller itself, and this is how I have made most of my live setups in Virtual DJ, Traktor, and Ableton Live.

I have been using an X-Session for a while myself and I can vouch for its reliability. I have never had a single problem with mine and I can unreservedly recommend it as an ideal controller for digital DJing.

FaderFox micromodul DJ1

FaderFox is a small German company that introduced a line of three small, cleverly designed MIDI controllers in 2004. The micromodul DJ1 (see Figure 7.4) is a controller unit especially made for computer DJs.

Figure 7.4 The FaderFox micromodul DJ1.

As you can see from this image, the DJ1 is purpose-built for DJs, featuring a compact layout that resembles a tiny DJ mixer. There is a full-size image of the unit on the FaderFox Web site; It measures only 7.09"×4.13"×2.76" and weighs less than one pound.

Its MIDI controls include a crossfader, two channel faders, six EQ knobs, two gain knobs, and a cue/monitor control. There is a filter section with two knobs and a button, an encoder knob to help you select and load tracks, eight deck control buttons, three special buttons, and

14 freely assignable, double-function buttons. The controls are all arranged as they would be on a DJ mixer, except that the DJ1 is considerably smaller than most mixers.

FaderFox claims that the DJ1 is "optimized for Traktor DJ Studio 2.0," Native Instruments' standard-setting DJ application, although it is not quite clear what this means (if anything). Nonetheless, the DJ1's logical arrangement of controls and small size are perfect for computer DJing with just about any DJ application. (See also Figure 7.5, the DJ1 being used together with Traktor.)

Figure 7.5 The DJ1 being used to control Traktor DJ Studio.

FaderFox's devices connect to your other gear via MIDI, so you will need an additional MIDI interface to connect the DJ1 to your computer. The DJ1 can run on four AAA batteries or can draw AC power via an adapter.

FaderFox also makes two controllers designed for use with Ableton Live (the LV1 and the LX1) that I will discuss further in the section on specialized and custom MIDI controllers below. These are the same size and shape as the DJ1 but have differing control configurations. I mention them because FaderFox has designed their devices from a modular perspective, so that two or more FaderFox controllers of the same or different types can easily be used together to control additional parameters in your software. In fact, these FaderFox units are so small that you could line up three or four of them together and still take up less space than many of the other MIDI controllers I am discussing here.

One drawback of the DJ1 is that the controls cannot be reassigned or programmed on the unit itself and it does not connect directly to the computer, so there is no possibility of remote editing its settings. However, as FaderFox points out on their Web site, there is no need to reassign the controls this way with many current software releases, as Traktor, Live, Reason, and many other popular music applications include some kind of "MIDI Learn" feature.

I first became aware of these FaderFox controllers soon after they debuted in August 2004. However, I have never actually been able to try one myself because until now FaderFox is still not selling their devices in the US—they will only ship to European addresses. The DJ1, as well as FaderFox's other devices, have received glowing reviews from users in many of the online forums I looked at while I was working on this chapter. Hopefully, their devices will become available in the US at some point in the future.

Behringer B-Control Deejay BCD2000

Behringer, a well-known German music technology company, offers a wide range of budget-priced audio and MIDI devices that bridge the consumer and low-end pro markets. They have recently entered the DJ MIDI controller market niche with a new hybrid audio/MIDI device they call the B-Control Deejay BCD2000 (see Figure 7.6).

Figure 7.6 The Behringer B-Control Deejay BCD2000.

Like the Hercules DJ Console, the BCD2000 combines the functions of a MIDI controller designed for DJs with a simple audio interface. It offers two large DJ CD player-style scratch/jog wheels that can be used for scratching, pitch bending, and quickly moving through a track to cue it up. It has MIDI controller buttons for transport functions such as play, pause, cue, loop, and pitch bend functions, as well as four user-assignable knobs and buttons for use controlling effects in your software.

In addition to its MIDI functions, there are also many analog controls on the unit that control its functioning as a DJ mixer, including three-bands of EQ on each channel (both knobs and kill switches), a crossfader, volume faders, and controls relating to the headphone cueing. It contains an integrated four-channel audio interface, and it connects to your computer via a USB connection.

There is also a mic input on the unit with a built-in preamp, as well as two line inputs with phono preamps. This means that you can attach turntables or CD players to it as well and combine their output with the mix from your computer.

All in all, the B-Control Deejay looks like an ideal solution for digital DJs. However, at time of writing I have not been able to try a sample unit (it is scheduled to be released in the second quarter of 2005, according to Behringer's Web site) so I cannot determine whether the BCD2000 is sturdy enough to be dependable in live performance or whether it is more of a toy for bedroom DJs to play with.

Mixer-Style MIDI Controllers

Another common type of MIDI controller often used by laptop music performers is the mixer-style controller. If you are playing back and mixing multiple audio tracks in performance using Ableton Live or any other DAW-style software, then this type of controller is the best choice to easily allow you to control the volume level, panning, effects, and other parameters associated with individual tracks in your software.

Evolution UC-33e

One of the most popular MIDI mixer controllers is the Evolution UC-33e (see Figure 7.7). Like Evolution's X-Session DJ controller, the UC-33e has earned a reputation among laptop musicians for its ease of use and durability in live performance. It is also very compact and lightweight compared to many comparable devices.

The UC-33e features a total of 47 assignable MIDI controllers, including 24 knobs, nine faders, and 14 buttons. As you can see in the picture, the knobs and faders are neatly arranged into eight vertical "channels," each containing three knobs and one fader, with one additional master fader and the assignable buttons off to the right. This arrangement makes it very easy to configure and use the UC-33e as your live mixer, assigning the controls from each channel on the UC-33e to a mixer channel in your application software.

Of course, you would not need to assign the controls this way; all of the controllers on the UC-33e are freely assignable and you can use any of them to control whatever software parameters you want. You can also use Evolution's Enigma software or the buttons on the UC-33 itself to edit its controller setup. You can store your setups in one of the UC-33e's 33 memory locations (hence the name). It ships with 30 pre-configured presets allowing quick

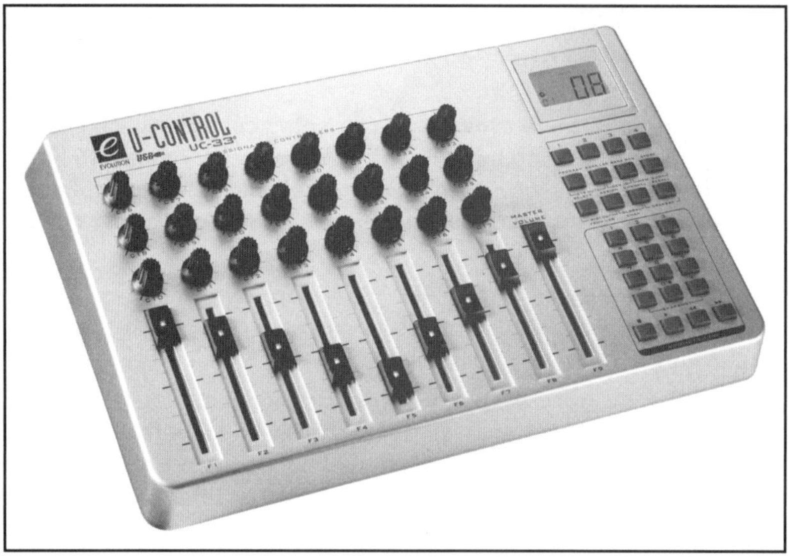

Figure 7.7 The Evolution UC-33e.

and easy access to the controls of the many popular music applications including Reason, Live, Logic, Cubase SX, as well as many of Native Instruments' software instruments.

Doepfer Pocket Fader, Pocket Control, and Drehbank

German company Doepfer Musikelektronik has been an innovator in music technology for more than two decades, developing and marketing a wide range of synthesizers, MIDI controllers, and other useful gear for electronic musicians. Among other things, Doepfer makes a variety of quality MIDI controllers that have proven themselves at live gigs around the world.

Doepfer controllers typically feature very sleek designs, with banks of faders and/or knobs arranged neatly in rows and columns. They are among the most generic controllers available, in the sense that the controls are not laid out like an analog mixer or other grouped arrangement, encouraging you to use them in a particular way. Rather, Doepfer controllers are like a blank slate, enabling you to create and assign whatever kind of performance setup you want. Many laptop musicians who change their performance setups frequently prefer these "generic" controllers for this reason.

Doepfer makes controllers ranging from very small to very large, but four of their controllers in particular will be of most interest to live computer musicians. Three of these are essentially the same in size as well as in their basic functioning: The Pocket Fader, Pocket Control, and Pocket Dial (see Figures 7.8, 7.9, and 7.10, respectively).

Each of these controllers provides a total of 16 independently assignable MIDI controllers in the form of either faders or knobs, as you can see in the photos below. The Pocket Control and Pocket Dial look very similar, the only difference being that the Pocket Control features

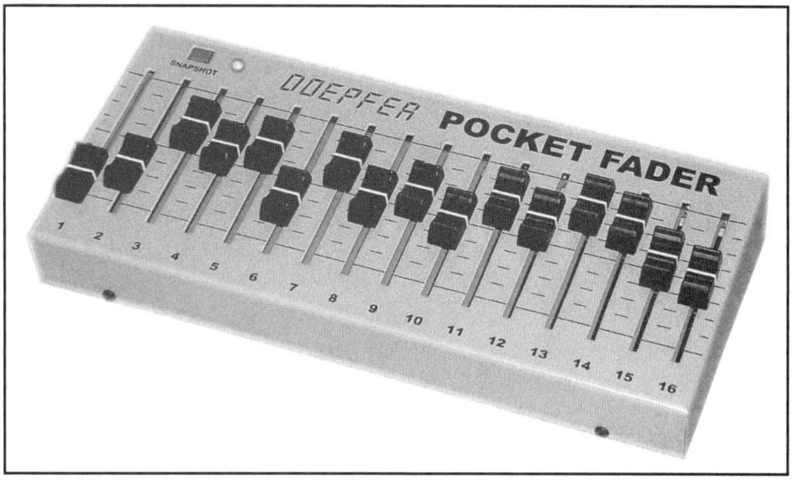

Figure 7.8 The Doepfer Pocket Fader.

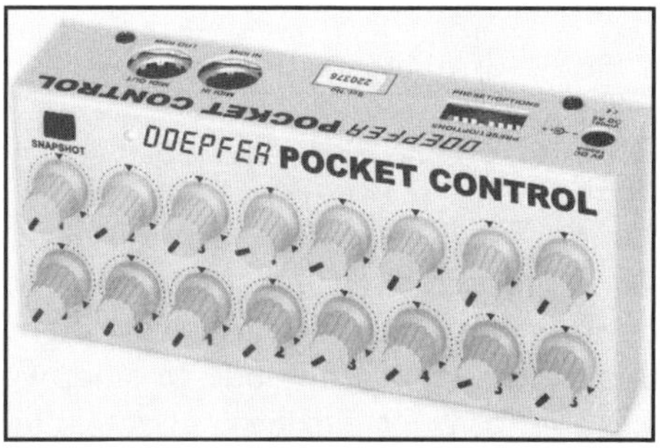

Figure 7.9 The Doepfer Pocket Control.

potentiometer-style controllers adjustable between fixed minimum and maximum points, while the Pocket Dial uses endless rotary encoders instead, with no fixed reference points.

Any of these three controllers is a great tool for the live laptop performer, providing easy control of 16 different parameters in your software. You can use one of these Doepfer controllers like a mixer if you want, just like the Evolution UC-33e, or you can assign its knobs or faders to control any other parameter in your software. Doepfer also offers a downloadable software application from their Web site that you can use to make MIDI controller assignments in their controllers.

According to the Doepfer Web site, supplies of the Pocket Fader are running low and it will soon be discontinued; however, the Pocket Control and Pocket Dial will continue to be sold. Which of these two is better for your needs as a performer depends on the application. The Pocket Control, with its fixed minimum and maximum points, is probably a better choice if you want to use the unit like a MIDI mixer and control mixer parameters such as volume, pan, and

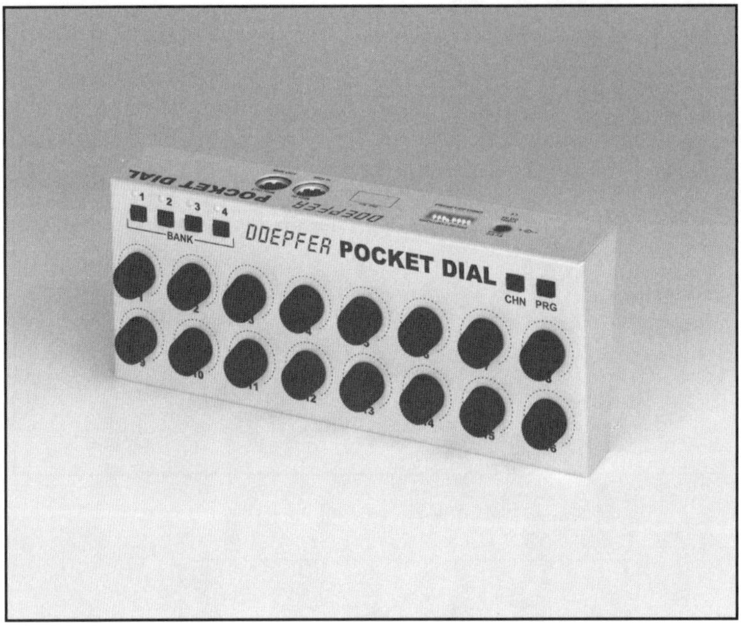

Figure 7.10 The Doepfer Pocket Dial.

effects sends. However, the Pocket Dial would better suit your needs if you want to control the parameters of software sound sources like VST instruments or effects. The Pocket Dial's rotary encoders enable it to operate in a relative controller mode in which any change you make is relative to the value that parameter already has. In other words, the parameter will change smoothly from its starting point as you move the knob rather than immediately jumping to the current position of the knob and causing a discontinuity in the sound.

For those laptop musicians who find that 16 controllers is just not enough for all the things they want to control live, Doepfer also makes larger MIDI control devices like the Drehbank (see Figure 7.11).

The Drehbank provides the user with four rows of MIDI controller knobs, each comprising 16 knobs, for a total of 64 individual assignable MIDI controllers. Besides its larger size and greater number of knobs, in other respects it is similar to the smaller Doepfer devices above. Saxophonist Andrew Pask of Cycling '74 (pictured in Figure 7.11), with whom I have done many live computer music performances, often uses his Drehbank to control various parameters in his MAX/MSP live rig. (Although how he can remember what he has assigned all of those 64 knobs to without writing them down is somewhat of a mystery to me!)

Note that none of these Doepfer devices can connect to your computer directly. You will need an additional MIDI interface to connect them.

Doepfer also makes the fascinating Pocket Electronic kit, enabling you to construct your own custom MIDI controller from whatever individual components you want to put together. I will

Figure 7.11 Andrew Pask of Cycling '74 looking down the rows of knobs on his Doepfer Drehbank.

describe more about this unique product in the section about specialized and custom MIDI controllers at the end of this chapter.

Behringer B-Control Fader BCF2000 and B-Control Rotary BCR2000

In addition to the DJ control device mentioned in the previous section, Behringer has recently introduced a number of inexpensive compact MIDI controllers that would be useful for laptop performers: The BCF2000 and BCR2000. These are quite similar devices but differ in the number and type of MIDI controllers they offer.

Looking first at the BCF2000 (see Figure 7.12), we see that it looks more or less similar to the Evolution UC-33e, with eight faders, eight knobs, and 16 buttons that can be freely assigned to control to any MIDI parameters in your software. The faders are motorized, meaning that once assigned, they will move and follow the level of the parameter they are assigned to as your arrangement plays back. With respect to live performance, this particular function would make the BCF2000 a good choice if you are playing back a multi-track arrangement from a DAW in live performance. It would also work well with any application in which you are mixing together the output from multiple audio tracks live.

The BCF2000 can connect directly to your computer via USB. It also offers one MIDI input as well as two MIDI outs, allowing you to connect additional MIDI devices. Like the Evolution products mentioned above, it is class-compliant under Windows XP and Mac OSX and does not require a software driver to operate.

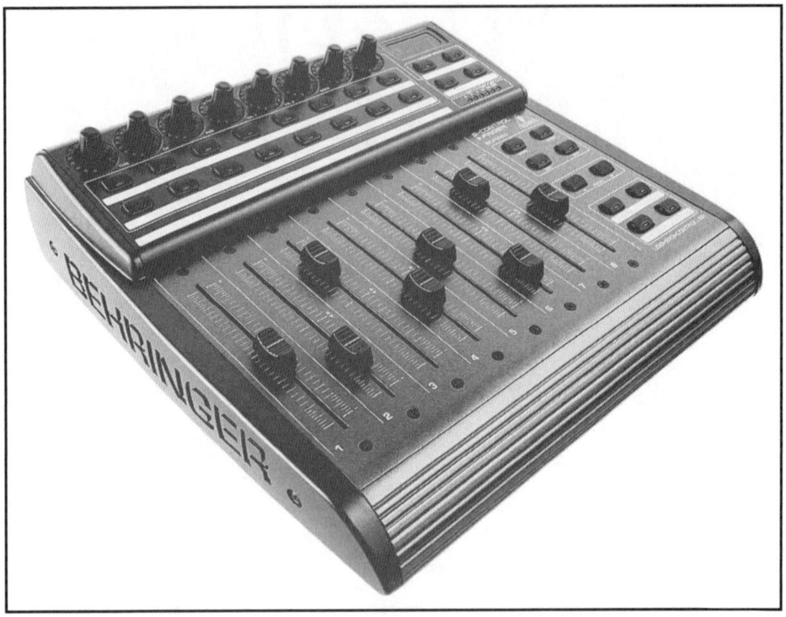

Figure 7.12 The Behringer BCF2000 B-Control Fader.

The controls on the BCF2000 can be programmed using the controls on the unit. When I last checked (April 2005) Behringer claimed that they would also be releasing their own librarian/editor software enabling remote editing of the BCF2000's controls and functions.

Behringer's BCR2000 B-Control Rotary (see Figure 7.13) is quite similar to the BCF2000 in design and function, except that it features rotary knob controllers exclusively rather than a mix of knobs and faders.

As you can see in the above image, the BCR2000 has a total of 24 rotary knobs and 16 buttons that can be assigned to control parameters in your software. In other respects it is identical in form and function to the BCF2000.

Keyboard Controllers

Many computer music performers are primarily interested in playback, mixing, and effecting pre-recorded audio material during their live performances, whether they are playing their own music or DJing a selection of the material of others. For these performers, one of the above DJ- or mixer-style MIDI controllers is probably the best choice.

However, other performers are interested in playing at least some of the parts of their music live using a keyboard controller or other input device. If you want to add live keyboard parts to your mix, here is a selection of some of the innovative keyboard input devices currently on the market.

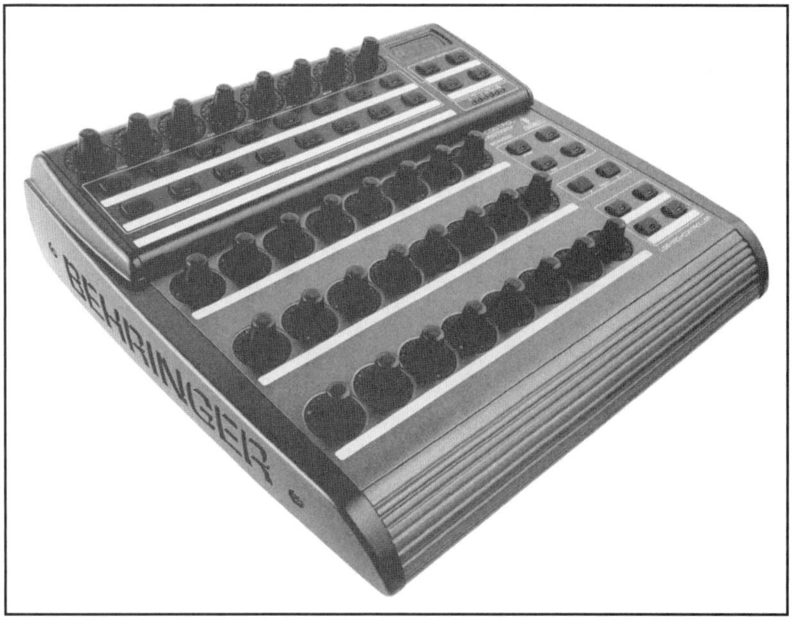

Figure 7.13 The Behringer BCR2000 B-Control Rotary.

M-Audio O2

One recent trend in the industry has been towards extremely lightweight compact keyboard controllers and the O2 keyboard from M-Audio (see Figure 7.14) is a good example. This type of small portable keyboard interface is ideal for many laptop performers who are not keyboard virtuosos and don't need a full-range keyboard but just want to use a keyboard controller to play some simple parts or trigger samples in performance.

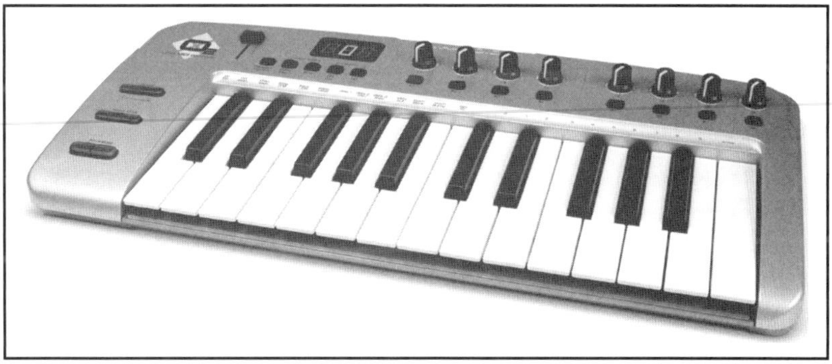

Figure 7.14 The M-Audio O2.

The O2 offers a two-octave, 25-key velocity-sensitive keyboard as well as eight knobs and eight buttons that can be freely assigned to control any MIDI parameter you choose. It has three small rocker controls on the left-hand side of the keyboard to control the modulation, pitch bend, and transpose the keyboard up and down by octaves.

The O2 connects to your computer via USB and requires no separate power supply. It is class-compliant in Windows XP and OSX, so no software driver is necessary. Like the X-Session and the UC-33e, you can use M-Audio subsidiary Evolution's Enigma software (available as a free download) to remotely edit the MIDI settings of the O2 and store them in the keyboard's preset memories.

The O2 is the successor to M-Audio's innovative Oxygen8 controller (see Figure 7.15), which started the trend towards compact keyboard controllers in the first place, and the two keyboards are similar in their overall functioning. However, the Oxygen8 is not compatible with Enigma and its functions cannot be remotely edited. It is worth mentioning here though, as it is probably the most common piece of MIDI equipment used by the current crop of computer musicians.

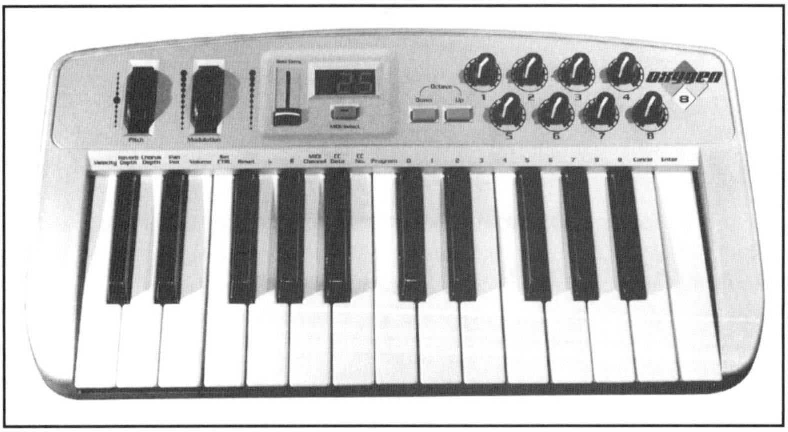

Figure 7.15 The M-Audio Oxygen8.

Edirol PCR-M1 and PCR-1

Edirol's PCR-M1 and PCR-1 keyboards represent their entries in this compact keyboard controller category. The PCR-M1 (see Figure 7.16) is similar in form and function to the M-Audio O2, and it offers eight knobs, six buttons, and two pedal jacks, all of which can be freely assigned to control any MIDI parameter. It also has a shift button that changes the assignable parameter in eight knobs and three of the buttons, which gives you a total of 27 controllable parameters accessible through the device in a given setup. It also has a rotary encoder that can be assigned to control various keyboard functions in performance. You can use Edirol's downloadable PCR-Editor software to remotely edit its settings from your computer.

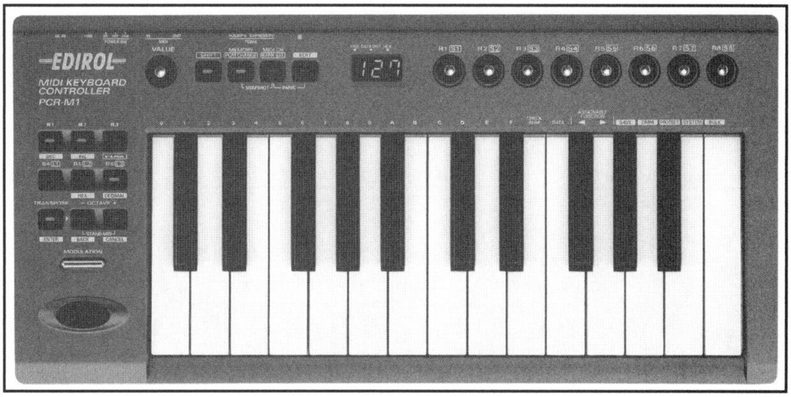

Figure 7.16 The Edirol PCR-M1.

Also like the O2, the PCR-M1 connects to your computer via USB and does not require an additional power supply.

Edirol's PCR-1 keyboard (see Figure 7.17) is similar to the PCR-M1 except that it also has a built-in audio interface.

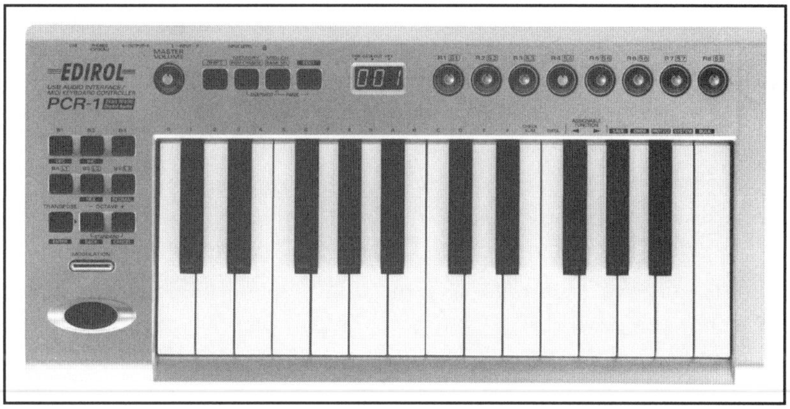

Figure 7.17 The Edirol PCR-1.

The PCR-1 offers one stereo analog input and output pair via RCA jacks on the back of the unit as well as a ⅛" stereo headphone jack that doubles as an optical S/PDIF output. Measuring only 17 ¾" × 8 11/16" × 1-⅛" and weighing only three pounds, five ounces, the PCR-1 is one of the most compact integrated audio/MIDI interfaces currently on the market.

M-Audio Ozonic

M-Audio's Ozonic keyboard (see Figure 7.18) is a good example of a larger class of integrated audio/MIDI controller. The Ozonic is significantly bigger and offers significantly more controls and features than Edirol's PCR-1, while still remaining easily portable.

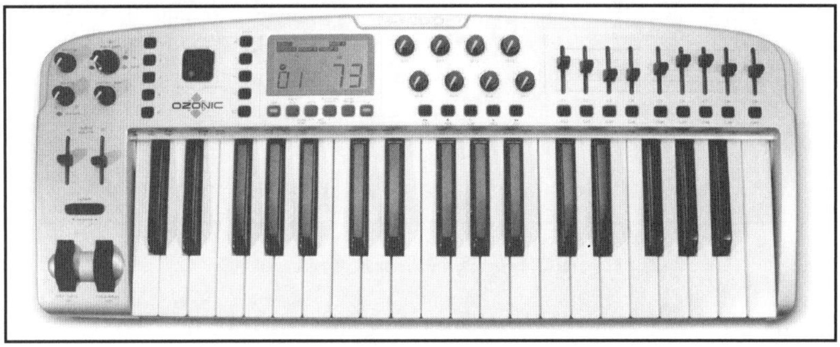

Figure 7.18 The M-Audio Ozonic.

On the MIDI side, the Ozonic has a 37-note, full-size keyboard with assignable aftertouch. It also has an external MIDI input and output port for connecting additional MIDI devices. Along with the keyboard, it has 40 assignable MIDI controllers including eight knobs, nine sliders, nine buttons, an X-Y joystick, pitch and modulation control wheels, two pedal inputs, and five transport control buttons that can be used to control the play, stop, record, and rewind functions of your sequencing software. There are small plus/minus buttons on the left side of the keyboard to transpose the keyboard by half-step or by octave.

All of the MIDI controls on the Ozonic are fully programmable and you can edit your setup using the buttons on the unit itself or by using M-Audio/Evolution's Enigma software for remote editing. You can store your setup in one of the Ozonic's 20 preset memory locations.

On the audio side, the Ozonic features four input and four output channels, including one XLR mic input with phantom power, a ¼" instrument input, and ¼" stereo line inputs. There are two pairs of stereo line outputs, also on ¼" jacks as well as a separate headphone output.

The Ozonic connects to your computer via a FireWire connection, and can be powered via the FireWire bus if your computer has a 6-pin FireWire port. (See the section on FireWire audio interfaces in Chapter 6 for more on FireWire.) If you are using a PC laptop, with a 4-pin FireWire port, you will need to use a separate power adapter.

The Ozonic is a very powerful controller for live performance, placing a range of controllers at your fingertips to adjust various software parameters in performance while still using it as a keyboard to play some parts of the music directly. For example, you could assign the bank of nine sliders to control the volumes of various tracks in a sequencer, while assigning the knobs to control various useful parameters of your effects or software instruments. The Ozonic's keyboard also features aftertouch, a feature not commonly found on MIDI controller keyboards, allowing you to transmit additional MIDI information to the computer by pressing down on a key more firmly after you have already played a note.

In addition, the built-in mic and line audio inputs of the Ozonic enable you to easily attach a mic or instrument to the unit and feed the signal through your software, adding live vocals, guitar, or other instrument to your music with no other equipment necessary.

Alesis Photon X49 USB/MIDI Keyboard Controller

The Photon X49 keyboard controller from Alesis (see Figure 7.19) is a standard MIDI keyboard controller in most respects, but it adds Alesis' proprietary AXYZ controller dome for added control. The AXYZ dome is a wireless controller that detects motion in three dimensions, allowing you to modify MIDI parameters assigned to it by waving your hand over it instead of touching a physical control. Only Alesis offers this particular technology at present, so if this type of controller appeals to you, then the Photon X49 is the keyboard for you.

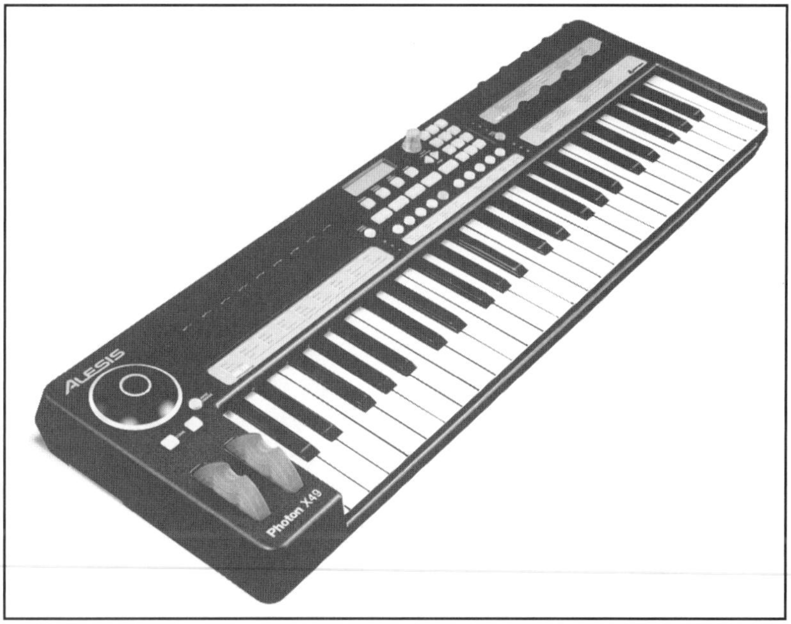

Figure 7.19 The Alesis Photon X49.

The Photon X49 offers ten rotary encoders, nine faders, ten backlit buttons, and dedicated transport controls for remote control of your software/hardware DAW. It runs on bus power from its USB connection to the computer, and is class-compliant under Windows XP and Mac OSX, so it does not require a software driver.

Korg KONTROL49

Another interesting keyboard controller with a unique interface is the Korg KONTROL49 (see Figure 7.20).

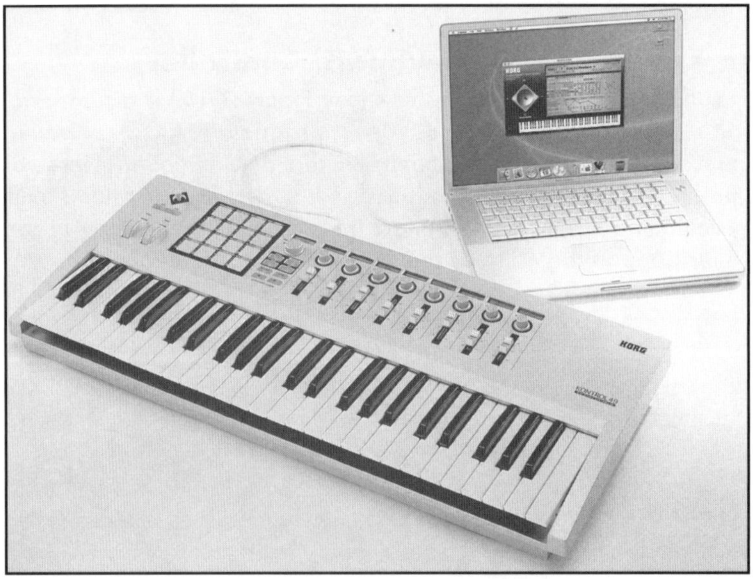

Figure 7.20 The Korg KONTROL49.

This MIDI device combines a 49-key keyboard with a four-way joystick, eight rotary encoders, and eight sliders. Unique among the keyboard controllers covered in this chapter, it also has sixteen MIDI trigger pads arranged above the keyboard in a 4×4 Akai MPC-style layout. These pads are very useful for programming drum patterns and triggering samples and effects live or in the studio. Hiphop producers in particular have always prized the Akai MPC controllers for their ease of use in programming beats. Although there are other MIDI devices from Akai and M-Audio that offer MPC-style pad controllers like this, it is also convenient to have them integrated into a keyboard controller.

Like most of the other MIDI devices here, the KONTROL49 connects to your PC or Mac computer via USB and receives power via the USB bus. You can program the MIDI functions of the keyboard by using the controls on the unit or by using Korg's Editor/Librarian software.

M-Audio Keystation Pro 88

The M-Audio Keystation Pro 88 (see Figure 7.21) is one of the largest dedicated MIDI keyboard controllers available on the market today. This kind of full-size keyboard controller might be overkill for some of today's digital DJs, but if you want to use a real piano-style keyboard in a performance, the Keystation Pro 88 is an extremely powerful and flexible choice.

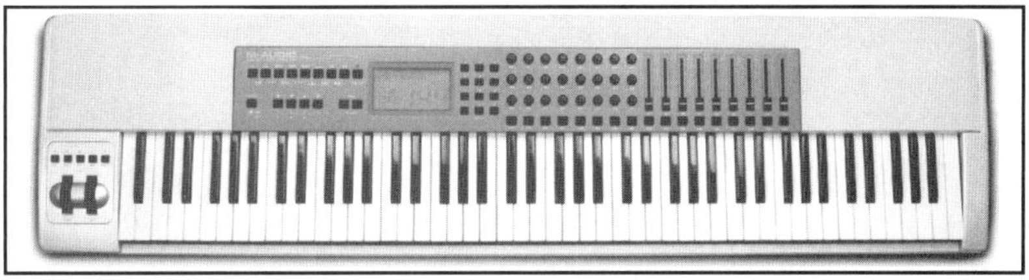

Figure 7.21 The M-Audio Keystation Pro 88.

The Pro 88 features a full-size 88-key hammer-action keyboard as well as a plethora of assignable MIDI controllers including 24 knobs, nine faders, 22 buttons, and assignable pitch and modulation wheels. It has four keyboard zones for layers and split, and ten non-volatile memory locations for saving all controller assignments. You can edit the Pro 88's MIDI settings using its controls or remotely from your computer via M-Audio/Evolution's Enigma software.

This keyboard connects to your computer via USB and is class-compliant under Windows XP and Mac OS X. Surprisingly, in spite of its large size it can draw all the power it needs from your computer's USB port and it does not require an external power supply.

With its full-size keyboard and so many controllers, the Keystation Pro 88 is wide open for experimentation and could be used effectively in a wide variety of software setups. It would be particularly useful for real keyboardists who are playing in a live band context but want to take advantage of the sounds available from today's crop of advanced software instruments.

Percussion-Style Controllers

For those without a background in keyboard playing (like myself, for example) who want to use some kind of MIDI controller device to trigger live events, there are also percussion-style controllers available as an alternative. These typically feature some kind of pad controllers instead of a keyboard interface, arranged in various configurations. We already looked at one keyboard controller above that incorporated trigger pads in its design, the Korg KONTROL49; now let's take a look at a few dedicated percussion controllers.

Akai MPD16

One of the principal innovators in the field of percussion controllers has been Akai, who have set the standard with their well-known line of MPC controllers and sequencers. The various MPC models differ in their particulars but all feature the familiar 4×4 grid of square trigger pads seen in Figure 7.22.

Most of the MPC units Akai has made have included many other functions along with these trigger pads. The MPC1000 unit pictured below is a MIDI sequencer as well as a controller. Of course, these sequencer units could be very useful for live performance, but my focus in this book is primarily on software-based computer performance rather than hardware-based sequencing.

Figure 7.22 The Akai MPC1000.

However, Akai does make one percussion controller unit that is strictly a MIDI controller: The Akai MPD16 (see Figure 7.23).

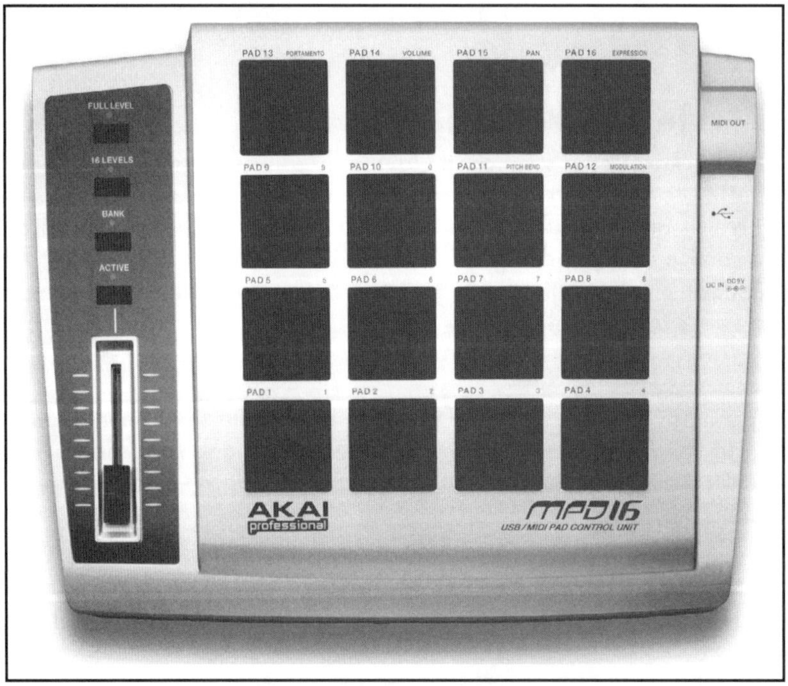

Figure 7.23 The Akai MPD16.

The MPD16 is a slimmed-down controller-only version of the larger MPC units. It features 16 assignable MPC pads as well as one slider control. It can connect directly to your computer via USB. You can use Akai's remote editor software to edit the MIDI note and controller data sent by the pads on the MPD16, but there is actually not much to set up on this unit anyway, as the pads send MIDI note and velocity data only. You can set them to whatever pitches you want, but they can only send note information and not other kinds of MIDI controller data.

You could use the MPD16 effectively live to play electronic beats, or to trigger a variety of samples that you have mapped across the pads. However, the range of possible creative applications for this particular unit are somewhat limited by the fact that the pads can only be configured to send MIDI-note data.

M-Audio Trigger Finger

The Trigger Finger is M-Audio's recent entrant into this product category, and at first glance (see Figure 7.24), it looks much like the MPD16. Looking more closely, however, there are some important differences.

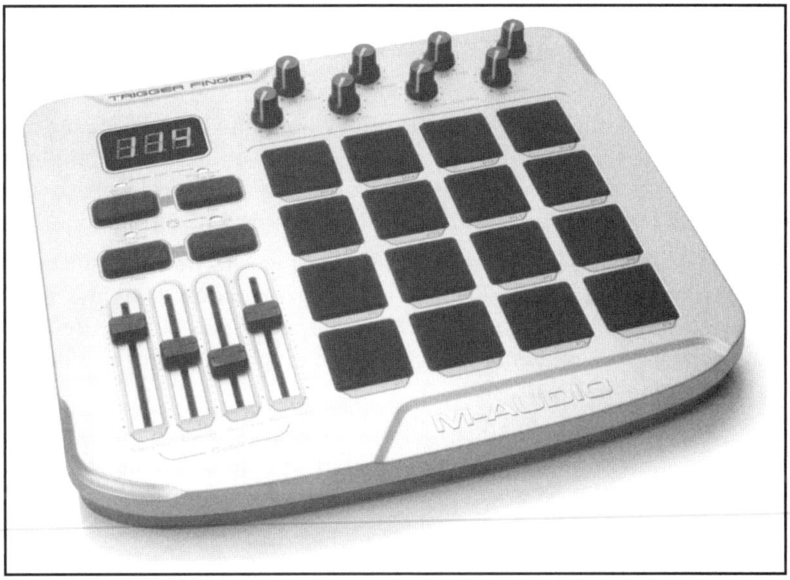

Figure 7.24 The M-Audio Trigger Finger.

Like the MPD16, the Trigger Finger has 16 pads laid out in the familiar MPC-style 4×4 grid, but also adds four sliders to the left of the pads and eight knobs above, all of which are assignable controllers themselves. There are also four buttons and a small display to enable the quick editing of the device's parameters. (The Trigger Finger can also be programmed using M-Audio's downloadable Enigma software.)

Although superficially similar to the MPD16, the extra MIDI sliders and knobs on the Trigger Finger make it a more useful choice for the gigging laptop musician. In addition, the pads themselves can be programmed to send any kind of MIDI controller message you want, not just MIDI note data. They are sensitive to aftertouch as well, opening up all kinds of additional creative possibilities.

For example, LA laptop performer Dream Electric played a live gig in April 2005 using Ableton Live and the Trigger Finger. Rather than triggering samples with the controller, however, he assigned its various pad controllers to trigger the "randomize" function in some of the various VST software effects he was hosting within Live. Thus, every time he struck one of the pads, one of the tracks of the music would suddenly change as the parameters of the effect was instantaneously reconfigured.

Like most of the other controllers in this chapter, the Trigger Finger attaches to your Mac or PC by a USB connection. It can draw power from the USB port and does not require an external power supply.

Roland HPD-15 HandSonic Percussion Controller

Another interesting percussion-style controller I have seen used in live computer performances is the Roland HPD-15 HandSonic, one of the more recent offerings in Roland's long line of drum and percussion MIDI devices. See Figure 7.25.

In contrast to the Akai MPD16 and the M-Audio Trigger Finger, the HPD-15 is both a controller and a synthesizer/sequencer, having a MIDI control surface as well as extensive banks of internal percussion sounds and hardware sequencer functions. Its central feature is a ten-inch-wide circular rubber MIDI trigger pad, divided into 15 discrete MIDI triggers.

This pad also features a built-in pressure sensor, enabling you to perform muting and pitch control effects by pressing on the pads just as you would on an acoustic percussion instrument such as a conga. In addition, the trigger pad also incorporates a technology Roland calls Positional Sensing, allowing the player to effect subtle changes in sound quality depending on exactly which area of the pad is struck.

Of course, you wouldn't have to use the HPD-15's built-in sounds or even use it as a percussion controller at all—you could also use it to trigger samples or change parameters in your software when struck, just as with the other controllers above.

The HPD-15 has only MIDI in and out ports for communication with other equipment, so you will need a dedicated MIDI interface as well to connect it to your computer.

Specialized and Custom Controllers

In addition to the basic types I have looked at so far, there are also many other types of specialized and/or custom MIDI controllers on the market that can be used to control your computer software in live performance. Although for most performance applications a basic mixer, keyboard, or percussion controller like the ones I have covered above will probably be the best choice, there will always be some performers whose ideas fall outside the

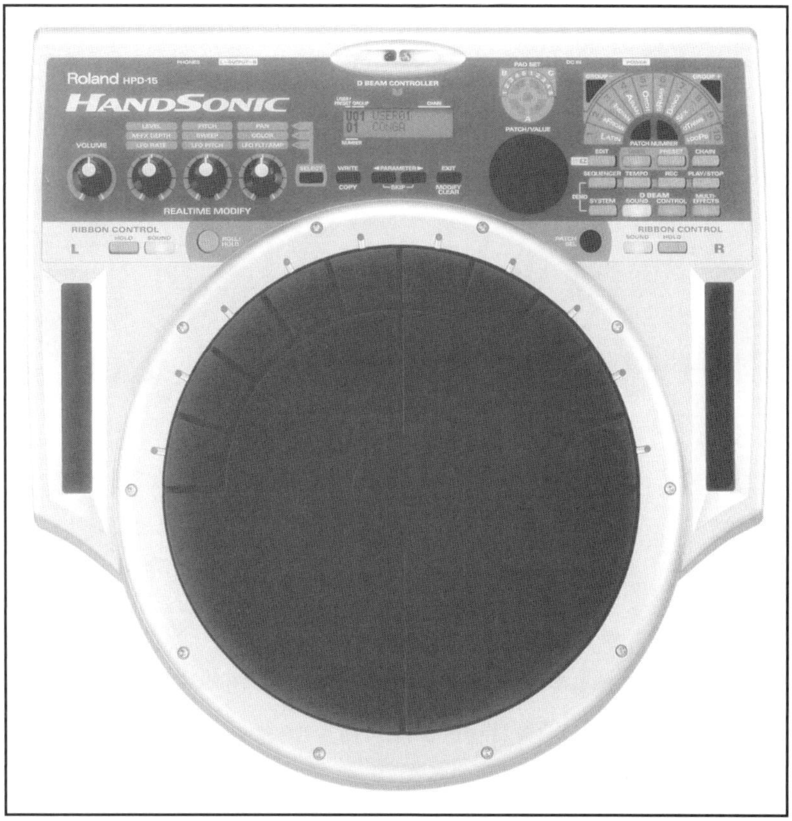

Figure 7.25 The Roland HPD-15 HandSonic Percussion Controller.

scope of what can be done with a standard controller. Some of these devices, like the Korg KP2 Kaoss Pad, are also a great add-on to a setup that already includes a principal MIDI controller device.

Korg KP2 Kaoss Pad

The first Korg Kaoss Pad effects unit/MIDI controller (see Figure 7.26) was introduced in 1999 and it quickly became a favorite among electronic music performers and DJs for its ease of use, unique touch-style interface, and powerful (though somewhat lo-fi) built-in effects.

The original Kaoss Pad featured 60 built-in effects programs and a unique touch-sensitive X-Y pad that let you control separate parameters on the horizontal and vertical axes, allowing you to do things like control the delay time and feedback of a delay line at the same time on the X and Y axes, or modify the cutoff and resonance of a filter with the sweep of a single finger. In addition, it had a standard MIDI out and you could use the touchpad as a MIDI controller, assigning it to whatever parameters you wanted to control in your software. I have

Figure 7.26 The original Korg Kaoss Pad.

one of these units myself and enjoyed using it on dozens of gigs until the power connection finally developed a short and worked only intermittently.

In 2002, Korg introduced an updated Kaoss Pad, the KP2 (see Figure 7.27), and took the opportunity to improve on their original design in a number of significant respects.

The KP2 improves upon the original Kaoss Pad in almost every respect, adding additional effects, a sturdier housing, a better touchpad, and important new features such as tempo detection and beat-syncing of effects. There are 100 effects programs in the unit, and with a built-in MIDI out port you can also use its touchpad to control any editable parameters in your audio software.

Although the Kaoss Pad is better known as a live effects unit than a MIDI controller, you can get amazing results by connecting it to your computer via MIDI and using its touchpad to control your virtual instruments or effects in a program like Ableton Live, which is why I am including it here. Both affordable and durable enough to be road-worthy, the KP2 is definitely the way to go if you want to incorporate a compact touch-sensitive MIDI control surface into your live setup. Whether you want to use the built-in audio effects when you perform (and you probably will), the Kaoss Pad's utility as a MIDI controller alone makes it worth the purchase price.

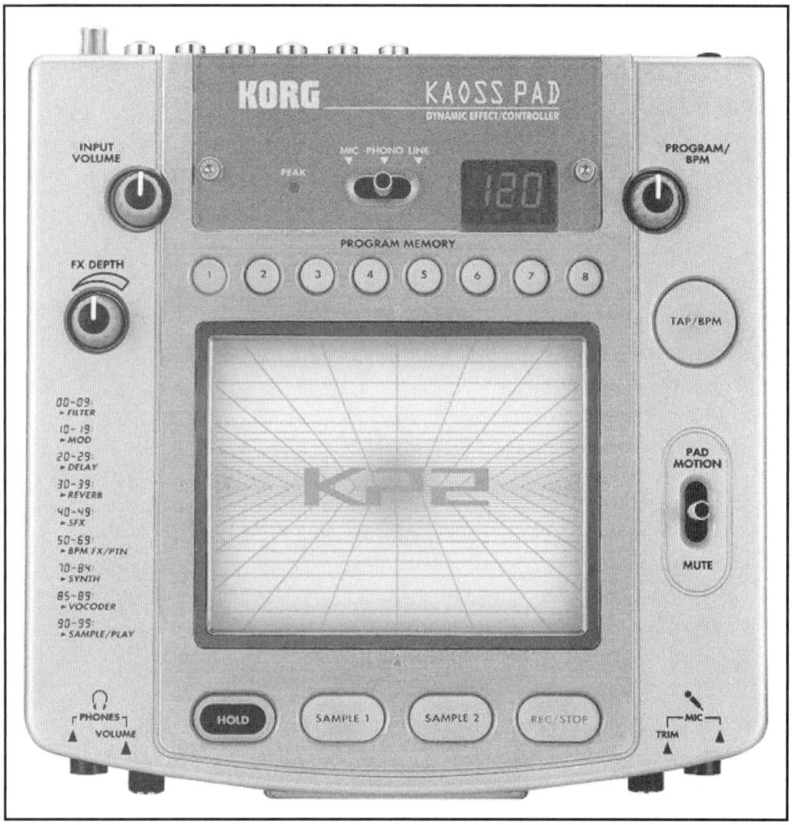

Figure 7.27 The Korg KP2 Kaoss Pad.

Korg also made another Kaoss Pad model called the Entrancer (see Figure 7.28) that adds video processing and effects as well to the capabilities of the unit. On-the-fly video processing is beyond the scope of this book but I highly recommend checking out the Entrancer if you are interested in this kind of thing.

FaderFox LV1 and LX1 Devices for Use with Ableton Live

I mentioned FaderFox's micromodul DJ1 unit in the section above on DJ-style MIDI controllers. FaderFox also makes two more similar controllers, the LV1 and LX1 (see Figures 7.29a and 7.29b respectively), which have been especially designed for use with Ableton Live.

FaderFox has designed these units to complement each other in the number and types of controllers that they provide for use with Live. The LV1 offers a selection of knobs and faders that can be used to control levels and effects parameters in Live, as well as transport buttons and a tiny X-Y joystick controller. The LX1 provides a panel of small MIDI buttons intended to trigger tracks, clips, samples, and other events in Live.

Figure 7.28 The Korg KPE1 Kaoss Pad Entrancer.

Like the DJ1, these two controllers connect to your computer via MIDI only so you need an additional MIDI interface to use them. They can be powered either by four AAA batteries or an AC adapter.

As I mentioned earlier in this chapter, however, the FaderFox units are not available in the US at the time of writing.

Doepfer Pocket Electronic

Doepfer's Pocket Electronic is a do-it-yourself kit that gives you the parts you need to build your own unique MIDI control device. Up to 16 controlling elements (see Figure 7.30) can be connected in one Pocket Electronic device transmitting 16 different MIDI messages at once. If you are interested in building your own gear, Pocket Electronic makes it relatively easily for you to create your own unique controller and develop fresh performance concepts.

The Pocket Electronic contains the electronics core of the company's Pocket Control device, with the possibility of connecting 16 input devices, but without the actual controls. The basic

Figure 7.29a The FaderFox LV1.

MIDI functionality of Pocket Electronic is identical to that of the other Doepfer Pocket Control devices I covered above.

Continuum Fingerboard

The Continuum Fingerboard (Figure 7.30), made by Haken Audio, is a unique "keyless" keyboard controller, somewhat analogous to a fretless bass or guitar in some respects. Individual instruments are made one at a time by hand and are quite expensive, but I wanted to include the Fingerboard here as an example of one of the directions that MIDI technology has developed in.

The Continuum Fingerboard resembles a standard piano-style keyboard in some respects: It is approximately the same size and is played with ten fingers using a pianistic technique. See Figure 7.31. However, like a fretless string instrument, it does not have discrete pitches but rather offers the user a continuous three-dimensional control surface (the third dimension in

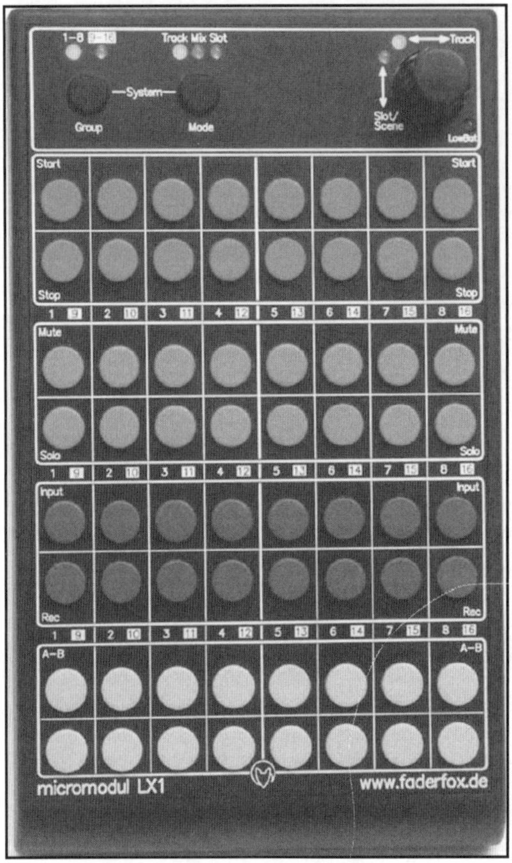

Figure 7.29b The FaderFox LX1.

this case being the amount of pressure you apply with your fingers when you touch the control surface).

The Fingerboard unit connects to your computer music via a standard MIDI port, so it must be used with an additional MIDI interface. It also has a FireWire port, though the documentation indicates that this is only to be used for communication with Symbolic Sound Corporation's high-end Kyma Workstation.

According to Continuum's technical documentation, the Fingerboard tracks and updates discrete MIDI values for the x, y, and z position of one to ten fingers every 1.33 milliseconds. The x dimension or side-to-side position of each finger provides continuous pitch control across the playing surface. A surface guide pattern helps you figure out what "notes" you are playing, as shown in Figure 7.32. Just as shown here, each "D" note on the actual Fingerboard has a circular mark for visual reference.

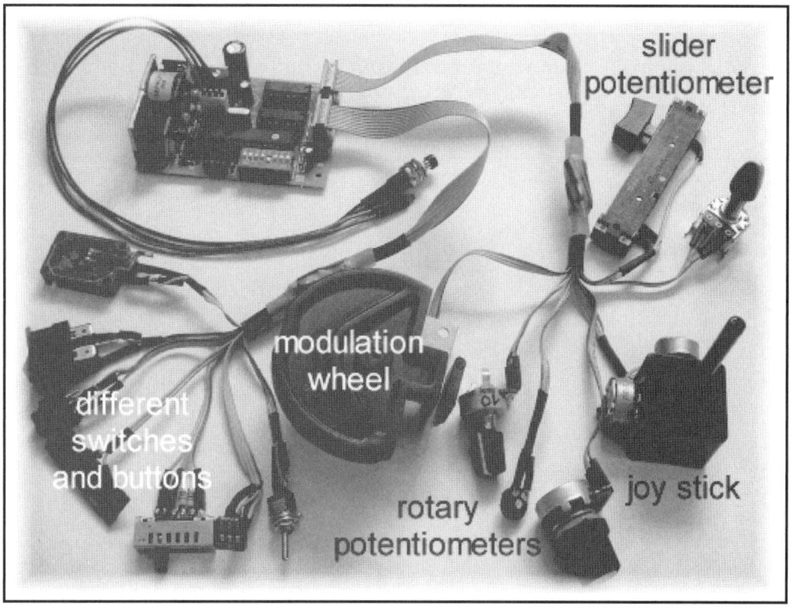

Figure 7.30 Some of the components of the Doepfer Pocket Electronic kit.

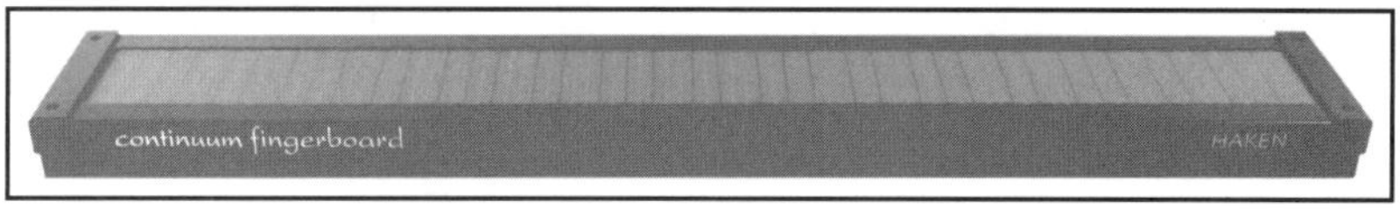

Figure 7.31 The Continuum Fingerboard.

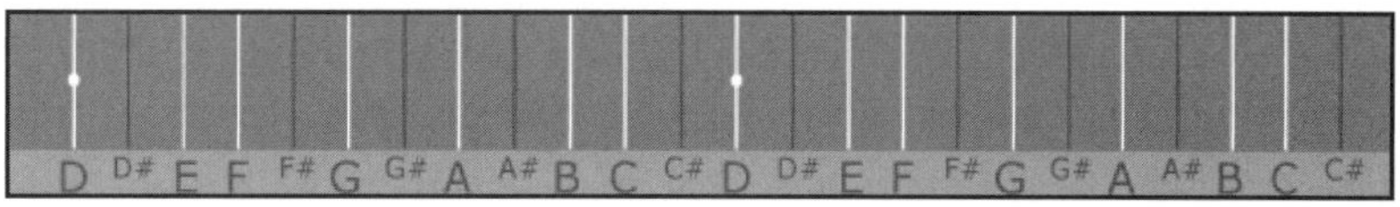

Figure 7.32 Two-octave section of the Continuum playing surface with note name markings added.

In addition to this x value, which determines pitch, each finger you place on the playing surface of the Fingerboard also outputs a unique y or front-to-back value as well as a z or downward pressure value. The y position of each finger provides additional control for each individual note, while the z (pressure) value allows for dynamic control, similar to what you can achieve with a MIDI keyboard that supports aftertouch.

It is difficult to describe the creative possibilities of such an elegant controller without actually seeing it in action. If you are interested in seeing and hearing for yourself what this controller is capable of, I highly recommend viewing the extensive performance videos Haken Audio have online at http://www.cerlsoundgroup.org/Continuum. Click the menu item "New Possibilities" to reach the video links.

Lemur

Another futuristic MIDI controller is the Lemur multitouch controller, made by French company JazzMutant and distributed in the US by Cycling '74 (see Figure 7.33).

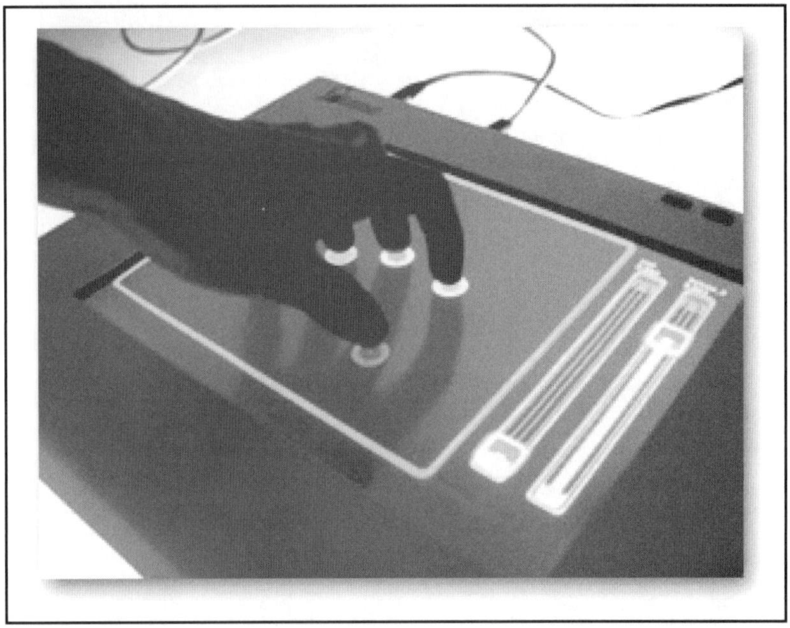

Figure 7.33 The Lemur.

As you can see, the Lemur is basically just a 12" LCD touchscreen display lying flat on a table. You use it by moving virtual objects on the touchscreen with your fingers. The Lemur uses proprietary touchscreen interface technology that can track multiple fingers simultaneously.

Using an editor application on your computer, you can design your own custom performance interface for the Lemur by dragging and dropping virtual switches, faders, and other objects into a facsimile of the Lemur's screen. Then upload your design to the memory of the Lemur (which connects to your computer via Ethernet) and you're ready to play.

You can also use the up and down buttons above the display to quickly change presets held in memory, completely transforming the interface you are using in an instant. As the Cycling '74 Web site puts it, "One moment you can be mixing by moving several faders simultaneously. The next moment you can be controlling a software synth with switches and balls that can be thrown around in a two-dimensional space."

Technically speaking, the Lemur isn't really a MIDI controller at all as it doesn't use the MIDI standard to communicate with other hardware. Instead, the Lemur uses the newer Open Sound Control (OSC) standard, which uses a standard 100baseT Ethernet cable instead of a MIDI connection. OSC is an emerging new standard for controllers that has a number of important advantages over MIDI: Virtually no latency, a higher data capacity, greater (32-bit) numerical precision, and easy configurability. To my knowledge, the only major audio software applications that currently support OSC are Cycling '74's own MAX/MSP, as well as a number of Native Instruments applications including modular synth Reaktor and Traktor DJ Studio, but other major software vendors are planning to add OSC support in future releases.

If you are interested in seeing the Lemur in action (and you really have to see it to get an idea of what it can actually do), I recommend the videos available from the manufacturer's Web site at http://www.jazzmutant.com/lemur_overview.php.

Unfortunately, at time of writing, the Lemur is not actually available for purchase yet, being scheduled for release later in 2005. Check the Cycling '74 Web site http://www.cycling74.com for more current information on Lemur availability in the US.

Eobody Sensor Interface Hardware

But just when you thought you'd seen everything, as if tossing virtual balls through the air on the Lemur touchscreen to control your soft synths wasn't strange enough already, here comes the Eobody Sensor Interface Hardware (see Figure 7.34).

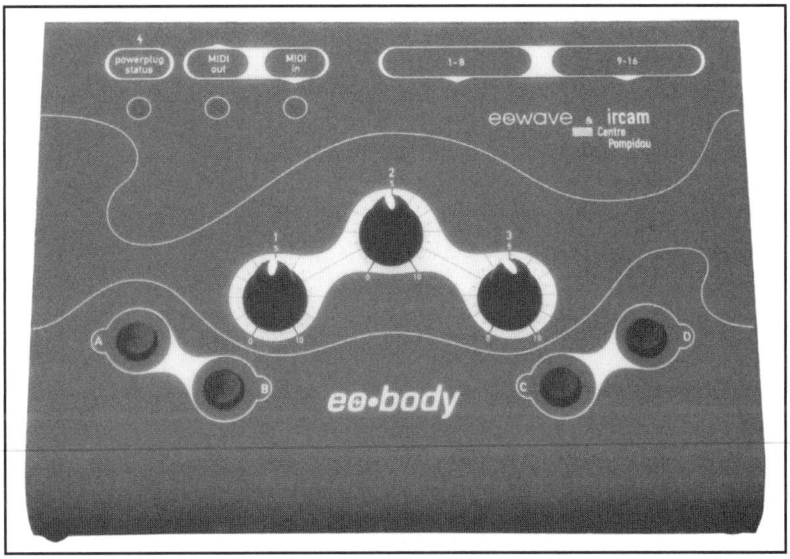

Figure 7.34 The Eobody Sensor Interface.

Sure, it looks harmless enough in the picture above, but this is just the base station. It is the attachments to the Eobody that really get crazy (see Figures 7.35a, 7.35b, 7.35c).

But perhaps I need to back up a minute and explain how this thing works first.

Figure 7.35a The Eobody Detection sensor.

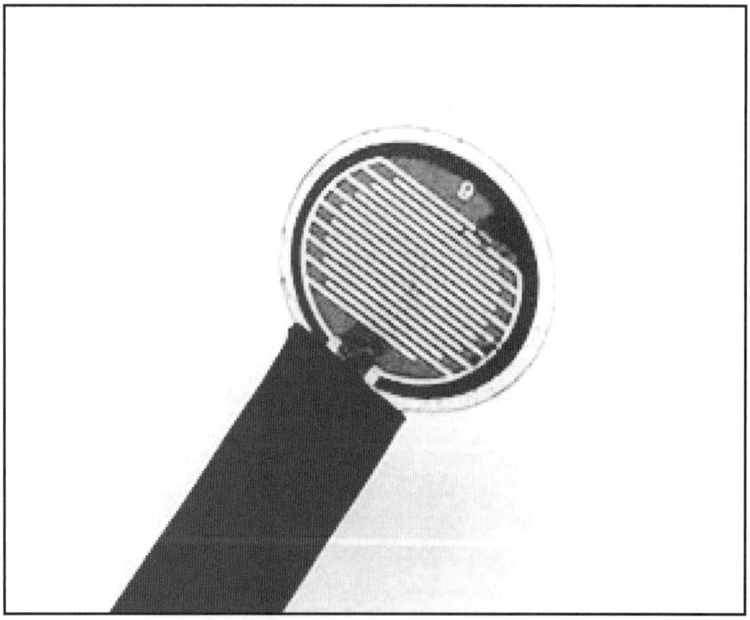

Figure 7.35b The Eobody 46mm Pressure sensor.

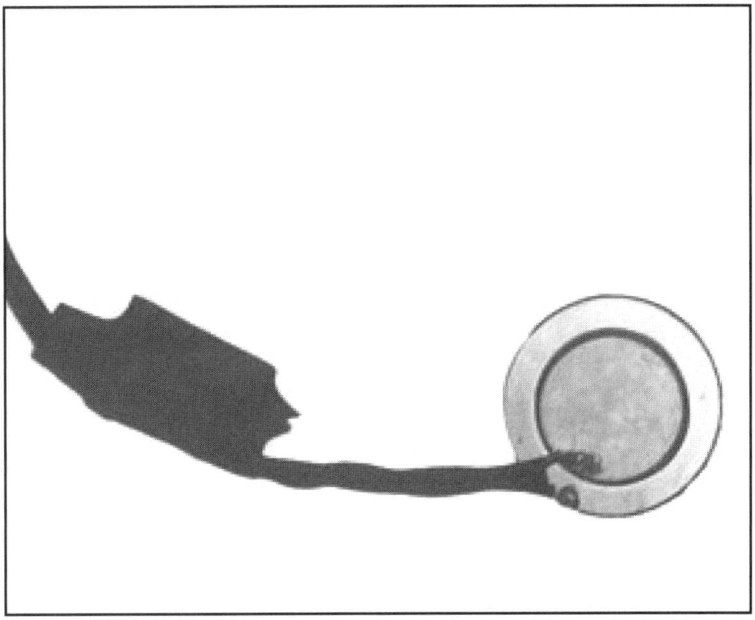

Figure 7.35c The Eobody Shock sensor.

The Eobody Sensor system is a unique MIDI controller system from French company Eowave comprising two main elements: The base station, which attaches to your computer, and sensors of various kinds, which are attached to the base station. There are a wide variety of sensors available for the Eobody system, including the following (details from the Cycling '74 Web site, the US distributor of the Eobody):

- Distance 20/80 sensor: Infrared distance sensors detect proximity within a 20-80 cm range.
- Small pressure sensor (size 20mm): Can be used as a trigger in response to impact.
- Light sensor: Detects light intensity.
- Movement sensor: Detects movement with mercury. Can be used to trigger and modulate events with your body.
- Position sensor (size 30cm): A ribbon controller that responds to touch by using position sensors. You can use them to modulate audio or video events, or for scratching applications. Ribbons may be attached to clothes or any other surface.
- Laser diode sensor: Useful for detection-based installations or in a matrix. Lasers can work in conjunction with light sensors to create a crossing point, for example.
- Large pressure sensor: Reacts to pressure modulation. Size is 38 mm.
- 2D G-force sensor: For dance performances and interactive installations.

- Position sensor (size 50cm): A ribbon controller that responds to touch by using position sensors. You can use them to modulate audio or video events, or for scratching applications. Ribbons may be attached to clothes or any other surface.

Basically, the Eobody system allows you to convert various kinds of analog data from the sensors into MIDI information, allowing for wholly new kinds of physical control of digital sound. The Eobody base unit is fully programmable via MIDI with the Eobody editor software, and connects to your computer via a standard MIDI connection.

How you use this kind of system is completely up to you, and you can probably see that these sensors open up huge creative possibilities. You could use temperature sensors on clubbers in front of the DJ booth to make the tempo of your tracks increase as the dancefloor heated up, or use light triggers to synchronize your effects with the lights in the venue you are playing. You could manipulate various software parameters by waving your arms in the air or stepping on various points on the ground where you have placed pressure sensors. The list of possible musical applications for the Eobody is endless.

For those interested, I highly recommend reading more about the Eobody system at http://www.eowave.com.

Now that we have covered all the gear you will need for live computer music performance, let's turn to the next chapter and start looking at some specific performance-oriented software and musical approaches.

8 Digital DJing

One of the most popular live music applications for computers is digital DJing: Using a computer and digital audio files to DJ in place of vinyl records or CDs. DJing with a computer has a number of distinct advantages over using vinyl and CDs, including:

- No need to carry large numbers of records and/or CDs to gigs... no more losing crates of records on the plane, no more wear on old records, etc.
- Carry a much larger selection of tracks with you to choose from when DJing.
- Spin your own original tracks live without having to make a test acetate pressing or at least a CDR first.
- Create your own custom "DJ tools" or special effects specifically for live performance.
- Play unreleased tracks and remixes in MP3 or WAV format that you have received from other producers.
- Set all your tracks to the same volume, saving you time matching levels when you are mixing live.
- Use software tools such as automatic beat-matching and beat-synchronized effects to create a more dynamic and interactive live performance.

Of course, there are also some disadvantages to using a computer for DJing as well:

- If you are already an experienced vinyl or CD DJ, you will give up some level of control if you try DJing with only a computer; however, you can try using a software application that allows you to control the playback of digital audio files with a turntable interface, such as FinalScratch2 or Serato Scratch.
- Vinyl records sound a bit better than digital audio files (or CDs for that matter)... Actually, while this is hotly debated, I'm willing to give this one a slight bit of credence based on the evidence of my own ears, but this is a trade-off I'm willing to make in exchange for all the incredible things I can do live with the computer that I could never do with records.

For me, the advantages of using a computer for DJing far outweigh the disadvantages, and I have been doing live gigs as a computer DJ since 1999. When I first started, there really wasn't any good software available for DJing on a computer, but now there are a number of applications that are well suited for professional use. In this chapter, I will cover the best of the current crop of DJ software titles and describe their basic workings. I will also include some information about advanced DJ performance techniques with the computer as well as some conversation with active digital DJs.

In many respects these various software applications work in similar ways and provide similar functions to the user, as they are all simulations of the traditional two-turntables-and-a-mixer setup DJs have always used. However, there are differences in how well these functions are implemented in each program, and I will cover these below.

Most of these applications are available online as free downloadable demos from the Web sites of the companies that make them. I would highly suggest getting the demos and installing them so that you can actually go through the program and try the controls yourself as you read my descriptions below.

How to DJ: Understanding the Basics

Before moving on to discuss any of these particular applications in detail, however, let's just have a quick overview of the basics of DJing. Although some readers of this book may already be experienced DJs with vinyl records or CDs and simply want to find out how to do their thing on a computer, others may be just starting out DJing for the first time, so a bit of explanation is in order.

I can't explain everything about the art of DJing here; that would be another book (and there are many available already). Let's just make sure we're all on the same page about what it is that DJs actually *do*.

At the most basic level, a DJ is simply selecting and playing pieces of music one after another. Which pieces of music you play, the order in which you play them, and how you mix from one track to the next are the crucial factors in determining the success of a DJ.

In order to mix tracks together smoothly, a DJ needs to have at least two independent sound sources to mix between. DJs first used two vinyl turntables for mixing, later adopting special DJ-style CD players to mix CDs as well. All of the DJ-style software covered later in this chapter supports at least two independent audio file players; otherwise it would be useless for its intended purpose. If you are looking at some DJ software application that can only play one track at a time, you should look elsewhere; this kind of application is useful only for creating an automated computer "jukebox" or managing playlists at a radio station, not live club DJing.

Which pieces of music you play and what order you play them in is up to you. This is where your artistic sense really comes in. You will have to figure this out on your own—you can't learn it from a book. However, you can improve your mixing through practice, as well as by going out every chance you get to hear great DJs spin and listen to how they mix *their* tracks.

From One Track to the Next

OK, you've started your set and put on the first track. You made a good choice for your opening beat and the audience is starting to get into it. You look through your music library and find another track to play, but now you need to smoothly mix it in with the first one. What to do?

Cue it Up

First of all, you need to load the new track onto your second (unused) playback device and cue it up for playback. When we are talking about *cueing* in reference to DJing, we are referring to the use of headphones to hear what you are going to play before the audience does. This allows you to match the tempo and beat of the two tracks together, find which part of the new track you want to play or where you want to start it playing from, and so on.

Here are a number of different techniques DJs use for making seamless transitions between tracks.

A Quick Crossfade

The easiest way to mix from one track to the next is simply to quickly fade down the first track as you fade in the next. You can do this either by using the separate volume controls for each track or by using a DJ-style crossfader to mix from one track to the other one. Listen carefully and experiment to make as smooth a transition as possible.

This technique is simple and obvious, but even experienced DJs will make transitions this way sometimes. In some cases, if the two tracks you are transitioning between are very different in their tempo or rhythmic feel, for example, this may be the only way you can mix them together smoothly.

The Ambient Breakdown

Another technique you can use when mixing two quite different tracks together is to insert a brief ambient/beatless interlude between them. Some dance tracks will already have an ambient intro or outro as part of the track; in this case, you can mix the beat of the incoming track in while the outgoing track is still playing its beatless outro and ensure a smooth transition.

Another method of doing this is to actually use a third, purely ambient track to cover the transition. Let's say you have a track with a beat playing and you want to bring in another track with a quite different rhythm. One way to do this would be by first mixing in another ambient track, and then fading out the first track entirely. Then quickly load the next beat track you want to use and fade it in over the ambient background track. This technique is especially useful if you want to give the crowd a bit of a breather by extending the ambient breakdown a bit between the two rhythm tracks.

Beatmatching

Most DJs who play for dance audiences will *beatmatch* most of the tracks they play over the course of a set, seamlessly matching the rhythms together so the beat never stops as one track is faded out and the next is faded in. Beatmatching between two records with nothing but turntables and a mixer is not particularly easy, and traditionally the ability to beatmatch has been one of the skills that set real DJs apart from imitators. By beatmatching most of your transitions between tracks, you can keep the beat continuous without interruptions and keep the dance floor jumping.

With most turntables or DJ CD decks, you have to use manual pitch controls to speed your tracks up and down and exactly match the speed of the incoming track to the one that is already playing. You may also need to briefly touch the surface of the record or nudge the playback of your CD back and forth with the pitch bend controls in order to get the two tracks to line up correctly.

The better DJ software applications available today, such as Traktor DJ Studio and Virtual DJ, provide the user with some kind of automatic beatmatching capability to help match the tempos together. See more about this in the sections on specific applications later in this chapter. These automatic beat-detection and -matching functions may not work perfectly in every case, but they can at least help you when you are mixing and make the job of beatmatching easier.

If the DJ software you are currently using has no beatmatching capability at all, you are working with a disadvantage and you would be well advised to switch to another program with better functionality.

Beatmatching is a crucial technique to master if you really want to be a good DJ. You may not want to beatmatch all of your transitions all the time, but if you never beatmatch anything, you will be seriously handicapped as you try to keep the vibe of the party flowing. Let's look at a few of the basics.

In order to start practicing beatmatching with a computer, find two tracks to mix with that are roughly the same tempo and genre. This will make it easier for you to mix them together. The easiest styles to practice mixing at first are any of those genres based around a 4/4 bass drum beat, such as techno, house, and trance.

To practice beatmatching, you need to start one track playing and then try to match the tempo of the second track to it. For purposes of my explanation here, I will refer to these as "Track One" and "Track Two." If you were playing a real gig, Track One would be the one that the audience is already hearing through the PA, while Track Two would be the one that you are listening to on headphones and cueing up in preparation for bringing it into the main mix. (Your DJ software will have a function that allows you to select which track you can hear via the cue output, routed to your headphones.)

Cue Starting

The first technique you need to practice in order to beatmatch is "cue starting." This means starting a track's playback exactly on a beat, from a "cue point" you have selected or set in the track. With a vinyl record, you need to move the record back and forth by hand and listen in order to find a beat to cue from, but this is made easier with most computer DJ software, because you can actually see the waveform of the track on the screen. In most cases, you can pretty easily find the beats and start playback from wherever you want (see Figure 8.1).

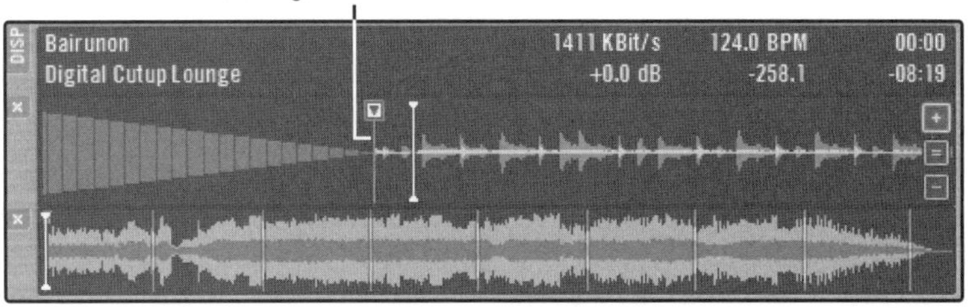

Figure 8.1 Finding the first beat of a techno track by looking at its waveform in Traktor DJ Studio.

Most good DJ applications also support the use of cue points in your tracks, which means that you can designate a number of different points from which you can begin playback and save these for future use.

Now, having found a cue point to start Track Two from, wait until an appropriate point in Track One and use the control in your software to begin playback. Basically, you want the downbeat of every bar in Track Two to coincide with the downbeats of Track One.

If your timing is good, you'll be able to start Track Two playing more or less in sync with Track One. However, if the tempos of the two tracks are not the same, they will soon start to drift out of phase with each other. This is something that every DJ tries to avoid the audience hearing, also known as a *train wreck* (not recommended).

There may be a short delay between the moment that you trigger the track to playback and the exact moment that it actually starts playing. This may be affected by a number of factors including the software you are using, the speed and power of your computer, the latency of your audio interface, and your audio buffer size setting. In any case, you can compensate for a slight delay once you get used to it, but the important thing is to get used to the feel of your own setup so you can control it precisely to get the results you want.

Note that when you are practicing at home, you can let the sound of both tracks play through your speakers or sound system simultaneously so you can hear what you are doing. However, once you get the hang of it a little bit, you should try practicing with only Track One coming through the speakers and Track Two only routed to your headphones while you are cueing and beatmatching it. This is how you will be mixing at your live gigs so you better get used to it!

Matching the Tempos

After *cue starting* Track Two so its first beat starts playing at the same time as a downbeat in Track One, you need to listen carefully in order to hear if the incoming track (Track Two) is rushing ahead or lagging behind the track that is already playing (Track One). This is not easy and may require considerable practice, to say the least!

Again, however, some DJ software applications provide us with visual cues as well to help us. In Atomix Productions' Virtual DJ software, for example, the waveforms of the two tracks are displayed in different colors (red and green) and superimposed over one another, so it is fairly easy to see whether they are in sync or whether one of the tracks is slowing down or speeding up in relation to the other.

Now, if the two tracks you are trying to sync are already running at exactly the same speed, and if you have cued Track Two to start in exactly the right place, your tracks will be playing back in perfect synchronization and you're ready to go!

However, chances are this will not be the case, and you will need to adjust the playback of Track Two in order to bring it into sync with Track One. There are several ways to do this, depending on what DJ software you are using.

Mixing with vinyl records, you can change the playback speed of a track by using the pitch control on the turntable, and you can adjust the exact playback point of a record by touching the vinyl lightly to adjust it.

You will typically have these same options available in your DJ software, but often your software will offer additional beatmatching tools as well.

For example, with Native Instruments' Traktor DJ Studio, you can adjust the playback speed of a track by pitching it up and down with the tempo fader, just as with a real turntable. However, you can also lock the pitch and adjust only the tempo while the pitch stays the same, which is impossible with a vinyl record. You can use Traktor's Pitch Bend buttons to make a track play faster or slower for a moment and nudge its playback position slightly ahead or behind in relation to another track, but Traktor also offers a Sync function that will attempt to match both the tempo and the playback position of your tracks automatically. Although this Sync function doesn't always work right and you shouldn't rely on it, this kind of feature can be quite useful in helping you get your tracks almost synced up, even if you still need to fine-tune the result a bit by hand.

Once you have the tracks synced, the result may look like this, with all of the beats (more or less) perfectly lined up together (see Figure 8.2).

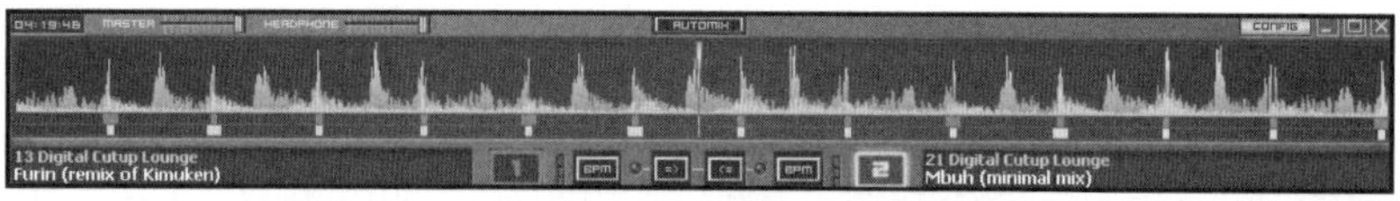

Figure 8.2 Two tracks synced in Virtual DJ.

If the two tracks are running at the same speed but are rhythmically out of phase, you will need to adjust the playback of Track Two using your software's controls in order to bring the two tracks into perfect sync.

Once you have the two tracks perfectly synced together, then you can use the controls on your DJ mixer (or the mixer controls in your software) to bring Track Two into the main mix so everyone can hear it. There are an infinite variety of ways to mix from one track to the next, depending on the tracks themselves and how they sound together, but here are a couple mixing techniques you might want to try.

Making a Smooth Transition

More often than not, you will probably want to make a smooth and gradual transition as you bring Track Two into the mix and then fade out Track One. Simply turn Track Two's gain up while turning down Track One and adjust accordingly, or use the crossfader on your mixer or in your software to mix from one to the other. Continue paying attention to the sync of the two tracks as well while you are doing this, in order to make sure that they are not drifting out of time with one another.

Dropping in a Beat

Another slightly trickier technique is to simply drop the new track into the mix abruptly. To do this, make sure the tracks are synced up and also check that Track Two is adjusted to nearly the same volume/gain level as Track One in your headphones. Then, simply bring the track into the mix suddenly by unmuting it or bringing the volume fader up very quickly to the same level as Track One. If the two tracks are well synced together, this can be a very dramatic and effective technique for bringing in a new track.

If you really want to make an abrupt change in the music, you can also try stopping playback of Track One at the same time as you bring in Track Two. You probably don't want to overuse this kind of abrupt mixing because it can kill the vibe of your set but, used sparingly, it makes an effective performance technique.

More DJ Mixing Tips

As you learn to mix and beatmatch with your favorite DJ software, here are a few more points about mixing that you should be aware of.

Watch Out for the Bass

One more point to be aware of when mixing tracks together is to watch out for the bass. Generally speaking, you don't want to mix heavy basslines or bass drum parts from two or more tracks together at the same time, because different bass parts usually sound very muddy when played together and this can make your music sound terrible. To avoid this, a good rule of thumb is that you should only have a strong bass part coming out from one track at a time. If Track One has a funky synth bassline, for example, you should roll off the low end EQ on Track Two when you bring it in, just in case it has another phat bassline that will conflict with the first one. You can do this with a DJ mixer or with the EQ or filter functions in most DJ software.

Playing a Whole Set

Although the techniques of DJing may take awhile for you to master, whether you are using records, CDs, or a computer to mix, you should always keep in mind that your ultimate goal is to be able to stop thinking about the mechanics and concentrate more on the overall musical statement you are making with your set.

The main factors that will give you your own personal style as a DJ and set you apart from others are the particular style of music you play, how you make the transitions between tracks, and how you construct your set as a whole.

Of course, you will need to decide what style of music to play yourself, and you will need to spend some time working on your mixing skills. When it comes to learning how to create an effective DJ set though, perhaps the best analogy is to tell a story.

Don't Start with the Climax

For example, when you tell a story you usually don't begin with the climax. So don't play your hardest/funkiest/hippest tracks right at the beginning; if you start out at too high of an energy level and you can't sustain it (or your audience gets tired), your performance will lose momentum in the middle and may become boring. Better to start out at a lower level and then build up to a climax later, or take an even longer view and construct a series of sub-climaxes that eventually lead to a peak towards the end.

Give the Audience a Break

Keep in mind that you do have to give the audience a break once in a while, especially if they're dancing. If you keep the energy level pumped up to maximum for too long, people will get tired and you'll start losing your crowd. Try playing some tracks interspersed throughout your set that are a bit more chilled out to create peaks and valleys in the energy level.

You can also use subtle variations in volume and tempo to shape the overall contour of your performance. Slow it down a bit and play just a bit quieter to cool things down a little, and then start bringing the tempo and volume back up later when you're ready to start building the music up towards a climax.

Record Your Sets

Many of the DJ software applications listed below offer some capability for recording your sets. One of the best ways to get better at pacing and putting together a set is to record your set and then listen to the results. Not only will you be able to hear any small mistakes in mixing you might have made while doing the recording, but when you listen back to the entire set, you'll get a much better sense of how all the tracks fit together as a whole.

Once you become good enough at mixing not to be embarrassed, start giving your mixtape efforts to friends as well and see what kind of feedback you get.

Traktor DJ Studio

Of the many DJ applications on the market today for Mac and Windows, one in particular has become the standard among the majority of today's digital DJs: Traktor DJ Studio by Native Instruments (see Figure 8.3).

I will cover Traktor's functions in detail in this chapter. In the process, I will also explain how to perform various basic DJ performance techniques on the computer. Even if you are not planning to use Traktor as your DJ application, I would recommend reading through this section and thinking about how to apply the techniques discussed to the application you are using.

Traktor provides computer DJs with an advanced performance interface suitable for pro use. It has all the controls you need to mix a seamless live DJ set, complete with effects, and combines functions including DJ mixing, live remixing, and demo mix production in one

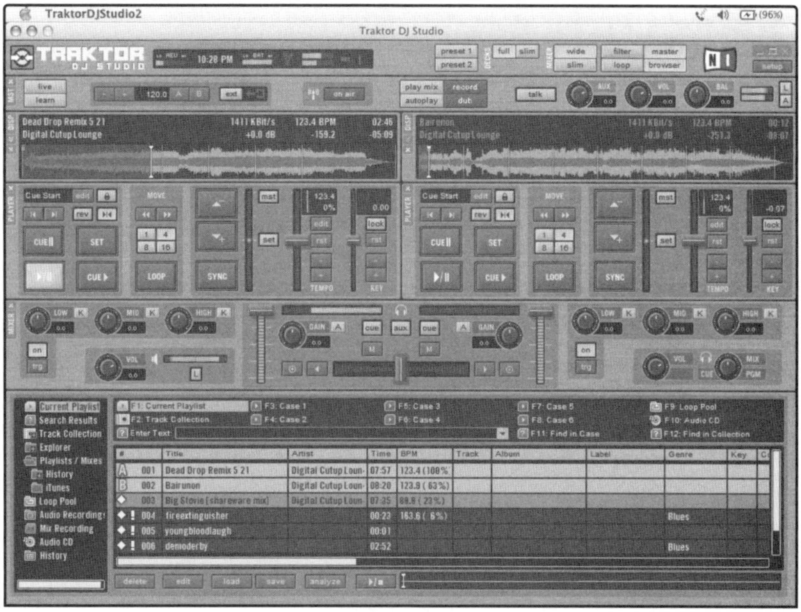

Figure 8.3 Traktor DJ Studio 2.6.

package. It offers two audio file players, a software DJ mixer including filters and EQ, automatic beat-matching technology, and the ability to set cue and loop points and save them. Traktor DJ Studio 2 can play back digital audio files in AIFF, WAV, MP3, AAC, WMA, Ogg Vorbis, and FLAC formats.

With interactive waveform displays and the ability to interface with any MIDI controller, Traktor DJ Studio is probably the most powerful integrated DJ software application currently available. You can control Traktor using the keys on your computer's keyboard or by using an external MIDI interface. You can even use a pair of digital timecode records played on real turntables to control the playback of tracks in Traktor if you use it together with Stanton's FinalScratch2 hardware interface (more on this in the section on FinalScratch later in this chapter).

There are a number of reasons why Traktor has become the standard among today's digital DJs: It has a powerful suite of features, it is stable and reliable, it will run on both Macs and PCs, and it has been constructed with the overall attention to detail and quality that we have come to expect from Native Instruments.

Let's look at how to set up Traktor and use it live. Note that all examples here refer to the current version of Traktor DJ Studio, version 2.6. (Note that Native Instruments also offers Traktor DJ, a less expensive entry-level version of the software.)

Setting Up Traktor's Preferences

Before using Traktor, you will need to configure its preferences. After launching the program, you can open the preferences by clicking the Setup button in the upper right-hand corner of the screen.

Audio Preferences

First, let's take a look at Traktor's audio preferences. It is important to set these correctly for best performance. Click Setup to open the preferences and then click the Audio button to open the audio preferences (see Figure 8.4).

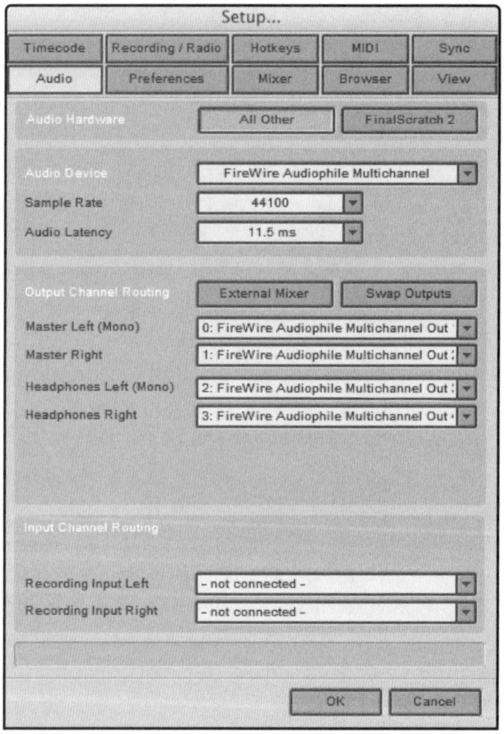

Figure 8.4 Traktor's Audio preferences.

First, the Audio Hardware section at top offers us the choice between setting up a Stanton FinalScratch hardware interface (specifically designed to work with Traktor) or any other type of interface. I will cover FinalScratch more below, so let's look at how to set up a third-party interface here.

After choosing All Other in this first section, the second section is labeled Audio Device. This is where you can choose your particular audio interface, which should appear in the drop-down menu here. If you don't have an audio interface, your computer's built-in audio output should also appear as an option, but this will generally not give very good performance (particularly on a PC).

Below this, you can select the latency time. You should set this as low as you can for best performance. However, if you are hearing glitches or artifacts in your audio when you are mixing, it may help to come back here and increase the latency slightly. Basically you want to adjust the latency as low as you can without causing audio problems. If you are unable to achieve an acceptably low latency time with your system, you probably need to get a better sound card or a faster computer!

For serious DJing, it is essential to use a multi-channel audio interface that can provide at least two pairs of stereo outputs, one pair for the main output and one for headphone cueing. If you have a multi-channel interface like this, you can assign the output pairs in the next section of audio preferences, labeled Output Channel Routing (see Figure 8.5). In this image, I have assigned the multiple audio outputs of my M-Audio FireWire Audiophile to the Master and Headphone output channels in Traktor.

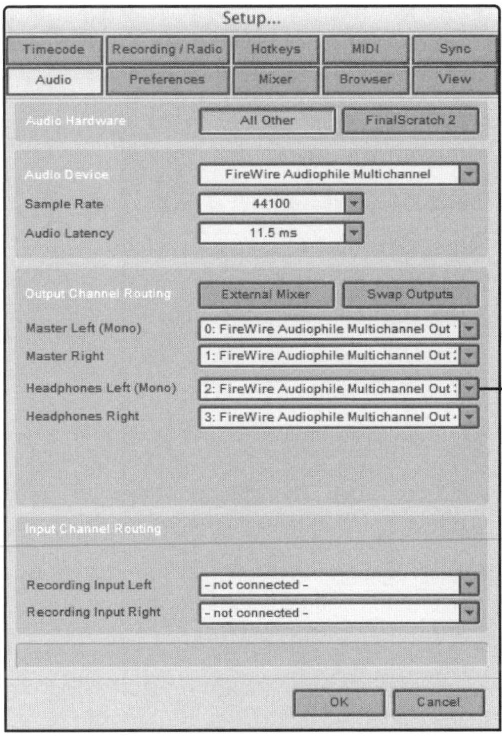

Figure 8.5 Assigning multiple audio outputs in Traktor.

You can still use Traktor with a stereo interface or even with your computer's built-in sound card if you don't have a separate audio interface, but you won't be able to do proper DJ cueing unless your interface has at least two stereo outputs.

The MIDI Preferences

After setting up Traktor's Audio preferences, click the MIDI button at the top to configure your MIDI options (see Figure 8.6).

All available MIDI devices connected to your computer will show up in the Interfaces section in the middle of this window, and you can make each of them active or inactive by double-clicking here.

Having made at least one MIDI controller active, you can make specific MIDI controller assignments by using the list of control parameters provided in the upper part of this window. Select All Controllers in the drop-down menu at the top to see all the parameters available to be controlled via MIDI in Traktor, or choose a specific subset of controllers to work with.

In order to assign a controller, first put Traktor into MIDI learning mode by engaging the Learn button in the middle of this screen. If you touch a control on your MIDI controller while this button is pushed in, you will see a CCxx message here showing the MIDI controller number

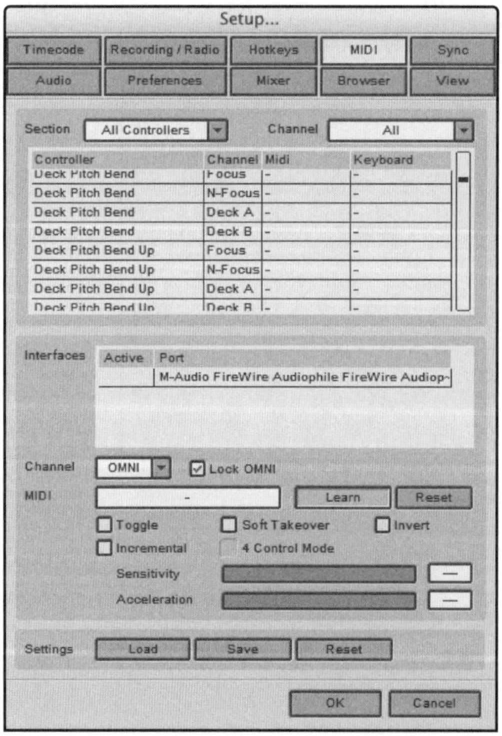

Figure 8.6 Traktor's MIDI preferences.

Traktor has detected from your interface. To make an assignment, simply click the parameter you want to control in the top part of this window, then touch the physical control on your interface you want to assign. In Figure 8.7, I have assigned the crossfader on my X-Session controller (which is registered as MIDI CC16 here) to control the crossfader in Traktor.

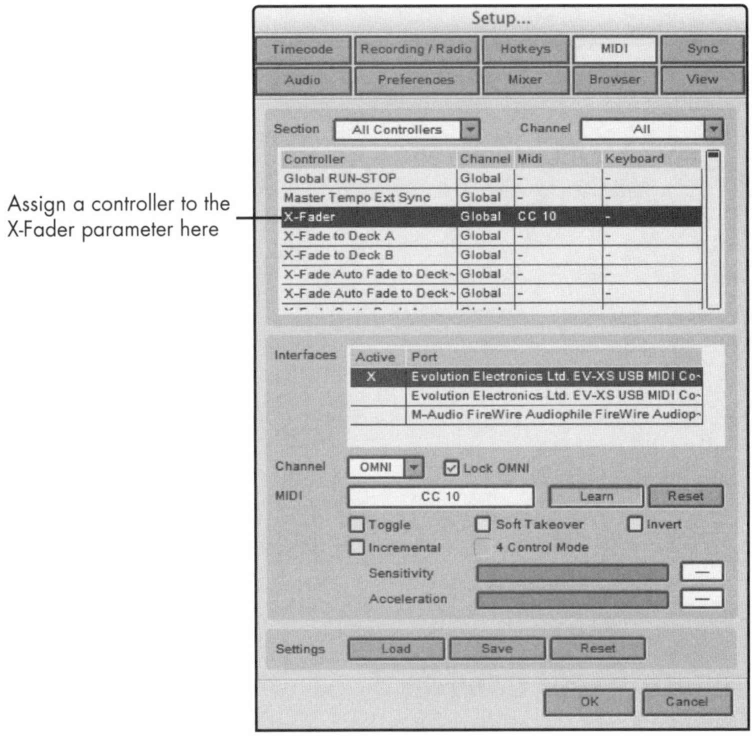

Figure 8.7 Assigning a MIDI controller to Traktor's crossfader.

Simply repeat this process to assign each control on your interface to control a parameter in Traktor.

As you can see, there is a long list of available parameters you can control in Traktor, and thus a wide range of customizable performance setups are possible.

The Hotkey Preferences

Similar to Traktor's MIDI preferences, you can also use the hotkey preferences in the program to assign keys from your computer keyboard to control any of Traktor's various functions (see Figure 8.8).

Just as with the MIDI preferences, simply click the Learn button below to engage the Hotkey learning function in Traktor, then select the parameter you want to assign, then click the key on the keyboard you want to assign to the parameter to set the Hotkey command.

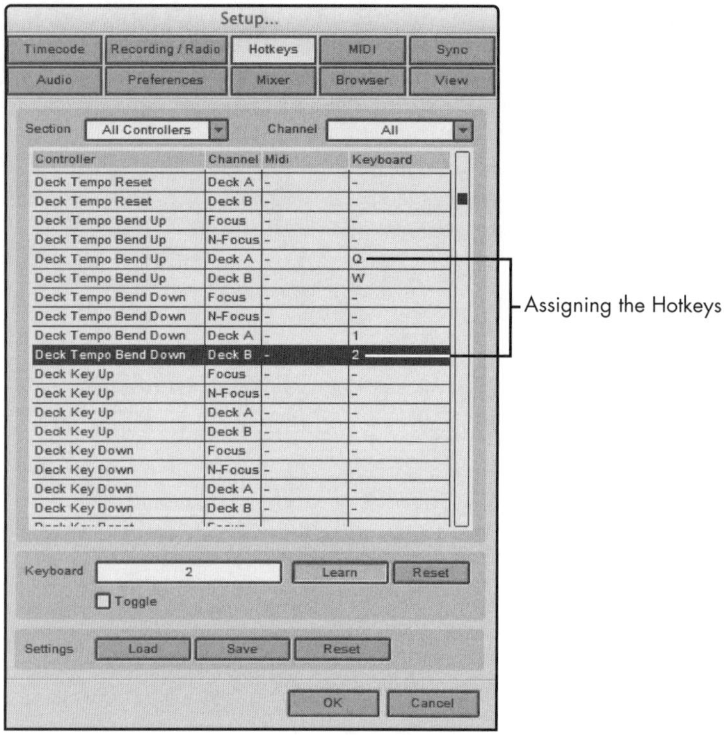

Figure 8.8 Assigning Traktor's Hotkeys.

The Traktor Interface and Controls

Now let's have a look at how Traktor's user interface is laid out and how to use it in performance. It is worth noting that most of the popular computer DJ applications have fairly similar interfaces, as they are all based on a traditional DJ setup.

Traktor's interface features a series of separate windows, most of which can be shown or hidden individually. Let's look at each of these briefly in turn and see what they do. I will not cover every feature of the interface in detail here, but I do want to call your attention to the most important on-screen controls.

The Head Panel

The Head Panel, marked with the Traktor DJ Studio 2 logo at left, provides a variety of basic information about your system and about Traktor's configuration (see Figure 8.9).

Figure 8.9 The Head Panel.

To the right of the Traktor logo, we can see the System Status Info display (see Figure 8.10), and there are several important points to be aware of here.

Figure 8.10 The System Status Info display.

First from left, there is a small LED-style meter labeled AEU. This stands for "Audio Engine Utilization." This meter shows the current level of CPU power on your computer being used by the Traktor DJ Studio 2 audio engine, expressed as a percentage. You should watch this AEU meter in performance and try to keep it below 70-80%. At you get closer to 100%, audio dropouts may start to occur.

The most common factor causing high CPU usage in Traktor is using the Key Lock feature to change the pitch of a track independently of its speed (and vice versa). If you are experiencing audio dropouts from high CPU usage, try mixing without using the Key Lock function.

Using backspins, scratches, and other effects within Traktor also requires additional CPU power that might cause spikes in the AEU meter.

There are also readouts showing the current time and your computer's battery level to the right of the AEU meter, which can come in really handy during a gig!

Further to the right, you can show and hide the Filter, Master, Loop, and File Browser panels of Traktor's interface panels in the Traktor display by using the Panel Buttons (see Figure 8.11).

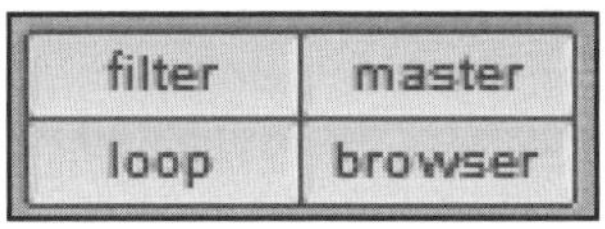

Figure 8.11 The Panel buttons.

The Setup button at the right side of the Head Panel opens Traktor's preferences.

Master Panel

Beneath the Head Panel is Traktor's Master Panel, which has a variety of controls relating to the overall functioning of the application (see Figure 8.12).

Figure 8.12 The Master Panel.

There are a few items here you should be aware of in particular.

The Live Button and the Learn Button

If you click the Live button so it is engaged, this locks certain critical features of TRAKTOR DJ Studio 2 from being changed accidentally. This is intended to be used when you are playing live, so you don't accidentally do something regrettable like close the application suddenly in the middle of your set or delete songs from playlists that you may want to play later.

Clicking the Learn button (see Figure 8.13) will open Traktor's MIDI preference panel so you can make or change MIDI controller assignments quickly and easily.

Figure 8.13 The Live button and the Learn button.

Master Tempo and External Sync

Next, you should at least be aware of these two tempo-related controls (see Figure 8.14).

Figure 8.14 The master tempo and external sync controls.

You can use the Master Clock here to control the master tempo that both of Traktor's Playback Decks will sync to. (Bear in mind that this is only one of the ways Traktor can sync tracks together, however.) Use the Ext button to toggle the output of MIDI Clock or OSC sync data to external computers or other devices. You can also use this button to send clock on and off messages to trigger any sync slaves that may be connected to your machine. These functions can be very important when you are attempting to sync two copies of Traktor together, for example. (Check the Traktor manual for more on how to do this.)

Main Volume Controls

The two knobs to the furthest right side of the Master Panel are Traktor's main volume controls: A master volume knob and a master balance knob (see Figure 8.15). (The knob to the left, marked Aux, is used to control the level of an external mic if you have one connected.)

Figure 8.15 The Main Volume Controls.

To the right of these there are two buttons labeled "L" and "A." The first of these activates a limiter on your main output, preventing audio distortion. The second button activates Traktor's Autogain feature, which will match the gain of each track you play with the track already playing, making it much easier for you to mix between them if you are using an external hardware mixer.

Filter Panel

The controls in Traktor's Filter Panel (see Figure 8.16) are simple and straightforward to use if you have ever used any type of hardware or software filter before.

Figure 8.16 The Filter Panel.

There are two sets of filter controls here: Independent filters for the left-hand and right-hand Playback Decks.

Use the Amount Knob on the left to adjust how much effect the filter has on the sound (from 0-100%). You can shape the curve of the filter with the rest of the knobs and buttons in this panel, including a low-cut knob, a filter width knob, a resonance knob, and two buttons which enable you to toggle between band-pass and notch-style filters.

The Filter Curve Display just above the knobs provides a graphic representation of the changes you are making.

Try assigning some of these controls to knobs on your external MIDI control and you will be able to make drastic changes to the sound of your tracks when you play live, enabling you to create smoother mixes or a more dynamic performance. Computer DJ RD White is constantly manipulating the filters when he plays live gigs with Traktor. (More on RD's live DJ setup later in this chapter.)

Loop Panel

The Loop Panel provides you with a number of controls that enable on-the-fly looping when you are performing (see Figure 8.17).

Figure 8.17 The Loop Panel.

You can easily select a section of a track to loop and keep it repeating as long as you want at any point during your performance by using these controls.

Use the Set/In button to set the beginning of a loop; click it a second time to exit the loop (see Figure 8.17). The loop created will be the length you have specified using the other buttons in this panel. If you have not specified a loop length, this button will only set a start point.

The Active/Out button sets the loop end after setting a starting point with the Set/In button.

The small left- and right-arrow buttons to the right of these buttons are used to move and/or resize the loop points. There is also a display that shows the increment that will be used. You can change this display by clicking it.

Below these buttons are the Loop Length buttons. You can use these to quickly set loops of four specified sizes. In the image above, they are set to Traktor's default sizes: One, four, eight, and sixteen bars. However, you can also change these values from a drop-down menu, accessed by control-clicking or right-clicking on the button you want to change.

The remaining controls in this section enable you to store your favorite loops for each track and have them available the next time you open the track in Traktor. Consult the Traktor manual for more on how this works.

Playback Decks

Below the Loop Panel are Traktor's actual Playback Decks, two of them (see Figure 8.18).

Figure 8.18 The Playback Decks.

As you can see, each of these has a waveform display on top of a panel of controls. These are used to control the playback of your tracks. The controls here are the most important in Traktor (they make your tracks play, otherwise you will hear nothing!) so I will cover them in detail here.

To load a track for playback in Traktor, simply drag it from the File Browser window below and drop it on one of these waveform displays. You will then see the artist name, song title, and elapsed and remaining time displayed on top of the actual waveform of the track as it plays back. There are also a number of customizable fields here that you can set to show additional information about each track such as its compression rate, tempo, beat counter, and so on. You can choose these options in the View tab of Traktor's preferences.

Once you have dragged a track onto the display and you can see its information in the display, simply click the Play/Pause button to begin playback.

As the track begins to play, you will see its waveform begin to scroll past in the display above. The current playback position is represented by a vertical line.

If you click and drag on the waveform display, you can drag the playback position back and forth just like a record on a turntable. This opens up some interesting possibilities depending on what kind of hardware interface you are using. For example, I saw Richard Devine play in February 2005 running Traktor on an Open Labs' "Neko" keyboard. The Neko has a built-in computer and touchscreen, and Richard was able to control the playback of his tracks and scrub them back and forth simply by touching the screen with his fingertips.

This would have been a neat trick if he hadn't set the keyboard on fire shortly afterwards, closing down the 2005 NAMM afterparty hosted by Native Instruments at the Blu Monkey bar in Hollywood. Do NOT try this at home, digital DJs (see Figure 8.19).

Figure 8.19 Richard Devine sets his Open Labs "Neko" keyboard on fire and attacks it with a bat.

More info on what not to do with an expensive piece of computer hardware can be found online at http://www.openlabs.com/press/newsflash-neko_fire.html.

The lower section of the waveform display area shows a larger-scale overview waveform, showing you how much of the track has played so far.

The Main Playback Controls

Traktor's main playback controls are found below the waveform display (see Figure 8.20).

Figure 8.20 The main playback controls.

As noted above, the Play/Pause button starts or stops playback at the current position. You can also use this button in conjunction with the Sync button to make a track start in sync with another track that is already playing.

Many of the other playback controls in this section of the interface are connected with setting and using cue points in your tracks. A cue point is a position in the track that you have preset so that you can quickly jump to it during a performance to begin playback.

For example, clicking the Cue/Pause button will cause playback to jump to the current cue point and stop.

Clicking this button again will start playback, which will continue until you release the button. Then the track will jump back to the cue point again.

Clicking the Cue/Play button, on the other hand, will cause playback to jump to the current cue point; playback then starts when you release the button.

Clicking the Set Button will set a cue point at the current song position.

Note however that this cue point will not actually be saved permanently unless you use the small Lock button (the one with a small padlock icon) found above the main playback controls.

Clicking one of the Cue Select buttons will jump to the previous or next stored cue point.

Clicking the Cue Lock button will lock or unlock the currently selected cue point.

The Reverse Playing button is one of my favorite functions in Traktor: This will reverse the playback direction of the track, great for special effects while DJing!

More Loop Controls

To the right of the main playback controls there is a reduced section of loop commands, similar in function to the controls in the Loop Panel, but quicker to access (see Figure 8.21).

Figure 8.21 Loop controls on the Playback Deck.

You can use the Loop button here to start a track playing in loop; the length of the loop in bars will be set by the Loop Length buttons above the Loop button. Use the Move arrows to move the loop back and forth through your track while keeping its length unchanged.

The Pitch and Tempo Controls

The pitch and tempo controls in Traktor allow you to change the playback speed as well as the pitch of a track while it is playing back, either at the same time or independently of one another. These controls are most important for getting your tracks to play in sync with each other, so you really need to work with them and get to know how to use them correctly (see Figure 8.22).

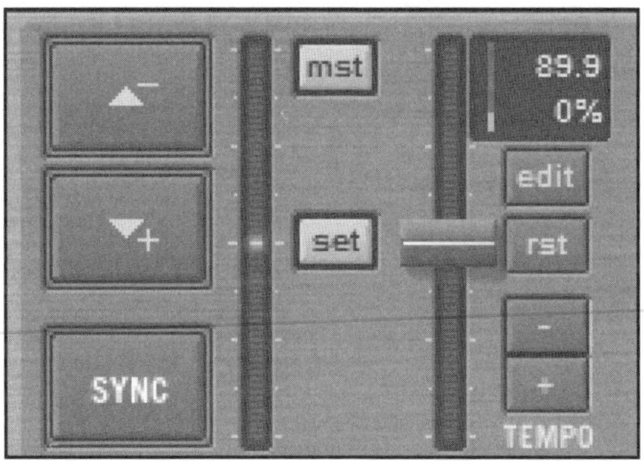

Figure 8.22 The pitch and tempo controls.

The pitch bend buttons will momentarily (while you hold them down) bend the playback speed of the track up or down, enabling you to quickly nudge the track ahead or behind in order to sync it together with another track.

After you release the pitch bend button, the pitch will return to what it was at before; the pitch bend buttons do not permanently change the playback speed. Thus, the effect of using these buttons is just like that of slowing down or speeding up a record slightly by lightly touching it while it spins on a turntable. In order to become a good DJ using Traktor, you will need to spend some time working with these pitch bend controls and get a good feel for how they work and how sensitive they are.

When you press the Sync button, Traktor synchronizes the speed and rhythm of the track playing in the opposite deck as best it can. Of course, this process works better with some tracks than others, and you shouldn't entirely rely on this function for mixing because Traktor can sometimes make mistakes. This depends largely on the style of music you are playing. Traktor can do quite well matching beats and syncing tracks with a strong 4/4 dance beat, such as most house, trance, and techno. If you are playing more rhythmically complex styles such as drum'n'bass, breakbeat, electro, or IDM, you will probably have to do a lot of the tempo-matching and beatsyncing yourself by ear, using Traktor's other controls to adjust the playback of each track by hand.

By pressing the Control key while you click the Sync button, Traktor will adjust only the rhythm of the track to fit the track on the other deck, without changing the playback speed of either track. This can help you to get two tracks exactly in sync once you have already got them playing at the same speed and you don't want Traktor to change the speed any more.

If you press the Sync button on a deck without a track playing, this will cause playback to start in sync with the track on the opposite deck.

The tempo fader gives you direct control over the playback speed of the track. The possible range of this fader can be adjusted in Traktor's preferences. The display here shows the current tempo of the track, as well as the percentage of tempo change you are currently applying to it with the tempo fader.

Clicking the tempo plus and minus buttons gives you finer control over the tempo. To make even finer adjustments, hold down the Shift key on the keyboard when you click these controls.

The Reset button resets the track to its original tempo and brings the tempo fader back to its center point.

Clicking the Edit button under the tempo display opens the Tempo Edit Dialog window (see Figure 8.23).

Use these controls to set the tempo of a track for future use. Check the Traktor manual for more on this.

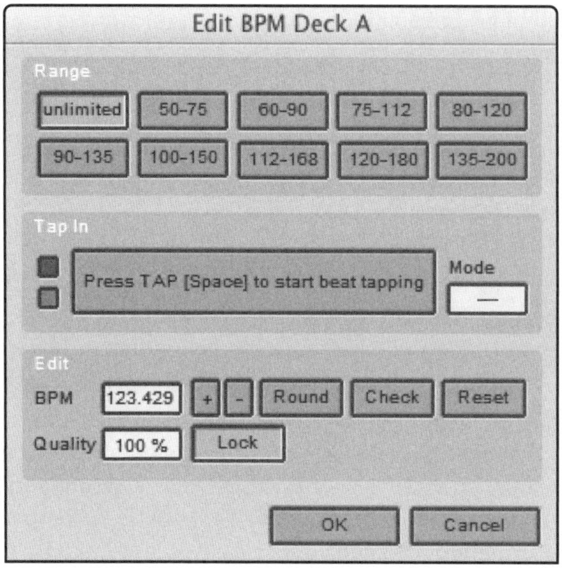

Figure 8.23 The Tempo Edit Dialog window.

The Key Section

The Key section (see Figure 8.24) allows you to make various adjustments to the pitch or key of your tracks as they play. Using these controls properly is particularly important if you are planning to play together with live musicians, for example, and you need to make sure that your music is in tune with the other players.

Figure 8.24 The Key section.

The most important control to be familiar with here is the Key Lock button, labeled "lock" on the screen. This button determines whether or not the pitch of a track will change when you adjust its playback speed. When you press "lock," Traktor will lock the pitch of the track at its current level. If you then go back and use the tempo fader or button controls to adjust the playback speed of the track, you will notice that the pitch does not change. Conversely, if this lock button is not engaged, the pitch and tempo controls will move together in tandem as you change either of them (go ahead and try it!).

It is important to note that using the Key Lock mode in Traktor will place a heavier load on your computer's CPU, which in some cases can cause audio dropouts, digital distortion, or other problems. If you are using this feature, keep an eye on the AEU meter in the Head Panel to make sure you're not overloading your CPU. Some computers may not be fast enough to support this feature even though everything else in Traktor seems to be working fine.

If you are DJing by yourself or with a partner, you will probably find that you get the best results by letting Traktor pitch the tracks up and down in order to change the speed; you will usually maintain the best sound quality this way. However, as mentioned below, if you are playing with live musicians, you need to use the Key Lock mode to keep the pitch steady so your tracks will be in tune with the instruments.

The Key Fader allows you to increase or decrease the pitch of your track plus or minus 12 semitones (half-steps). You can also use the plus and minus buttons here to change the pitch in increments of one semitone, or by one cent (1/100th of a semitone) if you hold down the Control key on the keyboard when clicking.

The Key Reset button (marked "rst") resets the pitch of the track to its original pitch.

Vinyl Panel

The Vinyl Panel is only visible when you switch from Software Control to FinalScratch2 Mode in the Audio tab of Traktor's Setup Dialog and then press the Vinyl button in the Head Panel. The Vinyl Panel will then open just below the Playback Decks (see Figure 8.25).

Figure 8.25 The Vinyl Panel.

By using the controls in this section in conjunction with Stanton's FinalScratch2 audio interface, it is possible to control Traktor DJ Studio via turntables with a special set of records. (These records have a type of digital timecode on them instead of music.) I will explain more about how to do this in the section on FinalScratch2 below.

The Mixer Panel

The Mixer Panel (see Figure 8.26) provides you with all the controls of a standard DJ mixer, and you can assign these to controls on an external MIDI controller as well to make DJing with Traktor more like DJing with a traditional setup.

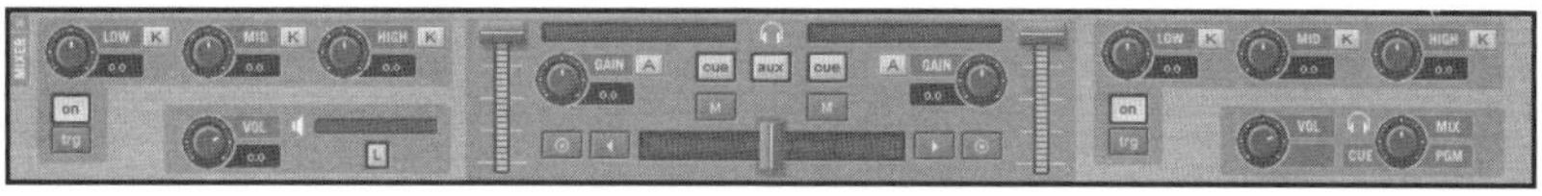

Figure 8.26 The Mixer Panel.

Note that you can use the wide and slim buttons in the Head Panel to toggle between two modes of viewing the mixer; the above image was taken in the wide mode, the one I usually prefer. Also, if you have selected the External Mixer Mode in Traktor's preferences, the Mixer Panel will be unavailable and the "mixer" button in the Head Panel will appear greyed-out.

The Channel Faders control the output volume of the decks. You can adjust the maximum output level of the fader with the Channel Gain knob. Clicking the small A next to the Channel Gain knob will cause Traktor's Autogain function to be activated, automatically adjusting the maximum gain appropriately.

The Crossfader

The crossfader is used to mix back and forth from one deck to the other, just like on a DJ mixer (see Figure 8.27).

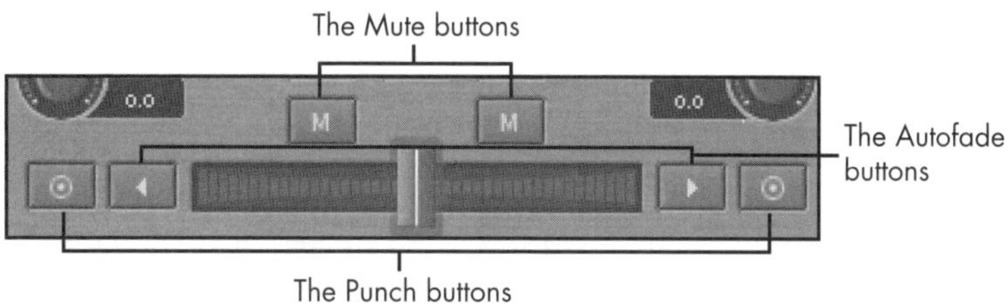

Figure 8.27 The crossfader.

This control will be most useful to you if you assign it to be controlled by a MIDI hardware controller, especially a DJ-style controller with a built-in crossfader like the Hercules DJ Console or the Evolution X-Session.

Clicking either of the Autofade buttons will trigger a smooth automated crossfade to that channel. (Note that the length of this automatic crossfade can be set under the Mixer Tab of the Setup Dialog.)

The Punch buttons are used to suddenly drop a new track in the mix with no warning (try it). In this case, you will only hear the track while you are actually holding down the button; the sound will be cut off when you release the button.

Clicking one of the Mute buttons will mute the respective track while you hold the button down. The sound will come back immediately when you release the button.

Headphone Cueing in Traktor

The Headphone Cue buttons in the center of the Mixer Panel allow you to select which deck, A or B, should be heard in the headphones (see Figure 8.28).

Figure 8.28 The Headphone Cue buttons.

Clicking the left or right Cue button will allow you to hear the sound from Deck A or B respectively, while clicking the Aux button will allow you to monitor the auxiliary input.

There are also a couple knobs in the lower right corner of the Mixer Panel that are used for headphone cueing (see Figure 8.29).

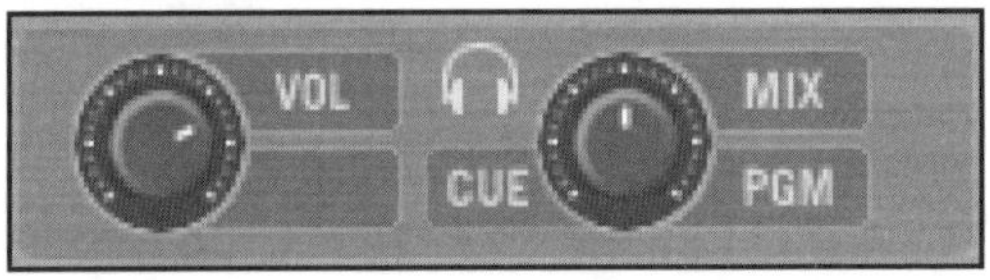

Figure 8.29 The Headphone level controls.

The Volume Knob here controls the volume of your headphones. The Mix Knob is used to adjust the balance between the CUE signal and the main output signal (PGM).

The File Browser Window

At the bottom of Traktor's main screen is the File Browser window (see Figure 8.30). This is where you can access all of the music files stored on your computer. You can show or hide the File Browser window by clicking the browser button at the top right of the Traktor interface.

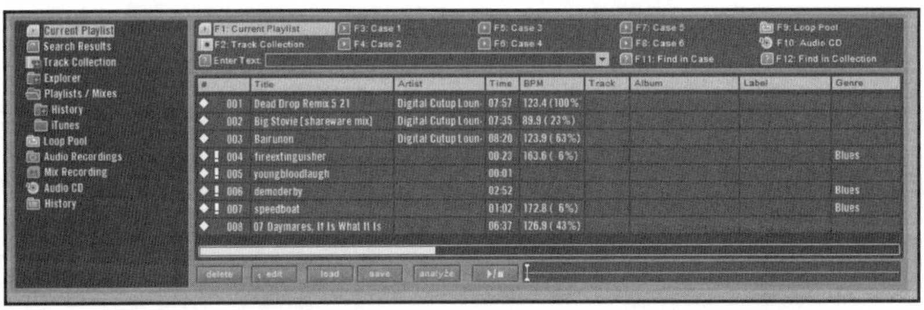

Figure 8.30 The File Browser window.

As described above, in order to play one of your tracks, you simply click on it in the File Browser and drag it onto one of the Playback Decks.

Traktor provides you with a variety of tools for organizing and analyzing your tracks. You can also save information about your tracks in a database for future use, so that, for example, your BPM settings and cue points aren't lost between performances.

I'm not going to explain in detail about Traktor's file management features, as they are fairly complex and are not directly related to performance. There are functions for sorting files into folders, searching for specific files, building playlists, and so on. Consult the Traktor manual for more on how these functions work.

I do want to add here that the way you organize your music files on your computer can have a great impact on your live playing style. You won't be able to play a track at a performance if you can't find it in your database while you are playing, and organizing your tracks according to some kind of scheme that works for you is one of the most important things to think about when you are getting ready for a gig. I can remember so many times during a show when I thought of the perfect thing to play next and then spent valuable minutes digging around fruitlessly in my files trying to find it... and then by the time I *did* find it, the perfect moment had passed.

Analyzing your Tracks

Before I move on, however, I do want to point Traktor's facility for analyzing the structure and waveform of your tracks. To analyze a new track, control-click the name of the track in the File Browser and choose Analyze from the small pop-up window that will appear (see Figure 8.31).

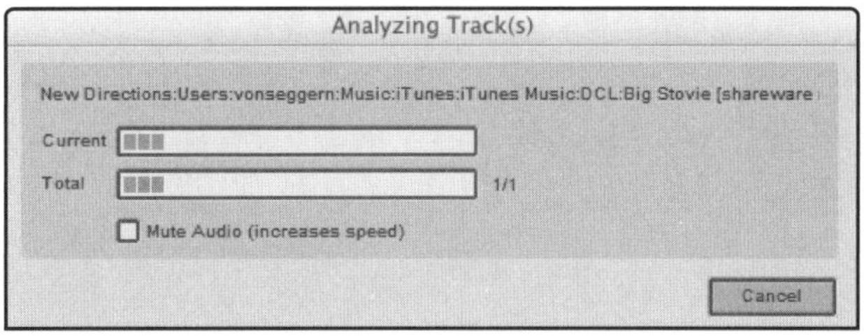

Figure 8.31 Analyzing a track in the File Browser window.

This will analyze the properties of the track and save them automatically in Traktor's database. This can take some time depending on the speed of your computer.

You can also analyze a group of tracks by selecting all of them together in the File Browser and then control-clicking and choosing Analyze.

After the track in question has been analyzed by Traktor, you will see its waveform as well as Traktor's estimated BPM for the track in the Playback Deck window when you drop the track there. Analyzing the tracks also helps Traktor in maintaining optimal audio quality as you change the track's playback properties.

Now that we've covered most of the important controls that you'll need to use to play a DJ set in Traktor, let's have a look at how one innovative electro DJ is using Traktor for his live sets.

Example: RD

RD White (better known simply as "RD" in the music scene) is one of the most influential figures in the Los Angeles electronic underground, both as a DJ and promoter. His experimental electro collective ELM Conceptions, started in 1997, have long been innovators in presenting some of the most cutting-edge electronic music on the planet on the West Coast, having hosted artists such as Phoenecia, Jega, Otto von Schirach, Crunch, and many others.

On any given weekend, RD can usually be found spinning his distinctive blend of precise, dark electro and IDM at an event somewhere in California or abroad, looping and mixing digital audio files in Traktor on his battered G4 PowerBook (see Figure 8.32).

Figure 8.32 RD.

RD got started in music playing guitar in various punk rock bands while he was in high school. He began DJing (with vinyl and turntables) as soon as he got to college, spinning a mix of dark trance and breakbeat records he had collected. Later, a friend introduced him to some of the more experimental strands of European electronic music and his tastes began to diverge more and more from the mainstream "electronica" that all the music magazines were talking about.

After DJing for a few years and mastering the art of mixing on the wheels of steel, RD started programming his first tracks using an Akai MPC1000 sampler/sequencer and a variety of other outboard gear. He made a number of tracks this way, sequencing everything on the MPC. (Some of his early tracks from this period have recently been released on Andrea Parker's Touchin' Bass label.) Then, after his collective hosted Florida IDM artists Phoenecia at a performance in Los Angeles, he saw them using Logic to create and perform their music and knew that he needed to get a computer himself for increased control over the sounds he was creating.

In 2002 RD bought his first PowerBook, one of the first G4 Titanium models, and began producing his own tracks on the computer in Logic. As he first learned how to use the computer to produce, he spent a lot of time online talking to other computer musicians, asking a lot of questions and learning everything he could about software-based music production.

He also began using early versions of Ableton Live and Traktor to perform live, as this enabled him to play his own unreleased music live instead of being limited to playing records by other artists. At first he experimented with mixing together loops from his own tracks in Ableton Live, effectively doing live remixes of his own material. Later, however, he found that he preferred to use a more DJ-style approach for playing live, using Traktor to play mixes of his own tracks together with those of other artists.

For RD, an experienced DJ, the most important thing during a performance is to stay in touch with the mood of the crowd and the ebb and flow of energy over the course of a set. He finds it easier to do this when he is mixing a selection of complete tracks together DJ-style rather than breaking his tracks down into their component parts. Pacing is everything.

Although now he uses his Traktor and his PowerBook for all of his live gigs and is more comfortable playing the computer than a pair of turntables, at first it was a bit difficult for him to switch to using digital audio files on a computer instead of vinyl records. On his earliest gigs with the computer, he simply plugged the laptop into one channel of a DJ mixer and mixed back and forth between the computer and records. Later he began using Traktor exclusively, but ran the channels from his sound card into an external DJ mixer in performance.

More recently, since getting his Evolution X-Session MIDI controller in 2003, he has switched to using an entirely computer-based DJ rig and has dispensed with the hardware DJ mixer entirely. In his current setup (described further below), he has assigned controls on his X-Session and his computer keyboard to most of the on-screen controls in Traktor that he needs to use in performance.

RD has now sold his turntables and is rarely seen mixing with vinyl anymore, although he still has a sizable record collection. The laptop can do whatever he wants as a DJ, so he doesn't miss spinning vinyl, and the computer also allows him to do some things that he couldn't do with records at all, such as looping and filtering.

RD's Hardware Rig

Currently RD is DJing with his 400MHz G4 PowerBook, one of the first of Apple's Titanium PowerBook models. This computer has been through a lot, including more than one trip to perform at Burning Man and numerous desert and warehouse parties, not to mention having had a lava lamp dropped on it at one point, but it is still going strong and RD rarely has a problem with it on gigs.

For an audio card, RD uses an Echo Indigo DJ PCMCIA card, which gives him two ⅛" mini-jack audio outputs he can use for the main out and for headphone cueing. As mentioned above, he uses an Evolution X-Session MIDI controller; more on how RD sets up his X-Session below.

RD's MIDI/Software Setup

RD DJs exclusively with the latest version of Traktor DJ Studio as he finds it can do pretty much anything he wants. In particular, he really likes the way Traktor handles looping, and he uses this function extensively when he performs.

The Evolution X-Session has a MIDI crossfader, two rows of eight knobs each, and ten assignable MIDI button triggers. Here's how RD has the controls mapped to Traktor.

First of all, he has the X-Session's crossfader mapped to the crossfader in Traktor. This allows him to cut and mix rapidly between two tracks playing in Traktor just like he used to do with a real DJ mixer.

The top row of knobs on the X-Session are assigned to control the parameters of the filters in Traktor. From left to right, knobs one through four in the top row are assigned to control the amount, low cut, width, and resonance controls of the filter on Deck A. Knobs five through eight are assigned to the same controls for Deck B's filter.

Moving on to the bottom row of knobs on the X-Session, RD has assigned the first three knobs here to control the low, mid, and high EQ for Deck A, while the fourth knob controls Deck A's gain. The fifth knob controls the gain for Deck B, and knobs six through eight control the low, mid, and high EQ for Deck B.

Note that he has placed the two gain controls in the center together; he wants to have these two next to each other so that he can most easily adjust the relative volumes of the two tracks without grabbing for the wrong controls.

RD only uses two of the buttons on his X-Session, to toggle the headphone cue for each track on and off: Button seven toggles Deck A and button nine toggles Deck B.

Note that most of these assignments are quite similar to the controls you would have on a real DJ mixer: EQ and gain knobs and headphone cue switches. (Most DJ mixers don't have a built-in filter, though; this is one advantage of Traktor.)

RD has also mapped Traktor's on-screen pitch bend controls to be triggered by keys on his PowerBook's keyboard, as these are the controls he most frequently needs to access when he is DJing, to nudge the tempo of the tracks together.

He has assigned the letter "Q" on the keyboard to pitch bend up for Deck A, and the number "1" to is pitch bend down for the same deck. Likewise, next to these, he has assigned the letter "W" to pitch bend up for Deck B, and the number "2" for Deck B's pitch bend down control. Figure 8.33 shows how this looks in Traktor's preferences.

He also uses the keyboard for one other function: Making fine adjustments in the tempo of his tracks when he is matching them together. He normally adjusts the tempo by clicking on the plus and minus tempo buttons in Traktor's on-screen interface. However, for finer adjustments, he holds down the Shift key on the keyboard while clicking the tempo; this causes Traktor's controls to move in much smaller increments when adjusted.

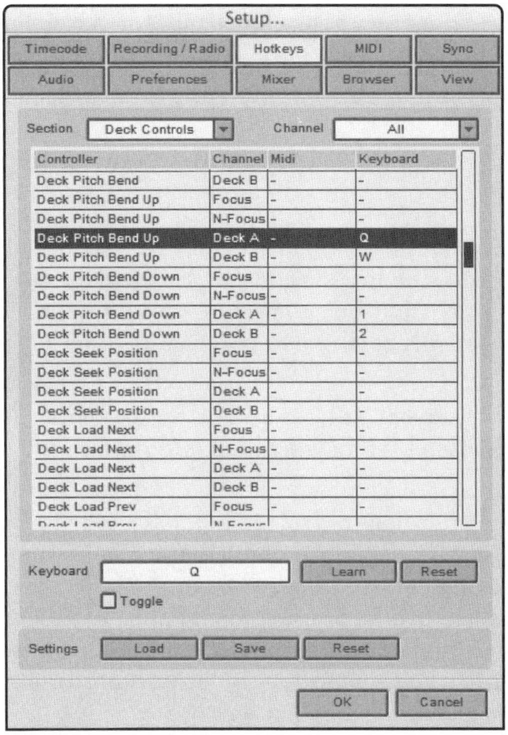

Figure 8.33 Setting the keyboard controls like RD.

Traktor vs. Vinyl

Although some of today's computer DJs (such as myself) have never touched a piece of vinyl or tried to mix with turntables, I have seen RD play vinyl once before and he's quite good at it. So why does he prefer to use Traktor?

There are a few main reasons why RD has gone all-digital in his DJ setup.

One of the most important factors is that much of the music he plays doesn't exist in physical form. Many of the tracks he plays were either produced by himself or other producers among his circle of friends. This may include, for example, the very latest mixes that may not have been released in any form yet, or may never be released at all on LP or CD.

This was the original reason RD started using a computer to perform; he took his ELM crew (himself joined by fellow electro headz Trichome and Ben Milstein) on a European tour a few years ago and he wanted to be able to play his own music live instead of just playing other artists' records. On that tour, he pulled all his tracks into Ableton Live and mixed them that way, but he soon found that with his background as a DJ, Traktor suited him much better.

In addition, Traktor offers the DJ more creative functions than a traditional turntables-and-a-mixer setup, and RD makes full use of these capabilities. In particular, he uses Traktor's filters extensively as well as its looping functions.

Tips and Tricks

I asked RD for a few examples of musical techniques he could pull off with this setup and he gave me some good ideas.

One thing he mentioned was that the filters in Traktor are capable of some really radical effects depending on how you manipulate the controls. However, you won't discover the true potential of the filters unless you assign their controls to an external MIDI controller, because you need to manipulate the controls at least two at a time in order to really find the limits of what the filters can do.

Filtering off a large swathe of frequencies from a track, for example, all of the highs or all of the lows, can also be a very useful technique when you are mixing two tracks together in Traktor.

RD also likes to use the looping functions of Traktor a lot to change up his tracks and keep his DJ sets fresh. An important point he mentioned about looping in Traktor was that you can use this function to help you mix together two tracks with very complex or irregular rhythms. For example, some IDM tracks may have a consistent beat in one part but have another section where the beat is much more chaotic and impossible to mix. In this case, all you need to do is engage Traktor's looping function during one of the sections of the track with a steady rhythm; then you can mix the next track together with this.

Or you can do this in reverse by looping a stead section of the track that you are about to mix in; after you've brought it in and mixed out the other track, you can turn the looper off and let the track continue on with whatever craziness is going to ensue.

RD also often uses the looper and the filter in conjunction with one another. For example, he might start looping a section of a track that he likes, then start using the filter to change its sound while it plays back.

RD and Trichome: 2x4 DJ Sets on Two Mac PowerBooks

Trichome (a.k.a. Barry Hewitt) has long been RD's DJing partner (although they play separately as often as they play together), and they have promoted and organized many underground music events in LA together as well. However, while both of them used to spin vinyl records at their events, Trichome has also moved to using Traktor now, although more recently than RD. They still play 2x4 DJ sets together, but both on computers instead of turntables.

Although Traktor has some built-in syncing capabilities (it can use either MIDI or the newer Ethernet-based OSC standard for sync), RD and Trichome still prefer to do it the old school way and rely solely on their ears and mixing skills to keep their computers in sync, using key commands and Traktor's on-screen controls to nudge and pitch bend their tracks together.

FinalScratch2

FinalScratch2 refers to an integrated hardware/software DJ system developed jointly by Stanton Magnetics and Native Instruments (see Figure 8.34).

Figure 8.34 A complete DJing setup based around the FinalScratch2 unit and Traktor.

Basically, the FinalScratch2 system allows you to use a pair of digital timecode records played on conventional turntables as controllers for the playback of tracks in Traktor. This is a simple but powerful concept that enables you to take your turntable skills honed on vinyl records and apply them to the digital medium.

The FinalScratch2 hardware system can be used with two different versions of Traktor. It is packaged together with an application called Traktor FS 2, which is a kind of "lite" version of Traktor with many of the more advanced features removed. If you have also purchased Traktor DJ Studio, however, you can use the FinalScratch2 system to control it.

Scratch History

Stanton was one of the first companies to introduce a technology aimed at controlling the playback of digital audio files via "controller" records spinning on turntables; the first FinalScratch system was introduced by Stanton and Native Instruments in 2001. Although the early systems had some problems and developed a reputation for not always working as well as people hoped, this technology has now matured to the point where it is a reliable basis for live performance, and there are countless DJs around the world using it.

Particularly in Europe, the use of FinalScratch systems has spread quite widely and some new clubs actually incorporate a FinalScratch system into the design of the DJ booth so that visiting DJs need bring nothing more than their own laptop computer full of music.

FinalScratch2 Hardware

On the hardware side, the FinalScratch2 system consists of a FireWire audio interface attached to the computer (see Figure 8.35).

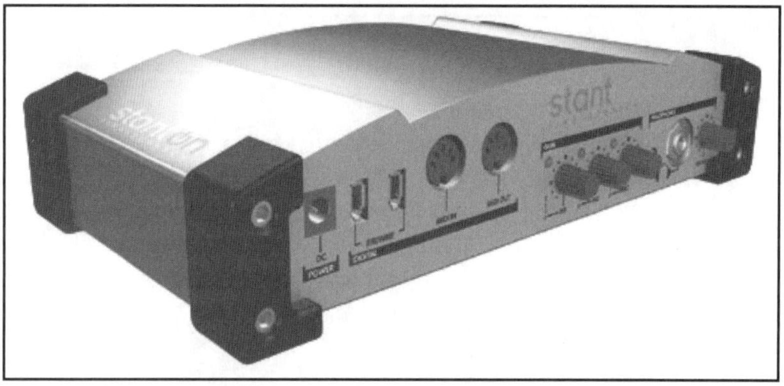

Figure 8.35 The FinalScratch2 hardware interface.

This unit offers 24-bit/96kHz audio quality, jacks for mic and line input as well as the RCA jacks for the turntables, and MIDI input and output as well. Here's how you hook it up:

Basically, you take the audio outputs from the turntables and plug them into inputs on the FinalScratch2 unit. Then, you run another pair of RCA cables from the audio outputs of the unit to the appropriate inputs of your DJ mixer. The FinalScratch2 unit is attached to your computer via FireWire. This will give you a setup that looks something like Figure 8.38.

You can then load tracks into the Playback Decks in Traktor and control their playback by using the digital timecode records on the turntables. The audio output comes from Traktor through the FinalScratch2 interface and then to your DJ mixer, and you use the mixer to play just like you would if you were using real records.

In fact, by changing a setting on the FinalScratch2 interface, you can monitor the direct audio output from the turntables through the interface as well. This means that you can even switch back and forth between playing digital audio files controlled by timecode records, and actually playing real records on the same turntables through the same setup!

Turntables in Control

Once you have everything set up properly, you can use the playback of two digital timecode records on your turntables to control the playback of your tracks in Traktor; this is the main point of this whole system. The way this has been implemented is both simple and ingenious. Basically, the timecode record contains encoded digital information that indicates numerically exactly how far the record has played at any point. This starts from zero at the beginning of the groove and tells the computer how far through the track to start playback.

FinalScratch2's tracking is quite good, much improved since the early days of this type of product, and it can track just about any DJ move you care to try on the decks, from cutting and mixing to scratching and fading.

Why FinalScratch?

You will all have to forgive me for not having much to say about FinalScratch2. I was a pro bass player before I got into computers, not a vinyl DJ, so I would never use this kind of system myself. If I started using turntables and records to DJ, I'd have to start from scratch and learn it all over again from the beginning.

I can well understand the appeal of these kinds of systems to vinyl DJs, however.

However, I did interview postdigital hiphop practitioners DJ Haul and Mason while writing this book and they made a pretty convincing case for the revolutionary potential of FinalScratch2's main competitor, Rane's Serato Scratch. More on this in the section on Serato Scratch below.

Virtual DJ

Virtual DJ (http://www.virtualdj.com), by France's Atomix Productions, is the main competitor to Traktor in the DJ software space (see Figure 8.36).

Figure 8.36 VirtualDJ.

I have enjoyed using VirtualDJ ever since it was first released in 2003, and have played countless DJ gigs with it and its predecessor, AtomixMP3. Honestly speaking, I have had a special place in my heart for the good people at Atomix Productions ever since they released AtomixMP3 1.0, the first version of their DJ software, in September 2000. As I described earlier in the book, AtomixMP3 was the first DJ software I found that had usable beatmixing capabilities, as well as being robust enough to be used reliably live. For me, AtomixMP3 was the missing piece of the puzzle that enabled me to start doing real DJ gigs with my laptop and caused me to embark (perhaps misguidedly) on a new career as a computer musician.

VirtualDJ Features: Comparison with Traktor

I covered Traktor DJ Studio in considerable detail above in part because I wanted to illustrate the features that a pro-quality DJ software ought to have. Traktor is not the only application that fits this description, but it has set the standard.

Having covered Traktor in detail already, though, I see little point in describing VirtualDJ at similar length, because the functions and capabilities of the two applications are quite similar. Instead, let's look at how VirtualDJ compares with Traktor in terms of usability and features.

For what it's worth, I have tried a quite a number of different DJ applications on both Macs and PCs, and I have found these two to be the best products currently available. I would highly recommend using one or the other of them for computer DJing. Here are some of the factors you ought to consider if you are trying to decide which one to use yourself.

Basic DJ Functionality

Both VirtualDJ and Traktor offer a similar basic package of DJing functions and features, the features that are essential in a serious DJing application:

- Support for playing (at least) two audio tracks simultaneously and mixing them together
- Support for multiple-output sound cards or multiple sound cards used simultaneously, so that you can play a track out to the PA while cueing another on headphones
- Basic DJ functions including three-band EQ, separate volume faders for each channel, headphone cue buttons, a crossfader, and so on
- Additional features to aid in beatmatching and mixing such as automatic syncing and savable cue points
- On-the-fly looping functions
- Reliable and robust (this is of course essential for live performance!)
- Compatible with external MIDI controllers

Although they are quite similar in their basic functionality, VirtualDJ's look and feel bespeaks a different overall design philosophy than Traktor's. Traktor sometimes seems to give us more detailed information and more control than we might actually need, and it sometimes seems a bit more difficult than it really needs to be to accomplish certain functions in the software. Working with VirtualDJ, on the other hand, tends to be a bit quicker and easier. It is just a bit simpler to install and configure the program and get going with it than it is with Traktor.

Automated Beatsyncing

Both Traktor and VirtualDJ offer some degree of automated beatmatching or syncing, and both of these suffer from similar limitations. Both programs will do pretty well at automatically syncing dance music tracks with a basic 4/4 bass drum beat (house, techno, and trance). These simple blocky rhythms are easy for their respective software algorithms to analyze and sync together. However, neither program fares very well at syncing together more rhythmically complex styles such as breakbeat or drum'n'bass.

Having said this, however, I have found that even for 4/4 based music, VirtualDJ's beatmatching algorithms seem to work a bit better than Traktor's version. Especially in the most recent versions of VDJ, once you have the tracks synced and you engage the program's "BeatLock" feature, they may play for minutes on end without ever drifting apart.

An interesting side note to the above is that VirtualDJ's BeatLock mode can produce some very interesting rhythmic overlapping and collisions even when it is wrong about the tempo. When it is wrong, it usually picks a tempo that has some mathematical relationship to the real tempo (such as ⅔ of the original tempo, ⅜ of the original tempo, etc.), and sometimes this results in patterns that can work rhythmically with a little clever mixing. For example, I used to collect MP3 files of Snoop Dogg a cappellas and mix them over techno and breakbeat music. Although the program could never figure out the tempo of the a cappella correctly, when it tried to match the tempo to the music I was playing, it seemed often to come up with some kind of relationship that worked and Snoop sounded great over the weird tracks I was playing.

Waveform Displays

One simple yet quite significant difference between Traktor and VirtualDJ has to do with the way they display the waveforms of the tracks on the screen. As we saw earlier, in Traktor, the waveforms are displayed separately, above their respective playback controls (see Figure 8.37).

Figure 8.37 The waveform displays in Traktor.

In VirtualDJ, on the other hand, the waveforms are displayed in different colors and superimposed on one another, like in Figure 8.38.

This is a seemingly small difference in the layout of the programs' user interfaces, but it makes a big difference when you are performing!

Because the tracks' waveforms are superimposed over each other as they play back together in VirtualDJ, it is very easy to see whether one of the tracks is drifting ahead or behind the other. By mapping keys on the computer keyboard to control the track pitch and nudge

Figure 8.38 The waveform displays in VirtualDJ.

controls, it is relatively easy to keep your tracks playing in sync, even in cases where the automatic beatmatching function is of no use.

Of course, you also need to listen to how the rhythms and sounds of the two tracks fit together while you are mixing, but VirtualDJ's innovative waveform display makes DJ mixing almost like a video game.

Since the waveform displays in Traktor are presented side-by-side rather than superimposed on each other, there are no visual aids like this to help you match the beats together.

Multi-Instance Support

Another cool feature of VirtualDJ not implemented in Traktor is multi-instance support, the ability to run more than one copy of the program simultaneously. This is important particularly if you want to use three or four separate decks simultaneously while mixing (which I often do when I DJ).

As should have been obvious from the descriptions above, both Traktor and VirtualDJ (as well as most other DJ applications on the market) are designed around the paradigm of mixing with two decks, and there is no capacity for adding further playback channels.

However, the designers of VirtualDJ later found a clever workaround to this problem that enables mixing on three or four decks at once without making any fundamental changes to the software. Instead of adding a third deck, they simply allowed more than one instance of VirtualDJ to be run at a time. As VirtualDJ is also fully skinnable (meaning that its interface can be customized by users), they then simply introduced a new multi-instance skin that only takes up half of the screen and can be oriented so that its waveform display is on top or bottom edge of the interface. By loading up two copies of VirtualDJ with this skin installed and selecting the appropriate options, you can get an integrated four-deck interface that looks like Figure 8.39:

Further, since now all four of the track waveform displays are scrolling through the middle of the screen (two above and two below), you can see how all the beats and rhythms of all four tracks line up with each other in time. This has got to be the greatest tool for multi-deck mixing that I have seen so far, and I used VirtualDJ like this for awhile myself before the problems I was having with my Compaq laptop led me to switch back to using a Mac for my live gigs.

PC vs. Mac

This brings us to one of the most significant limitations of VirtualDJ: It is only available for Windows PCs, while Traktor is available for both Mac and PC platforms. One of the most

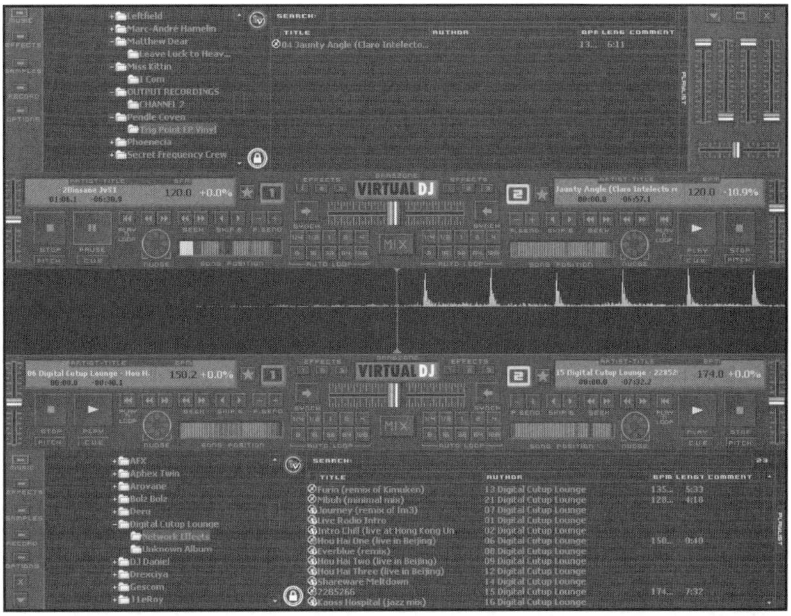

Figure 8.39 Mixing with four decks in VirtualDJ.

important factors in deciding what software application to use for performance is, of course, whether or not your chosen computing platform (PC or Mac) will support it, and on this point, Traktor wins hands down. One of the reasons I stuck with using Windows live for so long myself was that I liked using VirtualDJ so much, but when I finally switched back to using a Mac, I had to stop. I tried using Traktor myself for awhile, but then I started using Ableton Live for gigs and went a different route with my live performances anyway.

Built-in Effects

Another point where VirtualDJ and Traktor differ lies in their support for audio effects that you can apply to your tracks as they play back. While Traktor offers only its built-in filter, VirtualDJ can host a variety of different effects, many of which can be downloaded through the VirtualDJ Web site. These include plug-ins that can play your tracks in reverse, apply delay, phasing or flanging effects, slice and dice loops on the fly, create LFO-based effects like autopanning, and so on. New effects are being developed for VirtualDJ all the time.

And the Winner is... ?

Both VirtualDJ and Traktor DJ Studio are powerful applications suitable for live performance at any level, whether you are mixing in your bedroom or touring the world's top venues. They differ more in style than in functionality, so I would highly recommend trying them both (downloadable demos of both programs are available) before making a decision about which you prefer for laptop DJing.

Performance Technique: Using a Computer to DJ with Live Musicians

Another interesting performance technique made possible by applications like VirtualDJ is DJing together with live musicians. This can be a very dynamic way to play, with a percussionist, keyboardist, guitarist, or other musician adding excitement, energy, and creativity to your live set.

When I first got into electronic music myself I was already a pro bass player, so naturally enough my first gigs playing in dance clubs consisted of me playing funky live basslines together with a DJ friend: My roommate at the time, DJ Teng Boon, a Chinese-Canadian house, techno, and hiphop DJ well known in Hong Kong. However, I quickly became frustrated as I realized that DJs have to change the pitch of records up and down in order to get their tempos to sync together. Because of this, it is more or less impossible for an instrumentalist to play together with a vinyl DJ and keep their part in tune with the record.

I tried playing fretless bass with Teng Boon a couple times, giving me the ability to adjust my tuning a bit and match the pitch of the records, but this was quite difficult and I started thinking about other ways to combine live improvising musicians and DJ mixing.

When I started using a computer to mix, I quickly figured out that some applications (such as VirtualDJ and Traktor) will allow you to adjust the tempo of a track separately from its pitch. This is an essential capability to have if you want to play with live musicians, as it will enable you to keep the pitch unchanged from the original while still beatmatching all of your tracks. This will allow any musicians working with you to stay in tune with the tracks with no difficulty. Check the documentation for your particular application to see how to use the pitch and time-stretching capabilities in your software independently of one another.

This is what I did in the early days of our band Digital Cutup Lounge: Stephen and I would DJ a mix of tracks together while one or more jazz improvisers joined us for a live club session. Using VirtualDJ's predecessor software Atomixmp3, we were able to keep the pitch of all our tracks unchanged so that the improvisers would be able to follow us.

The only issue we found problematic with this approach was that some tracks we played were already out of tune with our live musicians even though we weren't changing the pitch in our software. This caused some major train wrecks at some of our first gigs as we would drop a new track and our musicians would try to play over it, only to find that it was far out of tune. This happened mostly with hiphop or drum'n'bass tracks that themselves sampled some older music; in this case, it was the samples that were out of tune in the original, so there wasn't much we could do about it. In order to avoid this problem, however, we started checking the pitch of all of our tracks beforehand with a synthesizer in order to make sure they were in tune, and I would recommend this solution to you as well if you are planning to have any live musicians play with you.

Serato Scratch

As we saw above in the section on FinalScratch2, with Traktor it is also possible to integrate the best of both approaches by using turntables to control the playback of your digital audio files in the software. VirtualDJ also offers this capability (although I have not tested this aspect of the program myself).

The other main contender in this category of applications is Rane's Serato Scratch (see Figure 8.40).

Figure 8.40 Serato Scratch.

Serato Scratch works similarly to FinalScratch2, in that a pair of special timecode records are played on turntables and used to control the playback of digital audio files on the computer. Also like FinalScratch2, Serato Scratch is not just a standalone software application but an integrated hardware and software system. The software comes from Serato, a small developer based in New Zealand, while the hardware, called the Scratch Live, is made by Rane (see Figure 8.41).

Basically, you hook this up just like FinalScratch. You connect the outputs from your turntables to the Scratch Live interface, which is connected to the computer via USB. The tracks are played in the computer and then output as two separate audio streams back to a conventional DJ mixer, and you mix just like you would if you were playing records. The diagram from Rane shows how it is all connected (see Figure 8.42).

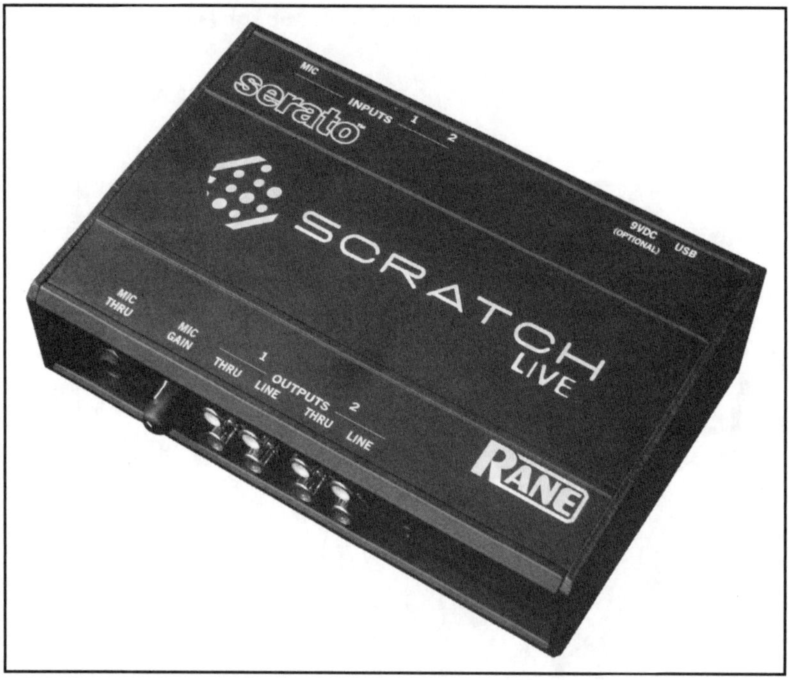

Figure 8.41 Scratch Live.

Serato vs. FinalScratch2

Comparing Serato Scratch to FinalScratch2 on a feature by feature basis, they are roughly equivalent in the sense that both provide sufficient functionality and reliably to be used in performance. (More information on Serato Scratch, as well as an impressive video demo, is available at http://www.rane.com/scratch.html#lit.) As in the case of comparing Traktor and VirtualDJ, your preference may depend on how the interface "feels" to you in performance, which is very subjective and difficult to put into words.

As I said before, I am not a turntable DJ myself, and it is impossible for me to really evaluate either of these applications on the basis of how they feel to play. I talked to a number of DJs who use these systems live, and found fans of both the FinalScratch2 and Serato Scratch systems.

One seeming difference did emerge in my informal poll of users, though: For various reasons, the Traktor/FinalScratch2 system seems to appeal more widely to dance/electronica producers, while the more recently released Serato Scratch seems to have made greater inroads among the hiphop community. One of the most interesting conversations I had on this topic was with LA hiphop duo DJ Haul and Mason.

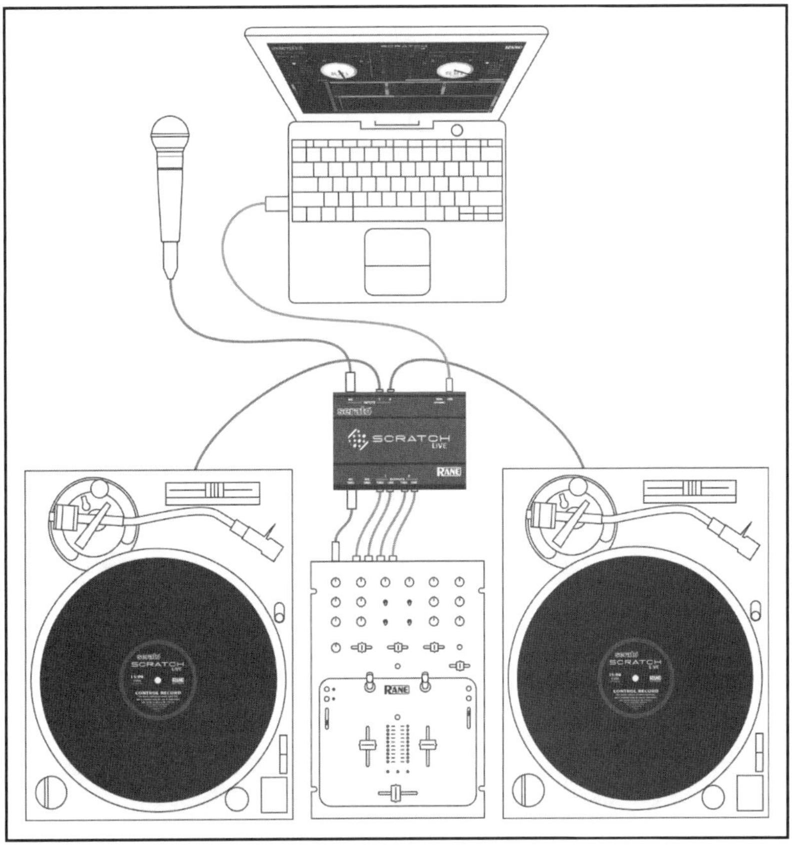

Figure 8.42 Connecting Serato Scratch.

Example: DJ Haul and Mason

DJ Haul and Mason (see Figure 8.43) have been mainstays of the LA hiphop scene for some years now, producing and gigging under their own name as well as participating in collaborations such as Afrodisiac Soundsystem and the Dakah Hip Hop Orchestra.

Haul and Mason are masters of spinning vinyl, scratching and cutting between records with incredible speed and dexterity at their live gigs. They are definitely vinyl purists in some sense, eschewing the use of any effects or outboard processing gear when they play live in favor of just playing and mixing records together. They told me that they had tried a number of systems for integrating computers with turntables for live performance, but always preferred the feel and sensitivity of playing real vinyl.

However, quite recently they have changed their live modus operandi and started performing with Serato Scratch instead. Now when they play live, each of them has two turntables and a mixer in front of him just as before, but they each have a Mac G4 laptop added to their

Figure 8.43 DJ Haul and Mason.

setup as well, and instead of playing hiphop vinyls, they are playing timecode vinyls that control the playback of tracks in Serato Scratch.

I had originally contacted DJ Haul and Mason in connection with this project because I had seen them using their Mac laptops on stage when they were playing at club Zanzibar in Santa Monica, and I wanted to find out how they were using them. I had heard they were using Ableton Live as well, so I was wondering if they were incorporating Live into their DJ sets somehow.

Contrary to what I expected, they told me that they only used Live in the studio, but they had recently converted to using Serato Scratch exclusively for their live performances. This surprised me because I had always assumed that hiphop scratch DJs would be the last to switch to any kind of computer-based system for performance.

They told me that they had never expected to switch to a computer-based system either, but that when they tried the Serato Scratch system, something about the feel of playing it appealed to them somehow. Although they said that they still found a slight latency/delay when using the turntables to control the playback of their tracks, after a little practice they were able to quickly get used to this and compensate for it, and they were soon able to pull off all of their turntable DJ mixing tricks on the Serato Scratch system. They decided to try using it for awhile, and before long, all the other benefits of using a computer-based DJ system began to sank in: No need to carry records to gigs, access to unreleased music, the ability to build your own custom DJ tools and play your own new tracks at gigs, and so on.

Now, having used the Serato Scratch system on countless gigs and found it to be reliable in performance, they have become enthusiastic converts to the world of digital DJing. Seeing them play at Zanzibar was an amazing demonstration of the potential of this technology. Even when I was watching them play myself I couldn't tell if they were playing real vinyl or controlling tracks on the computers they were using... although, in retrospect, the fact that they never seemed to change the records they were playing probably should have given everything away to me...

Other DJ Programs

There are many other DJ software applications available on the market now, ranging from shareware and freeware to expensive commercial applications designed for radio broadcasting, but I have chosen only a few of the best to cover here in any detail. As I mentioned above, Native Instruments' outstanding Traktor program has set the standard in this area, and my description of Traktor above shows the kind of features you should look for in other applications.

If you want to explore some of the dizzying variety of applications out there, I would recommend starting at the Shareware Music Machine page at http://www.hitsquad.com/smm.

9 Live Looping and Ableton Live

One of the most common performance techniques used by contemporary computer musicians is "live looping." This usually entails playing back and mixing together a collection of audio loops and samples of various lengths. Some performers also like to insert effects into the mix while the tracks and samples are playing back, enabling them to further manipulate the sounds live.

Looping is an extremely powerful and flexible technique and this basic idea can be employed in the performance of many different kinds of music. In the next two chapters, I will look at some of the best software to use for loop-based performance as well as various loop-based musical approaches for performance.

There are a number of different software packages on the market that you can use for live looping, but in this chapter I am going to concentrate specifically on performing with Ableton Live (see Figure 9.1).

Introduced on November 2nd, 2001 by the tiny German software company Ableton, Live has set the standard for software-based looping tools and live computer music performance in general.

Live has become by far the most popular software application for live computer music performance, and for good reason. At a typical computer music gig here in Los Angeles, virtually all of the performers will be using Live, except for those who prefer to perform with a digital DJ-style application like Traktor.

In this chapter and the next, I will cover Live's operation in depth, focusing specifically on how to set it up and use it for live performance. The information here will be more detailed than I have provided for any of the other software in this book. In subsequent chapters, I will look at some of the alternatives to Live for loop-based performance, such as radiaL, Reason, and MAX/MSP.

Note that you can easily download a demo copy of the latest version of Ableton Live directly from the Ableton Web site (http://www.ableton.com). If you don't already own Live, I highly recommend that you download a copy of the demo and follow along with the examples as

Figure 9.1 Ableton Live.

you read this chapter. It is also worth noting that many audio interfaces from M-Audio, Digidesign, and a number of other manufacturers currently ship with a bundled copy of Live Lite. This version lacks some of the features of the full version of Live but is certainly powerful enough to be used in performance. This is a good way to get started with Live if you are on a tight budget.

Note that Live 4 and later versions offer many options (such as MIDI support) not available in earlier versions of Live, so if you are using Live 3 or earlier, some of my discussions will not be applicable to the version you are using. My examples and screenshots in this book are based on Live 4.

There are a number of reasons why Live has become so popular:

- Stability and reliability
  Live is one of the most crash-proof audio applications I have ever used. Although crashes are not unheard of, if you are running Live on a clean, well-optimized computer system, crashes and freezes should be an extremely rare phenomenon.
- Elegant and powerful interface
  Instead of duplicating the complex functioning of an analog recording studio like other multi-track recording software (such as Digital Performer, Pro Tools, Cubase, and so on), the designers of Live completely rethought the design of their audio software from the

ground up. Live offers the user a stripped-down interface in which all controls you need to get to quickly for live performance are easily accessible.

- Flexible enough for any musical context
  Live is an extremely flexible and customizable piece of software, which makes it easy to adapt it to the performance of virtually any style of music. If you need to play back and control pieces of pre-recorded audio in performance, Live is probably the best tool available. More recent versions of Live have also added extensive MIDI capabilities to the program, including the ability to host VST software instruments such as Native Instruments' Reaktor synth or the MicroTonic drum machine from Sonic Charge (two of my personal favorites).
- Powerful time-stretching and looping features
  Live includes the most powerful time-stretching and syncing features of any audio software available, and this is one of its greatest strengths. After you have done a bit of preparation on your audio loops, you can simply drop any loop into your Live Set during a performance and it will start playing back at whatever tempo you have selected.

Now let's see how to start setting up Live for performance.

Setting Up Live's Preferences

Before you start using Live, you will need to configure its audio and MIDI preferences. After launching the program, you can open Live's preferences from the Options menu if you are on a Windows PC, or from the Live menu if you are using Mac OS X.

The Audio Preferences

After you open the preferences, click the Audio tab to open Live's Audio preference page (see Figure 9.2).

First, choose an audio driver type. In Mac OS X, your only choice is Apple's CoreAudio driver, but in Windows, Live can access MME/DirectX, ASIO, or Direct I/O (for use with Digidesign interfaces) drivers. Your choice will depend on what your audio hardware supports. If possible, you should always choose ASIO on a PC for best performance.

Once you have chosen the driver type, choose your device in the box below. On a Mac you will need to select a device for both input and output.

Below this you can select the buffer size setting, which determines the overall amount of audio latency in your system. In Mac OS X, you can adjust the buffer size right here in Live with a slider control, while on a Windows PC, you need to adjust the buffer size in the control panel of your audio interface. Some interfaces may require you to quit Live before you can adjust the buffer size.

Basically you want to adjust the buffer size as low as you can to ensure a responsive system in performance. However, if you adjust the buffer too low, at some point your system will be unable to keep up with the processing demands on it and you will start to hear pops and clicks

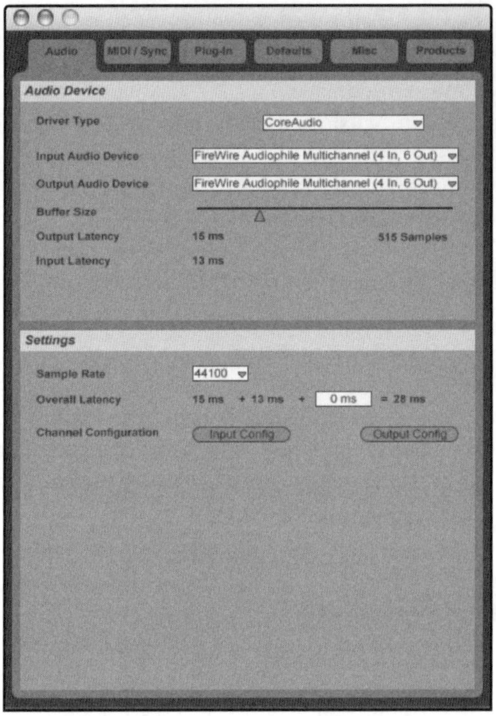

Figure 9.2 Live's Audio preferences.

or other artifacts in your audio. You should adjust your buffer size as low as you can, but back off and turn it a bit higher again if you start to hear audio artifacts.

You also need to choose which audio inputs and outputs are available for use in Live by clicking on the Input and Output Config buttons in the Settings section of the Audio preferences page. You will then see a sub-menu screen (see Figure 9.3) where you can make specific inputs or outputs active or inactive. You will probably need to do this if you are planning to mix audio from an external source (such as a microphone or synth) through your Live Set during performance, or if you want to enable extra pairs of outputs for headphone cueing or external mixing.

Each input or output pair can be used as one stereo channel or two mono channels. (You can set this up in the Live Mixer, as we will see below.)

You can activate as many inputs and outputs as you want here, up to the number that you actually have available on your audio interface. Always keep in mind, however, that having more inputs and outputs active will put additional load on your computer's CPU. For this reason, it is best to only activate the ins and outs that you are actually planning to use.

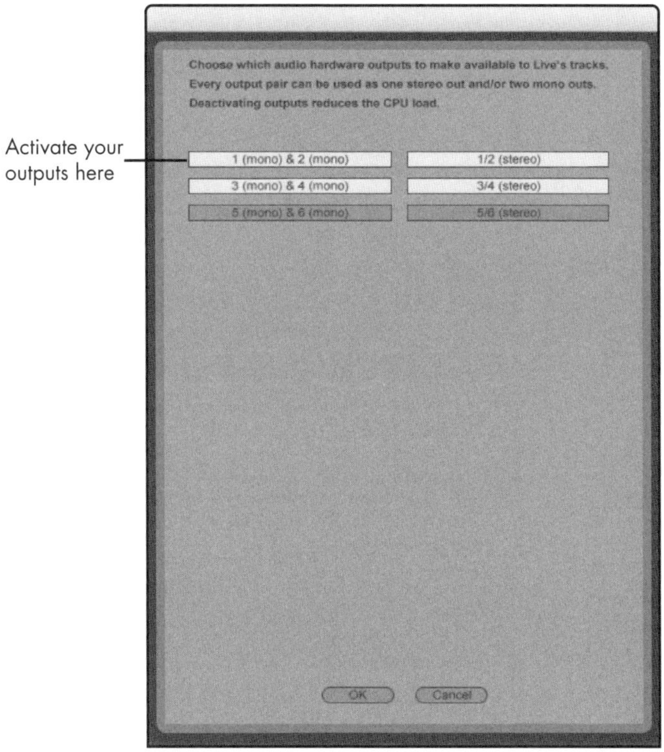

Figure 9.3 Activating outputs in Live's Output Config window.

Performance optimization is always an issue when setting up a computer for live performance, and you need to always keep this in mind.

The MIDI/Sync Preferences

After setting the Audio preferences, click the MIDI/ Sync tab to select your MIDI options (see Figure 9.4).

All available MIDI devices you currently have connected will show up in the Active Devices section at the top, and you can check the boxes next to them to make them active or inactive. Note that in Live you also have the choice of using your computer's keyboard as a MIDI input device, which can come in very handy for laptop performance in some cases. Also, the same device may show up under both input and output if appropriate.

The Remote Control section is where you will choose which external MIDI controllers or interfaces to use. You can use two MIDI input devices at the same time, as well as one output device.

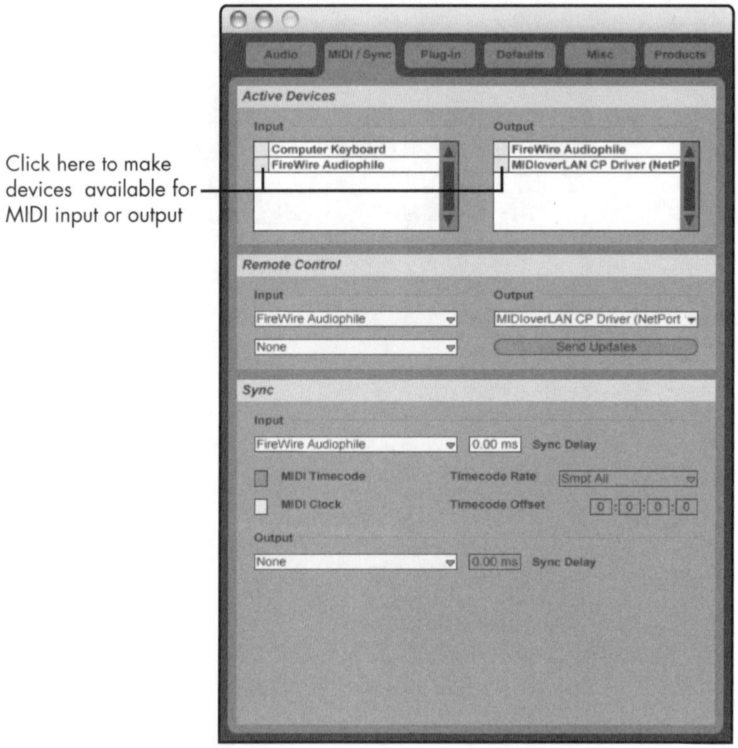

Figure 9.4 Live's MIDI/Sync preferences.

In the Sync section, you can choose which MIDI device you wish to sync to using either MIDI Clock or MIDI Timecode. MIDI Clock can be used to easily send or receive tempo and song position information to and from devices such as external sequencers or drum machines. You can also use MIDI Clock to sync multiple laptops running Live or other audio programs with each other in performance.

If you are syncing Live to an external device or computer using MIDI Clock but your audio is slightly out of time, you can use the Sync Delay setting to adjust the timing and bring everything precisely into sync.

I will explain further about the specifics of syncing with Live in the section on syncing Live in Chapter 10.

The Live Interface

Now let's look at how Live's user interface is laid out and how you can load your own audio and MIDI data into it for performance.

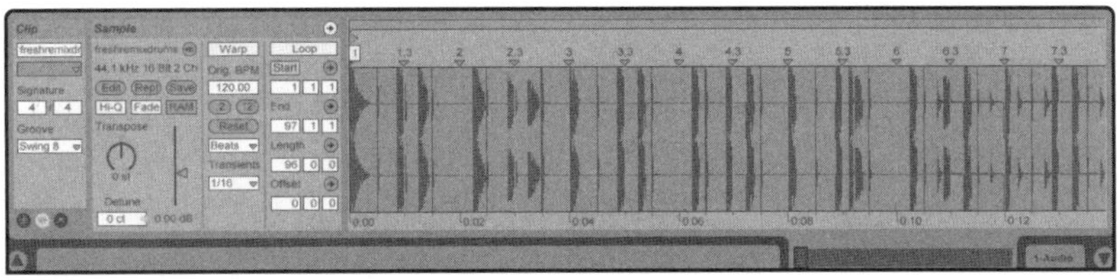

Figure 9.5 The Clip View window.

Audio and MIDI Clips

A Clip is the basic building block of audio or MIDI in Live. Each Clip can be as short as a single drum loop or as long as a complete song. Double-clicking on the Clip in the Session or Arrangement View will open the Clip View window at the bottom of Live's interface (see Figure 9.5), displaying all the properties of the Clip.

An audio Clip contains a reference to an audio sample on your hard drive. This can be a WAV file or AIF file. (You can also use Sound Designer 2/.sd2 files if you are on a Mac.) The Clip stores information about the sample's location, what part of the sample to play, and how to play it.

Samples are stored in Live's File Browser at the left side of the screen, and a new Clip will be created when a sample is dragged into a Clip slot. You can also create a new Clip by recording into a Clip slot, and this will create a new audio sample as well.

Once an audio Clip has been created, you can use Live's powerful Warping capabilities to manipulate it in various ways. For example, you can change the speed of a Clip independently from the pitch or vice versa. You can also correct the timing of a Clip or subtly alter its rhythmic feel.

MIDI Clips contain MIDI notes and controller envelopes. As with audio Clips, a MIDI Clip can be created by dragging a MIDI file from the one of Live's browser windows into a Clip slot, or by recording a new MIDI Clip into a Clip slot. You can also draw MIDI notes directly into a MIDI Clip with your mouse or trackpad in Live's MIDI Editor.

The Arrangement View and the Session View

Live has two screens in which you can work with your audio and MIDI data: The Arrangement View and the Session View. The Arrangement View is a linear layout of Clips along a musical timeline, while the Session View is a grid of Clips that you can launch at any time and in any order.

The Arrangement View and the Session View both have their own distinct uses and applications, and each can hold its own collection of Clips. Switching between these two views only changes the appearance of the Live Set and does not alter what is heard or what is stored.

You can switch back and forth between the Arrangement View and the Session View by using either the View buttons in the upper right-hand corner of the Live interface or the Tab key.

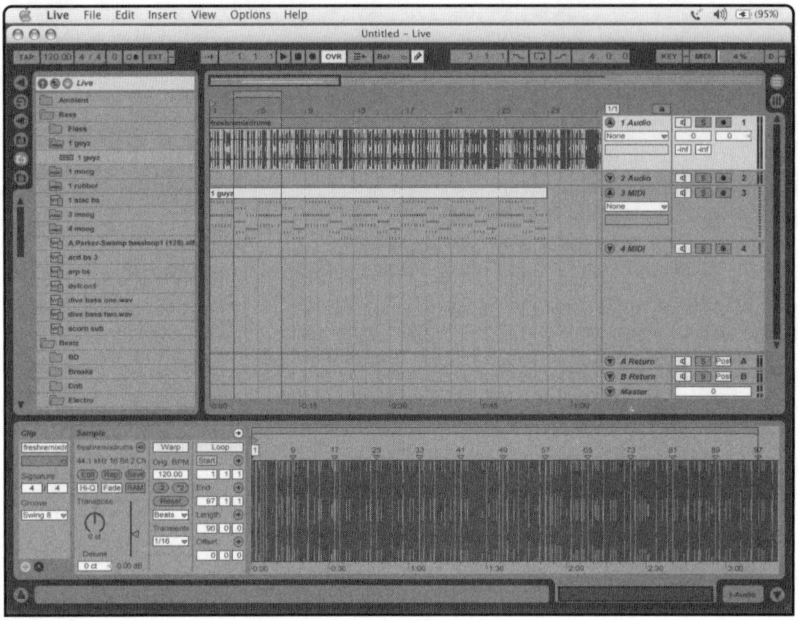

Figure 9.6 The Arrangement View.

The Arrangement View

The Arrangement View (see Figure 9.6) is laid out similarly to a more standard Digital Audio Workstation (DAW) application like Pro Tools, Digital Performer, or Cubase. The music is laid out along a fixed timeline where you can combine and arrange musical material of all types including audio loops, MIDI data, and sound effects.

It is possible to use the Arrangement View for live performance, playing back an entire arrangement with multiple tracks. This is how Jason Halbert uses the program with Kelly Clarkson, for example, as we saw in Chapter 2. However, when used this way, Live behaves more or less the same as other digital audio sequencers, and I will cover this type of live sequencing further in Chapter 11 instead of going into greater detail here. Please consult the Live manual for further information about how to use Live's Arrangement View for sequencing and arranging, as this is not my principal focus in this book.

The uniqueness of Live is found in the layout of the Session View. Here you can improvise and build ideas by spontaneously launching Clips in any order you want.

The Session View

The Session View (see Figure 9.7) is formed by the intersection of tracks (the vertical columns) and scenes (the horizontal rows). This forms a grid of small rectangular slots into which you can place audio or MIDI Clips.

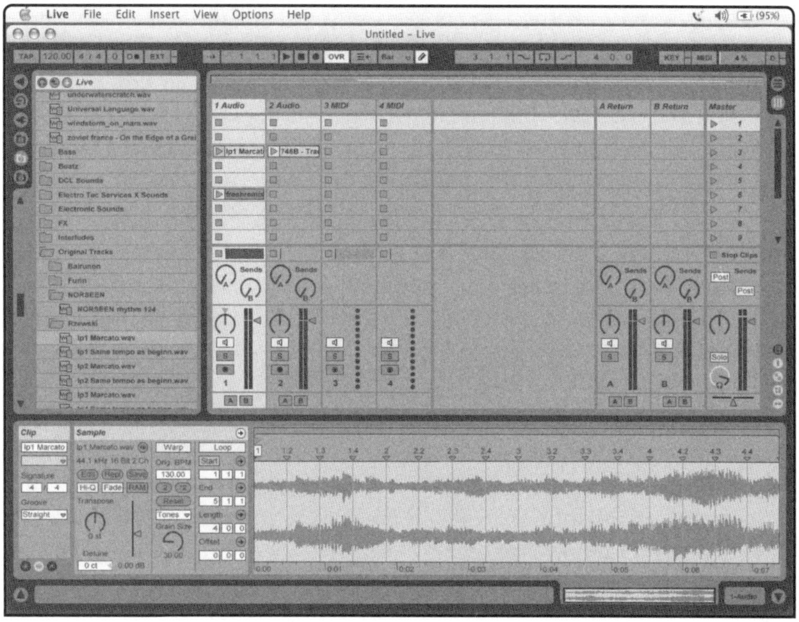

Figure 9.7 The Session View.

The Session View's tracks and scenes depart from the layout of most DAW-style applications in that there is no fixed timeline and no set order in which the Clips have to play, no matter how they are arranged on the grid. Because of this, the Session View lends itself well to intuitive mixing and improvisation in live performance, and this is one of the main attractions of Ableton Live for computer musicians.

You can launch individual Clips and start them playing back in the Session View simply by clicking on their small triangular Launch buttons (at each Clip's left edge). Only one Clip can play back on a given track at one time, so in many cases it makes sense to place many Clips of the same type (for example, drum Clips) on the same track. This enables you to rapidly switch back and forth between different Clips of the same type simply by clicking on them. As each one starts playing, the one that was previously playing will stop.

You can also select a Clip by clicking it with the mouse and then press the Enter or Return key on your computer's keyboard to launch it.

You can launch a whole row of Clips at once by using the small triangular Scene Launch buttons to the right of each row. This will simultaneously launch all the Clips in the row, allowing you to make quick and dramatic transitions in performance.

An empty slot that does not contain a Clip has a square button towards its left edge. This is the Clip Stop button. Clicking on this will cause any Clip currently playing on the same track to stop playing.

Any slot on the Session View grid (whether it currently has a Clip in it or not) can also be assigned to a key on your computer's keyboard or a button or key on your MIDI controller by using the Key or MIDI Map modes. Simply press the KEY or MIDI button in the Control Bar, click the slot you want to assign with the cursor, and then press the key or MIDI controller that you want to assign to it. A small indicator will appear, showing you what key or controller you have assigned. Then click the KEY or MIDI button again to exit the mapping mode. You can also use this procedure to assign keys or controllers to the Scene Launch buttons at right.

Virtually every control visible in the Session View can be assigned to an external controller via this method. For example, for performance it is often very useful to assign external keyboard or MIDI controls to Live's volume sliders, panning and send knobs, mute and solo buttons, or effects parameters.

Each track in the Session View has a Track Status field just below the vertical column of Clip slots. This indicates the playback status of the clip currently playing in that track. If the Clip is a loop, this field will show a circular icon with two numbers flanking it. The number to the left represents how many times the clip has played since it was launched, while the number to the right represents the length of the loop in beats. If the Clip is not a loop, the Track Status field will show a progress bar with a numeric display representing the amount of time remaining before the Clip ends, in minutes and seconds.

You can drag and drop Clips from a File Browser to any empty slot or even to a slot that is already occupied by another Clip, in which case the new Clip you are moving will replace the old one. You can also drag Clips between slots and tracks freely on the grid and arrange them however you want, for easiest access when performing.

Dragging several Clips at a time from a browser onto a track will cause the Clips to be arranged vertically onto this single track. On the other hand, by holding down the Control key (PC) or Command key (Mac) while dragging multiple Clips, the Clips will be arranged horizontally across a single Scene in your Live Set.

Live's Browser Windows

Live's Browser windows are where you can access all of your effects, instruments, samples, and saved Live Sets. Whether you are looking at the Session View or the Arrangement View, you will always have access to the Browser window at the left-hand side of the Live Set. You can show or hide this window by clicking on the Browser arrow at the top left-hand corner of the screen under the "Tap" button.

There are three types of Browser windows in all: The Device Browser, the Plug-in Browser, and the File Browsers. Let's take a brief look at each of them.

The Device Browser

Clicking on the Device Browser button will present you with a window containing all the built-in devices included in Live. (You can also access the Device Browser by clicking on View in Live's menu bar and choosing Live Devices.) Live's devices are split into three different folders here, labeled Instruments, MIDI Effects, and Audio Effects (see Figure 9.8).

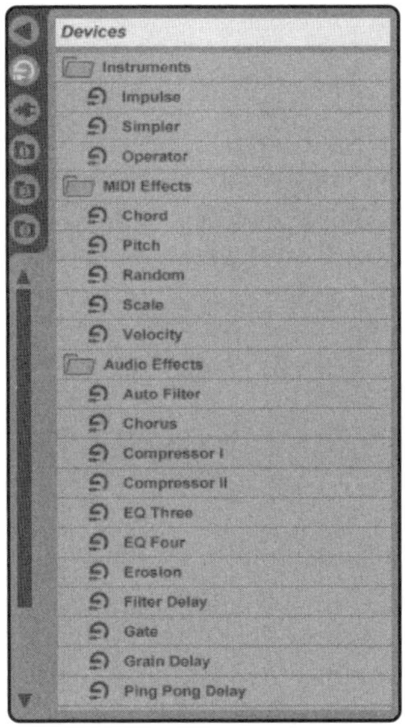

Figure 9.8 The Device Browser window.

To use a device, simply click on it here in the browser and drag it onto a track, or select a track and double-click on the device in the browser. Note that MIDI instruments and effects can only be used on MIDI tracks in Live, while audio effects can be used on audio tracks or MIDI tracks. However, audio effects can only be placed on a MIDI track if they come after a MIDI instrument in the signal chain (which generates an audio signal).

The first folder, labeled Instruments, contains Live's built-in virtual instruments. There are two of these included with Live 4, the Impulse drum machine and the Simpler sample player. Ableton also released their own FM software synthesizer for Live, Operator, and this will also appear here if you have downloaded the appropriate update of Live from Ableton and purchased an unlock key.

The next folder is the MIDI Effects folder. Live 4 contains five MIDI effects that can be used to process MIDI Clip data, including Chord, Pitch, Random, Scale, and Velocity.

The last folder in the Live Device Browser is the Audio Effects folder. There are 17 audio effects included here that can be applied to both audio and MIDI tracks.

I have included more specific information about Live's audio and MIDI effects below.

The Plug-In Browser

The Plug-in Device Browser can be accessed by clicking on the Plug-in Browser button, or by selecting Plug-in Devices from Live's View menu (see Figure 9.9).

The Plug-in Browser is where you can access the various third-party plug-in effects and instruments that are currently installed on your system. The Windows version of Live supports

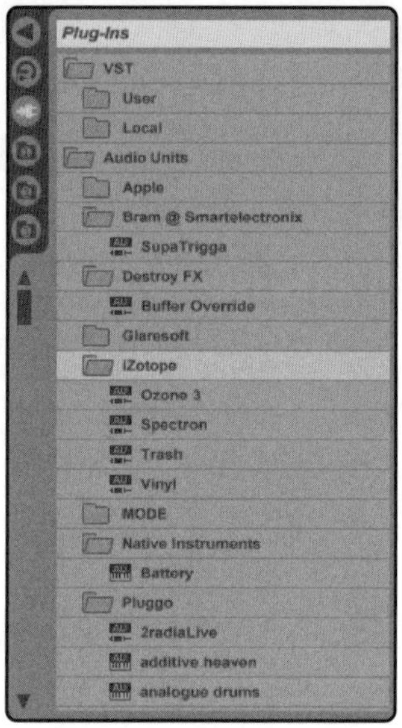

Figure 9.9 The Plug-in Browser window.

plug-ins written in Steinberg's VST format, and the Mac version adds support for Apple's own proprietary Audio Units format as well.

Note that the very first time you launch Live, there may be no plug-ins shown in the Plug-in browser even if you have already installed them in your system. In this case, you should check the Plug-in preference page in Live's Preferences and make sure that this is configured correctly so that Live can locate and access your VST and AU plug-ins.

The Plug-in Browser can contain both audio effects and MIDI instruments. You can tell them apart by their icons. Audio effects are represented by a plug-shaped icon, and MIDI instruments by a keyboard icon. Just as with Live's built-in devices, MIDI effects can only be used on MIDI tracks, while Audio effects can be used on both audio and MIDI tracks.

If you install a new plug-in while the program is running, Live will not detect it until the next time you restart the program. However, you can also use the Re-Scan button found in Live's Plug-in preferences to detect new plug-ins.

To use a plug-in, simply click on it in the browser window and drag it onto the appropriate track. You can also select a track and double-click on the plug-in to insert it.

When you view the parameters of a third-party plug-in in the Track View in Live, the plug-in's original user interface will be replaced with a Live panel similar to the interface of Live's built-in devices. You can view or hide the parameters for the plug-in by clicking the triangular button in the plug-in's title bar. Click on the wrench icon in the title bar to open a floating window containing the plug-in's original user interface and controls.

You can use either of these, the original interface or the Live-style interface, to control the parameters of the plug-in. However, you can only assign keyboard or MIDI controllers to the parameters of the plug-in by using Live's interface for the plug-in.

The File Browsers

The File Browsers are where you can directly see the files on your computer's hard drive and access your audio samples, MIDI files, and saved Live Sets. There are three File Browser folders you can choose, by clicking on the three File Browser buttons numbered 1, 2, and 3. You can also access these folders by selecting Files 1, Files 2, or Files 3 from Live's View Menu (see Figure 9.10).

Live provides three separate File Browsers to help you organize your samples and Live Sets efficiently, so you can quickly and easily find the files you need during a performance. The File Browsers are basically just pointers to locations on your hard drive. You can browse through the hierarchies of folders on your hard drive here, and use the down-arrow button at the top of the window to set a root directory for that window.

For example, on the iBook I use for live gigs, I have one File Browser set to the main Digital Cutup Lounge folder where I keep all the original music files I use for live performances. Another is set to the folder where I keep all my drum and percussion files specifically, as I need to access this folder most often during a gig. The third browser is set to the folder where I keep all the tracks by other artists I have cut up and warped for use in my Live DJ sets.

Another very important feature of the File Browser for live use is the Preview button, which looks like an up-arrow. If this is switched on, you can preview samples before they are dragged

Figure 9.10 The File Browser window.

into the Live Set simply by clicking on them in the File Browser. By default, you will hear the sound of the sample file through Live's main audio output, but you can also cause the previewed audio to be routed to a separate cue output (to your headphones, for example) if you have correctly set up a Cue Out on Live's Master track.

Audio samples appear in the File Browser with a small waveform icon. If the sample has been previously imported into a Live Set and Live has analyzed it, it will also have an additional little "note pad" picture on its icon. This indicates that Live has previously placed an analysis file (.asd) on your hard drive in the same directory as the audio file itself. Live's analysis files contain information regarding a sample's Clip settings, such as Warp mode and loop length.

MIDI files can also be accessed through the File Browser. Opening a MIDI folder in the browser gives you access to that MIDI file's individual MIDI voices or tracks.

You can also open an entire new Live Set through the File Browser window. Live Sets show up in the browser with the Live logo. However, it is important to note that audio playback will stop if you open a new Live Set during a performance! For this reason, it is usually best to set up one master Live Set for performance and use it to mix together all the music for your entire show, from beginning to end.

You can rename files in the browser by choosing Rename from Live's Edit menu, or pressing Control-E on a PC or Command-E on a Mac.

You can also delete files in the browser by using the backspace or delete key, or by choosing the Edit menu's Delete command.

The Transport Control Bar

Live's Transport Control Bar allows you to control the playback and recording of your Live Set, make tempo and global quantization settings, and activate MIDI or keyboard mapping modes for assigning parameters to external MIDI devices or to your computer's keyboard.

The Transport Control Bar is found across the top of your Live screen (see Figure 9.11). This Transport Control Bar is the same whether you are in Session View or Arrangement View. Toggling between these two views has no effect on the Control Bar.

Figure 9.11 Live's Transport Control Bar.

I will not cover every function of the Control Bar here (consult the Live manual for more on the other functions), but I do want to point out a number of controls accessible here that are very important for performance. Some of the other controls are also covered in some of the other sections below.

First of all, to the far left of the Control Bar is the TAP button (see Figure 9.12).

This button allows you to tap out the tempo for your Live session using the mouse, a MIDI control device, or a key on your computer's keyboard. All looped audio Clips as well as all MIDI data in your Live Set will follow the tempo you have tapped.

Figure 9.12 The TAP button in the Transport Control Bar.

If you tap five times in a row while Live is stopped (not playing), Live will quickly calculate the tempo and start playback on the fifth tap. This makes it easy to mix your computer tracks in with a group of live musicians that are already playing. Simply tap a four-beat count-off using the TAP button and you will join in with the rest of the group smoothly and easily at the correct tempo.

The more taps Live receives in a row, the more accurately it will calculate the tempo. Using a key or trigger on an external MIDI controller or a key on your computer's keyboard may provide more accurate results than tapping with the mouse.

For example, you can assign the letter "t" on your computer keyboard to control this by first clicking on the KEY button on the far right of the Control Bar. Then click on the TAP button and press the t key on the keyboard. You will see a small "t" appear on the button, indicating that you have made the assignment. Then click on the KEY button once again to exit the key-mapping mode.

To the right of the TAP button is the tempo indicator, which displays the current tempo (see Figure 9.13).

Figure 9.13 Live's tempo indicator.

In addition to controlling this with the TAP tempo button, the tempo can also be adjusted by clicking this indicator and dragging up or down, or by clicking and typing in the tempo you want. For even crazier time-bending effects, try assigning the tempo indicator to a knob or fader controller on your external MIDI controller.

In the center of the Transport Control Bar, you can see Live's playback position indicator showing you the playback time in bars and beats, and next to this, the standard Start, Stop, and Record buttons that you would find in most digital audio sequencing applications.

To the right of these, past the MIDI Overdub (OVR) button and the Back to Arrangement button, is the Global Quantization Menu, which is also important for live performers to understand (see Figure 9.14).

This sets the quantization that all Clips will follow when they are launched (providing that the Clips themselves are set to follow the global quantization setting, but this is usually the default). For example, if you set this to Bar (probably the most generally useful setting), then any Clip

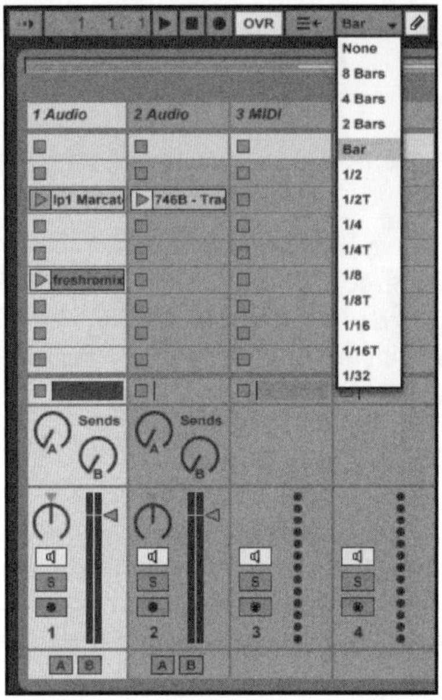

Figure 9.14 The Global Quantization Menu.

you launch will start playing exactly on the downbeat of the next bar that comes along after you click the Clip's Launch button.

It is important to understand how this works in order to keep all your Clips in sync during a live performance. If you set this value too small, for example, to ⅛ notes, then your Clips will all be triggered at different points within the bar and your loops will be out of sync with each other! To be safe, just leave this set to Bar unless you are trying to do something specific and you need to change it.

To the far right of Live's Control Bar you will find the Key and MIDI Map Mode switches (see Figure 9.15).

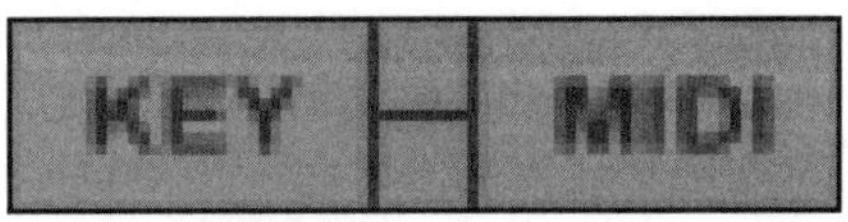

Figure 9.15 The Key and MIDI Map Mode switches.

These will allow you to assign MIDI controllers or keys on your computer's keyboard to control various parameters in Live, including launching Clips, adjusting Mixer controls, and manipulating VST software effects.

Making remote assignments like this is very important when configuring Live for a live performance, and this is why having an external MIDI controller is important for working with Live. You will find controlling everything with a mouse or trackpad too slow because you can only adjust one parameter at a time.

For example, you could map a number of Clip slots in the Session View to keys on your computer keyboard, and then use these keys to trigger the Clips in real time when you are performing. You could also assign the Clips to keys or buttons on your external MIDI controller.

The indicator boxes between the Key Map button and the MIDI Map button in the image above indicate when Live is sending or receiving controller messages.

To the right of the MIDI Map Mode button is the CPU meter, showing the current load on your CPU as a percentage (see Figure 9.16).

Figure 9.16 The CPU Meter.

Excessive CPU load may cause any number of problems and you should keep an eye on this now and then while you are performing.

Next to the CPU Meter and marked with a D is the Hard Disk Overload indicator, another important thing to watch when you are playing. This will light up red if Live cannot load audio from your hard drive in time to keep up with playback. This usually happens if you have too many Clips being recorded or played back from your hard drive at the same time. To compensate for this, you can assign individual Clips to load into RAM instead of stream from your drive. The more RAM you have, the more Clips can be played from RAM at once.

To the right of the Hard Disk Overload indicator are the MIDI Track In and MIDI Track Out indicator boxes. These indicators will flash when Live is sending MIDI from a track or receiving MIDI data into a track.

The Clip View

As mentioned above, when you first drag a clip from one of Live's File Browsers into either the Session or Arrangement View, you will see the Clip View window for that Clip open down at the bottom of the screen (see Figure 9.17).

Live's Clip View window is where you can view and adjust the properties of a Clip. To see the Clip View window for any existing Clip in your Live Set, simply double-click the Clip. Note that Figure 9.17 shows the Clip View for an audio Clip, but the properties of MIDI Clips can be viewed in this way as well.

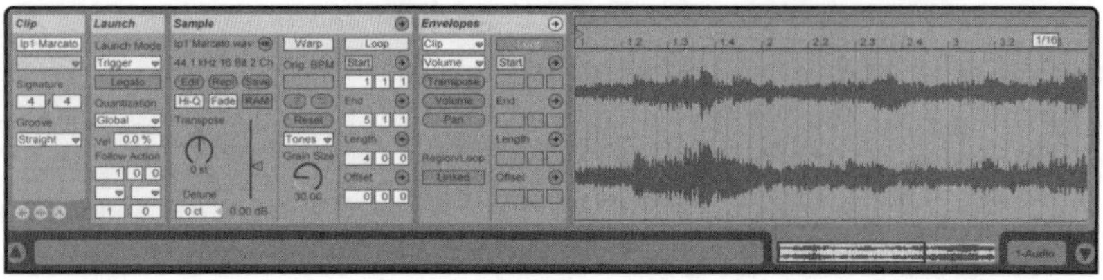

Figure 9.17 Return to the Clip View.

The Clip View window is divided into five sections. We can open or hide any of these sections by using the Clip View Box Selector buttons, located in the lower left-hand corner of the window.

The Clip Box

The first of these sections of the Clip View window is the Clip box (see Figure 9.18).

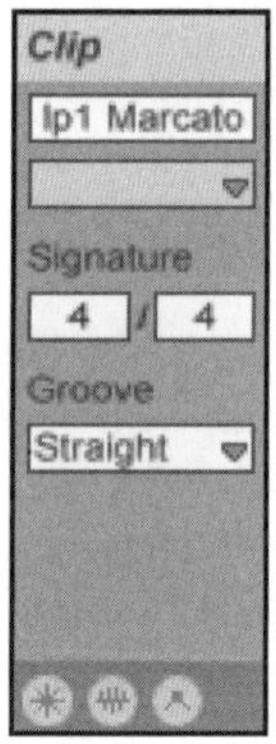

Figure 9.18 The Clip box in the Clip View.

The Clip box contains basic clip settings such as the name of the clip, the color used to represent it, its internal time signature, and the type of groove quantization that should be applied to it when we turn on the Control Bar's Global Groove function within our Live Set.

It is important to understand here that as always, any changes you make in Live are non-destructive and do not affect the actual audio files. Because of this, you can create any number of different Clips that refer to the same audio sample, giving each new Clip a unique name here in the Clip box, without affecting the actual audio sample located on your hard drive.

The Launch Box

Next we have the controls in the Launch box, which affect how a clip is launched when it is triggered (see Figure 9.19). Be aware this only applies to clips in the Session View; the Launch box does not appear in the Arrangement View.

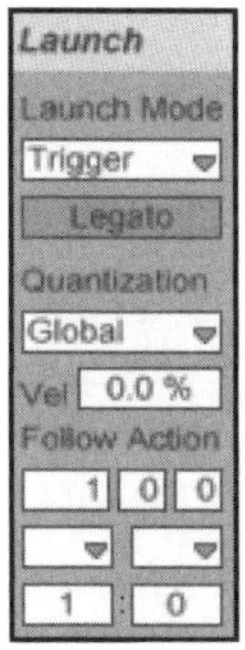

Figure 9.19 The Launch box.

The first selection to make here is the Launch Mode chooser box, which determines how MIDI up and down messages are interpreted for a particular clip. This setting can be important in preparing various live performance-oriented effects. There are four different modes that can be selected here: Trigger, Gate, Toggle, and Repeat. These affect the way the Clip will behave when you trigger it with an external MIDI controller.

In Trigger Mode, a MIDI down message starts a Clip playing back and MIDI up messages have no effect. This is what Clips in Live default to unless you change this in the preferences.

In Gate Mode, a MIDI down message starts playback of a Clip, while an up message stops it.

In Toggle Mode, MIDI up messages will have no effect. A Clip starts playing with the first MIDI down message, and will stop playing when it receives another down message. Thus, continued presses of a given MIDI key assigned to the Clip will toggle playback on and off.

In Repeat Mode, a Clip will be triggered repeatedly over and over again as long as the key or controller assigned to it is held down. The rate at which it repeats can be adjusted by the next setting, the Clip Quantization Chooser.

The button marked Legato toggles Legato Mode on and off. When a Clip with Legato Mode active is launched, it starts playing from whatever playback position the clip that was already playing in that track had reached. This sounds a bit confusing, but try it and you'll quickly see what I mean.

Legato Mode is also very significant for live performance because it allows you to rapidly switch back and forth between a number of different Clips without disturbing the overall rhythmic groove and sync. This is very useful for switching between multiple drum loops without interrupting the tempo, creating interesting changes and variations in the drum track.

These launch options are some of Live's most powerful features for live performance, allowing you to experiment with all kinds of creative ways to trigger samples on the fly during a show. I recommend loading up a sample and trying all of these in succession so you can understand better exactly what each mode does and how you can best take advantage of them.

Follow Actions

In the lower part of the Launch Box there are a number of small chooser boxes under the label "Follow Action." These are used to set up Follow Actions for a Clip, allowing you to create groups of clips that can trigger each other to play in sequence in a more or less unpredictable manner, depending on how they are configured. This unique function of Ableton Live can be put to a variety of powerful creative uses. As with many aspects of the program, complex variations can result from changing a few simple settings. This function has incredible possibilities for live performance, so let's take a closer look.

The Follow Actions enable you to create a group of Clips and set them up so that once you trigger the first one, each of the other loops will eventually be triggered as well in a kind of semi-unpredictable chain reaction. Once you trigger any one of these loops and start your Live Set in motion, each of them will sometimes repeat or sometimes trigger another loop in the group, creating endless subtle variations in the flow of the rhythm.

To understand how this works, let's look at how you could set up Follow Actions on a group of three drum Clips to create some complex rhythmic variations in performance.

As an example, I could create a group of drum Clips by dragging some drum loop samples from the File Browser onto a track in the Session View grid as seen in Figure 9.20.

Figure 9.20 A group of drum Clips in the Session View.

Note that these three Clips are in adjacent Clip Slots on the same Track, and that there is an empty Clip slot both above and below them; these things are what define them as a group. These three loops are each variations of the same basic pattern, which is why I have chosen them for this group. Now I want to set them up so that instead of just endlessly looping, they sometimes trigger each other in alternation, creating more variety in my live rhythms.

The first drum loop in the group is the main pattern, the simplest of the three. The second and third loops are more like fills or breaks.

Now here's what I'd like to do: When I launch the first clip, I want it to start looping for a while, and I want it to keep playing most of the time thereafter. However, I would like the other two loops to play once in awhile just for variety, and when they do, I would like them to sometimes play more than once before the main loop returns again. It is actually very easy to set this up in Live by using the Follow Actions.

There are three settings here in the Launch Box through which you can set the playback behavior of each Clip in the group, located just under the Follow Action label. The first setting is a time location expressed as bars, beats, and sixteenth notes. This is the Follow Action Time, and it sets the time during the playback of the Clip at which the selected Follow Actions will be applied. For my example, I am working with drum loop Clips that are four bars long and I want the Follow Actions to be applied at the end of one complete repetition, after four bars, so I would set this to four.

The next settings are the Follow Action choosers. These allow you to set two different possible Follow Actions for each Clip. If you click in the box, you will see the list of available Follow Actions. These are self-explanatory for the most part and you shouldn't have any trouble figuring out what they do. Basically you can set a Clip to play again, stop, or trigger one of the other Clips. The Previous and Next settings will trigger the previous or next Clips in the group, while the First and Last settings will trigger the first or last Clip. Choosing Any will cause one of the other Clips in the group to be triggered randomly.

Below the Follow Action choosers are the Chance A and Chance B controls. These set the chances that the Follow Actions will actually occur, and they are relative to each other. For example, if you set the first one to nine and the second one to one, Live will randomly choose the first action much more often than the second, approximately nine times out of ten.

For my example, I want the first Clip to repeat most of the time but sometimes trigger one of the other Clips. To accomplish this, I could set the first Follow Action chooser to Play Again, with a chance to be activated of three, and set the second one to Any, with a chance of one. So three times out of four, this loop will simply repeat again after it plays, but there is a one in four chance that it will trigger one of the other loops.

For the other two Clips in my group, I want the opposite behavior: I want them to repeat occasionally, but most of the time I just want them to play once and then go back to the main loop. To do this, I could set each of these two the same way: For the first Follow Action I could select Play Again, with a chance of one, and for the second Action I could select First, with a chance of three.

Set up like this, the main drum loop will probably repeat a few times after it is first triggered, and then eventually it will trigger one of the other loops. When one of the other, "fill" loops is triggered, it may repeat, but it will eventually trigger the first Clip again and begin the cycle all over from the start.

Obviously this is a fairly simple example, with only three Clips involved, but already, just through these simple settings, you can create some interesting and very usable variations in your drum tracks. By using more Clips and more Follow Actions, we can build up more complex structures if you want.

It is also important to remember that the Follow Actions settings you make are saved with the Clips, and you can easily make new groups simply by rearranging your Clips on the Session View grid.

As you can probably see already, although it is fairly simple to set up these Follow Actions, they are a very powerful creative tool. Besides adding interest to a rhythm track as we have seen, there are many other possible creative applications.

The Sample Box

The Sample box contains many settings that affect the audio sample and how it is played back (see Figure 9.21). I am not going to cover all of these settings in detail here, but there are a few that you should be particularly aware of as a live performer.

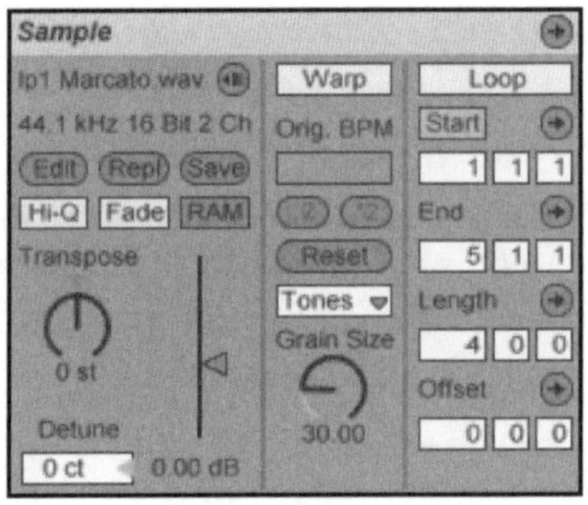

Figure 9.21 The Sample box.

First is the button marked Hi-Q, which activates Live's High Quality audio mode for that particular Clip. When High Quality mode is on, Live uses an advanced algorithm that provides better sound quality when doing audio transposition and sample-rate conversion on the Clip, but this will also use more CPU power in the process. In spite of the additional CPU load however, I nearly always select High Quality mode on my samples in order to get the best sound possible. This is one of the most important settings in order to get the best sound possible out of Live.

If you turn RAM Mode on by clicking the RAM button in the Clip View, Live will load the audio sample into the computer's memory rather than reading it off the hard disk during playback. This can be useful if you have too many tracks or clips for Live to playback at once and the disk overload indicator here is lighting up. However, of course, the number of samples you can load into RAM is dependent on the amount of RAM installed on your Mac or Windows machine.

The Reverse button, the leftward-facing arrow in a circular button just to the right of the sample name, is a feature added in Live 4 that allows you to quickly and easily reverse the sound you are playing back. When you click the Reverse button, Live will create a new sample with the same name as the original but with a letter R added to the end; this new sample will be a reversed version of the original sample and will be saved with your Live Set. In the case of very long samples, it may take a little while for Live to reverse the sound the first time you use this function.

MIDI Clips in the Clip View

The Clip View for a MIDI Clip is basically similar to that of an audio Clip, but with two differences: The Notes box replaces the Sample box, and the MIDI Editor appears to the right instead of the Sample Display (see Figure 9.22).

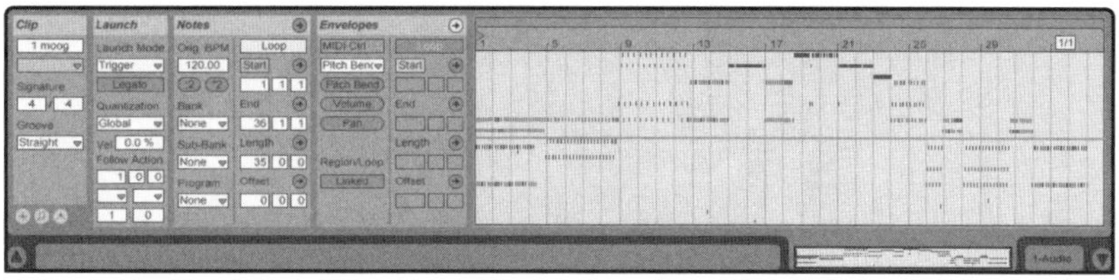

Figure 9.22 The parameters of a MIDI Clip displayed in the Clip View.

Within the Notes box, notice that there are Bank and Sub-Bank chooser boxes that allow you to send MIDI bank and program change messages to external MIDI devices such as synthesizers or samplers, obviously an important function for the live performer. This means that triggering a MIDI Clip can also send its bank and program change messages, so if you are triggering an external module, your MIDI Clips can carry the information of which sound to trigger, along with the note information they contain.

The Live Mixer

The Live Mixer allows you to mix signals together from various Clips and process them through effects before sending the result to the Master output. It is very important for you to have a solid understanding of how Live's Mixer works when designing and customizing your live performance setup, so I am going to cover the features of the mixer in detail.

The Mixer in the Session and Arrangement Views

First of all, there are two ways of viewing the Live Mixer, either vertically in the Session View or horizontally in the Arrangement View. Press the Tab key to toggle between the two viewing modes. These views present similar information about track volume, panning, muting, soloing, and so on, though it is laid out somewhat differently. For purposes of live performance you will usually be working with Live in the Session View, and I will concentrate here on working with this view.

You can choose what data is visible in the Mixer by using the View menu. Here you can choose to display or hide the Clips, Inputs and Outputs, Sends and Returns, Mixer controls, or the Crossfader. You can also use the buttons in the Mixer Section selector on the right-hand side of the screen to hide or display the mixer components.

Audio and MIDI Routing with Live's Ins and Outs

Now let's take a look at how to route the flow of audio and MIDI data into and out of Live. This is a very important topic to understand when you are setting up a Live Set for performance.

In Live, signal routing is handled in the Mixer's In/Out section, visible only in the Session View (see Figure 9.23). Each track has the same input and output routing options, with the exception of the Master track. To view the In/Out section in the Session View, simply choose In/Out from Live's View menu, or press the Control-Alt-I keys on a PC or Command-Option-I on a Mac.

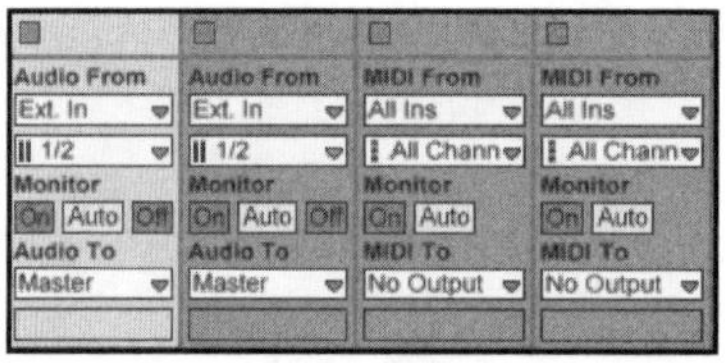

Figure 9.23 The In/Out section of the Live Mixer.

The In/Out section comprises a number of drop-down menus and buttons. The uppermost pair of menus, labeled Audio From or MIDI From, allow you to select the input source of the Track. The first menu lets you choose the signal category or source of the input, and the second menu lets you choose a specific input from that source.

For example, on an audio track, if you choose Ext. In (External Input) in the first Audio From drop-down box, you can select an input or input pair from your audio interface in the second box.

The next input choice here is any ReWire application you may have. This makes it possible to use additional ReWire-capable music software applications such as Reason in conjunction with Live. If you have Reason installed, choosing it at this point will make all of its 64 individual audio outputs available as individual input sources in Live. The default here is ½ Mix L, Mix R, which corresponds to Reason's main stereo output. If this option is selected, anything that is playing through Reason's main outs will be routed to the input of this particular track in Live.

Next is the Resampling input option. When this is chosen, the track will take Live's master output as the input source. This is a quick and easy way to record what you are doing in Live at any given moment and make it into a new Clip for use in future arrangements or performances.

Below the Resampling option you will see all of the other audio, MIDI, and Return Tracks in the arrangement, all of which are available as input sources as well, enabling you to easily record the output of any combination of other Tracks into one single Track.

On a MIDI track, the input options look a bit different. The default input choice for a MIDI Track is All Ins, the equivalent to the External In selection on an audio Track. This choice selects all external MIDI devices connected to your computer for input.

The next input choice is Computer Keyboard. This selects your computer's typing keyboard for use as a MIDI controller keyboard.

Next in the list is Configure, which opens up Live's MIDI/ Sync preferences and allows you to configure additional MIDI Input devices for use in Live. If the MIDI device you want to use is already connected to your computer but is not appearing here, you can use this option to make sure your MIDI preferences are configured correctly.

Your next MIDI input choices are any other MIDI tracks in the current Live Set. This option can be selected if you want MIDI notes playing on one Track to trigger another MIDI track that has a different MIDI instrument assigned to it.

After you select a MIDI input source in the first drop-down menu here, the second menu will give you the option of receiving input on all MIDI channels simultaneously, or selecting a single MIDI channel between one and sixteen for input instead. This feature can be very useful if you want to set up multiple MIDI controllers on one computer. By assigning each of them to different MIDI channels and assigning your Tracks in Live to only receive input on the same specific channels, you can use each MIDI controller to send data to a different Track in Live at the same time.

Below Live's input selectors are the Monitoring options. See Live's manual for more on these, but I recommend leaving them all switched to Auto (the default) for performance unless you are trying to set up a particular custom live monitoring setup for some reason.

Below the Monitoring section are the Track output menus, labeled Audio To or MIDI To. By default, all audio Tracks are routed to Live's Master output. Empty MIDI tracks are routed to "No Output" until a MIDI Instrument is assigned to the corresponding track; the track output then changes to an audio output and can be assigned just as the output from an audio Track.

Under the track output menu, you can choose Ext. Out (External Out) instead of Master, if you want. In the case of an audio Track, this allows you to directly route the output to a specific output or pair of outputs on your sound card. This can be useful for incorporating external effects into your live setup, for example, or for routing individual Tracks in Live to channels on an external mixer for greater control.

For example, one setup I have tried in the past was to connect outputs 5 and 6 of my M-Audio FireWire 410 audio interface to the inputs of my Korg Kaoss Pad, the outputs of which were then routed back to the main inputs 1 and 2 of the 410. Then I routed one of Live's Return Tracks to send audio to outputs 5 and 6, and I set up another audio Track to bring back the input from inputs 1 and 2 of my hardware interface. This setup allowed me to use the Kaoss Pad as an auxiliary effect on the Return bus, and I could send the output from any Track in my Live Set through the Kaoss Pad for processing by simply using the appropriate Send knob in the Live Mixer to send that Track's signal to the Return.

On a MIDI Track, you can also choose your MIDI interface in the MIDI To selector box. This will route all MIDI note data for that Track out through your MIDI interface to whatever MIDI synth or sound module you may have connected to it.

You can also route the output of a Track directly to another audio Track simply by choosing one of the available audio Tracks in the drop-down output menu. All audio Tracks in your Set will appear in this list as possible destinations for the audio.

One of the main reasons you would want to route the output of a Track to another Track like this is to create submixes. For example, if you have multiple drum and percussion Tracks in your Arrangement, creating a new Track and routing the output of all the drum and percussion Tracks to it will enable you to control all of the drum parts at once using the fader, pan knob, and other controls on the new drum submix Track.

To do this, first create a new track and name it Submix. Then, simply route the output of each of the drum tracks to the Submix track by choosing Submix in its Audio To drop-down menu. This concept can be very important in live performance, enabling you to control the output of many Tracks with a single controller on your MIDI device.

MIDI tracks also provide an additional output option. If you have a MIDI track with no MIDI or VST instrument assigned to it, you can route this data to another MIDI track instead.

The final output option for each track is "Sends Only." If this option is selected, the output of the track will only be available to Live's Return tracks, and nothing will be sent to the Master output. In this case, the amount of signal sent to the Return tracks is controlled by the track's appropriate Send knob, and the Track's volume fader will have no effect.

The Mixer Controls

Now let's look at the Mixer controls for each track, located below the input and output display (see Figure 9.24). These are similar in function to the controls of a standard analog mixer.

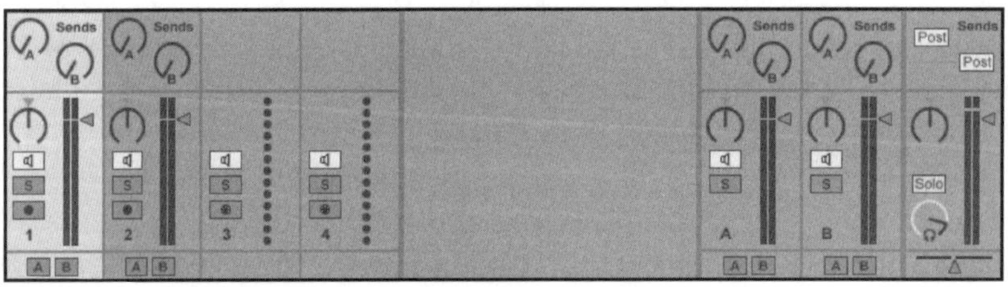

Figure 9.24 The Mixer track controls.

The Sends control specifies how much of a track's output is sent to the respective Return track.

The Meter control shows us the track's output level, adjustable by using the track's Volume fader.

The Pan control adjusts the track's left to right panning. You can reset this control to zero by clicking on the little orange triangle at top center.

The Track Activator switch is used to mute or activate the track.

The Solo switch solos the track by muting all the other tracks. Tracks will be soloed one at a time with the next one soloed muting the last in turn. However, you can change this by deselecting the Exclusive Solo option in Live's Preferences (located on the Misc page). You can also solo more than one track at a time by holding down the Control key (PC) or Command key (Mac).

The Solo buttons can also be used to activate Cueing if we toggle Live into Cue Mode using the Solo/Cue Mode switch located on the Master track. When you activate this, you will see the "S" Solo buttons turn into little headphone icons indicating that they are now Cue buttons (see Figure 9.25).

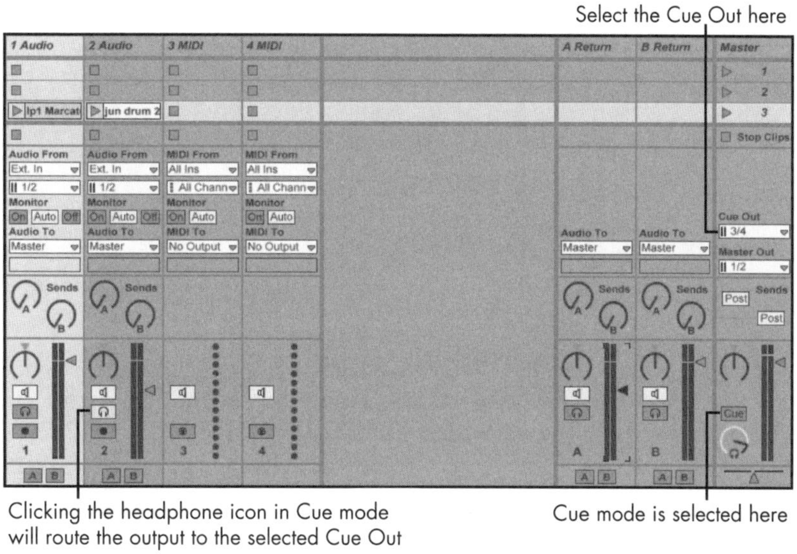

Figure 9.25 The Live Mixer in Cue Mode.

This Cue function in Live allows you to cue your Clips in headphones before introducing them into the main mix. See the next section on Sends and the Master output for more information on how this works.

The Sends and Returns

Live's Mixer also features Return tracks and associated Send knobs in addition to audio and MIDI tracks (see Figure 9.26).

These cannot host audio or MIDI clips but are used primarily for effects routing. There are a number of reasons you might want to do this:

- To make creative use of the Sends and Returns to add effects to your tracks in a live performance situation
- To conserve system resources by running just one copy of an effect on a Return channel and routing your audio tracks to it as opposed to creating multiple copies of the effect on each track, which is very CPU-intensive

Let's look at a few of the ways you can most effectively use the Returns in live performance.

Figure 9.26 The Return tracks.

When you first open a new Live Set, you will see this default setup: Two audio tracks, two MIDI tracks, two Return tracks, and one Master track See Figure 9.27.

For each audio or MIDI track, the Send knobs A and B control how much of the signal is sent to the corresponding Return tracks, A and B, in addition to the signal going to the Master (see Figure 9.28).

Note that the Return tracks have Pre/Post toggles that determine if the signals they receive from audio or MIDI tracks are sent before or after the respective mixer stage controls such as volume, pan, and so on. This can have an immense impact on the audio output. If this is set to Pre instead of Post, for example, then we will still hear the signal from this track through the Return even if the track's volume fader is all the way down. This can cause some big surprises in performance if you're not careful!

The most obvious use of these Sends and Returns is to use them just like the Auxiliary Effects Send bus on an analog mixer. This is the way I set up my iBook with my external MIDI controller for my live performances, so let's take a look at how this works.

First I set the effect I want to use on the Return track. For example, I usually use Live's built-in Ping Pong Delay as one of my effects for live performance. I select the Return track by clicking on its Track Name, then look in Live's built-in effects and click and drag the Ping Pong Delay onto the Return Track (see Figure 9.29).

Now, while the track is playing back, I can turn the Send knob up and down and it will send more or less of the signal to the Return track and through the Ping Pong Delay.

There are a number of reasons why you might want to route effects this way rather than inserting them into the individual tracks. In this example, I have set up the Ping Pong Delay

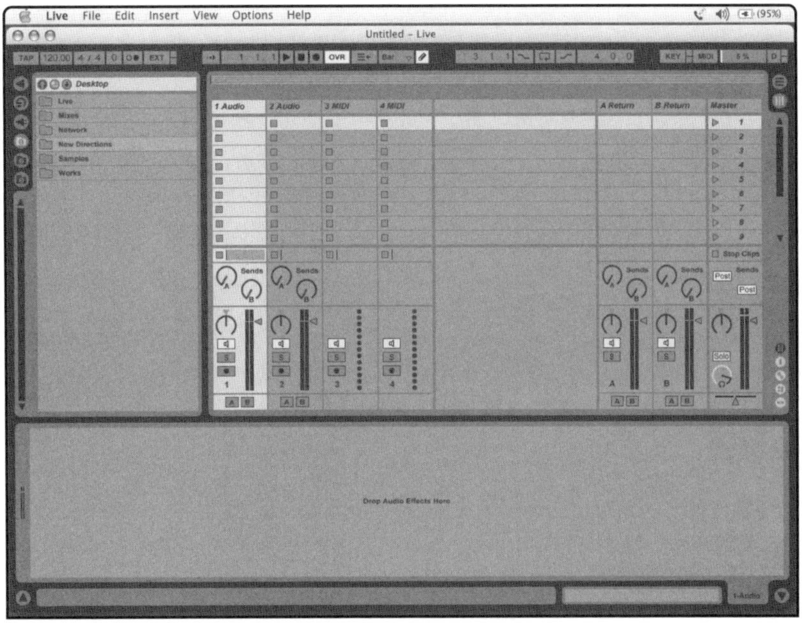

Figure 9.27 Live's default Live Set.

on one of the Return tracks of the Live Set I use for live performances because I use this effect quite often and I might like to apply it to any of the tracks I am playing at different points in my set. By creating just one Ping Pong Delay on Return A rather than one for each of my audio and MIDI tracks, I can more easily control the delay effect from my external MIDI controller in addition to conserving a lot of system resources.

Another helpful use of the Sends and Returns is to create a drum submix and compress it in order to make your live drum mix sound punchier or heavier. Let's look at how to set this up.

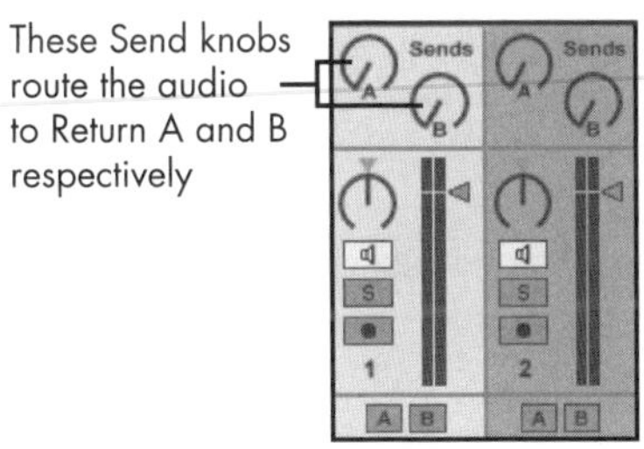

Figure 9.28 The Send knobs for each track.

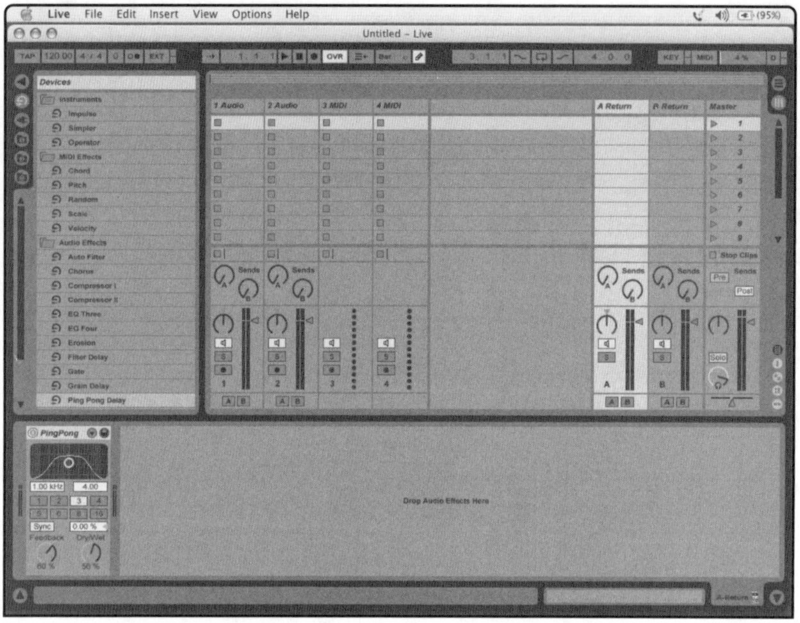

Figure 9.29 Inserting the Ping Pong Delay on Return A.

In Figure 9.30, I have set up two audio tracks for my drum loops. I have turned each track's Send B knob all the way up so that the full signal of will be sent to Return B. I have also set the Audio To chooser of each track to Sends Only, so that the signal of each will only be sent to the Returns and not directly to the Master output.

As you can see in the above image, I have placed Live's Compressor II effect on Return B. By adjusting the compression settings on this effect, I can get a fatter, more powerful drum sound without affecting other tracks that I don't want to compress so much, such as vocal tracks or ambient pads.

More specific information about how to set up effects in Live can be found below in the sections on audio and MIDI effects.

The Master Track

Live's Master track also has several important controls that you need to be aware of when you are configuring your Live Set for performance (see Figure 9.31).

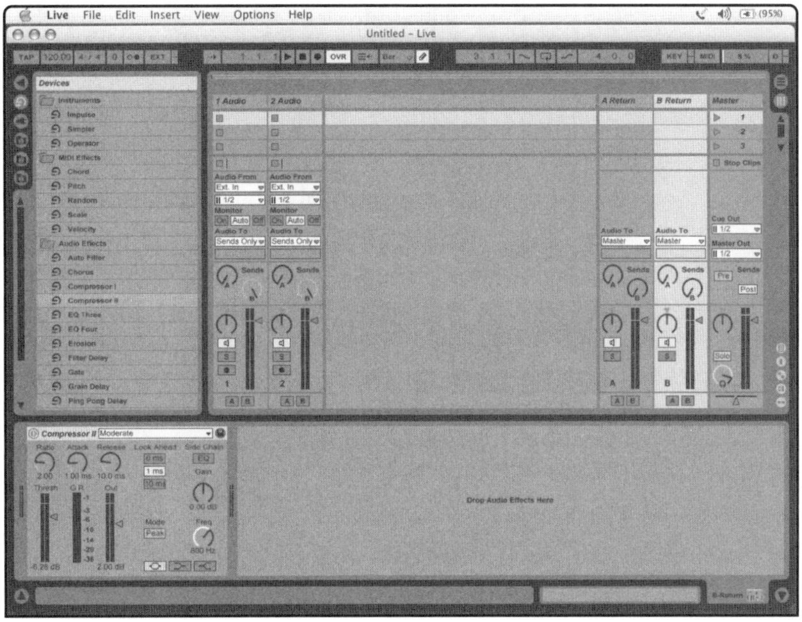

Figure 9.30 Setting up a drum submix on Return B.

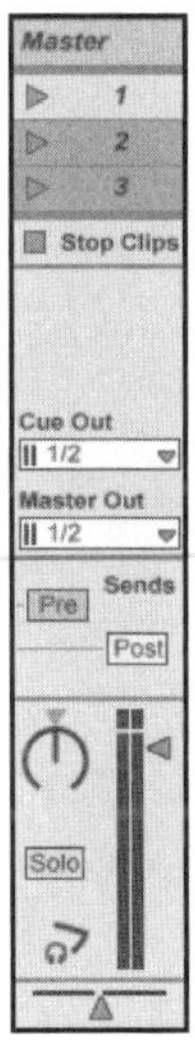

Figure 9.31 Live's Master track.

The Master Out chooser box lets you select which physical output on your audio interface to use for the main output.

The Cue Out chooser selects the output on your hardware interface to be used for headphone cueing. You must select a different output pair here than you are already using for the Master Out.

If you don't see all the outputs of your sound card available here, look in Live's Audio Preferences and click the Output Config button to make sure that all of your card's outputs are activated for use in Live.

The Cue Volume control changes the volume of the cueing output (i.e., your headphones in most cases).

The Solo/Cue button (set to Cue in the image above) determines whether you are in Solo or Cue Mode. When Solo mode is selected, you will see small "S" buttons on each track that function as Solo buttons. When Cue mode is selected, each of these will change to a small headphone icon instead (see Figure 9.32).

Figure 9.32 The headphone cueing button on an audio track.

This switch behaves just like the Track Activator switch, except that it routes the audio to the selected Cue output instead of Live's Master output. The main Track Activator button still controls whether or not the signal is sent to the main output, thus a track can be sent to both the Cue Out and Master Out at the same time.

If you are using Live with a multi-channel audio interface, this Cueing function can be used to listen to selected tracks in your headphones before you mix them into the main output, just like a DJ cueing up the next track on headphones while the last track is still playing. I use this feature at my live performances with my M-Audio FireWire Audiophile. The Audiophile also has a headphone A/B switch on the front so I can actually alternate between hearing the main mix or the cue mix in my headphones.

Note that when you have Cue Mode set up like this, clips auditioned within the File Browser will also be heard through the Cue Out instead of the Main Out.

You can also use Live's Master track to host plug-ins that modify the sound of your overall mix, such as a compressor/limiter, a loudness maximizer, or a harmonic exciter. In Figure 9.33, I have placed iZotope's Ozone 3 VST plug-in on the Master track to pump up my final output and add a bit of exciter to the high frequencies.

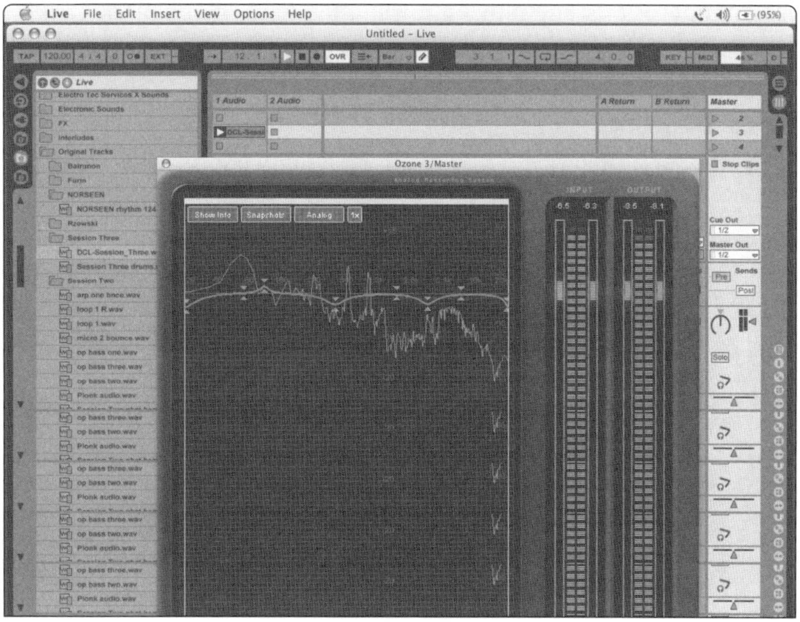

Figure 9.33 Using the iZotope Ozone 3 on the Master track.

More information about how to use effects in Live is found in the sections on audio and MIDI effects below.

The Crossfader

In addition to the other mixer controls, Live also includes a crossfader that can be used to create smooth transitions between tracks. Live's crossfader works like a typical DJ crossfader, and it allows you to mix from the tracks assigned to two separate groups, A and B. You can assign any of your tracks to either A or B by using these buttons at the bottom of the tracks, and you can then fade between the two groups using the crossfader, which can of course be assigned to an external MIDI crossfader or knob on your MIDI controller. Tracks that have not been assigned to group A or group B are not affected by the crossfader and will play on regardless.

You can use Live's crossfader to set up all kinds of interesting live performance applications. If you have ever DJed or used a DJ mixer to play live, you may already be familiar with the wide variety of DJ-style techniques you can perform with a crossfader. My Evolution X-Session MIDI controller has a DJ-style crossfader built-in, and I usually assign this to Live's crossfader when I play.

For example, one technique I like to use a lot is to set up some drum and percussion Clips playing and assign some of them to A and some of them to B. Then I can use the crossfader to cut back and forth rapidly between the two sets of rhythm Clips, while all the Clips remain playing in perfect sync.

If I have an ambient pad or bassline playing, I will often leave it unassigned. In this case it will keep playing on unaffected while the rhythms flip back and forth maniacally underneath.

Using Effects in Live

Live has quite a number of built-in audio and MIDI effects that can be inserted in your tracks to modify the output. You can also use third-party effect or instrument plug-ins in VST (PC and Mac) or AU (Mac only) format in your Live Sets.

Let's look at some of how to set these up. Remember, creative use of effects in Live can really add a lot to your live performance.

Audio Effects

To insert one of Live's built in audio effects in a track, first double-click the track's name at the top of the screen. This will open the Track View window for that track at the bottom of the screen (see Figure 9.34), and you will be able to see any effects or instruments already present on the track, if any.

Next, click on the small Ableton Live symbol at the left edge of the screen in order to open the Live Device Browser and show all the built-in effects and instruments available (see Figure 9.35).

Looking in the Audio Effects folder, we can see the list of built-in audio effects in Live, including filters, compressors, EQs, delays, and other interesting effects. Many of these can also be found in other software, but a few of them are unique to Live. Try using the Grain Delay for some wild granular synthesis-based sounds, for example.

To insert an effect on the selected track, simply click on the effect in the Device Browser and drag it to the Track View window. The effect will appear in the window as shown in Figure 9.35, and you can see and adjust all the parameters of the effect here.

If you have an external MIDI controller, you can easily assign your knobs or faders to control any of these effects parameters. Just click the MIDI button in the Control Bar to turn on Live's MIDI mapping function, click the parameter you want to control, and then move the external controller you want to assign to the parameter. When Live receives the MIDI input, you will see a small symbol appear which indicates which MIDI channel and controller number have

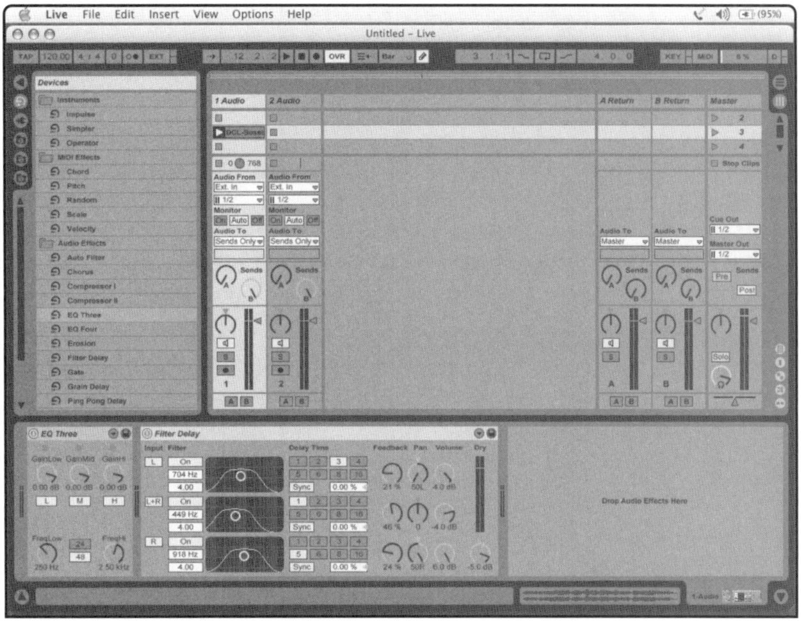

Figure 9.34 The Track View window.

been assigned to that parameter. Then click the MIDI button again to turn off the MIDI mapping mode.

You can keep adding as many effects as you want here in the Track View. The main limitation is the CPU speed of your computer. The CPU meter in the Control Bar gives us a constantly updated readout showing what percentage of your CPU resources you are currently using. Using a lot of effects on our tracks (particularly resource-intensive effects such as reverbs) can quickly eat into your available CPU resources, particularly on older and slower machines. If this meter starts running towards the top, at 80 or 90%, you will start to encounter some unpredictable problems such as stuttering or jerky audio playback. For this reason, you should always consider how to make best use of your system resources when you are designing a Live Set for performance, and don't use any plug-ins you don't actually need.

One good way to conserve CPU resources in Live to is to make good use of the Master track and the Return tracks, which can accept the input from several tracks and mix them together before going through an effects chain. For example, instead of using a reverb on each individual audio track, you could use just one reverb on a Return track and send the output from each track to that Return.

The signal flow in Live's effects chain flows from left to right, and there are small level meters before and after every plug-in in the chain showing us how strong the signal is at each point

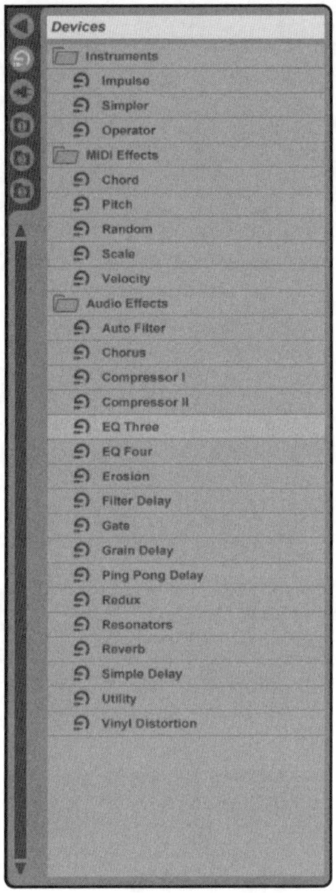

Figure 9.35 Live's built-in effects.

(see Figure 9.36). Basically, you want to make sure that you are getting a good strong signal level as the sound is passed from effect to effect in the chain.

Don't worry about running these too hot and peaking the signal. While it *is* important not to peak the Mixer's volume faders or the Master fader since this may cause digital distortion, there is infinite headroom in the effects signal chain, so you don't need to worry about peaking the meters here. The purpose of these meters is simply to show you what is happening to your signal at each point in the chain, whether it is getting stronger or weaker or dropping out entirely.

For example, if you can't hear anything from a particular track, it may be because the sound is being filtered down to nothing by one of the effects. Looking at these meters can tell you how far the audio is getting in the chain before it drops out.

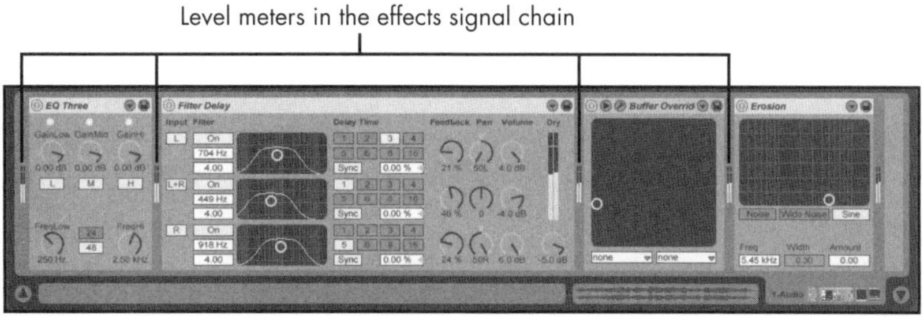

Figure 9.36 The effects signal chain in Live.

When inserting additional effects, the order in which they are placed in is very important; this will make a big difference to the final sound. You can click and drag the effects around in the Track View window to rearrange them and experiment with various combinations.

You can remove a device from the effects chain by clicking on it and pressing Delete.

Use the Activator switches at the upper left-hand corner of each effect to turn it on or off. When an effect is turned off, it does not consume any of your CPU resources, so you can switch some effects off to temporarily reduce CPU usage if you are experiencing performance issues.

If you place so many effects in the chain that you can't see them all in the window at once, you can use the scroll bar at the bottom to move back and forth and see different parts of the chain.

Built-In MIDI Effects

In addition to its audio processing capabilities, Live also has a number of built-in MIDI effects that can be inserted in your MIDI tracks to modify their playback, allowing you to alter the pitch, velocity, or other parameters of your MIDI Clips in performance.

There are also three built-in MIDI instruments you can use for playing back your MIDI Clips: Simpler, which basically does the same thing as a sampler (hence the name); Impulse, which is like a software drum machine; and Operator (available as a paid upgrade to Live), Ableton's FM-based software synthesizer.

You can place MIDI effects or instruments in any MIDI track in your Live Set. However, you need to understand the order in which they must be connected. Here's how it works.

MIDI Clips play back MIDI note and controller data, and this MIDI data can be modified by applying MIDI effects. MIDI effects must come first in the signal chain on a MIDI track.

For example, in Figure 9.37 I have inserted the Scale MIDI effect on a track in order to modify the pitch data of the track's Clips as they play back.

Next in order are MIDI instruments. After your MIDI data has run through whatever MIDI effects you have inserted in the track (if any), the data then needs to pass to a MIDI instrument

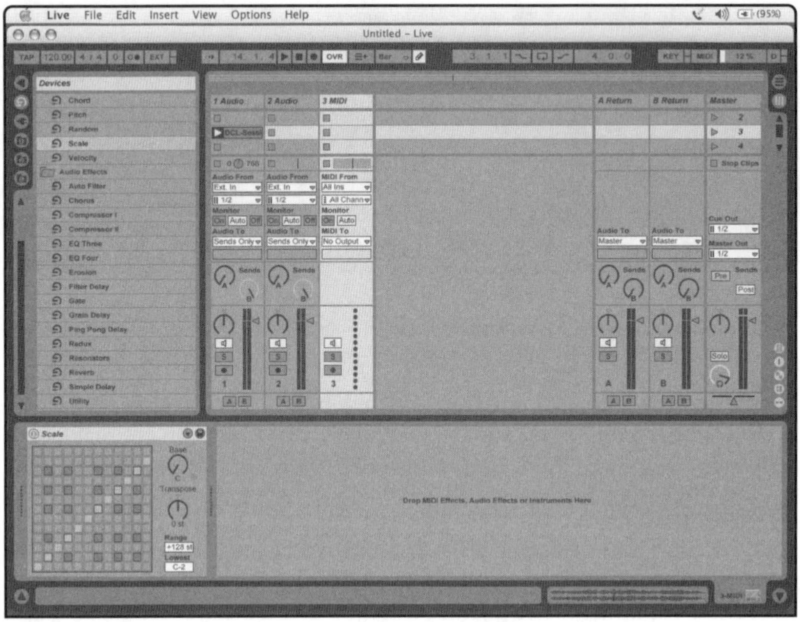

Figure 9.37 Inserting the Scale MIDI effect on a MIDI track in Live.

to actually trigger sounds that we can hear. In Figure 9.38, I have inserted a copy of Impulse after the Scale MIDI effect and loaded one of Live's built-in drum kits as sound sources.

In addition to Live's built-in MIDI instruments, you can also use other VST or AU MIDI instruments in Live. (See the next section for more on how to use VSTs and AUs in Live.) Even a powerful software synthesizer like Native Instruments' Reaktor can run smoothly inside Live as a plug-in MIDI instrument, and receive MIDI input data from Live's MIDI clips and effects.

After our MIDI data has triggered the playback of audio via a MIDI instrument, we can then insert any audio effects to complete the signal chain. In my example setup here, I have added Live's Compressor II effect next in the chain to fatten up the sound of the drum sounds coming out of Impulse, and then placed the Ping Pong Delay at the end of the chain. In performance I might assign the activator switch of the delay to a button on my MIDI controller and then turn it on only when I want to trigger some special delay effects at the right moment in my set.

Live's MIDI effects are placed in tracks in the same way as audio effects. Double-click the track's name at the top of the screen to select it, then click on the small Ableton Live symbol at the left edge of the screen in order to open the Live Device Browser. Looking in the MIDI Effects folder, you can see the list of built-in MIDI effects (see Figure 9.39).

To insert an effect on the selected track, simply click and drag it to the Track View window. For example, in Figure 9.40 I have inserted the Velocity effect on a MIDI track.

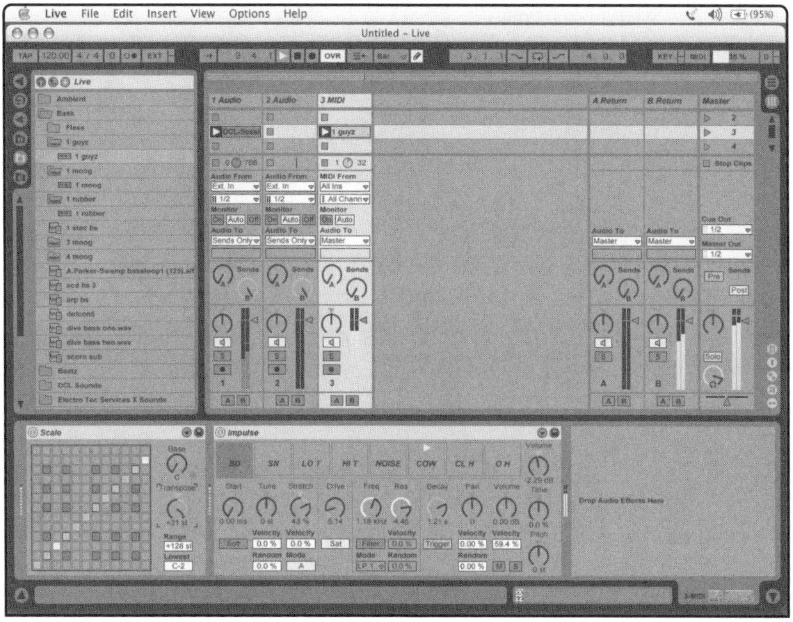

Figure 9.38 Placing Impulse next in the signal chain.

This MIDI effect works in a similar fashion as an audio compressor; however, instead of compressing the actual output signal volume, it merely limits the MIDI velocity values to a narrower range. This is quite useful for making a MIDI drum loop sound more solid, for example.

If you have an external MIDI controller, you can easily assign your controller knobs and faders to modify various MIDI effects parameters by using Live's MIDI mapping mode, just as with audio effects.

You can keep adding as many MIDI effects as you want. The main limitation here is the CPU speed of your computer. However, MIDI effects take much less CPU power than audio effects.

Some MIDI instruments, on the other hand, can require much more processing power, and the number of MIDI instruments we can use simultaneously in our Live Set is significantly limited by system resources. Live's built-in MIDI instruments, Simpler, Impulse, and Operator, seem

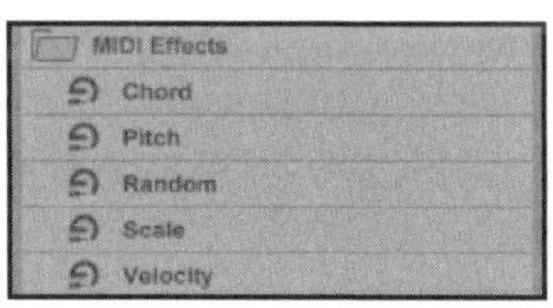

Figure 9.39 Live's built-in MIDI effects.

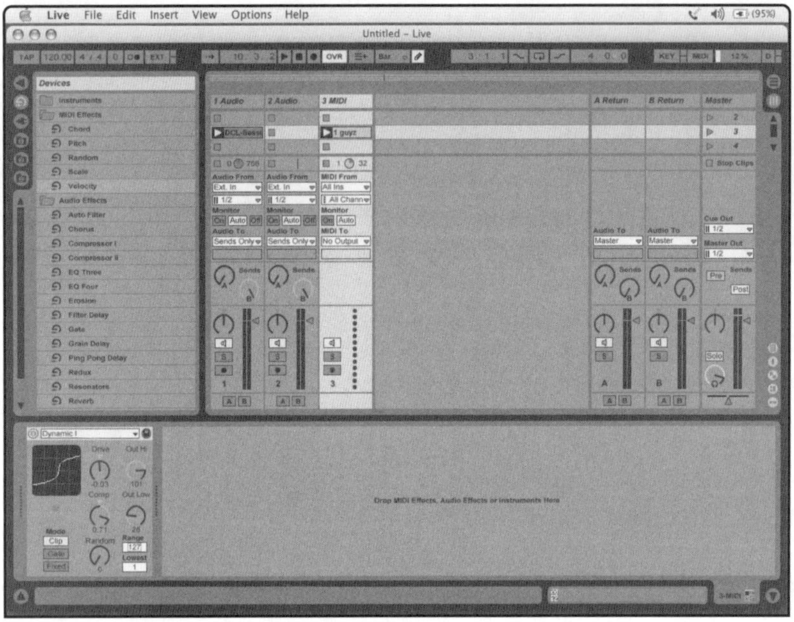

Figure 9.40 Inserting the Velocity effect on a MIDI track.

to require relatively less CPU resources than some "heavier" third-party instruments, and this can be an important consideration in setting up a Live Set for performance.

For example, when I am performing with Suspect.Seen (a laptop duo project with Sariah Storm), I focus on playing beats and rhythms on my computer while Sariah mixes ambient sound textures and effects. I play a lot of MIDI drum patterns when I play with Sariah, and when we first started doing live gigs together, I experimented with using Native Instruments' popular Battery drum sampler as the sound source for my MIDI drum loops (see Figure 9.41).

However, I don't have a lot of raw power to spare on my 1GHz iBook G4, and I soon found that if I tried to do very much with Battery while I was playing live, I would often run into performance problems. I later switched to using two or three copies of Live's Impulse drum sampler instead; this configuration seemed to use less CPU power and run better than even one instance of Battery.

Just as with audio, the MIDI signal flow in Live is from left to right, and there are small MIDI level meters before and after every plug-in in the Live signal chain registering the MIDI signal at each point. In the case of MIDI tracks, these will register a signal reading if MIDI data is being passed through from the Clip and through each MIDI effect before being passed finally to a MIDI instrument and generating audio.

Figure 9.41 Native Instruments' Battery drum sampler running as a plug-in in Live.

Plug-In Effects and Instruments

As I just mentioned in passing, you can expand Live's capabilities by using third-party plug-in effects and instruments (like Battery) in either VST (PC and Mac) or AU (Mac only) formats. This opens up access to hundreds of additional effects and instruments for use in Live, vastly increasing your options for performance.

Inserting a third-party plug-in effect in a track works the same way as using one of Live's built-in effects. First click on a track's Track Title Bar to select it; then click on the small plug symbol at the left edge of the screen to open the Plug-in Device Browser, showing all the VST and AU plug-in effects and instruments you have available on your system for use in Live. Effects will appear here with a small plug icon, while instruments will have a keyboard icon. To insert a plug-in on the selected track, simply click on it and drag it to the Track View window.

If you don't see your preferences available here when you first start Live, you may need to check Live's plug-in preferences and make sure they are configured correctly. To check this, open Live's preferences and click the tab labeled Plug-In. Then you will see the Plug-in preferences page (see Figure 9.42).

Let's look at how to activate your VST plug-ins first.

If you are using Windows, check the Use VST Plug-in Custom Folder setting and set it to On. Below this, next to where you see VST Plug-in Custom Folder, click the button that says Browse.

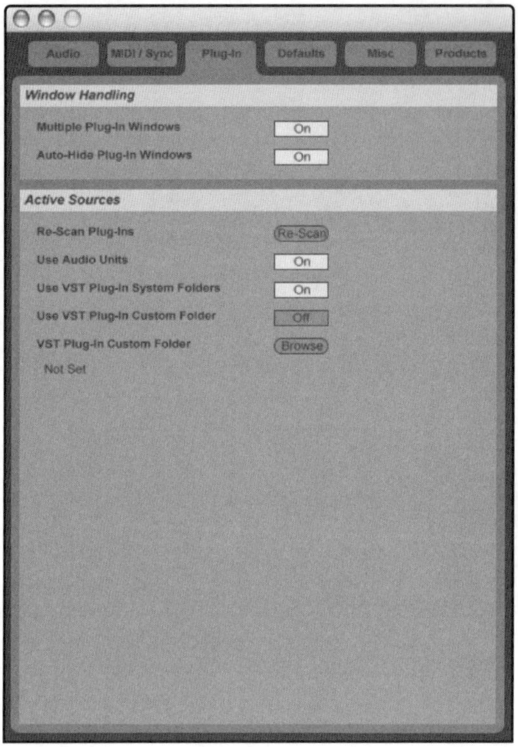

Figure 9.42 Live's Plug-in preferences.

This will open a file browser dialog box where you need to specify where your VST plug-ins are saved on your computer.

Sometimes Windows will already know the location of the VST plug-in folder and it will be chosen here automatically when you first check it. If not, you can simply browse to the correct folder and select it. In most cases, your VST plug-ins will be installed in the folder Program Files → Steinberg → Vst Plug-ins unless you have previously set up a custom location for this yourself.

In Mac OS X, the default location for your VST plug-ins is the folder Library → Audio → Plug-Ins → VST on your main system hard drive. If your VST plug-ins aren't showing up in Live, try clicking the Re-Scan Plug-ins button. If this doesn't work, double-check the folder indicated above to make sure your VST plug-ins have been installed in the proper location.

On the Mac, you also need to make sure that the setting labeled Use Audio Units is set to On in order to make your AU plug-ins available in Live as well.

When using third-party plug-ins in Live, you may notice that they look different in Live. The original graphic interface of each plug-in is replaced in the Track View window by the standard Live effects interface, just like the interface used by Live's built-in effects (see Figure 9.43).

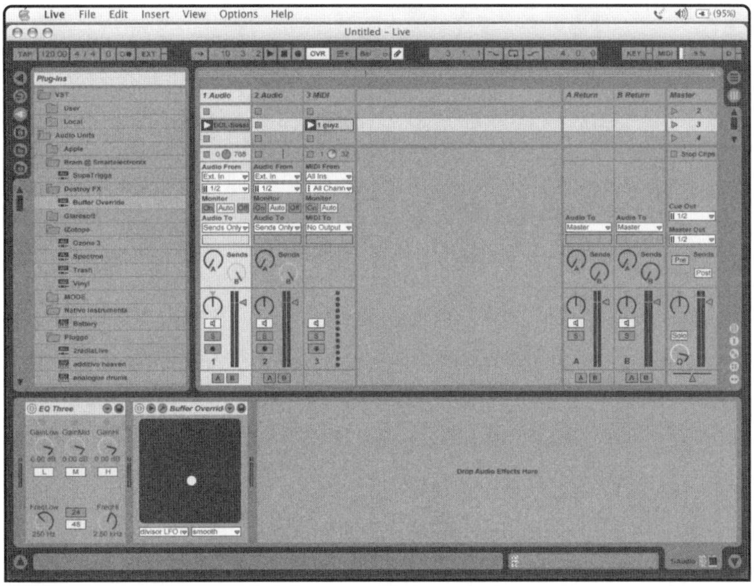

Figure 9.43 The DestroyFX Buffer Override Plug-in as it is displayed within Live.

However, you can still see the plug-in's original graphics by clicking the small wrench icon at the top edge of the plug-in window. This will open a new plug-in window floating above the main Live window (see Figure 9.44). This window will float on top of the main Live window until you close it.

If you click the small triangular button on the top edge of the plug-in's Live interface, a wider display will open, showing all the parameters of the effect (see Figure 9.45).

If you have an external MIDI controller, you can use this interface to easily assign various controller knobs and faders to modify effects parameters in Live, just as with Live's built-in devices.

However, note that you cannot use Live's key and MIDI mapping functions to assign controllers to the plug-in settings when you are working in the pop-up window containing the plug-in's original interface. Controllers can only be assigned to the parameters as they are visible in Live's interface.

Now let's move on and look at some more performance-oriented applications of Live.

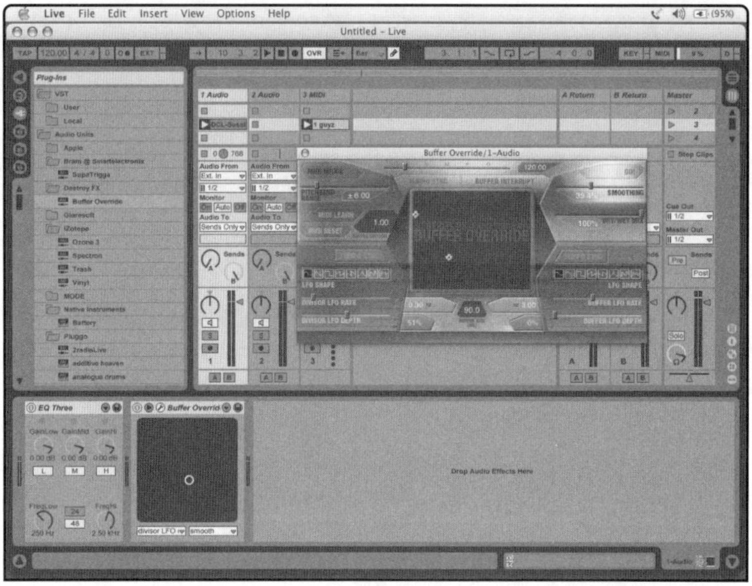

Figure 9.44 The original interface of the DestroyFX Buffer Override plug-in, displayed in a floating pop-up window in Live.

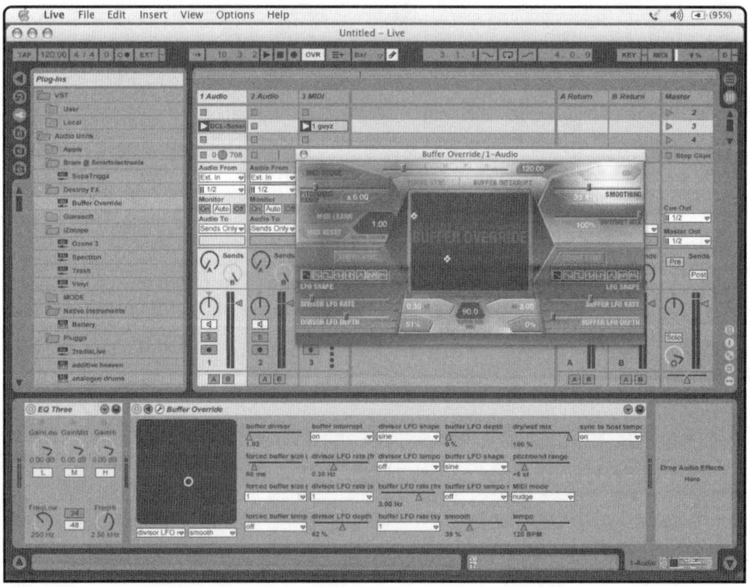

Figure 9.45 Expanding the Live interface to show all the assignable parameters of the DestroyFX Buffer Override plug-in.

10 Performing with Ableton Live

Let's move on now with our exploration of Ableton Live and look at some techniques that are especially useful for live performance.

Working with MIDI Instruments Live

Many computer music performers use Ableton Live primarily to mix together an assortment of audio Clips that they have created. In fact, earlier versions of Live (before version 4) had no MIDI functions at all and could only handle working with audio material.

However, the introduction of MIDI functionality with the release of Live 4 has opened up a variety of new performance possibilities. In particular, using MIDI software instruments such as synths or drum machines in your Live Sets offers you the ability adjust a variety of parameters in live and make your performances more dynamic. Let's look at how you can set this up.

Once you have inserted a MIDI instrument, it will appear in the Track View window. In Figure 10.1, I have inserted one of the mode software synthesizers from Cycling '74 on a MIDI track.

There are two main ways to use a MIDI instrument live: You can either play it directly with a keyboard or other external MIDI controller, or you can trigger it with MIDI Clips in your Live Set while adjusting some of its assignable parameters to alter the sound.

If you want to use a MIDI instrument for live playback with a keyboard, first make sure that your keyboard controller is selected in Live's MIDI/Sync preferences in the Remote Control section. Then, after you have inserted a MIDI instrument into a track in Live, you need to click the track's Record button so that the live MIDI input from your keyboard triggers the MIDI instrument you want to use.

Whether you are playing notes on an instrument live or triggering it with notes from a MIDI Clip, you may also want to control some of its parameters live with your controller. Clicking the small triangular button at the top edge of this plug-in window will reveal all assignable parameters for that particular plug-in in the Track View window (see Figure 10.2).

Figure 10.1 A mode software synthesizer inserted in a MIDI track.

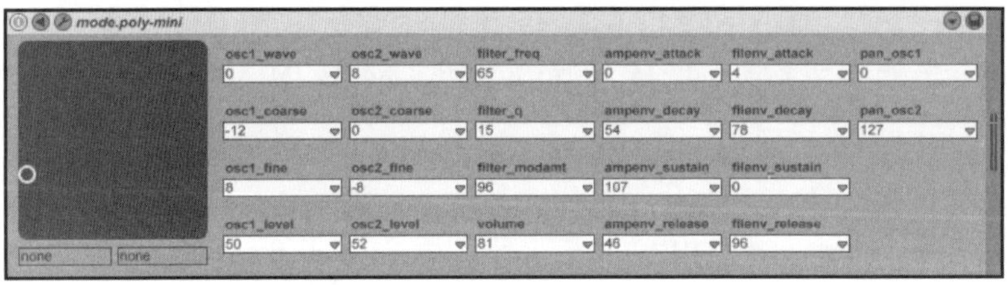

Figure 10.2 The assignable parameters of the mode software synth.

When working with MIDI instruments live, remember that you can use the Device Activator button in the upper left-hand corner of the interface to make each instrument active or inactive. When a plug-in is inactive it doesn't consume any system resources, and this can be an important point to keep in mind when configuring your Live Set.

For example, you may have a number of different powerful MIDI instruments that you want to use in your performance, but your computer may not be powerful enough to run all of them at the same time. In this case, you can simply insert all the instruments you want and configure them so they are ready to use, but only make the one you want to use at a given time active. I sometimes assign the buttons on my X-Session controller to these Device Activator switches so I can easily turn various instruments and/or effects on and off when I play, always paying close attention to how high I am pushing the CPU meter in the upper right-hand corner of Live's Transport Control Bar.

In the row of buttons below the Device Title bar, you will find a drop-down chooser box that lets you choose between an instrument's various preset sounds (see Figure 10.3). Use this to quickly switch between different patches in performance.

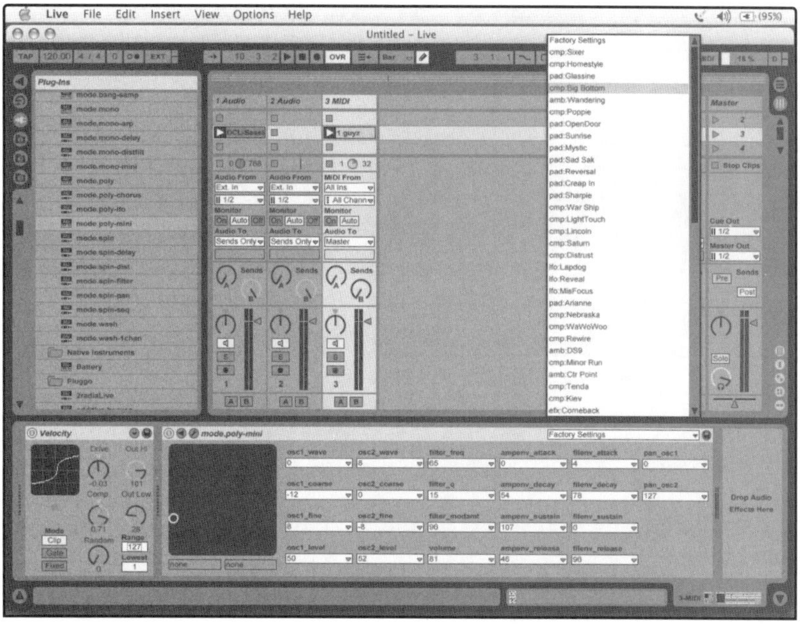

Figure 10.3 Selecting presets from the mode software synthesizer.

You can also use the two small buttons to the left of this chooser to save new presets that you have created or load presets you have saved previously.

The XY Controller

As you have no doubt noticed already, the left-hand part of Live's instrument interface is occupied by a large black square with a dot inside it. This is the assignable XY controller window. The XY controller allows you to control any two parameters of an instrument or effect by using this graphical interface. This can be a very powerful technique for performance, so let's look at how to use it.

By using the two pull-down menus below the XY controller, you can select which of the instrument's parameters you want to control here. Once these parameters have been assigned, you may control them both simultaneously in real time by moving the dot in the XY controller around the controller window. There are all kinds of possibilities here, depending on what kind of instrument you are using, so you need to experiment with various parameters yourself to figure out which ones can create the effects you want when played live.

In many cases, it can be helpful here to have some understanding of how synthesizers and samplers actually work when you are trying to determine which parameters would be most effective to control live.

For example, I have learned from experience that two of the most dramatic synthesizer parameters to control live are the filter and resonance controls, which may appear in different configurations within different software synths. In Figure 10.4, I have set the XY controller in Live to control the filter and resonance parameters of the Cycling '74 mode synth.

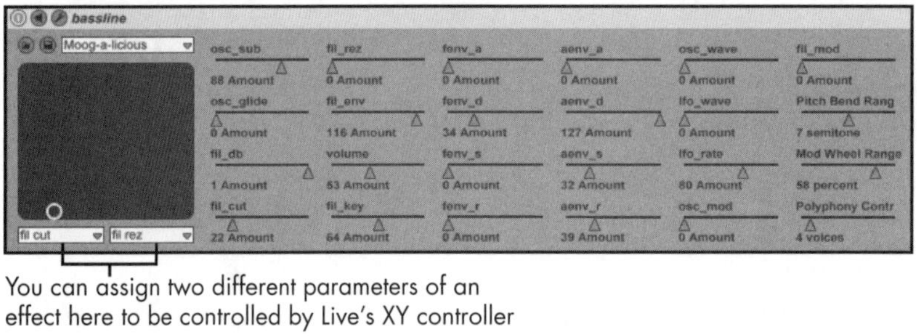

Figure 10.4 Assigning parameters in Live's XY controller.

Try assigning and controlling the filter and resonance controls in any software synths you may use to create some dramatic effects.

Live's Built-In MIDI Instruments

As mentioned above, you can use all kinds of third-party VST and AU software instruments in your Live Sets. However, Live's own built-in instruments provide you with a set of simple and powerful software tools already, so let's look at how you might use Simpler, Impulse, or Operator in performance.

Simpler

Simpler is Live's simple built-in audio sampler (see Figure 10.5). It can play back samples as well as having some of the processing capabilities of a synthesizer. You can load an audio sample into Simpler and then use its processing controls to apply envelope, filter, LFO, volume, and pitch changes. Triggering samples live in Simpler with an external keyboard or other MIDI controller can be an exciting performance technique, so let's take a look at how to set this up.

The window at the top of Simpler is the Sample View window. The Sample View displays a waveform, or graphic representation of any sample you load into Simpler. To load a sample into Simpler for playback, simply drag an audio sample from one of Live's File Browsers or a Clip from the Session or Arrangement Views onto this Sample View window and you will see its waveform appear here.

Just below the Sample View are the sample controls, which determine how the sample is to be played back when you trigger it. The Start control defines where you want the sample to

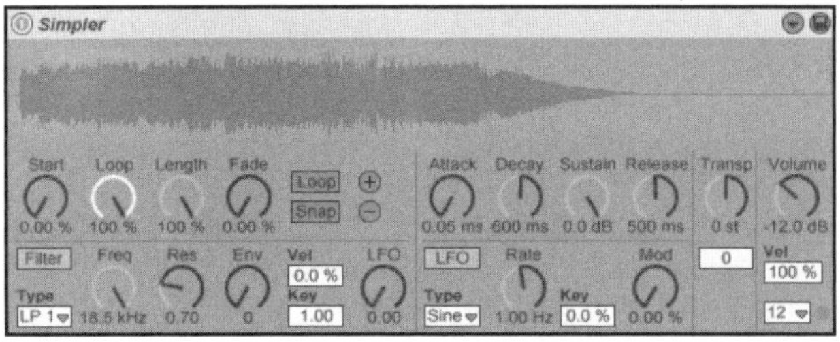

Figure 10.5 Simpler.

begin and the Length control defines how long you want it to play before it stops. These are both expressed in percentages of the total length of the sample.

For example, if you want the sample to start playing a quarter of the way from the beginning of the original sample, set Start to 25%. If you want it then to stop playing halfway through the original sample, set Length to 50%. As you change these parameters, the active part of your loop will be highlighted in the Sample View (see Figure 10.6).

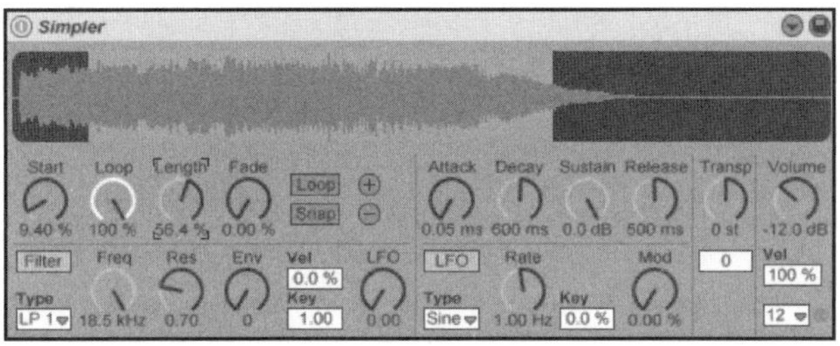

Figure 10.6 Changing the Start and Length parameters.

The control located between Start and Length is the Loop control. This is used in conjunction with the Loop button, located just to the right of the Fade control.

You can use these controls to set whether or not you want your sample to continue playing back in a loop if you continue to hold down its MIDI trigger. If the Loop button is inactive, Simpler will view the sample as a one shot and play it from beginning to end once when it is triggered. If the Loop button is active, Simpler will treat the sample as a loop. The Loop control can then be used to define the length of the loop. Experiment with these to see what kinds of sounds you can get by looping different parts of a long sample, for example.

The Fade control activates an automatic crossfade for smoothing transitions between the beginning and the end of a playing loop. This can be very helpful when you are looping a sample and want the loop to sound seamless.

Just to the lower right of the Fade control is the Snap button. Sometimes adjusting loops points can cause glitches or artifacts in the audio due to mismatched start and stop points, or differences in volume and dynamics in the sample. When the Snap button is active, any

Start, Loop, and Length adjustments you make will automatically snap to the nearest zero-crossing, a safe place for the parameter to be set, in order to keep your audio free of glitches and artifacts.

To the right of the Loop and Snap Buttons are plus and minus buttons. These will let you zoom in and out for a better view of the currently selected area of your sample.

Simpler also includes envelope, filter, LFO, and other controls that can affect the sound of your sample as it plays back. All of these can be assigned to external MIDI controllers as well. Consult the Live manual for more information on how these work.

Impulse

Impulse is a drum-oriented sampler that allows you to load up to eight different drum samples and process them using its built-in filter, envelope, saturation, time-stretching, panning, and volume controls (see Figure 10.7).

Figure 10.7 Impulse.

Although Impulse is ideally suited for use as a drum sample player, it can be used to hold a bank of any eight samples and play them back in any combination when triggered by an external MIDI controller. This can be very useful in live performance: Use it to hold any eight samples that you want to trigger live while other loops or textures are playing at the same time on the Session grid. Impulse is also a perfect match for MIDI sample trigger controllers like the M-Audio Trigger Finger or the Korg Kontrol49.

At the top of the Impulse interface you'll see eight cells or sample slots. This is where you will load your drum samples. For purposes of control by an external MIDI controller, the sample slots are automatically set to the eight white keys on your keyboard beginning with the pitch C3 (or middle C). Thus C3 D3 E3 F3 G3 A3 B3 C4 is the complete set of pitches that will trigger the slots in Impulse. If you are trying to trigger sounds in Impulse but are hearing nothing, you may be playing some other pitches that do not match these.

Just as with Simpler, you can load a sample into one of Impulse's slots by clicking and dragging an audio sample from one of Live's File Browsers or an audio Clip from the Session or Arrangement Views. Then you should see the name of the sample appear in the slot it was dragged into.

When you roll over a sample slot with the cursor, a triangular play button accompanied by two small rectangles will appear. You can click on the play button to hear the sample that is loaded in that slot. This is useful for auditioning samples, but if you are using Impulse live, this method of triggering is usually not accurate enough to be useful.

The rectangle to the left of the play button will mute the sample. The rectangle on the right side of the play button will solo it. If you can't hear some of the samples you have loaded into Impulse, it may be because one of them is soloed, thus muting the rest.

You can modify the sound of each of these eight samples individually by using the parameter controls below the sample slots. For example, if you click on the leftmost sample slot, it will be highlighted. Now any changes made to the parameters below will only affect the selected sample. If you click on the next sample slot to the right, you will then move to modifying its sound, and so on. These controls affect various aspects of sample playback including the start point, tuning, time-stretching, dynamics, filter settings, envelope, panning, and so on.

At the far right of Impulse, there are also a few global parameter controls that affect the playback of all eight samples loaded into the instrument, including master volume and pitch controls as well as a Time control that allows you to adjust the time stretching and decay of all samples simultaneously.

Warping and Syncing Samples in Live

Another of the most powerful and unique features of Live is its ability to play all audio samples in sync with the tempo of your Live Set. This is accomplished by setting "Warp Markers" at particular points in a sample. In addition to syncing the tempo of your samples, these Warp Markers can also be used to "warp" or alter a sample's rhythmic flow. See Figure 10.8.

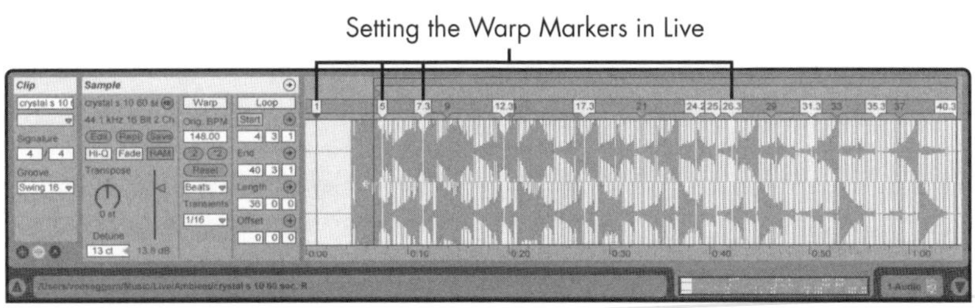

Figure 10.8 The Sample View showing Live's Warp Markers.

In order to mix together a set of samples and tracks for a live performance, you will usually want to make sure that they all play back in sync so everything will work together rhythmically. In order to do this, you will need to do a little preparation first as far as checking tempos and setting Warp Markers.

Whereas in a digital DJ application like Traktor you can just drop in a track and use the application's built-in beat-syncing functions and keyboard controls to nudge it into sync with whatever is already playing, in Live you do all the work of synchronizing your beats and riffs beforehand, while you are preparing for your performance at home. Then when you go out to play, all you have to worry about is the order, arrangement, and mixing of your clips; as long as they have been properly prepared and warped beforehand, they will be always be in perfect sync whenever you drop them into your Live Set.

Here's how the Warp Markers work: As an audio sample plays back and loops, the Warp Markers force specific points in the sample to be played back at specific musical times. You can use any number of Warp Markers to alter the rhythmic flow of a sample, to better fit the feel of the other samples in a Session or to create entirely new rhythms.

When you bring a new audio sample into Live by dragging it from a File Browser, Live will try to calculate the original tempo. It will usually be correct, as long as the original sample is already cleanly cut and edited into an even loop, for example, in a two- or four-bar pattern. Many samples from commercial CD-ROMs are already cut into even loops in this way, so they can be used as loops in Live with no additional preparation.

In order to play the loop in sync with the tempo of your Live Set, two Warp Markers will be automatically placed at the beginning and the end of a sample when it is first dragged into a Live Set. These Warp Markers are visible in Figure 10.8 in the Sample View.

The Loop Bar above the sample indicates the length of time that will be played as a loop if the Loop button is engaged.

The number labeled Orig. BPM shows us the estimated loop tempo that Live has conveniently calculated for us. Often if the tempo is off it will be wrong by a factor of 2, half or double. You can easily fix this by clicking the two buttons below: Use the *2 button to double the tempo and the :2 button to halve it.

The Reset To Default button restores all Warping settings back just as they were when the sample was first dragged into the Live Set from a File Browser window.

On the other hand, if you drag a sample into Live that is *not* cut into an even loop, it will play back out of sync with the other loops in your Live Set. In this case, you need to move the Warp Markers around manually by clicking on them and dragging them to match up with the rhythm of the sampled loop. Even if the beats of your sample are uneven, such as in a poorly played drum loop, you can compensate by placing Warp Markers on each beat or subdivision of a beat. Live will then pull everything into sync as it plays.

You can create as many Warp Markers as you want by clicking on the grid markers in the Sample window of the Clip View. You may need to create more Warp Markers in cases where you have a sampled loop with an uneven rhythmic flow. Just remember that you can place as many Warp Markers as you need on the beats of a sample in order to make it sync with the other Clips you are using.

Note that Warping and syncing your Clips with Live's Warp Markers is not a completely transparent audio process. The more drastically you alter the playback of an audio sample, the more degraded the audio will sound. Looking below the Orig. BPM setting, you will see another setting accessible from the Sample View that indicates the method of time-stretching that has been selected for the sample. In order to get the best sound quality when using

Live, it is very important to pay attention to this setting and to set each sample to play back via the time-stretching method that will make it sound the best.

You may even be using samples in your Live Set that do not need to be Warped at all, for example, a long ambient pad or a recorded vocal track. In this case, be careful that Warp mode is not turned on at all for best audio quality. Long sounds in particular will sound best if they are not Warped.

The different Warp modes are basically varieties of granular resynthesis, and these techniques have been named according to what types of sounds they will work with best. You should take these as a guide and experiment with the various settings to see which sounds best for a particular sample.

Beats Mode will usually sound best for drum and percussion loops. This mode basically works by splitting up the sound into equal segments before stretching them. The size of these segments is determined by the selection made in the Transients drop-down menu below when Beats Mode is selected. If Beats Mode is used on other kinds of sounds, like a pad loop for example, this slicing action may add a kind of rhythmic pulsating effect to the sound. While this is usually undesirable, you may also want to use this as an effect in some cases.

Tones Mode is usually the best choice for samples with a musical pitch structure, such as solo instrument, bass, or vocal parts. When using Tones Mode, you can also experiment with the Grain Size setting to see what sounds the best for a given sample. This setting affects the way Live divides up the sample before stretching; Grain Size will determine the "resolution" of the granularized sample.

Texture Mode usually works best with more complex sounds with an unclear pitch structure, for example, orchestral textures, noise, nature sounds, or even an entire song arrangement with multiple instruments. Just as in Tones Mode, you can adjust the Grain Size here for better results. There is also a Flux control, which adds a degree of randomness to Live's time-stretching algorithm in Texture Mode.

The last of Live's time-stretching modes is Re-Pitch Mode, which differs from the other modes in that instead of using a granular resynthesis technique to time-stretch the sample without affecting the pitch, Live simply repitches it, playing the sample at a faster or slower speed as necessary to adjust the tempo. This is analogous to the way a DJ spinning vinyl will speed up or slow down a record to match the tempo of different songs.

Selecting Re-Pitch Mode will often provide the best audio quality of any of Live's time-stretching modes, but there are some drawbacks to it. Be aware that changing the tempo of a Clip by re-pitching will (by definition) change the pitch as well as the speed. This will cause the Clip to sound out-of-tune with other Clips in your Set (providing that it was in-tune in the first place, of course), which may be a crucial consideration depending on what you are doing. Also, in Re-Pitch mode, all other controls for controlling the pitch of the Clip are disabled, so there is no way to fine-tune the pitch either.

For example, at some of my performances I play the computer by myself in a kind of mixed live/DJ mode, mixing together my original material with Clips and loops I have made from tracks by my favorite artists. When I am playing like this, I am usually only mixing two or three different Clips together in Live at any given time, usually whole tracks or sections of tracks. In this case, I usually prefer to set the Clips I am using to Re-Pitch mode because of the superior sound quality I can get.

However, I also do performances with live musicians improvising along with my electronic tracks, and in this situation, pitch is an important concern as well. In this case, I need to keep my Clips in tune and not re-pitch them, because otherwise they will be out-of-tune with the live instrumentalists who are playing along with me. (This is a familiar problem to any musician who has ever tried to play along with a vinyl DJ spinning records, only to find that all the records are out of tune because the DJ has pitched them up or down to sync them together.) In this situation, I will switch all the Clips I am using to Beats, Tones, or Texture Mode instead to keep them in tune.

More Expert Tips for Using Live Live

Here are some more tips that will prove especially useful as you set up your Live Set for performance.

Assigning MIDI and Keyboard Controls

Although I have already covered the basics of how to assign MIDI controllers or keys on your computer keyboard to control various parameters in Live by way of some of the other topics I have discussed so far, I want to give a brief recap of this process here and point out some particular points you should be aware of when assigning controls in your live setup.

Using the Computer Keyboard as a Controller

As mentioned previously, it is possible to use your computer's typing keyboard as a controller in Live. There are actually two distinct ways you can do this.

The first way is to directly assign the keys on your computer keyboard to control various functions in Live. When assigning parameters to the computer keyboard, note that only *letter* (the a-z keys) assignments will be accepted. Live will not allow you to assign numbers, symbols, or function keys to any parameter.

To enter the Key-mapping mode, press the KEY button in the Control Bar (see Figure 10.9). You can also use the keyboard shortcuts Control-K (PC) or Command-K (Mac) to enter this mode.

Figure 10.9 The Key map mode button in the Transport Control Bar.

When you do this, all of the controls available to be assigned will be highlighted on the screen. Note that only those controls that are highlighted can be assigned. Click the control you want to assign, and then press the key that you want to control it. A small letter will appear showing you what key you have assigned. Then click the KEY button again to exit the mapping mode.

It is important to remember that the keys on the computer keyboard will only send note on or off messages. (The same is true for the keys or buttons on an external MIDI controller as well.) For this reason, you will probably want to use the keys to control toggle switches in Live such as the Track Activator and Effect Activator buttons. If you want to assign controls to continuous parameters such as volume or pan, it is better to use a fader or knob on an external MIDI controller for this purpose.

Simply repeat these steps for any parameter that is highlighted.

You can assign individual track slots to play and stop as well. Figure 10.10 shows a row of slots that all have keys assigned to trigger them. Some of these slots are empty and some already have Clips loaded in them.

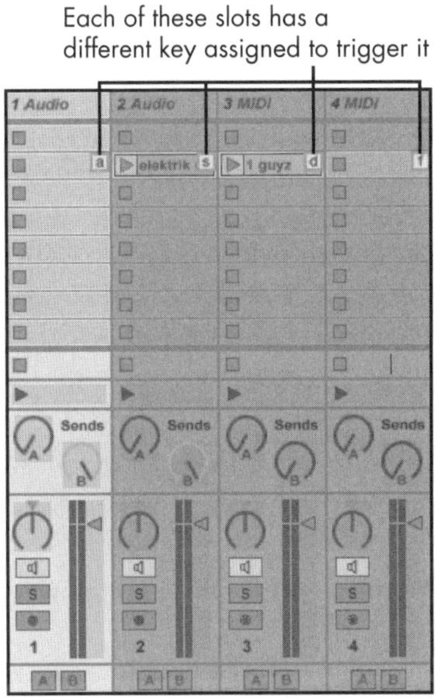

Figure 10.10 Assigning keys to trigger slots.

When you are creating a setup like this, keep in mind that the assignments you make are connected to the track slot itself and not the Clip that resides in it. Even if you drag a new Clip into the slot, the parameter assignments for that slot will remain.

In my own Live setup (described further below), I often use these Key assignments to control various mute and toggle switches in my MIDI software instruments, giving me a fine level of control over exactly which sounds are playing.

If you want to delete a key assignment that you have already made, simply enter the Key-mapping mode by clicking the KEY button, click the setting you want to delete, and use the backspace or delete keys on your keyboard to delete it.

In addition to assigning the keys on the keyboard to trigger events directly like this, you can also use the computer keyboard as a small MIDI keyboard. This is covered in the next section.

Working with an External MIDI Controller

The procedure for assigning a MIDI controller to control Live's parameters is basically the same as assigning a key on the computer keyboard.

To enter the MIDI mapping mode, press the MIDI button in the Control Bar (see Figure 10.11). You can also use the keyboard shortcuts Control-M (PC) or Command-M (Mac) to enter this mode.

Figure 10.11 The MIDI map mode button in the Transport Control Bar.

When you do this, all of the controls available to be assigned will be highlighted on the screen, the same ones available in the Key-mapping mode. Again, note that *only* those controls that are highlighted can be assigned. Click the control you want to assign, and then press the key, knob, or fader on your MIDI controller that you want to control it. A small indicator will appear showing you what MIDI channel and controller number you have assigned. Then click the MIDI button again to exit the mapping mode.

Again, remember that keys, buttons, or pads on a MIDI controller will only send note on or off messages. If you want to assign controls to continuous parameters such as volume or pan, it is better to use a fader or knob on an external MIDI controller for this purpose.

Simply repeat these steps for any parameter that is highlighted to assign a MIDI controller to it.

Syncing Live

Another powerful and creative feature of Live is its ability to synchronize with other MIDI devices or software. Live can act either as a MIDI master or a MIDI slave depending on how it is configured. Among other things, you can sync multiple computers running copies of Ableton Live, allowing you to perform with one or more other computer musicians.

Knowing how to sync Live is very important for all kinds of live performance applications. I will cover the basics of setting this up here. There are also some interesting examples of Live sync setups in the Approaches section later in this chapter.

Setting the Sync Preferences

In order to set up Live for syncing, first you have to configure the Sync preferences, on the MIDI/Sync page of Live's preferences window (see Figure 10.12). We looked at these briefly above but let's go over them in detail here. This is important because if you have only one thing set incorrectly, the sync will not work.

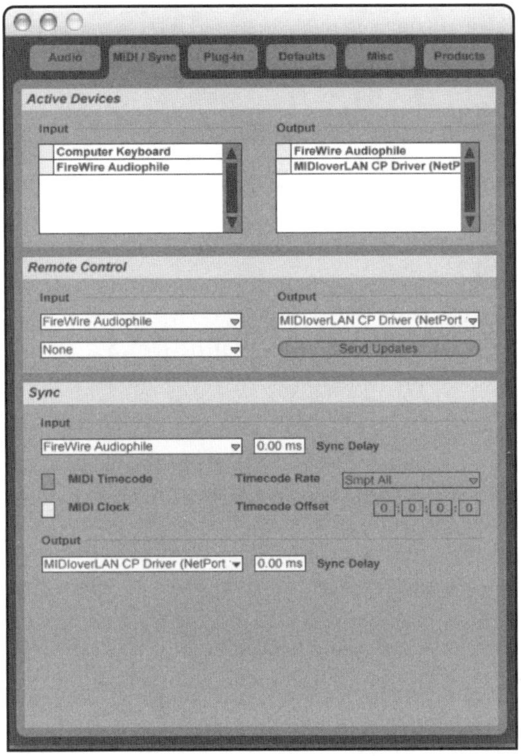

Figure 10.12 Live's MIDI/Sync preferences.

Your MIDI input and output devices are listed at the top of this screen. You need to enable at least one input or output here, depending on whether you want to use this computer as master or slave.

At the bottom of this preference screen is the Sync section of the panel (see Figure 10.13).

Use these to select the MIDI device you want to use for the sync input or output. If this machine is going to be the MIDI master, you need to select a sync output. If it is going to be a MIDI slave, you need an input selected.

If this machine is configured as a MIDI slave, you also need to specify what kind of sync signal Live will be looking for or receiving at the specified input, MIDI Clock or MIDI Timecode. Live

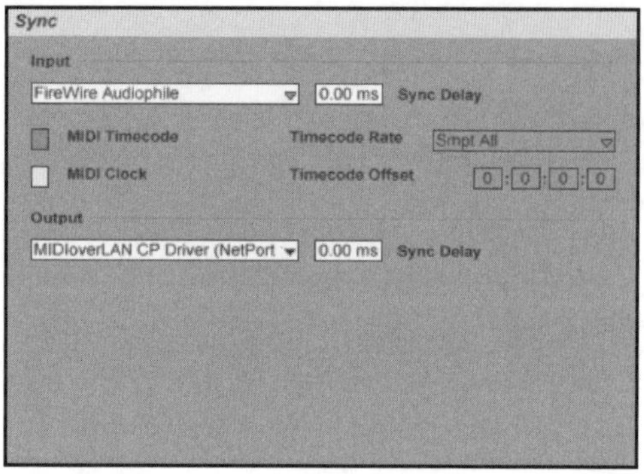

Figure 10.13 The Sync section of the preferences.

can sync to an external MIDI signal in either of these formats. If Live is the master however, it will only transmit MIDI clock.

If you want to synchronize an external MIDI device to Live, just enable the MIDI sync output here, connect the external device via your MIDI interface, and then make whatever settings are necessary on the external device for it to be the MIDI slave.

Syncing to an External MIDI Device

There are two indicators in the Transport Control Bar that give you a visual indication of when Live is sending or receiving sync (see Figure 10.14).

Figure 10.14 The sync indicators in the Transport Control Bar.

When Live is sending sync messages, the lower of these two indicators will flash in tempo, letting you know that MIDI sync is being transmitted. When Live is receiving sync messages from an external source, the upper indicator will flash.

To make Live the MIDI slave to an external source, click the EXT button. When this is active, Live will then follow all start, stop, tempo change, and other MIDI sync messages from the external MIDI master.

There are a couple important points to remember when using this mode. After you click EXT and put Live in MIDI slave mode, Live will not actually start playing until it has received a MIDI start message from the MIDI master. If the master is already playing when we first click EXT, it may need to be stopped and started again in order to send a MIDI start command to all the MIDI slaves chasing it.

Be aware that when Live is syncing to MIDI clock, it will follow song position information as well as tempo information. This means that when it first receives a MIDI start message from the master, it will immediately jump to whatever bar number the master is at. This doesn't matter if you are simply triggering Clips in the Session View, but if you have Clips laid out on the Arrangement, it can create an unintended abrupt change by jumping ahead.

Also, once you have clicked EXT and the external sync mode is active, you will not be able to stop Live with its own Transport controls. You need to first click EXT again and take Live out of MIDI slave mode to make its own controls active again.

MIDI Clock and MIDI Timecode

Although it is more common in live applications to sync to MIDI clock information, in some cases (when syncing Live to video, for example), you may want to sync to MIDI timecode instead.

To sync to MIDI timecode, MIDI Timecode is chosen in the MIDI Input Sync Type menu, and there are two more settings to configure (see Figure 10.15).

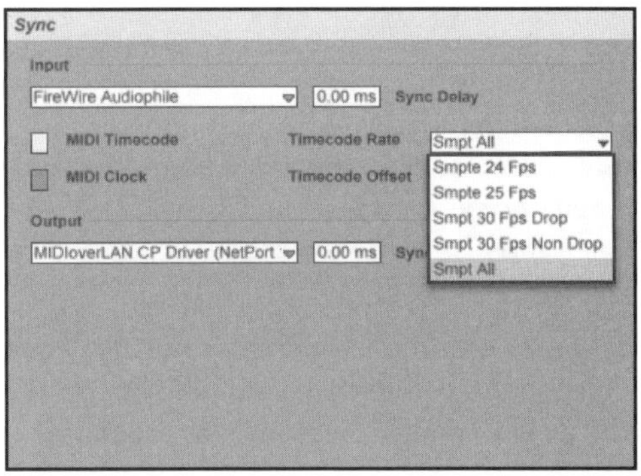

Figure 10.15 The MIDI Input Sync Type menu in the MIDI/Sync preferences.

The MIDI Timecode Frame Rate chooser selects the type of timecode to which Live will synchronize. All of the usual frame rates for video work are available, from 24fps up to 30fps, with both drop and non-drop formats available.

If you choose SMPTE All, Live will automatically detect the timecode format of incoming sync messages.

You can also set a SMPTE time offset using the Timecode Offset setting. For example, you might want to do this when synchronizing Live's start point with that of an external video source.

Sync Delay

There is also a pair of settings here in the MIDI/Sync preferences labeled Sync Delay. These can be set independently for Input and Output. This allows you to adjust Live's playback behind or ahead of the external sync signal.

This is often necessary when syncing two computers together, for example. Reasonably exact syncing between two (or more) computers is very important when you are doing live gigs, otherwise your rhythms will not be exactly synced and your performance will sound like a mess!

Here's how you can fine-tune this.

When setting up a new MIDI sync configuration between one or more computers running Live or other external devices/software, it is best to check the sync timing by playing some kind of drum or percussion sample from both machines and listen to see if they are perfectly in sync.

You can also turn on Live's metronome on both machines to check this (see Figure 10.16).

Figure 10.16 The MIDI Input Sync Type menu in the MIDI/Sync preferences.

Of course, Live's metronome will sound exactly the same no matter what computer it is played from, so if you are using the metronome as a test on two machines, you may not be able to tell which is which! In this case, it may be better to play back two different percussion loops on the two computers instead.

If you can hear that your computer or external devices are not in sync, then you need to adjust the appropriate Sync Delay here in the preferences until they are in sync. If you click one of these settings and drag up or down with your mouse or trackpad, you can nudge Live's playback gently back and forth in time in order to bring it into sync with another computer or device.

Having Problems Syncing? You May Not Be Alone...

Although it is pretty easy to set up MIDI sync between two computers running Live by following the procedures I have outlined above, sometimes you may run into problems although you have set everything up correctly. I have encountered two main problems when syncing Live.

The most common problem I have seen is that you set up everything right and the MIDI master machine shows that it is sending a MIDI signal out, but the MIDI slave machine doesn't detect an incoming signal on its end. In this case, rebooting the MIDI slave machine (or both machines for that matter) seems to solve the problem most of the time, so this isn't really a big issue.

However, I have noticed another problem as well when I am trying to do this. In many cases, it seems that Live's tempo wavers and changes significantly when it is trying to sync to an external MIDI clock signal. You can see if this is happening simply by watching the BPM indicator in Live: It will keep changing up and down within a range of a few BPM on either side of the actual tempo. This is not necessarily a problem with Live and it can happen with other MIDI software sequencers as well. However, this is a serious issue for performance because it can cause rhythms and beats on the slave machine to play out of sync with the master machine, completely defeating the purpose of syncing them in the first place.

Ableton refers to this problem on their Web site and advises that you will get tighter MIDI sync by reducing the audio buffer size on your sound card, but this has not helped much in my case—the problem still remains, no matter what combination of MIDI and audio hardware I use. I have even tried using a MIDI connection via Ethernet for greater bandwidth and stability using Music Lab's MIDI over LAN CP software (see http://www.musiclab.com/products/rpl_info.htm for more on this), but even this has not helped much. (MIDI over LAN is a very interesting technology, however, and I would definitely recommend checking out the above link if you are interested in this.)

One solution to this problem might be to use an external MIDI hardware sequencer to generate the master clock signal and slave both laptops to this. I have experienced problems even with this kind of setup, however.

On some recent duo laptop gigs I have played in LA with Dream Electric, we've found that we actually get better results by not using the MIDI sync and simply syncing our computers together by ear, DJ-style. Here's how we do it.

Let's say that my partner is already playing something and I want to sync to his beat and join the mix. No problem. This is actually pretty easy to do even without using MIDI sync.

First of all, to make things easiest, I'll click the metronome switch in Live and turn on the metronome click. I have my Cue out in Live set to go only to my headphones, so only I (and not the audience) can hear the click.

Then I just look over at my partner's computer and see what tempo he's playing at—let's say he's at 130BPM. So I set my copy of Live to play at 130BPM as well.

Then, just like a DJ playing a record, I try to hit Live's Play button and start playback on a downbeat in my partner's music. I try to drop it in as close as I can, but if it's not exactly on target that's OK because it's easy to fine-tune.

If I can get the playback pretty close to where I want by dropping it in like this, then I listen to my metronome click in my headphones and try to match it up with the playback of my partner's music. I can make fine adjustments in the playback by simply nudging the BPM indicator in Live up and down to adjust the playback speed. (To adjust the BPM setting, click the BPM and then use the up and down arrow keys on the keyboard to nudge it up and down in increments of 1 BPM.)

For example, if the playback of my computer is lagging slightly behind my partner's, I can click the BPM and nudge it up from 130BPM to 131BPM for a second. As I do this, I listen carefully to the metronome click in my headphones until it gradually slides into sync with the rhythms of my partner's music. As soon as they are in sync, I nudge the tempo back down to 130BPM.

This is basically the same way that a DJ syncs two records together, except in this case you already know the BPM of the music you want to sync to, so it is actually much easier than mixing vinyl.

After getting two copies of Live in sync by ear like this, they will stay in sync for quite some time. After awhile they will inevitably start to slowly drift apart, however, so if you are playing together with a partner like this and syncing the tempos by ear, you need to constantly pay attention to whether or not your rhythms are syncing up. Again, this is no different than how a vinyl DJ works, and it is actually a lot easier to keep two computers in sync than two records. If you are having problems getting the MIDI sync in Live to work properly, try doing it this way.

Performance Approaches Using Ableton Live

As I've made clear above, Ableton Live provides you with incredible flexibility when configuring a Live Set for performing.

In this section, we will explore specific ways of configuring Live for live performance. As you read through these pages, try going through with your own copy of Live and creating a similar setup in order to better understand what I'm talking about here.

Most of these are setups I have used myself at gigs. Like most computer musicians, it seems like I am constantly in the process of reconfiguring and "improving" my live rig, always tinkering here or there around the margins in order to give myself greater power and flexibility for live performance.

Using Live as a DJ Tool

I didn't cover digital DJing with Live in Chapter 9 because it is so much more than just a DJ application. However, you *can* set up Live for DJing if you want, and with a little preparation, it is potentially one of the most powerful DJ software tools on the market. One of the reasons Live is so universally popular among live computer musicians is that you can build almost any setup you want with it, and this includes a replica of a standard DJ setup.

If you want to use Live as your DJ application, here's how you could set it up.

For a basic DJ setup, you can start by making a Live Set with just two audio tracks, no MIDI tracks, and no Returns. This would look like Figure 10.17.

Notice that I have assigned the track 1 Audio to the A side of Live's crossfader, and 2 Audio to the B side. Then, using a MIDI controller with a built-in crossfader like my X-Session and assigning it to control Live's crossfader, I can do all kinds of DJ-style effects with the crossfader: Mixing between two tracks, using two copies of the same track at the same time to create various special effects, beat juggling, etc.

Just as in my standard Live setup for solo gigs (described above), I have assigned the Cue Out in Live to channels 3/4 on my FireWire Audiophile, allowing me to do headphone cueing like a DJ as well. However, I don't need a DJ mixer as I can do everything a DJ can do with my computer setup.

Although this kind of setup will allow you to mix track after track in sequence like a DJ, DJing with Live is somewhat different than DJing with a standard DJ-style application such as we looked at in the previous chapter.

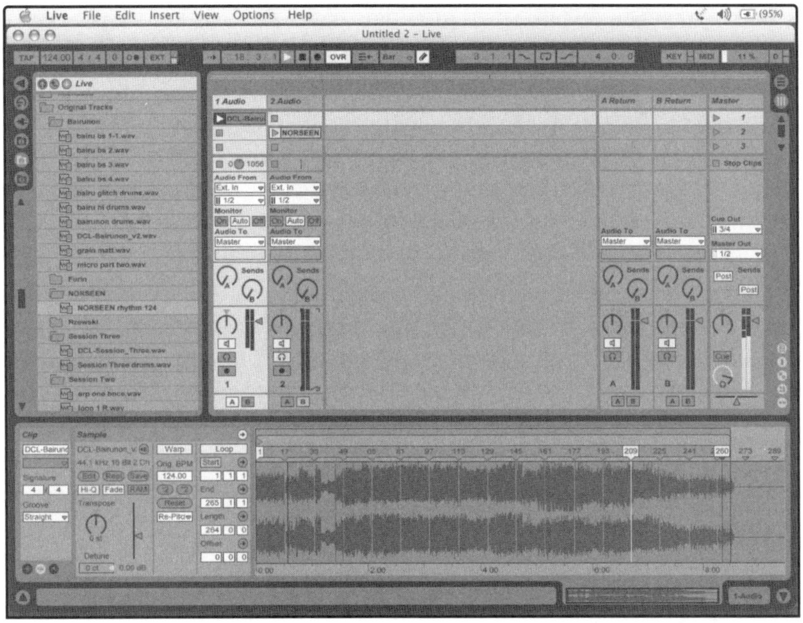

Figure 10.17 A very basic DJ setup in Live.

For one thing, Live requires you to prepare your tracks in advance by Warping them.

With a standard DJ application like Traktor or Virtual DJ, you are able to change the playback speed of a given track on the fly as well as slightly nudging its current playback position back and forth using the computer keyboard, allowing you to manually adjust two tracks to get them in rhythmic sync for mixing. Many DJ applications also provide you with some kind of automatic beat-matching tool that can help you to get the tracks in sync.

In Live, however, you need to take a different approach to get the tracks in sync. Basically, you have to prepare any tracks you want to play ahead of time by placing Warp Markers in them to provide Live with an accurate tempo map for playback. However, once you have done this, you never have to do it again, and if you have done a good job placing the Warp Markers accurately, your new track will automatically play in sync with the other Clips in your Live Set at whatever tempo you have set. This means that you will be able to mix much more smoothly and accurately when performing.

Also, it is more difficult in Live to quickly jump to different parts of a track. In most DJ-style applications, you can drop a track on one of the playback decks and then click on its visual representation to jump to different parts of the track, just as you do when you drop the needle on a vinyl record at various points.

This is more difficult in Live, however, because when you start a Clip playing in Live it will always start at the beginning, and there is nowhere to click on its visual representation to change the playback position. You can affect the playback position indirectly by adjusting the loop points and start offset position in Live's Clip View window, but these controls aren't really meant to be adjusted on the fly and are awkward to use live.

However, it is quite easy in Live to cut a track into short loops or somewhat longer segments and save these. Then you can play these whenever you want in your set. This is a very useful and important technique for DJing in Live because it allows you to extract and use only the parts you like within a given track. How many times have you heard a great track or a great rhythm ruined by one bad section? When DJing with Live, you can simply make loops out of the parts of the track you like and then use those to DJ rather than the original.

Personally I have switched to DJing with Live after using various digital DJ applications over the last few years. It does require more preparation beforehand in terms of Warping and cutting up tracks and loops from tracks for live use. However, once you have your material prepared, DJing with Live allows you to explore all kinds of new mixing techniques that would be impossible with a standard DJ setup.

Also, with some experimentation you will find that most of the techniques I described in the previous chapter on digital DJing are possible with this kind of DJ setup in Live as well, although you may end up executing your DJ tricks somewhat differently in the Live environment.

My Solo Setup as Digital Cutup Lounge

Most recently, I have been doing solo laptop gigs in Los Angeles under the name Digital Cutup Lounge. As mentioned earlier in the book, I started DCL together with partner Stephen Ives in Hong Kong in 1999, and we are still making music together now. However, I now live in LA and Stephen lives in southwest England, so when I perform as DCL here in LA, I usually play solo.

I use Live together with an Evolution X-Session MIDI controller, which has two rows of eight knobs each, ten assignable buttons, and a crossfader. In my solo setup, I have tried to work out how to get the most out of my X-Session controls by mapping them to the most important controls I need to access in Live. For my audio interface, I use an M-Audio FireWire Audiophile, which gives me the ability to easily cue on headphones when I'm mixing (see Figure 10.18).

When I play a solo set as DCL, I usually play a mix of my own music and cutup samples of music by other artists. In other words, my approach is somewhere halfway between DJing (mixing together a series of tracks by other artists) and playing a "live PA" comprising my own material exclusively. To best facilitate this style of playing, I have created a hybrid Live Set that combines some features of a DJ mixer-like setup with others more oriented towards "live" performance.

Figure 10.19 displays a screenshot of my current Live setup settings.

There are a total of seven tracks in all. I have arranged them the way they are for a number of reasons, and not all of them are set up the same way. Here's a list of the tracks in order and what I use them for:

- 1 left, 2 ctr, and 3 right

  I use these three audio tracks to play audio loops and complete tracks (see Figure 10.20).

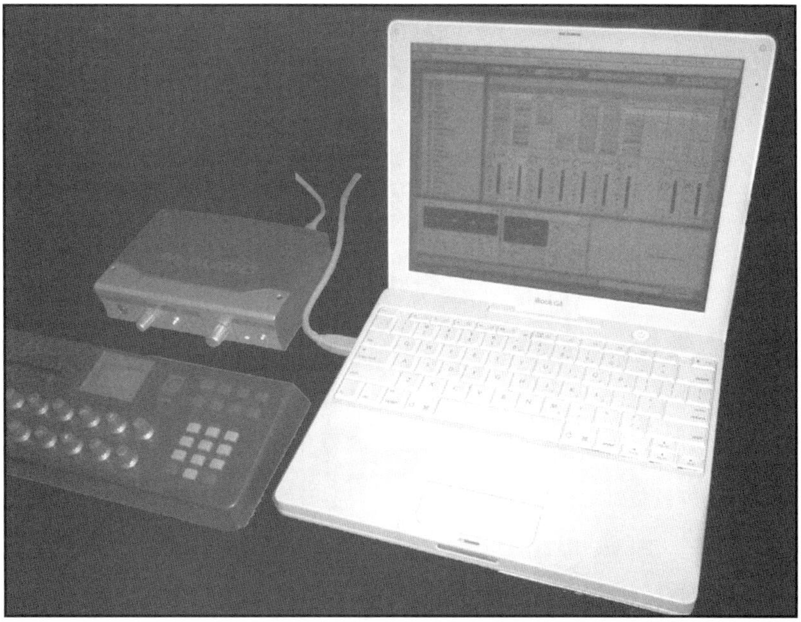

Figure 10.18 My current live hardware setup.

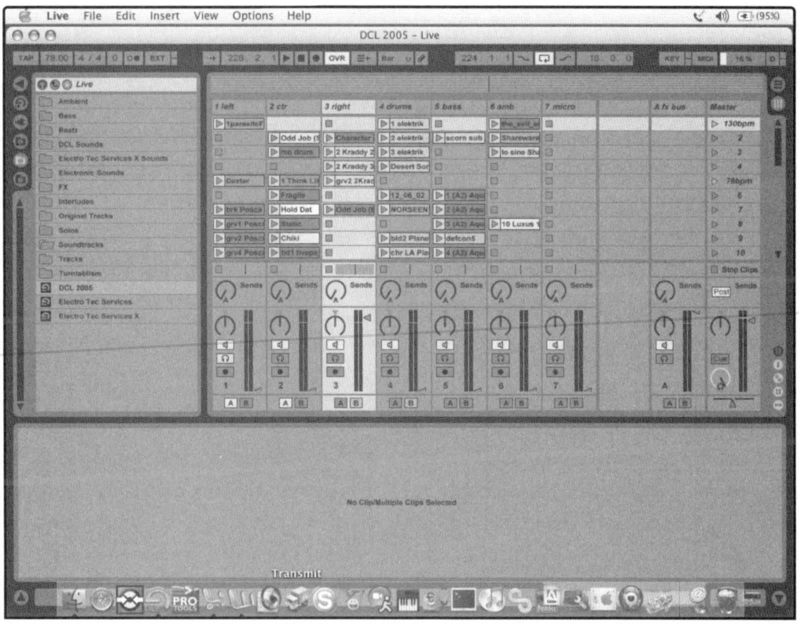

Figure 10.19 My current Live Set for solo DCL gigs.

Figure 10.20 Tracks 1 left, 2 ctr, and 3 right.

Although they are named "left," "ctr," and "right," this is not because they are panned to different sides. This is how I have assigned them to Live's crossfader to facilitate DJ-style mixing between the various tracks. "left" is assigned to the "A" or left-hand side of the crossfader, "right" is assigned to the "B" or right-hand side, and "ctr" is unassigned, meaning that it will always be heard when triggered and will not be affected by crossfader moves.

These tracks each have one effect placed on them, Live's built-in EQ Four effect. I have set these up like bass EQ kill switches such as can be found on many of today's DJ mixers, a high-pass filter set at around 400Hz. I have mapped the activation switches of these EQs to buttons on my X-Session. When I press one of these buttons and engage the EQ, most of the bass frequencies will be cut from that particular track. This can really help a lot when you are mixing two, three, or more different tracks or loops together simultaneously.

- 4 drums

  I use this audio track primarily to play drum and percussion loops (see Figure 10.21).

  It contains one EQ Four effect set up as a bass EQ kill switch just as on tracks 1-3, as well as three additional effects particularly suited to how I like to process drums. These days I am using the SupaTrigga effect to slice and dice my drum patterns on the fly and give them more variety, as well as the DestroyFX Buffer Override effect to "enhance" my drums with a slew of out-of-time chop-ups and glitchy artifacts. I am also using the Audio Rate Pan plug-in, part of the Pluggo package of plug-ins made by Cycling '74, which obscures and mystifies the issue further with a variety of weird complex panning presets to start tweaking.

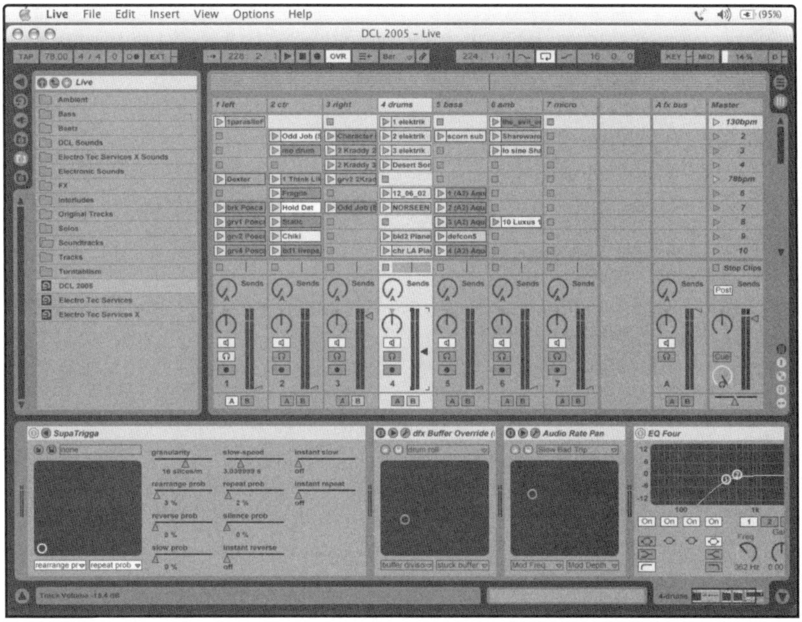

Figure 10.21 Track 4 drums.

I have mapped the activation switches of each of these effects to one of the buttons on my X-Session. By turning these effects on and off in different combinations and modifying their parameters while I play live, I am able to achieve an incredible range of live drum textures, from solid 4/4 grooves to complete postdigital glitch meltdown.

- 5 bass

  I use this audio track pretty much exclusively for playing bass loops and samples, and it is set up for this purpose (see Figure 10.22).

  This bass track hosts an EQ Four effect like the other tracks, but I have set it up a bit differently. This EQ is set up as a low-pass filter, and I have assigned one of the knobs on my X-Session to control the frequency that the filter acts at. This allows me to do interesting filter effects on my basslines in performance.

  I have also placed Cycling '74's Comber plug-in effect here on the bass track and mapped its activation switch to a button on my X-Session. I sometimes activate this during a gig to trigger big sweeping comb filter effects on my bass loops, which I can accentuate even further by moving the knob controlling the filter frequency on the EQ Four.

- 6 amb

  I use this audio track mostly for playing back ambient tracks, pads, and sound effects (see Figure 10.23).

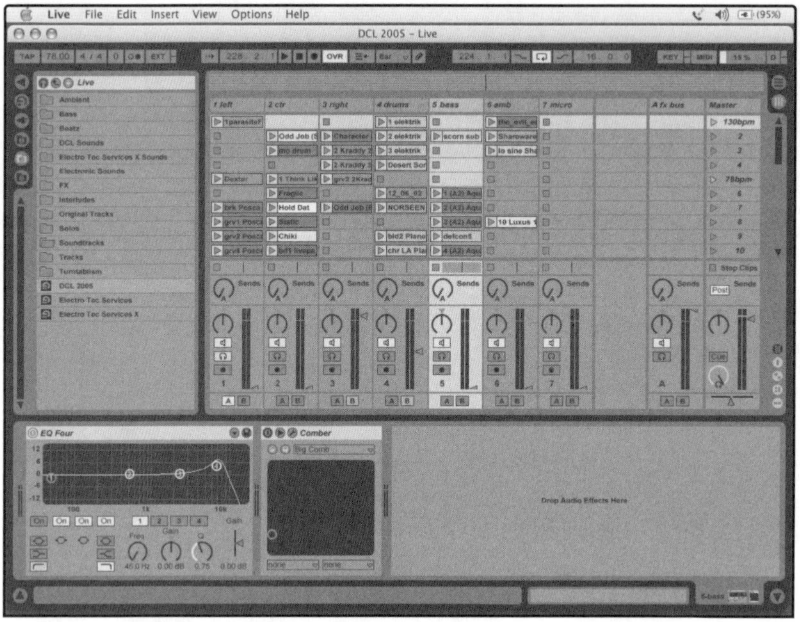

Figure 10.22 Track 5 bass.

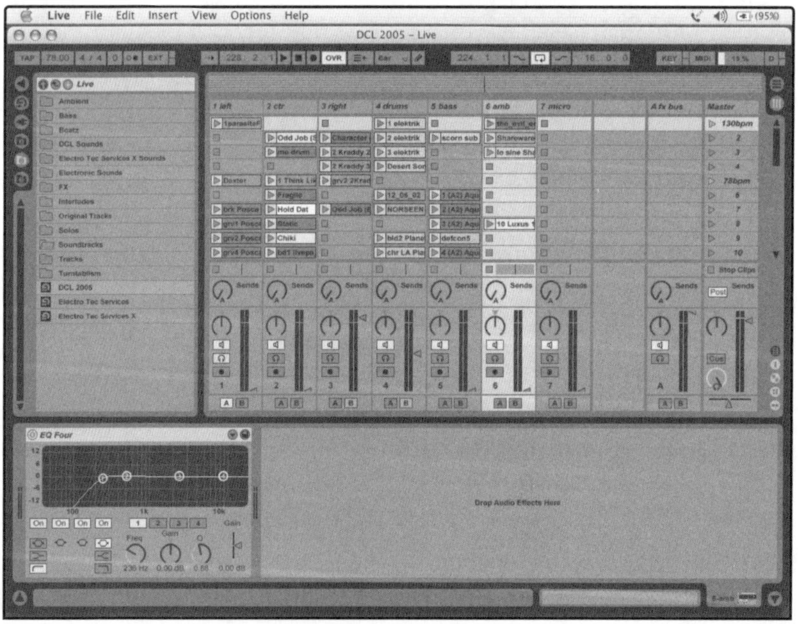

Figure 10.23 Track 6 amb.

As you can see in the image above, the only effect on this track is the EQ Four, set up as a bass EQ kill switch just like the first four tracks.

- 7 micro

This track is a MIDI track, the only one in my live setup. It hosts the Sonic Charge MicroTonic VST instrument, a software drum synthesizer than can play back from a set of eight different drum sounds at any one time (see Figure 10.24).

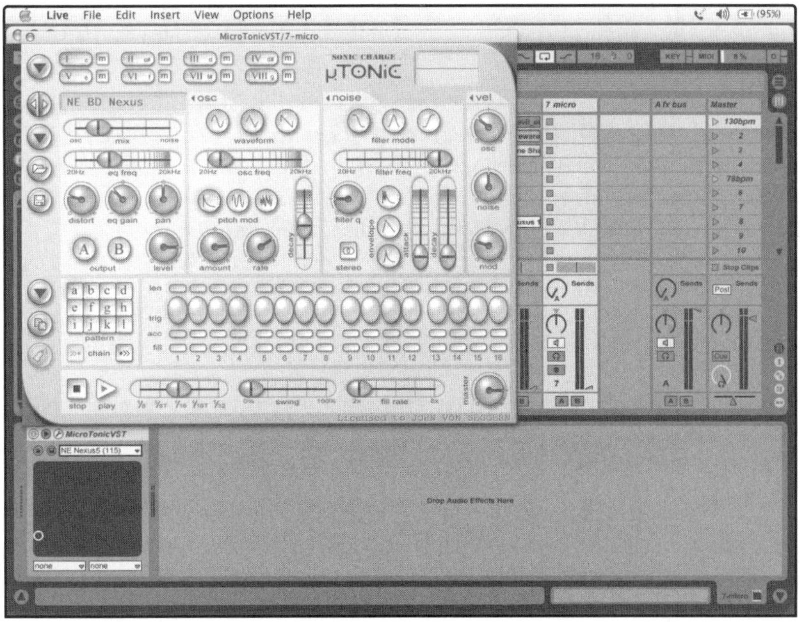

Figure 10.24 Track 7 micro, hosting the MicroTonic VST instrument.

I use the MicroTonic as the sound source for playing back various MIDI drum loops and adding these to my live sets. Often I will set up a simple hi-hat or percussion part playing on the MicroTonic and then drop this in the main mix to build up the energy of the rhythms I am playing.

This track has no audio effects on it at all. To more precisely control the sound of the MicroTonic in performance, however, I have assigned eight keys on my computer's keyboard to control the eight instruments on the MicroTonic, controlling each instrument's mute switch to turn it on and off.

When I play live, I trigger a complete MIDI groove loop in one of this track's Clip slots, or use the built-in sequencer of the MicroTonic to play a complete MIDI pattern with 6-8 separate instrument parts. When I first start this playing, I usually mute all eight instruments with the keys so no sound is heard at all. Then I can selectively mute and unmute the parts with the keys on the keyboard to create endless variations on the sound. When

I have exhausted the possibilities of a particular MIDI groove or pattern, I can trigger a different MIDI Clip or change the bank of sounds I am using in the MicroTonic to get a whole new set of possibilities.

- Another advantage of using a MIDI software instrument live in performance like this is that I can tweak and change various parameters of the MicroTonic while I am playing. In one setup I used playing with Sariah Storm in Suspect. Seen, for example, I assigned one of the knobs on my X-Session to control the fundamental oscillator frequency (Osc1 Freq) parameter of the first instrument on the MicroTonic, the bass drum. This let me change the frequency of the bass drum over time and generate all kinds of crazy phat bass drum vibrations.
- This was a cool effect for a while, but later I decided that it would work better to vary the bass frequency in a regular pattern instead of doing it with a knob and dialing in the frequency by hand. I did this by adding automation envelopes to some of my MIDI drum Clips and making the bass drum frequency oscillate up and down in regular patterns this way. (See the Live manual for more on using automation envelopes.)
- A fx bus
- This return track is hosting two dubby effects for live use: Live's built-in Ping Pong Delay and Reverb (see Figure 10.25).

Figure 10.25 Track A fx bus.

I have inserted these effects on a return track like this because I might want to use them on any of the other tracks at various points in a performance. Rather than putting delay and reverb on each track, it is much more convenient to put them on this return and then use my MIDI controller to route the output from the other tracks to this track when I want delay and reverb.

Now let's look at how I have assigned the controls of my X-Session to control the various parameters in my Live Set. The X-Session has two rows of eight knobs each, as well as a DJ crossfader and ten assignable buttons (see Figure 10.26).

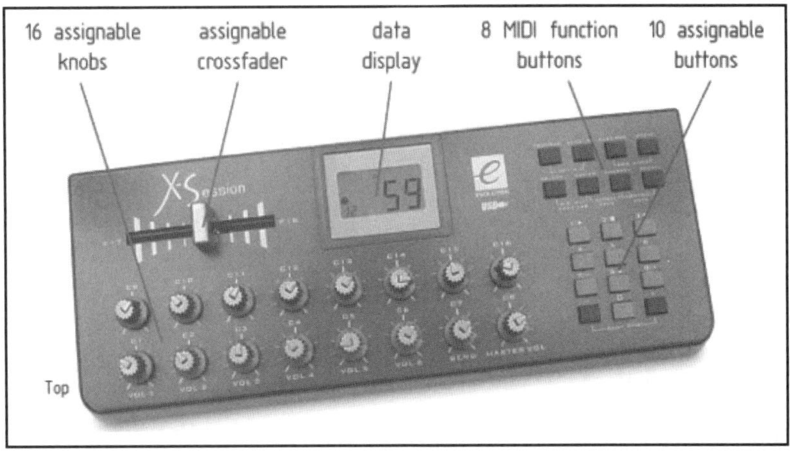

Figure 10.26 The controls on the X-Session.

In the first place, I have assigned the crossfader on the X-Session to control the crossfader in Live.

I have assigned the lower bank of knobs to control the track volumes, one through seven. This is where I mix all the tracks in and out. The last knob, number eight, is assigned to my master volume.

Most of the upper row of knobs are assigned to control the Send knob on each track. This sends the signal to the return track, "A fx bus," and thus through the delay and reverb.

One exception to this scheme is the fifth knob from the left in the upper row. Track five in my Live Set is the bass track, and I don't need the option of sending my bass loops through the delay and reverb as this won't sound good anyway. Therefore, I have assigned this knob to control the frequency of the low-pass filter I have set up in the EQ Four effect inserted on this track. This enables me to do filter sweeps and adjust the EQ of the bass track while I play.

Now let's look at how I have the ten available buttons on the X-Session assigned (see Figure 10.27).

Figure 10.27 The ten assignable buttons on my X-Session controller.

Buttons one through four and six are assigned to control the activation switches of the EQ effects I have inserted on the respective track. They are acting like the bass EQ kill switches on a DJ mixer, a separate kill switch for each of these tracks.

However, track five is the bass track, so I don't need a bass EQ kill on this track. Instead, I have assigned button number five to control the activation switch of the Comber filter on the bass track. I often like to flip this filter on and off during a performance, so this is a good use of this button.

Buttons seven through nine are assigned to control the activation switches of the various crazy effects I am using on track number four, which hosts my drum tracks and loops. In my current setup, button number seven is assigned to control the SupaTrigga effect, button eight controls the DestroyFX Buffer Override, and button nine is assigned to the Audio Rate Pan plug-in. This gives me easy control over endless variations in my drum patterns.

This setup is a good example of how to get the most out of Live and an external MIDI controller in a live performance situation. This setup gives me easy access to a variety of controls that adjust crucial aspects of the overall sound, like the track volumes, the effects return, and the bass EQ kills.

These ideas provide a good starting point, but ultimately you will want to build your own Live Set to give you the ability to create the sounds YOU are looking for and get to them quickly and easily.

This is part of the elegance of the design of Live. It provides incredible flexibility for creating and customizing your own setup, in conjunction with whatever external MIDI and audio equipment you want to use.

Now let's look at a few other examples of possible live setups.

Upcoming DCL Band Gigs in SE Asia: 2 Laptops Plus Bass, Drums, and Keys

As this book nears completion, I am just getting ready to travel to Malaysia and Singapore, where I will do a few live gigs with a larger version of our Digital Cutup Lounge project. For this mini-tour I will play computer and bass, joined by my partner Stephen using both a PC and a Mac laptop; drummer Jun Kung using a regular acoustic drum kit (see Figure 10.28); and keyboardist Jondi Mac, playing a wearable keyboard controller connected to a Roland XV-5080 synth module (see Figure 10.29).

Figure 10.28 Jun Kung: Asian singer/musician, also DCL's favorite drummer.

Figure 10.29 Jondi Mac: Man of the world and keyboardist extraordinaire.

We have tried quite a few different ways of incorporating live musicians into our DCL performances, and this is the best combination of people and instruments that we have come up with. Over the past year we have had shows in Hong Kong, Bangkok, Kuala Lumpur, and Singapore with this line-up. Here's how we hook everything up and make it work.

For this configuration, I run Ableton Live on my laptop and make it the MIDI sync master. I run sync out of my computer and connect it via a Midiman Thru 3×8 interface to Stephen's PowerBook, which is also running a copy of Ableton Live. Stephen's PC will be set up purely as a DJ machine, not synced to the two Macs. We plug all three computers into a Stanton DJ mixer, the same model we've been using for all our gigs in the past several years (I think we're on our fourth one now or something like this...).

We also connect Jondi's XV-5080 module to the MIDI sync coming from the Thru 3×8. This enables Jondi to sync the internal effects and oscillators in the module to the tempo sync information I am sending from Live, very important for the dance-oriented kind of music we play.

Along with all this electronic gear, I play my Fender fretless bass plugged directly into the DJ mixer (it's easier for me to control the level this way) with no effects, and Jun is playing regular acoustic drums with no electronic craziness added either.

For our upcoming performances, Stephen will begin by DJing some downtempo tracks on his PC using VirtualDJ and I will add some effects and ambiences from my Mac. Then when we are ready to start the more groove-oriented part of the night, we will start mixing together on the two computers, syncing them together by ear or handing off the main groove to one another over the course of the set. We will play a combination of bits and pieces of our own material, finished original tracks, and loops cut from other artists' tracks.

As always, we will have no fixed plan for the overall performance; we like keeping things loose and spontaneous. There *are* a few key tracks we will probably drop in at various points in our set, though. Most of the time when I play with Stephen, though, anything goes. We don't usually have fixed roles as far as who will play which type of part; our musical relationship is more of a free-for-all.

Jondi and Jun will play along with us, interpolating additional keyboard, synth, drum, and percussion parts to the mix. I will join on bass at some points as well, depending on what Stephen plays and what direction the music goes in. The trick here is for the instrumentalists to *add* to the flow of the computer music instead of simply *duplicating* it; at least, this is the approach we try to take. Although as an instrumentalist it seems relatively easy at first to stand on stage and simply "play along" with the computer tracks, in practice it is quite difficult to fit in with the flow. However, Jun and Jondi are both very good at this and always manage to find creative ways to make the music more interesting and dynamic.

One of the great advantages of this setup for me is that I can play computer or bass depending on what is happening musically. If I stop playing computer and switch to bass for an extended period, Stephen is more than capable of keeping everything going on the computer(s) without me. Then I can rejoin the mix on computer again whenever I feel inclined.

[a]pendics.shuffle

Kenneth James Gibson (see Figure 10.30) is one of the LA computer music underground's local celebrities, with releases on half a dozen European and American labels under several different pseudonyms.

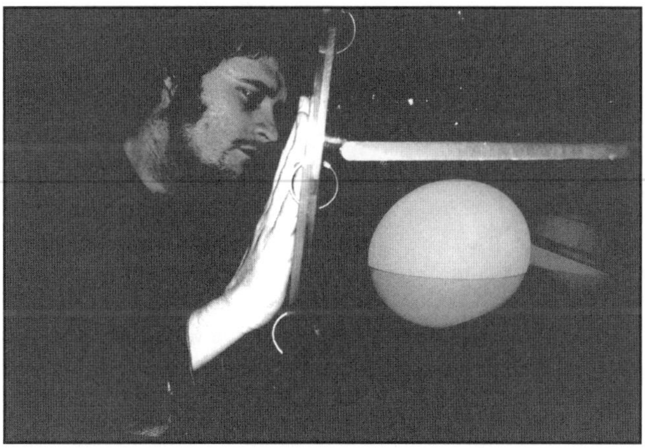

Figure 10.30 Ken Gibson a.k.a. [a]pendics.shuffle.

[a]pendics.shuffle, his most frequently-used recent alias, combines subtly destabilized funky house grooves with all kinds of experimental synthesizer squalls and postdigital glitch collages floating on top. His frequent live laptop sets in California have become legendary for pushing the sonic envelope while still keeping the dance floor pumping.

Before getting into electronic music, Ken played guitar in the rock band "Furry Things" in the early 1990s, resulting in two albums and a number of other releases. He started his Eight Frozen Modules solo electronic project in 1994. His first solo electronic release came under this name in 1995. Back then he used an Ensoniq EPS sampler, using it to play back his own guitar loops among other things, and then recorded multiple layers of samples into a four-track tape machine.

Ken has played many live electronic gigs over the years with varying equipment, but began using a computer live in 2002 because of the added power and flexibility it could provide for performance. He started with an early version of Ableton Live running on a Windows PC and later began using Traktor as well, to play DJ sets of his own material.

KENNETH JAMES GIBSON (Los Angeles)

[a]pendics.shuffle aka Eight Frozen Modules is one Kenneth James Gibson. Exploring the boundaries by scaling and shaping sounds, he creates a hybrid that can bounce from giggling mania to panicked oblivion. Gibson has spent many years releasing music on such labels as City Slang, Orthlorng Musork, Phthalo, Tigerbeat6, Lo recordings, and Orac, to name a few. He also records under the following identities: The Premature Wig, dubLoner, Reverse Commuter, and Electronic Music Composer.
Quote taken from http://www.createfixate.com/april05/april05pr.html.

Currently Ken performs running Ableton Live on his PC laptop and uses an X-Session MIDI controller to control everything in Live. However, Ken's approach to setting up Live for performance is quite different than how I do it.

Whereas I tend to think in terms of vertical channels when I'm mixing and use the Live Mixer more or less as I would a DJ mixer, Ken has his channels assigned according to the type of audio Clips each will hold, for example bass, drums, vocal, effects, and so on. Then he has a whole series of each of these types of Clips loaded up on his tracks, and he can trigger a whole horizontal row of them together by using the Scene Launch buttons on the right-hand side of the live interface (see Figure 10.31).

Working this way, he can still mix and match different bass loops and drum loops together if he wants, for example, and he can let any combination of Clips play on for as long as he wants before moving on or changing anything. At the same time, he always knows that when he presses the next Scene Launch button in sequence, everything will jump to a completely new sonic configuration, just like putting a new record on a turntable. This gives him the ability to focus his attention on small details as well as shaping the pacing of his set as a whole. He can also trigger effects live on any of the various instrumental parts he is working with.

Figure 10.31 Ken Gibson's Live setup.

Prof

Réné T.A. Lysloff is a professor of ethnomusicology at the University of California, Riverside, specializing in the study of the gamelan music of Indonesia. In recent years however, he has become an active performer of computer music as well.

Although Réné performed with various rock bands when he was younger, and did incidental music for a documentary in the early 80s using an early Moog synthesizer, he didn't get involved in electronic music performance until the late 1990s. In the course of his academic work, he became interested in the societal dynamics of the nascent online music culture that he saw emerging on the Internet, on sites devoted to the exchange of MOD files and (later) MP3s. He wrote a few research papers exploring the phenomenon, and before long started writing his own music with some of the software he found online. Later he started using Logic to produce his music and more recently has begun using Ableton Live for his performances.

Réné has spent considerable time in Indonesia over the years, studying music, doing ethnomusicological research, and teaching in Indonesian universities. On his most recent trips, he has begun doing laptop performances with Ableton Live at various large art and music festivals there. He has performed his own music solo as well as collaborating with a gamelan drummer and an expatriate American DJ from Santa Cruz now resident in Bali, DJ No.e, who uses a second computer synced to Réné's to trigger her own sounds and samples.

Réné's Rig

For his live performances, Réné uses a G4 PowerBook 933MHz with 1GB RAM installed. He is currently using an Emagic A62m USB audio interface, and an M-Audio Radium61 MIDI keyboard controller.

When Réné plays live, he makes extensive use of Ableton Live's MIDI capabilities. He usually has two or three MIDI tracks setup in Live and he loads these with various software synths or samplers.

Réné prepares for live gigs by getting together a set of MIDI clips that he wants to use. Typically these are melodies, riffs, or rhythms that he has recorded in MIDI using his keyboard controller. He has made these into MIDI Clips that he can play as loops in Live, using the MIDI data to trigger whatever sounds he wants from the synths and samplers. In addition, he often uses Live's Follow Actions feature to enable his MIDI clips to trigger one another in succession in various complex patterns.

By record-enabling any of the MIDI tracks, Réné can use his Radium61 keyboard to play the software instrument on that track live. In this way, he can play live while his MIDI loops are playing in the background.

Assigned Reading: Music and Technoculture

In addition to being an innovative laptop performer, Réné T.A. Lysloff is also one of the foremost theorists of music and technology writing today. For those of you reading this book who are interested in some more advanced ideas on these topics, I would highly recommend *Music and Technoculture*, a collection of recent cutting-edge writing on the subject co-edited by Dr. Lysloff. It is available online from Amazon, among other places.

Remote Viewing

Remote Viewing is a live electronic dub band I play with in Los Angeles with two of my co-workers at M-Audio, Steve Nalepa and Matt Piper (see Figure 10.32).

Our setup is a good example of how to use multiple computers together live, each running a copy of Ableton Live.

When we do Remote Viewing gigs, laptop beat scientist Steve Nalepa plays rhythms and samples in Live on a Mac iBook, mixing and controlling them with an Oxygen8 keyboard controller. He sends a MIDI sync signal out of the Oxygen8 and then into a Midiman Thru 3×8 (see Figure 10.33), which splits the MIDI sync so that our two other computers running Live can receive the same sync signal.

Keyboardist Matt Piper runs Propellerhead's Reason software running inside Live via ReWire, on a powerful Dell PC laptop. He uses an M-Audio Radium61 keyboard controller to play the software synthesizers and samplers in Reason, and then processes the sounds using the effects in Live.

Matt has assigned the knobs and faders on his Radium keyboard to control various parameters in the Reason synths and the effects in Live, giving him a powerful degree of control over his sounds when he performs. All of the effects he uses in Live are automatically in tempo with

Figure 10.32 Steve Nalepa and Matt Piper.

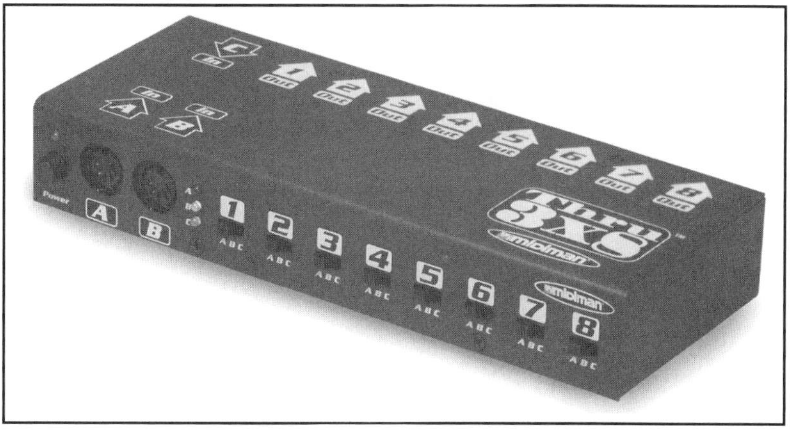

Figure 10.33 The Midiman Thru 3×8.

the MIDI sync signal. (Note: there is a much more detailed description of Matt's trippy keyboard setup in Chapter Thirteen.)

When I play with Steve and Matt in Remote Viewing, I play dubby fretless bass guitar the majority of the time (see Figure 10.34), but I also have my iBook synced to the Thru 3×8 via a MIDI cable connected to the MIDI IN of my X-Session, running yet another copy of Ableton Live.

When we do Remote Viewing gigs, Steve plays most of the main beats and grooves from his computer and I have mostly percussion loops and sound effects loaded up on my

Figure 10.34 Author with Fender fretless bass—a real musical instrument!

machine, dropping some of these in the mix when I'm not playing the bass. I also have some ambient pad loops that I will fade in from time to time.

Recording from Session to Arrangement

Another powerful and creative function of Live is its ability to record all the moves you make in the Session View into the Arrangement View. This means that you can start recording and improvise in the Session View, whether you are actually performing or are home in the studio, and every move you make will be recorded in the Arrangement View. Then you can go back later and do further editing or arranging to create a more finished track or mix.

Although this is not strictly speaking a technique for live performance, I decided to include this section at the end of the chapter here because this unique feature of Live is a fantastic tool for you to record your live sessions. As many of us know, we often get our best musical ideas while we are just "playing around" with a new instrument or technique, and Live makes it easy to record your spontaneous inspiration for use in future compositions.

This is extremely useful for creating a live demo mix, for example. Just start recording and make a long continuous mix of your live material just like you would on a real gig, then go back and edit and change anything you want. Presto, an instant live demo, and with all of the mistakes edited out, you have no excuse for not sounding like a superstar. Now go out and get some gigs!

Here's how this works: Basically, whenever the Record button is on in the Control Bar, Live will record all the moves you make in the Session View into the Arrangement (see Figure 10.35). This includes any clips you launch, as well as any changes you make with the mixer controls or effects.

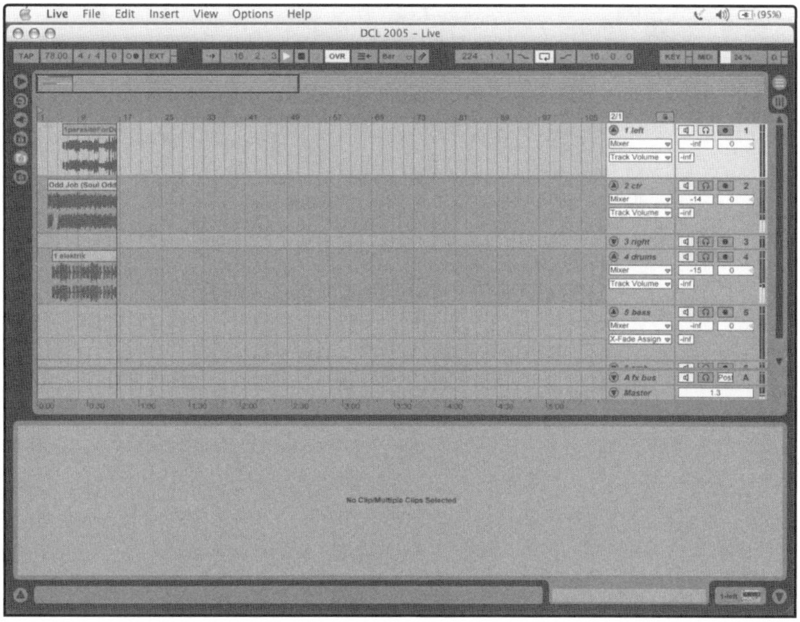

Figure 10.35 The Record button in Live's Control Bar.

To see how this works, try making a simple recording yourself. Simply drag a few clips into your Live Set and press Record in the Control Bar. Trigger some of the clips and let them play while adjusting their relative levels, panning and so on by using Live's Mixer controls.

When you are finished recording, simply click Stop in the Control Bar. Then switch into the Arrangement View by pressing Tab on the keyboard to see what you have recorded. You will see all the Clips you launched laid out on the Arrangement View timeline, as well as any automation data you may have recorded. If you go back to the beginning of the Arrangement and listen to it again, you will hear exactly what you recorded played back again.

When you are recording this way, you are not actually recording any new MIDI or audio data. Live is simply recording all the moves you made while the Record button was engaged, while the actual audio samples on your hard drive remain unchanged.

Remember that only one Clip can play at a time on any given Track, whether in the Arrangement View or the Session View. For example, if a Clip is already playing on Track 1 in the Arrangement, but we then switch back to the Session View and launch a different Clip on that Track, the new Clip will start playing and the Clip that was already playing in the Arrangement View will be muted.

When this happens, the Back to Arrangement button will light up in the Control Bar to remind you that what you are hearing is different than what is actually recorded in the Arrangement. Clicking this button will cause everything to revert back to the settings in the Arrangement.

Well—that should be enough to get you started looping with Ableton Live!

Now, if you're not already looped enough from reading about all those different performance setups, let's turn to the next chapter and learn more about looping. I will also introduce some other software tools you can use for this style of performance.

11 More on Looping

Mixing together audio or MIDI loops of various lengths on the fly is a powerful performance concept, as we have seen in the last two chapters on Live. While Ableton Live is by far the most widely used software application for this purpose in the current music scene, there are also other programs you can use in this capacity. In this chapter we'll have a quick look at some of the alternatives to Live for loop-based performance, as well as some of their individual pluses and minuses. I'll also include a little background on the art of looping and where it originated.

> **LOOPER'S DELIGHT (Internet Mailing List)**
>
> Looper's Delight is a cultural and informational resource for musicians creating with audio loops of every sort. Loop based music essentially involves the repetition of audio samples, or loops. From that basic premise looping moves off in numerous directions, encompassing a wide range of techniques for building, manipulating, and using loops. The technique crosses many musical boundaries and appears in a wide range of musical styles and genres.
> (Quote from http://www.loopers-delight.com/history/Loophist.html.)

Music History in a Loop

Although today loop-based performance is most commonly associated with various genres of electronic music, it actually has a long history in many of the world's musical traditions. Loop-based music is actually a very ancient technique that long predates the electronic and digital musical instruments we use today. Before diving straight into the practical material, here's a quick look at where the idea of loop-based performance came from.

Looping Around the World

Looping repeated melodies and repeating song structures are commonly found in musical cultures around the world. Looping is a pervasive structural element in world music traditions ranging from the Javanese gamelan to Indian tabla drumming to the Shona mbira music of

Zimbabwe. Looping and repetition are also crucial structural elements in much modern popular music including rock, pop, and electronica.

In part, this may be simply because repeated patterns are the easiest to remember, but early Man also discovered the powerful consciousness-altering mental effects that can be induced via the repetition of musical patterns. Many of the world's great religious traditions developed specific techniques for using repetition through breath, voice, song, and music to induce various altered states of consciousness in order to get closer to God, the Ultimate, Nirvana, Krishna, or whatever name they gave their goal. These variously included the repetition of Indian mantras, the Gregorian chanting of Christian monks, and the music and dance of the Sufi Whirling Dervishes of Turkey, just to choose a few well-known examples.

Looping in the 20th Century

Modern loop-based performance using technological means to loop audio material got started in the 1960s with minimalist composers like Terry Riley, Philip Glass, and Steve Reich, who used tape loops to repeat short fragments of audio material over and over again.

Riley has been famously quoted as saying that "Although repetition is a major force in music, it was never used in this way before," and he was one of the most significant innovators in developing early audio looping technologies such as tape loops and tape delay feedback systems.

TERRY RILEY

I was asking the engineer, describing to him the kind of sound I had worked with in Mescaline Mix. I wanted this kind of long, repeated loop and I said, "Can you create something like that?" He got it by stringing the tape between two tape recorders and feeding the signal from the second machine back to the first to recycle along with the new incoming signals. By varying the intensity of the feedback you could form the sound either into a single image without any delay or increase the intensity until it became a dense chaotic kind of sound. I enjoy the interplay between the two extremes. This engineer was the first to create this technique that I know of, this began my obsession with time-lag accumulation feedback. It took me quite a while before I could afford to buy two good tape recorders to run this process in my own studio.
(Quote from http://www.loopers-delight.com/history/Loophist.html.)

Riley, Reich, and Glass all created pioneering tape loop- and delay-based pieces in the 1960s that became very influential among later electronic musicians, and these ideas were later developed further by performers such as Robert Fripp, Brian Eno, and Jon Hassell.

Looping Today with Computers and Software

Today, we can use computers and software to play back and combine our loops in performance, opening up far more creative possibilities than existed before with tape-loop systems or digital delay effects. Numerous software packages exist that allow us to play back many loops simultaneously, mixing them together and adding effects in performance.

Other Looping Software: Alternatives to Live

In Chapters 9 and 10 I included extensive information about how to use Ableton Live to playback and mix audio loops in live performance. Although Ableton's software is by far the most popular for use in this type of performance mode, there are alternatives you can use for live looping. Let's take a look at a few of them here and see what some of their advantages and disadvantages are.

Acid (PC)

Acid (see Figure 11.1) was first debuted by Sonic Foundry in 1998, and it brought something of a revolution in loop-based audio production.

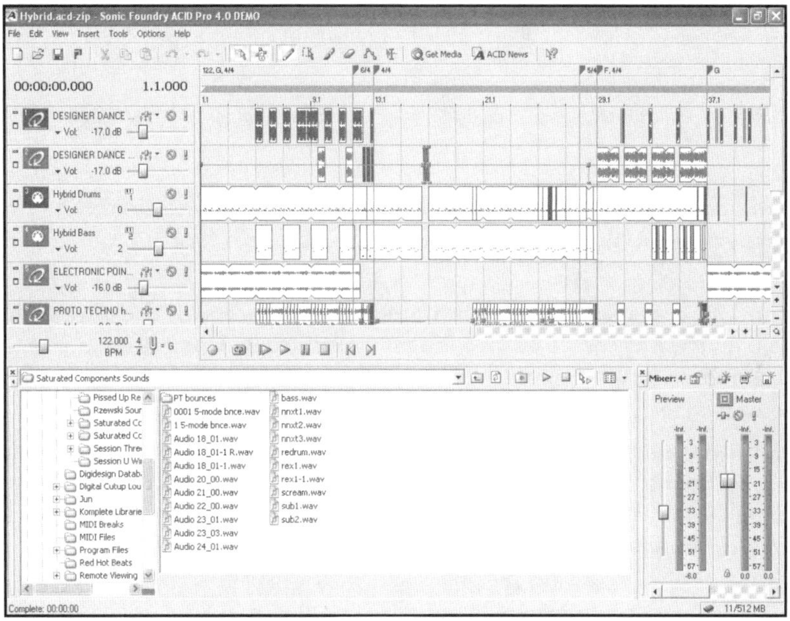

Figure 11.1 Sonic Foundry's Acid.

Before Acid, it had been possible to synchronize audio loops together in your main DAW software but it was something of a chore, requiring you to chop each loop precisely at beginning and end and then time-stretch them one by one until they matched up with the tempo grid of your composition. The genius of Acid was to introduce automatic time-stretching and looping features that made synchronizing loops and samples far easier than it had been previously.

Acid made quite a splash in the audio software marketplace when it was first introduced, and quite a few Mac-based studios running DAWs like Digital Performer or Pro Tools ended up installing dedicated Windows systems just to run Acid, in order to take advantage of its powerful loop-based music creation tools. However, although there have been several major upgrades of the software released, Sonic Foundry never seemed to deliver on the promise of their early breakthrough with this software. Acid eventually lost ground in its own market niche as more powerful alternatives became available from other manufacturers.

In many respects, Acid is similar to Ableton Live. Indeed, the Ableton Live project seems like it began in part as an attempt to take the basic concept of Acid and make it work better for live performance.

> **RUTGER DE GROOT (Ableton, Berlin)**
>
> A lot of the musicians working at Ableton have been using versions of Acid before Live was released. One thing we always hear from these users is that they are excited by the fact that they are now able to bring their compositions "to life," by rebuilding them (with the same loops) in Live. In Live the song can be "played" and improvised with, rather than just being a fixed composition. One can now take its songs on stage and perform them.
> (Quote from http://www.ableton.com/index.php?main=press&sub=press-release-020603.)

Ableton has now succeeded in this goal, in the estimation of most observers, and as a consequence, Live has now supplanted Acid as the preferred audio looping tool for both stage and studio.

Although Live and Acid are similar, Acid has a number of particular drawbacks that in my judgment make it an inferior choice for *live* looping specifically. Compared to Live, its sound quality is inferior, and it is significantly less stable. It lacks most of the live performance-oriented features of Live and is designed more for use as a studio production tool.

To be fair, it is worth mentioning that the various Sonic Foundry software applications—including Acid and Sound Forge—are now owned by Sony, and they have made a major facelift of Acid with the latest version, 5.0. Notwithstanding the new features introduced by Sony, however, Acid was never really designed for live performance in the first place and it is much less suitable than Live for this purpose.

Reason

After the first version of Reason (see Figure 11.2) was released by Sweden's Propellerhead Software in the fall of 2000, computer musicians immediately started trying to think of creative ways to use it in live performance.

For those not familiar with Reason, it can be thought of as an entirely self-contained virtual electronic music studio, all modeled in software and contained in your computer. The current version of Reason offers a mixer, synthesizers, a drum machine, samplers, and effects (see Figure 11.3), all controlled by the application's own built-in sequencer (see Figure 11.4).

Reason can be used as a brilliant performance tool in some applications, and I will have more to say about Reason in the subsequent chapters on live sequencing and sound generation. However, it is not very well suited to use as a live looping tool, and I mention it here because

Figure 11.2 Reason.

I would not recommend using Reason if you are interested in exploring looping as a performance technique.

Reason can be used most effectively live as either a software sequencer or as a standalone sound source that can be controlled/played from an external MIDI controller. However, I have also seen people use it as a kind of software looper, setting up banks of independent Dr. Rex software loop players in their Reason setup (see Figure 11.5) and using these to play back and mix a selection of different loops on the fly in performance.

If you already have Reason and you want to experiment with this kind of setup, simply create a mixer device and add as many Dr. Rex Players as you want to use below. Then assign some knobs or faders from your MIDI controller to control the faders on the Reason mixer, with other MIDI controllers assigned to various EQ or effects parameters if you want.

With this setup, you can play back a variety of loops and samples in the Dr. Rex Players and mix their output on the fly through the Reason mixer by using your MIDI controller. You can also open up new loops during performance and keep adding to the mix.

Figure 11.3 The virtual studio rack in Reason 3.0.

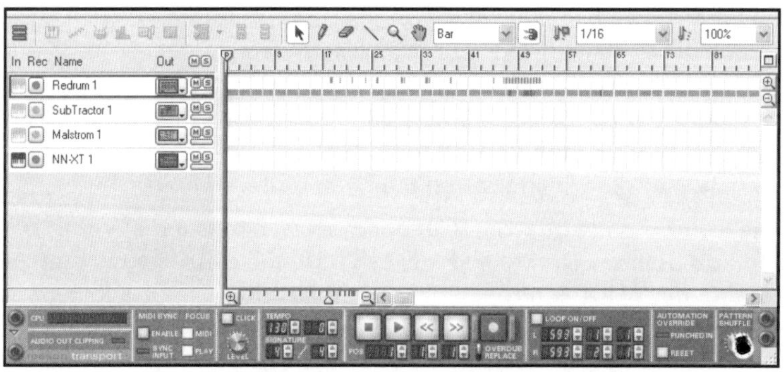

Figure 11.4 The sequencer window in Reason 3.0.

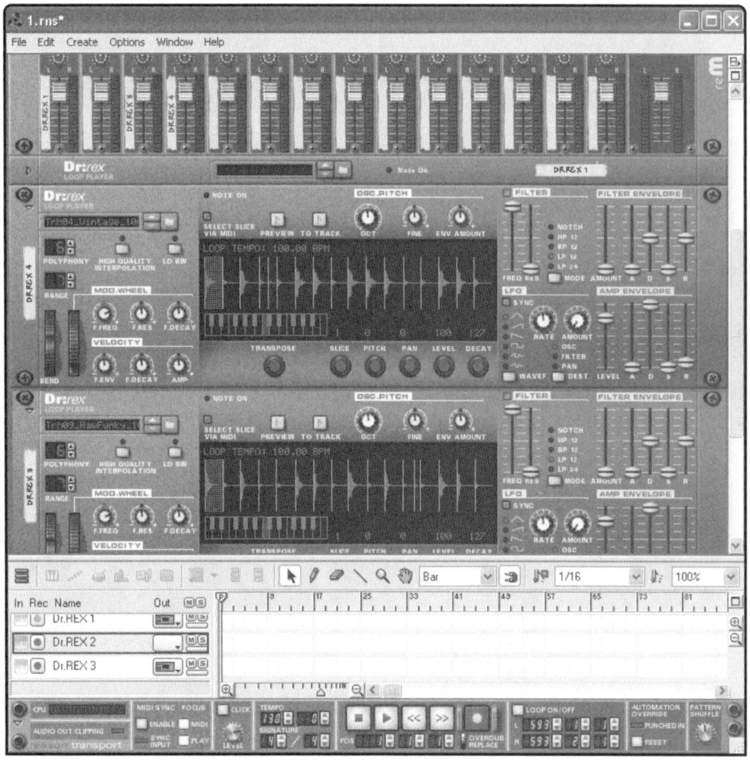

Figure 11.5 Using a rack full of Dr. Rex Players and the Reason mixer as a live software looping device.

I know musicians who have used this kind of setup in Reason extensively for live gigs. However, in spite of Reason's other virtues, it is not really designed for live *looping* and Ableton Live is far superior to Reason in this kind of application for a variety of reasons (no pun intended).

radiaL

radiaL is an application for live loop-based performance designed by jhno of Cycling '74. radiaL takes its name from the fact that it uses circular displays to indicate loop playback rather than the vertical/horizontal Session and Arrangement Views of Ableton Live (see Figure 11.6).

This radial interface is certainly unique, and it may inspire you in a different creative direction to work with this non-linear data view. You can load various loops into the channels in radiaL, automatically synchronizing them, and use live EQ and effects on them as they play back.

Although radiaL has not become nearly as popular among loop-based musicians as Ableton Live, it is certainly a viable alternative for loop-based performance, and it does offer some creative possibilities that Live lacks. Here's a brief overview of how it works.

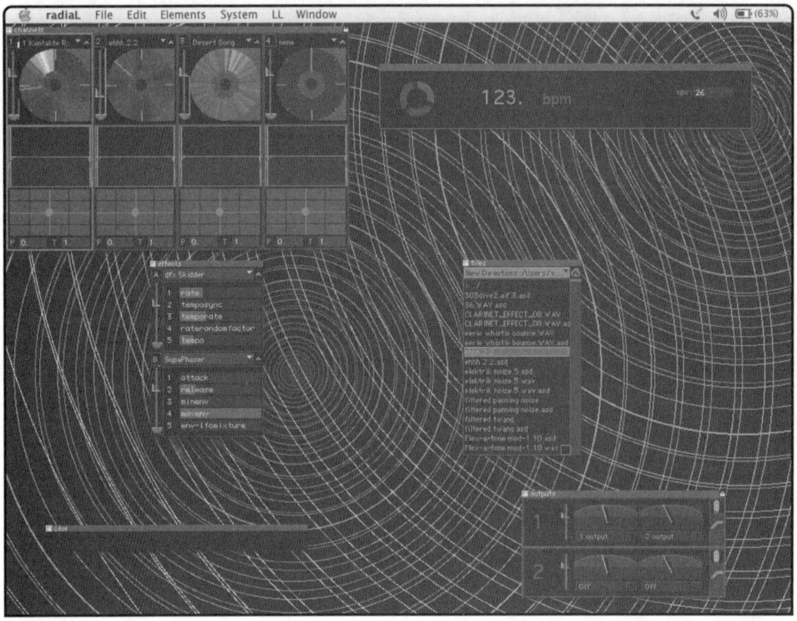

Figure 11.6 radiaL.

radiaL's Interface Windows

As shown in Figure 11.6 above, radiaL's interface is divided among six windows. The first of these is the Channels window (see Figure 11.7); this is where you load audio loops to be played back and manipulated.

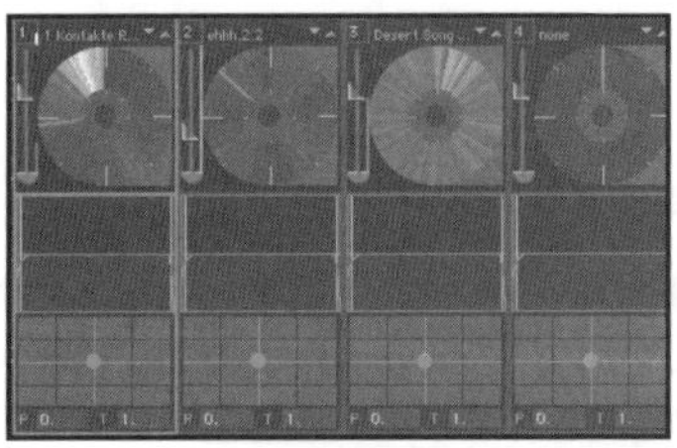

Figure 11.7 radiaL's Channels window.

When you first open the program, you will see four radial channels as shown in the image above, but you can add more as long as your computer's CPU, RAM, and hard drive speed are enough to keep up with the added load.

The Files window (see Figure 11.8) displays a list of the audio files available for playback on your computer. Simply drag and drop a file from this window into the Channels window to move it to a channel.

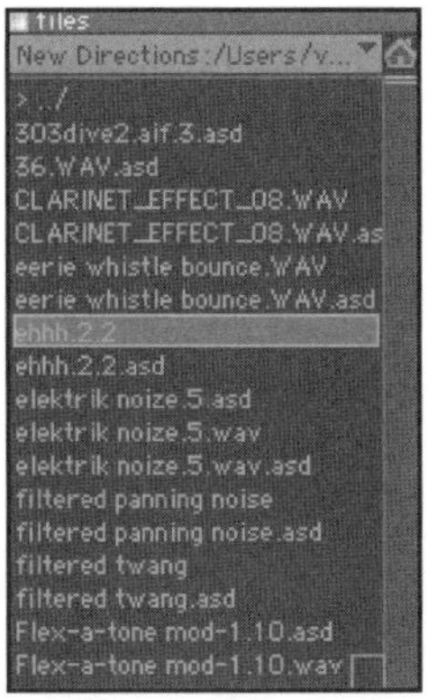

Figure 11.8 radiaL's Files window.

The Effects window (see Figure 11.9) is where you can access your VST plug-ins.

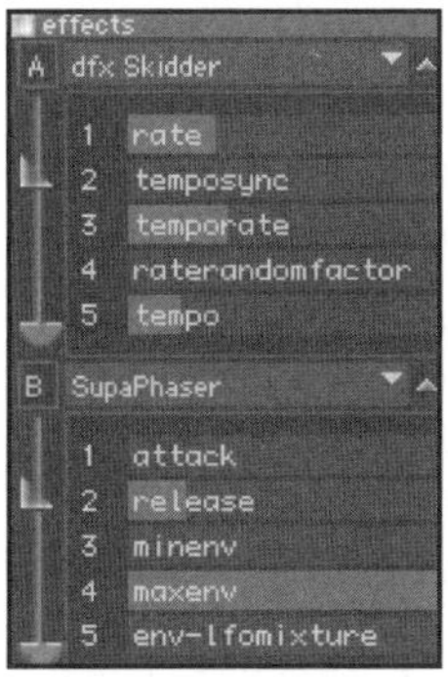

Figure 11.9 radiaL's Effects window.

The Outputs window (see Figure 11.10) offers us a master fader and level meters.

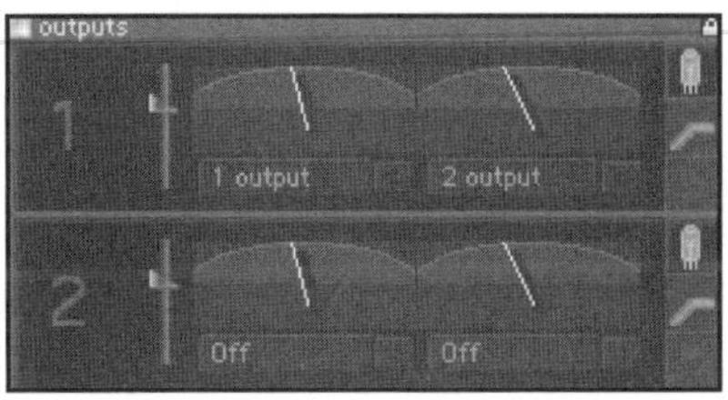

Figure 11.10 radiaL's Outputs window.

The Top window (see Figure 11.11) shows us the play status and the tempo.

Figure 11.11 radiaL's Top window.

Strangely enough, you may notice that there don't seem to be any start and stop buttons anywhere. This is because radiaL starts playing as soon as you drop an audio loop onto one of the channels... and it just keeps on going around and around... and around... and around...

Working with Loops in radiaL

radiaL's rotary dials offer some unique possibilities for loop playback control. For example, let's say you have one loop playing back and the playback indicator is steadily sweeping around the radial indicator. If you click your mouse inside the circle and drag across part of it, say from 25% to 50%, now the loop will only play that quarter-section of the whole circle over and over again.

Try clicking and dragging in the center ring to increase or decrease the amount of loop played. Or, double-click in the center to play the whole loop again. These operations will begin to give you a sense of how radiaL differs from Ableton Live. Although it is less powerful overall and lacks many of the advanced functions offered by Live, radiaL does offer an intuitive and spontaneous approach to loop-based music making that some performers find attractive.

You can also alter the playback of loops in radiaL in a number of other ways. Of course you can change the volume, or add filter, pitch shifting, and time shifting effects. As noted above, radiaL also supports VST plug-ins, so you can use many of your third-party plug-ins in radiaL as well. radiaL also offers ReWire support, opening up the possibility of using it in conjunction with Live, Reason, or other programs for a truly maniacal live setup.

MAX/MSP, Audiomulch, and Other Modular Software

In addition to software applications made with some degree of looping functionality built in such as Live, Acid, Reason, or radiaL, it is also possible to design your own looping machine for live performance using one of the modular software environments such as MAX/MSP or Audiomulch. There is more information about using this type of software to design your own live performance setup in Chapter 14, but I just want to note in passing that many of these object-oriented environments include loop players among the assortment of devices available.

This makes it a (relatively!) simple matter to design a setup with an array of loop players attached to some kind of software mixer, allowing you to mix and match loops together on the fly while you are performing. Christiaan Virant (whom I discussed towards the beginning of the book) built his own loop-playing application in Audiomulch just like this and used it for quite a few club gigs before finally getting early versions of Live and Reason.

If you are interested in this topic, see Chapter 14 for more on designing your own live application.

12 Live Sequencing

Live sequencing refers to the use of an audio/MIDI sequencing application (such as Pro Tools, Logic, Cubase, etc.; see below) in a live performance. In this chapter we'll look at some of the possible creative applications for using this type of software live.

Since sequencing is essentially a process of creating fixed musical structures, the inclusion of a chapter on sequencing in a book on live music performance is a bit strange. If you have created a complete MIDI sequence that plays all the parts of a song using VST instruments in your sequencer, for example, then what is there left to do in performance? You can just click the play button in your software and the whole song will play back from beginning to end, with no need for any human interference...

However, in actuality, sequencers can play many useful roles in live performance. Using a sequencer live doesn't have to be boring; it all depends on how it is used.

What is Sequencing, Anyway?

Audio/MIDI sequencer software (also often referred to as "DAW" or "Digital Audio Workstation" software) is the control center for computer-based music production. Powerhouse applications such as Pro Tools or Digital Performer provide you with a virtually unlimited number of audio and MIDI tracks for recording, arranging, and mixing your compositions.

The power and capabilities of the various sequencer applications has advanced tremendously over the years, fueled by the massive increases in affordable computing power as well as the intense competition between the various companies producing the software. If you're unfamiliar with this topic, here's a breakdown of the basic capabilities of these workhorse applications:

- They include a virtual mixing console offering various basic studio effects such as delay, reverb, chorus, compression, EQ, and so on, as well as some degree of support for plug-in effects and instruments from third-party manufacturers.
- They can record external sound sources directly through the inputs of your audio interface attached to the computer.

- They can record MIDI data from an external MIDI controller.
- They offer limitless nondestructive editing of recorded audio and MIDI material.
- They allow direct import of audio samples (from commercial sample collections or other sources), such as basslines, synth pad sounds, or drum loops.
- The MIDI data in the sequencer can be used to trigger plug-in software instruments hosted in the sequencer itself or external hardware modules (such as synthesizers or drum computers) connected to the computer via a MIDI interface.

As should be evident from this list, sequencer software is primarily designed for recording, editing, and mixing, not live performance.

Software

What software should you use for live sequencing? There are a lot of sequencing applications on the market these days, but there are only a handful of major applications that I would recommend.

If you don't yet own one of these, I would advise investigating further before investing in one or another. These applications are expensive, and learning a sequencer is a major commitment of time and energy as well, so once you learn one fairly well, you may be reluctant to change. Better to try and pick the right one from the beginning and learn it well.

One good idea is to try and find out what software other people in your genre of music are using to record and produce their music; at least you can't go too far wrong this way.

The Big Five

When we're talking sequencers, there are basically five major software applications to consider, plus one newcomer that is coming up fast. If you have already been recording and producing music with a computer for a while, you might already be familiar with one of these. Here are the five "majors" as it were, and the companies who make them:

- Pro Tools (Digidesign); see Figure 12.1
- Logic (Apple); see Figure 12.2
- Sonar (Cakewalk); see Figure 12.3
- Digital Performer (Mark of the Unicorn); see Figure 12.4
- Nuendo/Cubase (Steinberg); see Figure 12.5

I don't want to spend time here debating the various pros and cons of the five major sequencers, as it would be a fruitless (and thankless) task. Each seems to have its partisans, who have been known to argue with a near-religious fervor. (Only Mac vs. PC debates are comparable in their vehemence.) Many books could be (and have been) written about these complex applications, and it is difficult to know enough about all of them to make any meaningful comparison between them.

Figure 12.1 Pro Tools.

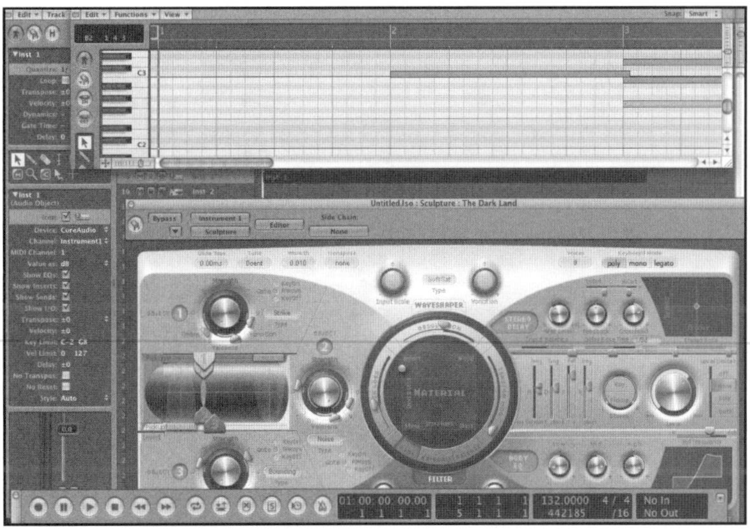

Figure 12.2 Logic.

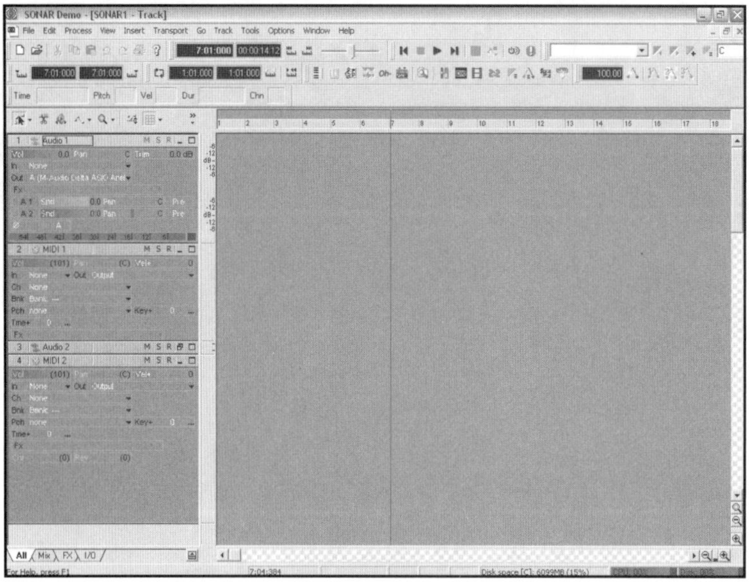

Figure 12.3 Sonar.

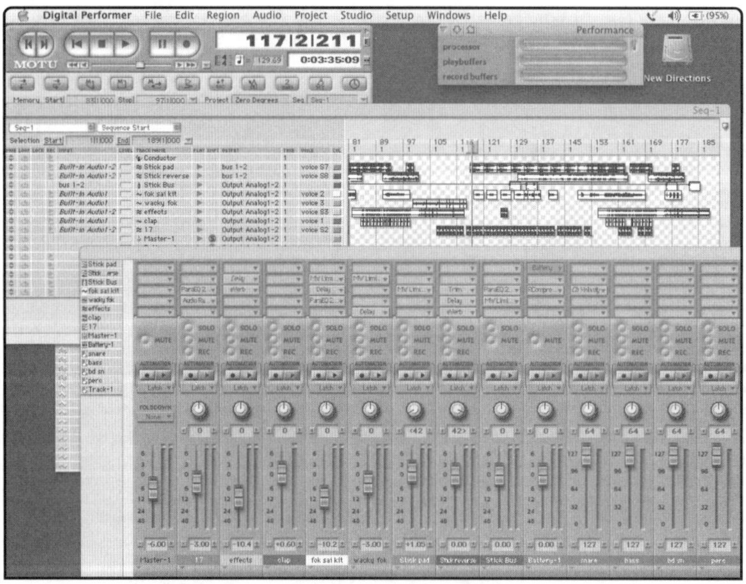

Figure 12.4 Digital Performer.

Figure 12.5 Cubase SX.

The important thing is that all five of these are powerful, pro-quality applications that provide a wealth of features and options for recording, sequencing, production, and mixing. Any of them would work fine in a live situation as well– if running on sufficiently powerful hardware, of course!

Ableton Live Again

The newcomer on the audio sequencer scene is Ableton Live. Live crops up in several different places in this book because it is so flexible and can be used in so many different ways as a live music tool.

When Live was first introduced, it seemed aimed primarily at the live performance market and didn't really compete with the five major sequencers. It could only work with audio tracks and loops (no MIDI), and its sequencing and arranging capabilities were limited.

However, with later releases, Ableton added more sequencing capabilities as well as the capability to work with MIDI and software instruments (in VST or AU format), and with the release of Live 4 in 2004, Live really started to come into its own as a production and sequencing tool. Although Live may lack many of the complex features of Pro Tools or Nuendo, it is plenty powerful enough to produce complete tracks, and it is beginning to compete more and more with the other sequencers.

Reason

Propellerhead's Reason software also comes up a few times in this book, again because it is flexible and can be used live in a number of different roles. Reason isn't really a full-fledged competitor to the other sequencers above because it only works with MIDI and not audio for one thing, and also because you can only work with Reason's built-in sound devices, such as the Subtractor synth and the NN-XT sampler.

However, I wanted to mention Reason in this chapter anyway because there are a significant number of performers who produce and perform their music almost entirely with Reason. Although Reason's limited number of devices and lack of audio recording support would seem to limit its creative possibilities, it is possible to import any sound into Reason by using its built-in samplers, and I am still surprised by the wide range of music and sound that different artists manage to produce with it.

If you use Reason to play back complete tracks in performance, it will function in a similar fashion to the other sequencing applications covered above, with similar capabilities and limitations.

Performance Approaches

When we talk about sequencing we are basically talking about the playback of a fixed musical arrangement. Once we start it playing back, the sequence itself will not change, and all of the various parts of the song will play through in order just as we arranged them beforehand. There are many different ways you can integrate this basic concept into a live performance, however. In the rest of this chapter, I will illustrate some of the possible ways you can use a sequencer live, as well as some specific examples of how to set this up.

Although I will refer to one or another sequencing application in the sections below, keep in mind that most of the concepts I mention here could be implemented with any of the programs covered above.

Playing a Complete Sequenced Live Set

One approach to playing live with a sequencer is simply to play your entire set out of the sequencer, with all the parts pre-recorded in the computer either as MIDI or audio data. Although we usually produce our music one song or track at a time in a sequencer, for live performance it can be very advantageous to combine all of your sequences together into one massive mother-of-all-sequences that contains your complete live set from beginning to end.

Performing this way has a number of advantages.

For one thing, there is no need to open a new song file before playing the next song. This is very important, as it can take a few minutes to open a new song file in a sequencer and this is often impractical for performance.

Another important point is that preparing the entire set ahead of time in the sequencer allows you to carefully sculpt the transitions between tracks, especially important if you are playing dance-oriented music.

In addition, doing your live show this way has the advantage of security. You know more or less what will happen in the show before it begins (barring any hardware or software problems, of course!).

On the other hand, there are disadvantages as well. The most obvious is that if you prearrange your entire live set in advance, you lose a lot of the spontaneous excitement that a looser, more improvisational performance style can bring.

There are ways to introduce improvisation and spontaneity into even a completely sequenced set, however. Let's look at one psytrance artist who does his performances this way and see what techniques he uses in order to keep his live sets exciting and fresh.

Prophei

Prophei is a producer of psychedelic trance, industrial, and other electronic music styles based in Long Beach, California (see Figure 12.6).

Figure 12.6 Prophei.

Prophei has been writing his own music with computers and sequencers since 1991, when he was in high school. At that time, he used an Apple Macintosh Plus to run an early MIDI sequencing application called Master Tracks, controlling various Roland and Yamaha synthesizers. His first live music performance with a computer was while he was still in high school, singing his original songs while the Mac Plus played the sequenced electronic backing tracks behind him.

PROPHEI (Long Beach, California)

Prophei has been writing music for over 15 years. For him, what started out as an emotional necessity has become a spiritual journey. Prophei reaches out to the soul with a colorful psychedelic soundscape designed to lift the listener to a new level of being. Major importance is placed on an utmost honesty in presentation, and a dedication to artistic purity. Many different pieces of self exist in each human being, much like the pieces of a puzzle. Peace within ourselves occurs when we become able to assemble these pieces into a unified whole. Much like this, Prophei strives to use his many different musical projects to describe these pieces of himself, and help achieve a balance and unity in his life through them. His greatest goal is to help others do the same utilizing his music as a catalyst.
(From Prophei's online bio at http://www.prophei.com.)

Later he started producing psychedelic trance tracks and playing live trance sets at clubs and festivals. Most of his live gigs in the last few years have been solo performances of his psytrance music. Prophei uses Pro Tools for his sequenced live performances, here's how he does it.

Prophei Hardware

Prophei's current live rig is centered around a 1GHz G4 PowerBook with 512MB RAM running Pro Tools M-Powered, the recently released version of Digidesign's Pro Tools sequencer that is compatible with a variety of audio interfaces from M-Audio. He uses an M-Audio FireWire 410 audio interface and runs its eight analog outputs into eight input channels of a 32-channel analog mixing board.

Prophei doesn't use an external controller to manipulate the parameters in his sequencer software, preferring to use the analog mixing board for live mixing and for sending various parts of his arrangement through a variety of outboard effects units, using the auxiliary send and return channels of his mixer. He also carries a number of hardware synthesizers and samplers with him to live gigs, including an Akai MPC 2000 XL, a Yamaha AN1x, and a Nord Lead.

With the channels from Pro Tools (via the FireWire 410) and all of his outboard gear connected, here's how Prophei sets up his live mixer:

First of all, eight channels of audio run direct from Pro Tools out through the FireWire 410; although he often uses as many as 32 tracks as a time for his live sequences, he breaks them down into four stereo buses within the software and then sends the resulting eight channels of audio output to the mixer. This allows him to arrange his software tracks into groups of similar sounds (drums on one stereo output, pad sounds on another, bass sounds on another, and so on) and retain considerable control over his live mix in performance.

The next four mixer channels are returns from Prophei's outboard effects, so he can use these to adjust the level of the effects in the mix.

The next six or so channels are used for the outboard synthesizers and samplers, one stereo pair for each instrument.

Prophei Live on Stage!

When Prophei goes out to do a live show, he is basically playing back a single gigantic Pro Tools sequence that may contain an hour or more of continuous music (see Figure 12.7). While in the wrong hands this kind of approach can be lifeless and boring, Prophei uses a number of performance techniques to keep his live sets fresh every time he goes out to play.

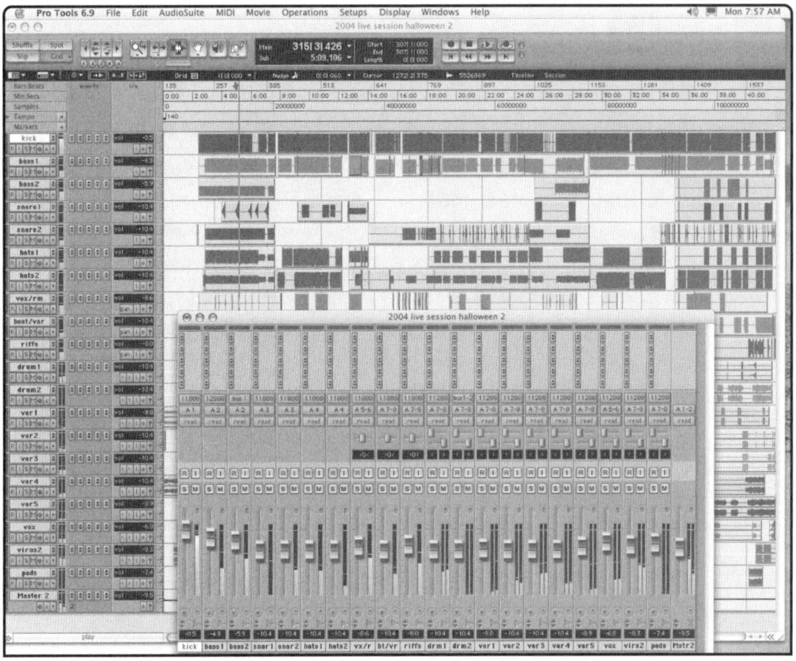

Figure 12.7 One of Prophei's live Pro Tools sequences.

For one thing, he very actively uses the faders on the analog mixing board to change the live mix and make various parts of the music more or less prominent over time. Sometimes he might drop out the drums entirely, for example, or mute everything except the bassline to create a sense of ebb and flow in the music.

He uses the sends and returns on the mixer to send various parts of the music through his outboard effects and then back to the mixer again. This allows him to put the effects on only certain elements in the music and create exciting live sound effects in tune with the vibe of the audience.

In addition, he uses the hardware synthesizers and Akai MPC sampler to add live keyboard synth parts to the music and trigger samples, giving his music an additional live dimension.

Prophei also pays a lot of attention to the way his music sounds in the particular venue he's playing in. Since he still has the different parts of the music separated on his outboard mixer, he is able to carefully balance the levels of the various tracks and the EQ of each track so that his music sounds the best it can in that specific context.

Prophei Whys and Wherefores

Prophei has spent a lot of time thinking about how to construct a live rig that would best suit his music and the kind of situations he usually performs in (large outdoor dance events, for the most part) and when I interviewed him, he had a lot to say about how he has put together his hardware/software setup.

In the first place, the reason he plays live using a sequencer is that he has spent a long time arranging his tracks just how he wants them to be, and he wants to keep this same structure in performance rather than rely on a more improvised style of performance.

He uses Pro Tools as his live sequencer because he uses it to produce his tracks as well. This makes him easy for him to take his latest material straight from the studio to the stage. In addition, merging a number of different song files into one long sequence is particularly easy with Pro Tools. Simply drag and drop a Pro Tools song file onto another Pro Tools sequence that is already open and the program will open a dialog box asking you how you want to merge the tracks of the two song files together. See Figures 12.8a and 12.8b.

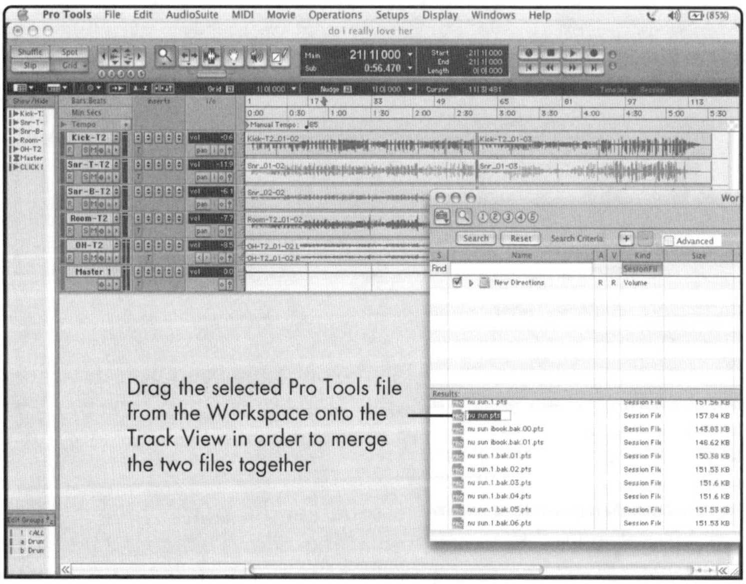

Figure 12.8a Merging song files in Pro Tools.

Prophei also believes quite strongly that Pro Tools sounds perceptibly better than any of its sequencer competitors, and this is another reason he prefers to use it for live gigs. In his view, a live performer is responsible for making their music sound the best it possibly can by

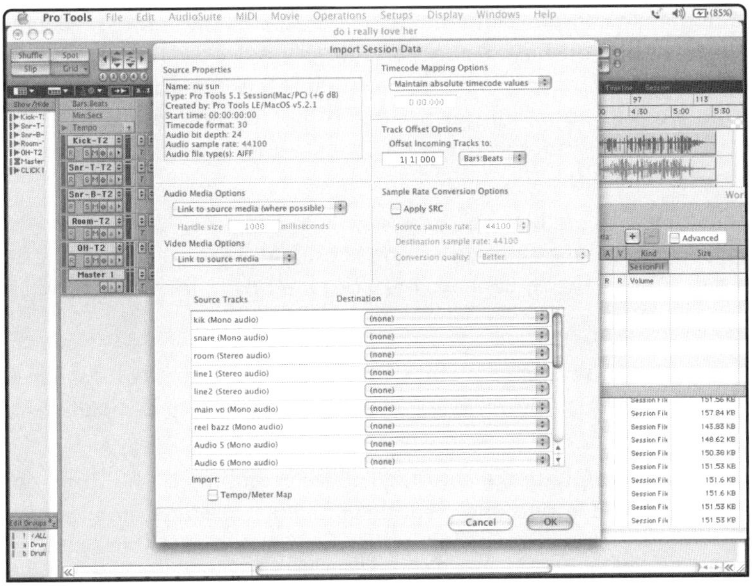

Figure 12.8b The Import Session Data dialog with options for merging Pro Tools song files.

whatever means possible, and he feels that his music sounds the best when it is played directly out of Pro Tools.

Does it Work?

The inevitable question: How well does it all work on the gig?

In fact, this is another reason Prophei uses Pro Tools to do his sequenced performances: Its high degree of stability. In all of the many live computer gigs he has done over the past several years, under the most demanding of conditions (in the desert, for example), he has only had problems with his setup once or twice, and he swears by the stability of his current setup... after testing it thoroughly at home, of course!

For more information on Prophei and links to hear some of his music, check http://www.prophei.com.

Augmenting a Live Band

Another widely popular use for a sequencer in live performance is to augment a live band and add extra parts to the music that none of the musicians are playing live. Let's consider how and why you might use this approach to add sequenced parts to your band's live performances, and look at some of the specific ways that a sequencer can be integrated into a live band setup.

As I described in Chapter 1, computers and sequencers are widely used by major international pop artists to back up their live bands in concert and make the live performance sound more like the album, adding, for example, some of the actual sounds and effects from the album to the live mix. Pop artists often do this to add parts from their recordings to their live performances, such as electronic drums and percussion, samples, or sound effects. Pop audiences are more inclined to want to hear live performances that sound more or less "just like the album," so it is especially important to recreate specific effects or sounds from the original recording that fans will recognize.

I have already explained something of how the live computer musicians working with Madonna and Kelly Clarkson use Digital Performer and Ableton Live to play back some of the backing parts these artists use in concert; here are the basics for this kind of setup.

Keeping in Sync

The main issue in integrating a sequencer with a live band is the necessity for the live musicians to keep in time with the parts playing from the sequencer. There are basically two ways you can do this.

On the one hand, you can simply make sure that all the members of the band can hear the music playing from the computer loud and clear through their on-stage monitors and are able to play along accordingly. This approach can work well in many situations, particularly when there is no live drummer in the band and the sequencer is the rhythmic foundation of the band. In this case, the live musicians can simply play on top of the sequenced beats and rhythms and syncing is unlikely to become an issue. However, monitoring the computer parts this way always carries the risk that the musicians may in their enthusiasm start playing louder than they were during the sound check when the levels were set, drowning out the sequencer in their monitors and getting out of sync with the sequenced parts.

Another way to keep the band in sync with the computer is by using a click track to keep the live drummer, in time. This is the method used in most large pop concerts, where it is essential to give as "perfect" a performance as possible and there is little room for mistakes. In this case, the live programmer will generate some kind of metronome click from the sequencer and run this out along with the music in a special monitor mix, which the drummer listens to on headphones. The other musicians in the band cannot hear the click, but as long as they keep time with the live drummer, they will be in time with the sequencer as well.

Staying Flexible

As Mike McKnight (programmer for Madonna) observed in the interview I quoted in Chapter 1, even when working with a sequencer it is sometimes necessary to jump ahead or behind in the sequenced arrangement during a performance. When I was doing pop music gigs on bass in the late '90s, for example, sometimes we would start playing a song together with a computer sequence, perfectly in time, only to be thrown off when the singer missed his/her cue and entered in the wrong measure, on the wrong beat, with the wrong lyrics, or whatever. The session musicians I was working with usually had no problem quickly adjusting to and compensating for the singer's mistake by following him/her; however, this caused a new problem because the band was no longer together with the sequenced parts on the computer.

This is one of the main things the on-stage programmer needs to look out for. In our case, what usually happened was that the programmer would first fade out all of the computer parts so that the audience wouldn't be able to hear anything wrong. Then he would try to jump ahead in the sequence to some known reference point in the song, such as the chorus or an instrumental breakdown and begin playback from there at the same time that the band reached that point. This was always a tricky process and it didn't always come out exactly right, but as McKnight said in his interview as well, when you're working with a star, the star is always right, and unfortunately the poor computer programmer is left to pick up the pieces when things go badly wrong...

STG

STG is a self-described "cyberpunk" band from Southern California (see Figure 12.9). They have been playing together in one form or another since 1989, and have been using some kind of sequencer to augment their live shows for nearly that entire period.

Figure 12.9 STG.

Although STG has a full band lineup when they play live, featuring two guitarists, a bassist, a vocalist, a drummer, and a live keyboard player, they use a sequencer as well to add electronic percussion and various synthesized sound effects to their live performances. While in the early days of the band they used an Atari 1040ST running the Master Tracks MIDI software and triggering various outboard hardware modules to play live, on their recent 2005 reunion gigs, they have been using a Mac PowerBook G4 running Ableton Live in sequencer mode.

Figure 12.10 shows one of STG's live sequenced arrangements in Live.

STG's music is a loud intense mix of industrial, punk, and electronic influences, and the computer rhythms would likely be lost in the din at some points if the musicians didn't have a way to stay in time with the sequencer. To avoid this problem, they run a live mix of the electronic drum and percussion parts to drummer Brandon via headphones, and he plays the live drums

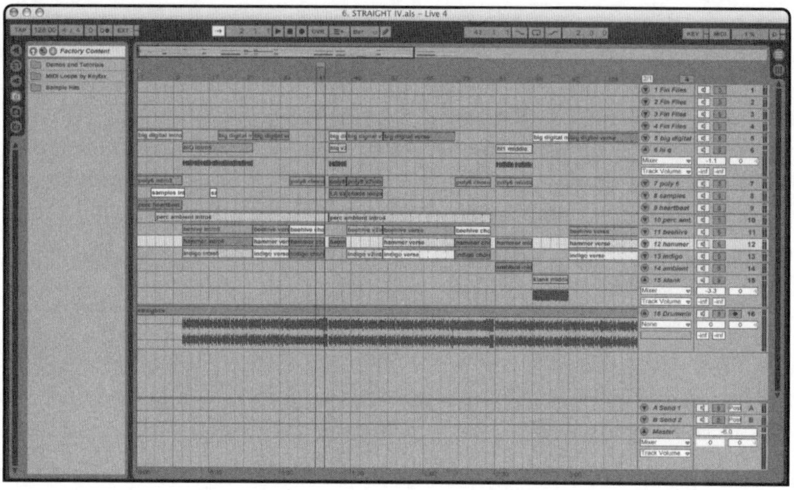

Figure 12.10 An STG arrangement in Live showing the sequenced parts.

in time along with the sequenced parts, keeping the whole band in sync with the computer. Also, STG prefers the combination of the live drummer playing on top of the electronic rhythms—this is the sound they are going for.

STG has a live synthesist/keyboardist in the band in addition to the computer, and he usually plays any distinct keyboard parts live, for example, melodies or riffs. The computer is reserved for playing electronic beats and sound effects that would be impossible or impractical for the musicians to play live on their instruments.

The computer arrangements for STG's songs are completely sequenced from beginning to end; there is no improvisation with the computer parts. One of the band members simply triggers playback in Live at the beginning and the sequence starts to play, joined by the musicians. While this kind of approach is potentially boring as there is no flexibility in the arrangement, in STG's case, this slight drawback is more than made up for by the raw live energy of the instrumentalists and vocalist in performance.

STG is a good example of a band whose sound is predominated by the live instruments (bass, guitar, drums, etc.) and vocals, but still manage to incorporate electronic sounds in a significant way. Of course, this kind of approach could be applied to any type of music. STG's setup is a good model to work from if you are trying to do something similar with your band.

13 Live Sound Generation

Most of this book has been about playing music live with a computer where the music is at least partially pre-recorded. For example, if you are DJing with the computer, you are playing back a series of entirely pre-recorded tracks, whether your own or those of other artists. The creativity and interactive quality of the performance comes in how you mix the tracks together, how you arrange them in sequence, what tracks you choose to play in reaction to the crowd, and so on.

Similarly, if you are playing live using Ableton Live or some other loop-based software, you are mixing together chunks of music and audio, loops, effects, and so on. This approach can make for a very dynamic live performance, but just as with DJing, you are basically playing back and mixing chunks of audio that you have previously created.

I have concentrated on these types of approaches in this book because they are used by the majority of today's computer music performers.

However, you can also use the computer live as a standalone sound source. Many exciting new software applications aimed at this market have been released recently, and with the dropping prices of computer hardware, it seems likely that this type of use will increase considerably in coming years. We can expect to see more and more musicians using computers live to replace racks of hardware synthesizer modules or other outboard gear.

There are a number of powerful advantages to using a computer for these functions instead of a dedicated hardware device, as we shall see throughout this chapter. A contemporary Mac or PC is more powerful than most dedicated hardware modules and, crucially, it is much more flexible. While synthesizers and samplers often become outdated quickly as music technology continues to change and progress, if you are using a computer, you can always get new software in order to update your sounds.

You can also carry any amount of software you want to a gig, and even use a variety of different applications during the course of one performance if you want to draw from a wider range of sounds. It is certainly much easier to bring along a laptop computer and a lightweight MIDI controller keyboard than a rack of heavy outboard equipment! Used as a standalone sound generator, the computer can replace a hardware synth or sampler module, for example.

With the widespread availability of lightweight MIDI controller keyboards, it has become increasingly common to see a keyboard player using a MIDI keyboard and a laptop computer running a software synthesizer, in place of a dedicated hardware synthesizer. With the huge number of software instruments available, a computer is potentially a much more powerful and creative tool that any dedicated hardware instrument could be.

Using the computer this way is basically a simple setup. You can use a MIDI keyboard or other controller to play while the computer takes the place of the sound module you might have used in the past. You will need a good-quality audio interface as well, to send the audio output of your software to the PA.

One important point to consider when setting up your software instruments this way for live performance is syncing together with other members of your band. Although you may be playing everything yourself on the keyboard live, it still may be useful for you to sync together with other computer musicians in the band in order for the effects and oscillators in your software to synchronize to the same clock signal as the other players.

There are dozens, if not hundreds, of software synthesizers and other virtual instruments that can be used in this capacity on a typical computer system. I am not going to discuss these instruments in great detail here—that is a topic for another book, and Course Technology offers a numbers of other books specifically covering this, such as *Sampling and Soft Synth Power* by Michael Prager—but I will discuss a few of the more common systems and look at an example setup to give you some ideas.

If you are interested in further exploring the range of software synths available, a good place to start would be the software synthesizer page on the Shareware Music Machine at http://www.hitsquad.com/smm/cat/SOFTWARE_SYNTHESIZERS. Another excellent Web site with extensive information about virtual software instruments and effects plug-ins is the KVR Audio site at http://www.kvraudio.com.

Steinberg's V-Stack and the VST Standard

Steinberg's VST (Virtual Studio Technology) for software effects and instruments, first launched in 1996, is one of the most common plug-in standards. It is most widely supported plug-in standard among other manufacturers, and there are literally hundreds of VST instruments and plug-ins available, both commercial products and freeware/shareware.

It is possible to play live with VST software instruments but you will need a VST host application to run them in. You could use any of the major audio/MIDI sequencer applications that provide VST compatibility for this purpose, such as Steinberg's own Cubase/Nuendo, Ableton Live, or Acid. For example, you could create an audio channel in Cubase, load a VST instrument in one of its slots, record-enable the track, and then you would be ready to play.

However, if your principal interest is live performance and not recording, it is somewhat awkward to use a sequencing program like Cubase as your VST host. It has many features that are unrelated to performance, and the entire layout of the program is oriented towards recording.

Steinberg provides a simpler solution for those who want to play VST instruments live: V-Stack. This is a 32-bit VST host designed expressly for the needs of computer performers playing live. It provides a virtual equipment rack that allows you to load up as many as 16 VST instruments simultaneously, controlled via an onscreen virtual mixer (see Figure 13.1).

Figure 13.1 The instrument rack and mixer in Steinberg's V-Stack.

Using a dedicated standalone application like V-Stack to host your virtual plug-in instruments instead of a sequencer like Cubase provides a number of advantages in performance. For example, you can quickly access relevant keyboard functions that allow you to transpose, layer, and split your VST instruments across the range of your MIDI controller. You can also insert VST effects on your instruments in the V-Stack mixer as well as using the mixer's EQ, send, and return features for further signal processing.

Using V-Stack to Expand Your Studio

Although my focus here is on using software for live performance, I should also point out in passing that a live plug-in instrument host like V-Stack can be a powerful production tool as well, particularly if you have two or more computer systems (either Mac or PC) in your studio. Having two separate computer systems allows for the possibility of running your main sequencer/recording software on one computer while using a second system to run virtual instruments. This can be a far more powerful and flexible studio setup than you could create using only a single machine. V-Stack supports a number of connectivity protocols so that it can be used in this kind of scenario, including Steinberg's own VST System Link technology as well as Propellerhead's ReWire standard.

Other Virtual Instrument Hosts

There are also a number of other standalone virtual instrument hosts that you can use that provide similar functionality to V-Stack. For example, Rax from Granted Software (see Figure 13.2) is a host application for Mac OS X that can host instruments in Apple's Audio Units (AU) format instead of Steinberg's VST format.

Figure 13.2 Rax.

Your choice of which host to use will depend in part on what plug-in instruments you want to use and what formats they support. Many plug-ins support two or more formats (AU, VST, DX, etc.), but some are available in only one, so this is an important point to keep in mind when you are putting together your software rig.

Reason

As noted already in this book, Propellerhead Software's Reason is a powerful music software application that combines virtual synthesizers, samplers, and effects together with a built-in sequencer. Reason can be used live in a variety of ways, as we saw in the chapter on live sequencing, but it can also be a good sound source for a live keyboard player.

To use Reason like this, simply create a Reason song file containing whatever modules and devices you want to have available for live performances. Reason has two different synthesizers, two samplers, a loop player, and a drum machine as well as many different effects, so there are a lot of possibilities. Reason 3.0 has also introduced the new Combinator device, which can be used to combine two or more devices in a single patch.

Figure 13.3 shows a sample live rack set up in Reason 3.0.

Figure 13.3 A live rack setup in Reason.

Set up your Reason song something like this, a number of different modules attached to a mixer. Then select your MIDI controller in Reason's preferences and use Reason's MIDI learning mode to assign your faders and knobs to control various parameters of the devices you are working with. For example, try assigning controllers to the frequency and resonance knobs of the synths and samplers for some wacky filter sweep possibilities.

In this configuration, you might not have to touch the computer very often as most of the basic controls you need to use in Reason can probably be assigned to controls on your MIDI device. However, if you want to switch between using different devices while you're playing, you will need to use the cursor to select a different active channel for MIDI input. In Figure 13.4, you can see the small MIDI plug image on the Subtractor channel that shows which channel is currently active.

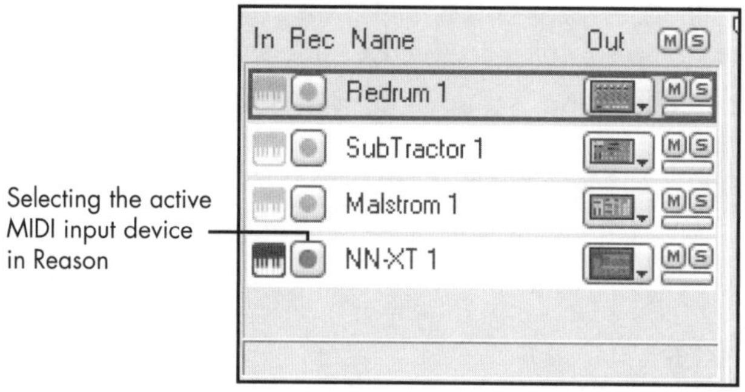

Figure 13.4 Selecting the active MIDI channel in Reason.

Keyboardist Matt Piper uses Reason as part of a more complex setup that also uses Ableton Live; for more on how to configure Reason for live performance, see my description of Matt's rig in the next section.

Ableton Live Again

"Oh no," you're probably thinking, "we already had 100 pages on Ableton Live in Chapters 9 and 10. Won't this guy ever shut up about it?"

However, Ableton Live tends to crop up again and again in any discussion of live computer music, precisely because it can be used in performance in so many different roles.

In the present discussion, while Ableton Live is not exactly a sound source/instrument itself, I bring it up again here because in many ways, it is an ideal host application to use for playing software instruments live.

Live can host both VST and (on the Mac) AU format virtual instruments and effects for live use, on as many channels as you want, and you can hook up one or more MIDI controllers to play them.

It also supports ReWire, allowing it to host Reason as well.

These basic functions are all supported by other audio/MIDI sequencers as well, of course. However Live's unique layout is designed for ease of use in live performance, so it is better suited for this role than any of its competitors.

To see how this works, and how to use Reason and Live together, let's look at a setup used by one virtual keyboardist and improviser here in LA.

Matt Piper's Performance Setup with Live and Reason

Matt Piper is a 33-year-old keyboardist and music technologist (see Figure 13.5).

Figure 13.5 Matt Piper.

Matt started playing piano and guitar while growing up in rural Illinois, and started using computers to write music in 1991 after relocating to California. His first computer music studio featured an Atari 1040ST with 4MB of RAM running an early MIDI-only version of Cubase.

Matt used Cubase and the Atari to control a variety of external hardware sound sources via MIDI, such as an e-Mu Proteus synth module and a Roland sampler. These were connected to a mixer and then recorded on a Tascam TSR8 8-track ½-inch reel-to-reel tape machine.

However, at this time, the computer didn't generate any of the sounds—it only controlled them, triggering playback from the synths and samplers. Now Matt uses a computer live to create all of the sounds he uses in performance.

Matt sees the computer as a very economical and adaptable tool, capable of near-infinite expandability and complexity. "The computer is like an instrument," he told me, "but more than a single instrument, it's really more like an 'instrument construction set' that allows you to create whatever kind of instrument you want to use in software. In some cases, the instruments you construct can be somewhat unpredictable..."

Matt has created a software setup for himself for his live gigs that is truly unique and reflects his characteristic musical personality. He uses both Reason and Live together in combination in his rig; let's take a look at Matt's hardware/software setup and see how it works.

Matt's Hardware Setup

Matt uses a Dell Inspiron laptop computer together with an M-Audio FireWire Audiophile interface, as well as an M-Audio Radium61 keyboard controller. This is a good setup for him for several reasons.

The Dell laptop has plenty of CPU power and RAM and can handle pretty much any combination of applications and plug-ins that he wants to use.

The FireWire Audiophile gives him two separate stereo outputs; one pair is routed directly to the main PA while he uses the other pair for cueing up new sounds on headphones.

The Radium61 (see Figure 13.6) features eight knobs and eight faders, all MIDI-assignable to control various parameters of Matt's software. He uses these controls extensively in performance to modify his live sounds.

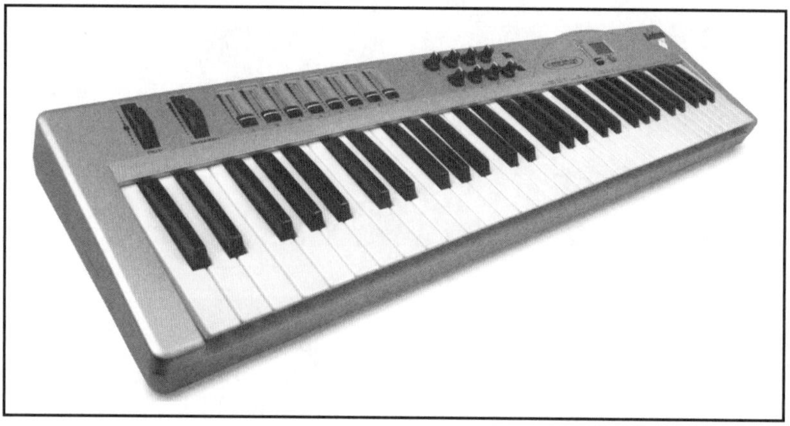

Figure 13.6 The M-Audio Radium61.

Matt's Reason Setup

First let's look at Matt's Reason setup. All of his live sounds originate from Reason's samplers and synthesizers, and he uses a lot of them to give himself a wide range of sounds to choose from.

Matt's live Reason setup is shown in Figure 13.7.

Here we can see that Matt's Reason rack has the Reason mixer at the top and then a series of software sound modules connected below. Matt's Reason setup includes:

- One mixer, receiving the outputs from all the software instruments below (see Figure 13.8); the master volume control of the mixer is controlled by one of the knobs on the Radium keyboard.
- One NN-XT sampler loaded with a set of high-quality Rhodes electric piano samples; the output from this instrument then goes through a phaser and a chorus/flanger effect before reaching the Reason mixer (see Figure 13.9), and the on/off/bypass switch of the phaser is mapped to a knob on the Radium.
- Another NN-XT sampler loaded with a set of high-quality clavinet samples; the mod wheel on Matt's Radium keyboard is assigned to control a wah-wah-like effect on this sampler, giving him the ability to play very guitar-like rhythms and phrasings.
- Three more instances of the NN-XT, which Matt uses to hold an assortment of sampled instrument sounds such as a tambura, a digeridoo, and a Hammond organ.

Figure 13.7 Matt Piper's Reason setup.

Figure 13.8 The Reason mixer.

- Seven instances of Reason's Malström synthesizer, preset to a variety of pads and weird sound patches (see Figure 13.10).

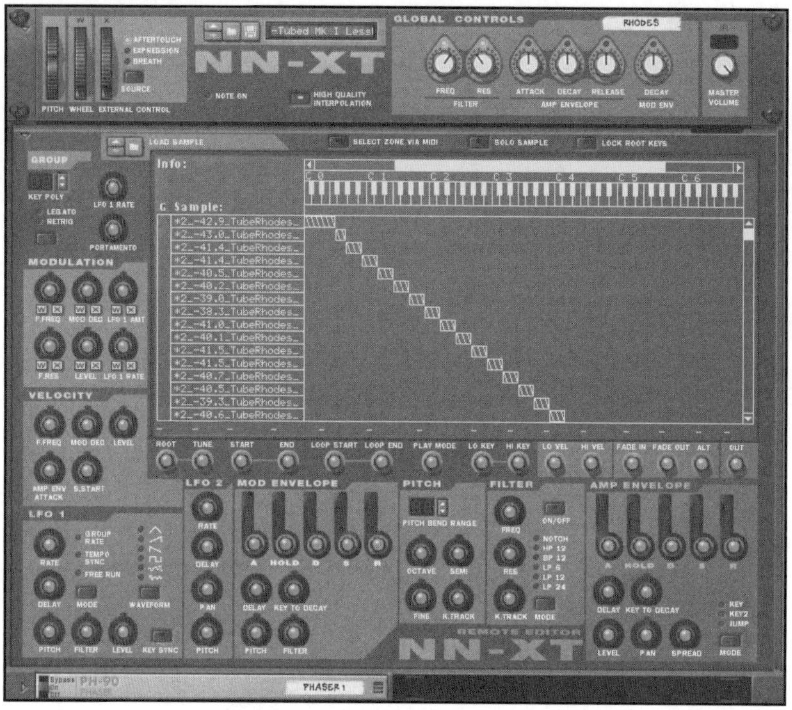

Figure 13.9 The NN-XT Rhodes.

Figure 13.10 Seven Malströms.

- One Matrix sequencer device connected to one of the Malström synths; this Matrix is constantly playing a weird little sequence that Matt has programmed, he uses this to play a pattern on the Malström while using the mod wheel on his Radium to do a filter sweep on the sound (see Figure 13.11).
- One Subtractor synth loaded with a sine wave patch, with legato and portamento turned up; various controls on Matt's keyboard are assigned to change the LFO waveform and other LFO parameters live...this patch is good for theremin-style leads as well as solid deep subbass sounds (see Figure 13.12).
- Another Matrix sequencer is set running in a constant sine wave pattern, and Matt uses this to create an autopanning effect on the Rhodes NN-XT by running the Curve CV output of the Matrix to the Pan CV In on Channel One of the mixer (see Figure 13.13a and 13.13b).

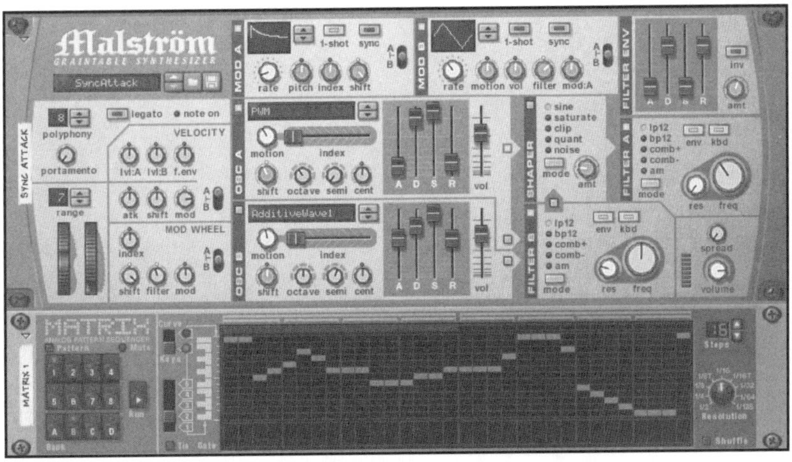

Figure 13.11 Atonal Matrix arpeggiation action.

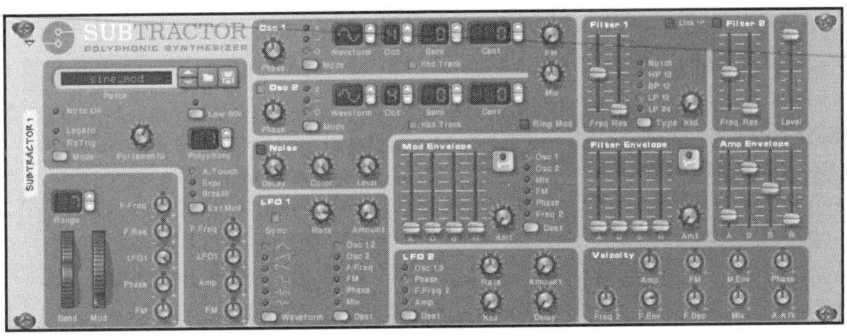

Figure 13.12 Sine wave Subtractor.

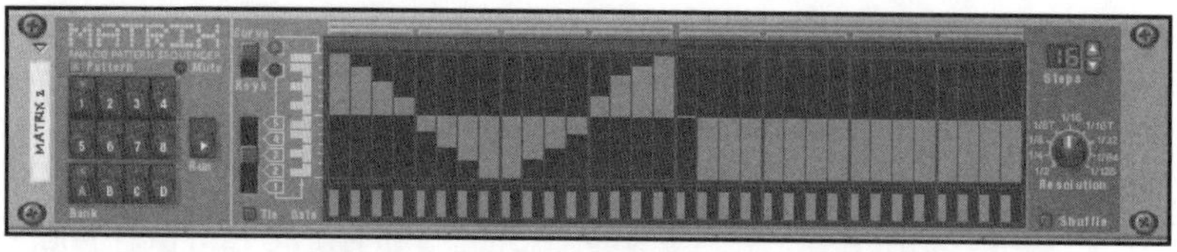

Figure 13.13a Using the Matrix for autopanning.

Figure 13.13b Rear view showing connection between Matrix and NN-XT.

As noted above, the output of all of the sound-producing software modules are routed into the Reason mixer. This is where Matt adjusts the levels of all his devices.

The output of the Reason mixer is then routed to a stereo audio channel in Ableton Live via ReWire. This is set up within Live as described below.

Matt's Live Setup

In Matt's setup, Live is the ReWire host application and Reason is the ReWire slave. To make everything work properly, he opens Live first and then opens Reason, having already configured an audio channel in Live to take the input from Reason (see Figure 13.14).

Figure 13.14 Matt's setup in Live.

As you can see, the Audio From field of the first audio channel is set to Reason. This will automatically appear as a choice in Live if you have Reason installed on your computer. Note also that the Monitor switch in Live is set to On. This enables us to hear the audio output from Reason at all times, even if the Live sequencer isn't running.

Matt has Live set up to accept a MIDI clock input as well. When playing with one or more other computer musicians, he will typically take a MIDI output from one of the other musicians and sync his setup to the incoming MIDI clock signal. (See Figure 13.15 to see how this is set up in the preferences of Live.)

Although Matt doesn't make much use of live sequencing, syncing to MIDI clock in this way will synchronize many of the effects and oscillators in Live and Reason to the master tempo and make all the sequenced rhythms and delays line up correctly.

Matt has placed a series of audio effects on his main audio channel here, including:

- Redux (see Figure 13.16).
- Matt only uses the downsample parameter of this bit-eroding effect in Live, and he has assigned it to one of the faders on his Radium keyboard so he can sweep across the range of possible settings.

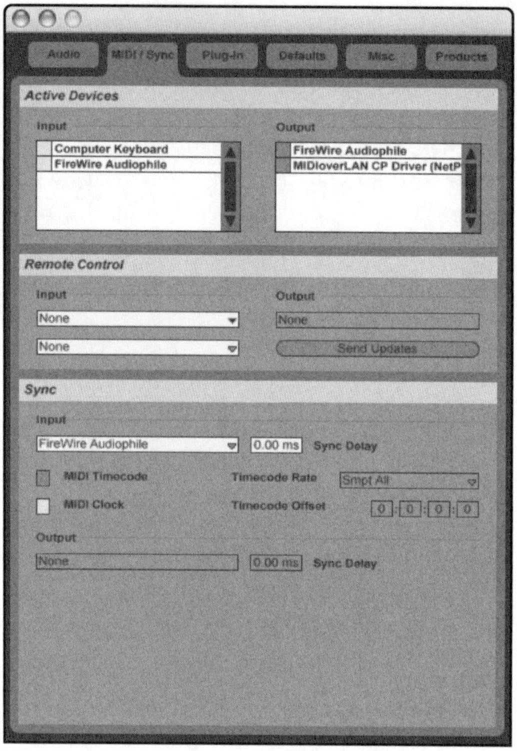

Figure 13.15 Receiving sync through the FireWire Audiophile into Live.

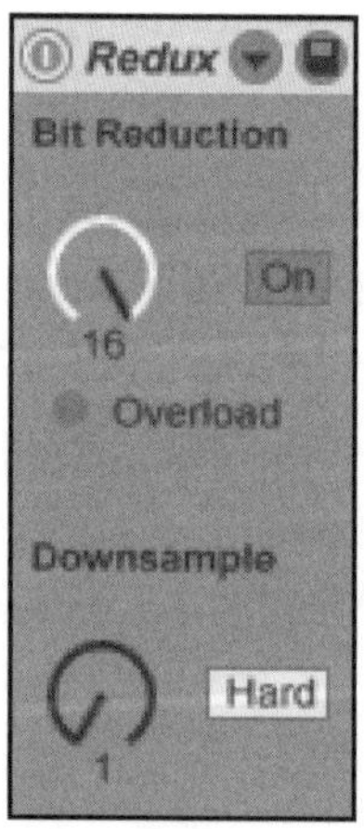

Figure 13.16 Redux.

- Ping Pong Delay (see Figure 13.17).

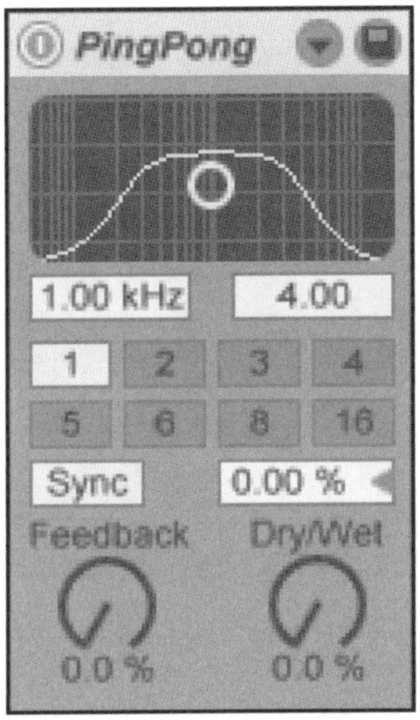

Figure 13.17 Ping Pong Delay.

- On this effect, the note division, feedback, and dry/wet mix parameters are all controlled by faders on the Radium.
- Grain Delay (see Figure 13.18).

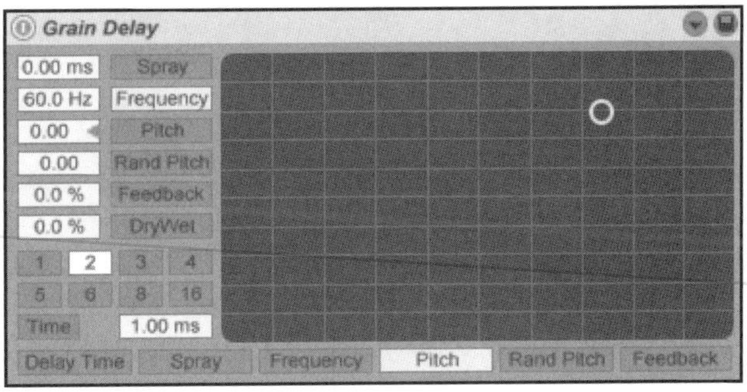

Figure 13.18 Grain Delay.

- Matt has the feedback, delay time, and dry/wet controls of this effect mapped to external controllers on his keyboard, enabling him to create shifting delay feedback effects while simultaneously changing the delay time, "which sounds really weird," according to Matt.
- Compressor (see Figure 13.19).

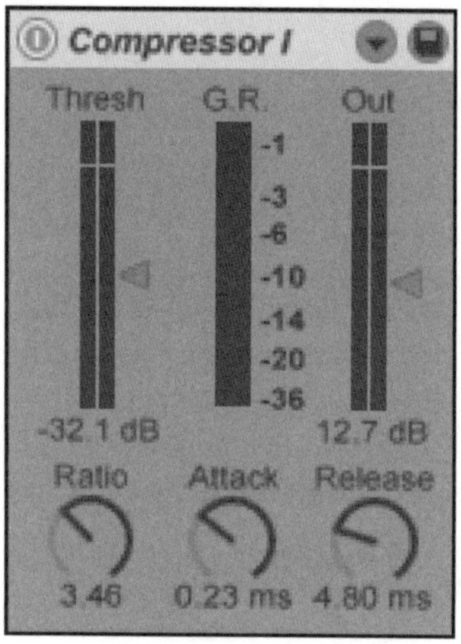

Figure 13.19 Compressor I.

- Matt has inserted Live's Compressor I effect at this point in the chain to limit possible uncontrollable cascading feedback coming from these first few delay effects.
- Reverb (see Figure 13.20).

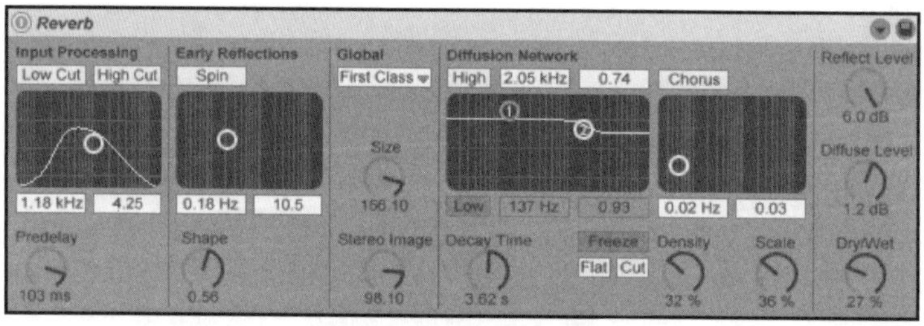

Figure 13.20 Reverb.

- Matt uses Live's built-in Reverb effect for a little live Reverb, and has the dry/wet control mapped to a controller on his keyboard so he can easily adjust the reverb mix whenever he wants.

After passing through this effect signal chain, the output of this first channel passes to the master output in Live and then out channels ½ on Matt's FireWire Audiophile. This is the main output and it goes directly to the PA system.

As seen above, however, Matt also uses a second audio channel in Live that takes the pre-fader output of track one as its input in the Audio From box. This track's output is routed to hardware outputs 3/4 on the FireWire Audiophile, and he monitors this output with his headphones.

The Live volume faders for both of these audio channels are mapped to controls on Matt's Radium keyboard, allowing him to quickly and easily adjust the main volume and cue volume in performance. By turning the main channel down to zero and listening only to the cue output on channels 3/4, he can cue up new sounds in his headphones and get everything sounding just how he wants before he introduces it into the main mix.

Matt's MIDI Controller Setup

In the above description of the virtual instrument rig Matt has constructed in Live and Reason, I have mentioned how he has assigned controllers from his Radium61 keyboard to various parameters. Let's also take a look at the overall layout of how he has assigned these here so you can get an idea of what it is like to use Matt's setup on a gig.

The Radium61 keyboard that Matt uses has eight faders and eight knobs, all MIDI-assignable, numbered sequentially from one to sixteen. Here's how he has laid them out:

- Fader 1: Feedback of Ping Pong Delay in Live
- Fader 2: Dry/Wet mix of Ping Pong Delay in Live
- Fader 3: Note Division setting of Ping Pong Delay in Live
- Fader 4: Feedback of Grain Delay in Live
- Fader 5: Dry/Wet mix of Grain Delay in Live
- Fader 6: Delay Time (in milliseconds) of Grain Delay in Live
- Fader 7: Dry/Wet mix of Reverb in Live
- Fader 8: Downsample control of Redux in Live
- Knob 9: Rate of LFO1 on the Subtractor in Reason
- Knob 10: Amt of LFO1 on Subtractor
- Knob 11: Waveform of LFO1 on Subtractor
- Knob 12: Bypass/On/Off switch on the Phaser in Reason (which is affecting the sampled Rhodes sound)
- Knob 13: Activation switch of the Compressor in Live
- Knob 14: Volume of cue audio channel in Live (routed to audio out 3/4; Matt uses this output for headphone cueing)
- Knob 15: Master volume of Live
- Knob 16: Master volume of the Reason mixer

Of course I am not suggesting that you should set your live computer music system up exactly like Matt Piper's—although I *would* recommend it as an interesting experiment. I have described Matt's setup in detail here because it is a good example of how you can build a custom software setup that perfectly suits your performance style—in effect, designing your own live instrument.

Matt has set up his rig this way because it gives him quick access to a wide variety of his favorite sounds and effects in performance, and gives him easy control over various parameters within his software. Your own ideal setup will depend on what kind of music you want to play and what kind of sounds you want to use. Hopefully this description of Matt's fairly complex performance system will have given you some ideas about how to set up your own live rig.

14 Designing Your Own Live Applications

Chapters 8 through 13 demonstrated techniques for live performance using a variety of commercially available music and audio software. Though I have shown you how to design your own custom performance setup with programs such as Ableton Live and Pro Tools, so far I have limited myself to talking about only off-the-shelf software applications for performance.

However, there are also a number of software environments available for the live computer musician that enable you to actually get down to a deeper level and create your own custom software applications. While this may end up being a lot of work, if you are willing to invest the time and effort, it can pay off by helping you create a unique performance interface that best suits your musical style.

I don't want to go into too much detail about how to design your own applications here, but I want to briefly mention some of the more widely used environments that can be used to create your own performance applications and give a couple examples of what can be done with these.

Max/MSP

Many readers of this book will have at least heard of the powerful audio software environment known as Max/MSP, published and supported since 1999 by Cycling '74 (http://www.cycling74.com). In my experience, only a tiny minority of today's computer musicians actually have any experience with Max or even understand what it is exactly.

In the simplest terms, Max is an object-oriented programming language aimed specifically at creating multimedia applications. While there are other applications and environments available that provide similar functionality, Max has established itself as the international standard for multimedia programming.

Here's the description of Max/MSP from the Cycling '74 Web site:

"Max/MSP is a graphical programming environment, which means you create your own software using a visual toolkit of objects, and connect them together with patch cords. The basic environment that includes MIDI, control, user interface, and timing objects is called Max."

This image of a patch made in Max shows what these objects and patch cords look like in the Max environment (see Figure 14.1).

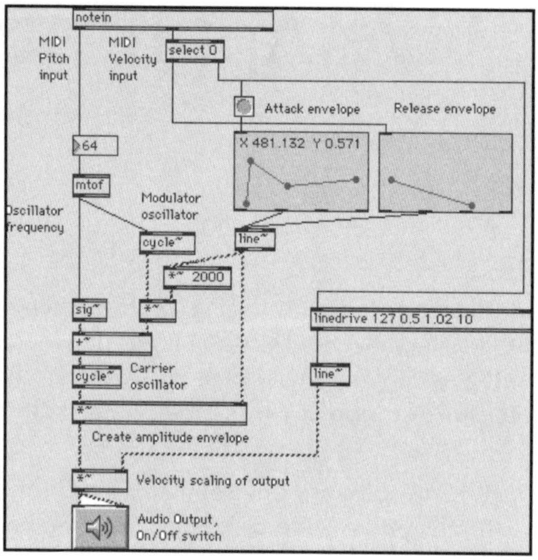

Figure 14.1 A simple patch written in Max.

Here you can see how you can use simple modules connected by virtual patch cords to create larger, more complex software objects in Max. You can then connect these together to make even larger-scale, more complex objects, and so on. Thus, by combining sets of objects together, you can make any kind of audio, MIDI, or video processing device that you desire.

Of course, if you are just starting out with Max, the task of writing your own synthesizer or effects processing device from scratch might seem a bit daunting. However, part of the appeal of Max is that you don't have to start from scratch, as there are innumerable patches and objects made by others that are readily available for you to use. Cycling '74 itself sells two basic packages that are crucial building blocks for audio and video applications: MSP, a set of audio processing objects, and Jitter, a set of matrix processing objects optimized for video and 3-D graphics. Most people using Max for audio development today are using the MSP set of audio processing objects with it as well, so in practice the environment is often referred to as Max/MSP. (Also see the sidebar "Where Did Max/MSP Come From?").

In addition to these packages, there are also a plethora of Web sites where you can download Max patches made by other users. There are complete synthesizers, DJ mixers, video effects processors, and other software devices available online free of charge, built entirely within the Max/MSP environment, as well as high-level building block objects that will ease the task of developing your own patches in Max.

Where Did Max/MSP Come From?

Max was first developed for the Macintosh in the mid 1980s at IRCAM by Miller Puckette. In 1989, IRCAM started work on a real-time synthesizer card for the NeXT computer produced by Ariel called the IRCAM Signal Processing Workstation (ISPW). Puckette ported Max to the NeXT and ISPW and added a set of objects to do audio on the card. Max combined with the audio was known as Max/FTS and was widely used at IRCAM and about 30 other centers and individual studios around the world. A single card with two processors was about $12,000, not including the computer.

Max was first released commercially by Opcode Systems, Inc. in 1990. It was chosen as Software Innovation of the Year by the readers of Keyboard Magazine in 1991. Since 1999 it has been published and supported by Cycling '74.

In 1996, Miller Puckette, now at the University of California San Diego, began developing a new program, Pd or Pure Data, aimed at the new generation of powerful microprocessors. The goals of Pd are different than Max/FTS, but it shares the ability to do real-time signal processing by connecting objects together. Initially developed on the SGI platform, Pd now runs on Windows, Linux, and MacOSX. Shortly after Pd was started, David Zicarelli decided to add audio processing for PowerPC computers to the existing Opcode Max environment. Max/MSP is the result. It uses the Pd signal processing infrastructure, and adds features inspired by Max/FTS but not yet implemented in Pd, along with new innovations and user-interface enhancements appropriate for the Opcode Max environment.

From the Cycling '74 Web site (http://www.cycling74.com/support/questionsmsp.html).

If you really want to design your own live software applications in Max/MSP, you will have your work cut out for you. I would recommend looking for some online tutorials or purchasing a book on the subject. However, for a look at what you can create in Max/MSP, let's take a look at the live setups of two computer musicians in Los Angeles: edIT and Andrew Pask.

edIT

edIT is a glitch-hop producer and laptop performer (see Figure 14.2).

Figure 14.2 edIT.

He first became known around town as a resident at the Konkrete Jungle drum'n'bass and hiphop weekly from 1998 to 2001, spinning underground and indie hiphop using vinyl and turntables. He was very active as a hiphop DJ at this time, playing several gigs a week at venues all over Southern California. On his own Web site, found at http://www.complexplayersclub.com, he refers to himself as:

"...cpc's very own crunk master extraordinare and los angeles' very own golden child of the dirty southwest. if edIT was a baller on the and1 mix tape tour, they'd call him the 'yellow fever' aka 'you know this well' aka 'i don't need to say no more'...notoriously known for blowing up spots with the jiggy cut-up sound..."

Eventually he became interested in producing his own music and began buying computer music equipment and software. He started offering his services as an engineer to local MCs and producers, recording their beats (often programmed on a hardware sampler like an Akai MPC) and raps, and mixing and editing the tracks into finished productions. Later he started making his own music, and his increasingly experimental tracks eventually led to his 2004 solo CD on planet-mu, *Crying Over Pros For No Reason*.

edIT still performs frequently in Los Angeles and on tour, but now uses a Mac PowerBook exclusively for his live gigs instead of vinyl and a pair of decks. He doesn't DJ anymore, at least not in the sense of playing DJ sets of other artists' music. Instead, he uses a DJ-style software application he wrote himself in Max/MSP to play live mix sets of his own original tracks.

The Crunk Master 3000

edIT's custom DJ application is called *Crunk Master 3000*.

edIT built the Crunk Master 3000 in Max/MSP because he couldn't find the features he wanted for playing live in any of the commercially available DJ applications.

edIT's application is similar to the other DJ programs (such as Traktor or Virtual DJ) that I mentioned in Chapter 8 in implementing most of the standard DJ functions such as two playback decks, a crossfader to mix between them, DJ-style EQ controls, and pitch and nudge controls to help beatmatch tracks together.

edIT can match two tracks' tempos together manually in the Crunk Master 3000 by clicking the controls on the screen, just like he used to do with vinyl records. Or, if he already knows the tempo of the tracks, he can simply type in their BPMs and the Crunk Master 3000 will automatically match the next track's BPM to that of the track currently playing. This is a very useful feature for him when playing sets of his own music as he already knows the exact tempos of all of his original productions.

edIT plays live with nothing but his 12" Mac PowerBook G4, manipulating most of the controls of the Crunk Master 3000 with the trackpad and cursor, although he has mapped the transport functions of the playback decks (play, pause, rewind, and so on) to keys on his computer keyboard for quicker access.

There are also built-in audio effects including a comb filter, an LFO filter, a degrader, and a filter delay, as well as VST support for third-party plug-ins.

An important feature of the Crunk Master 3000's user interface not found in other DJ software is the use of X-Y controller windows for controlling the effects.

These X-Y controller windows allow edIT to easily create wild audio effects live by tracing curves with the trackpad. These are similar to the X-Y controllers in Ableton Live, but I have not seen this type of control interface implemented in any of the commercial DJ software packages.

edIT reports that the Crunk Master 3000 is very stable in performance, and I have seen him play live many times myself without ever having a problem.

Although the Crunk Master 3000 is not radically different than some of the major commercial DJ applications such as Traktor, it is custom tailored to the way that edIT wants to perform his music live. In particular, I have seen him make extensive use of effects in his live sets, using combinations of effects and sounds that would be impossible to realize in any other DJ software that I am aware of. The Crunk Master 3000 is a good example of how you can use Max/MSP to create a live software interface that perfectly suits your own performance style.

Although creating your own DJ application in Max/MSP is far from easy, in the Crunk Master 3000 edIT has designed a simple and usable interface for himself without getting distracted by the endless complexity possible in the Max/MSP environment. As he puts it himself on his Web site:

"it's simple. we be droppin' sirens up in this piece. we rocks the party that rocks the body. ain't nothing complex about it. and that's the truth."

Andrew Pask and Live Control

Andrew Pask is a saxophonist/clarinetist and computer musician from New Zealand (see Figure 14.3).

Since arriving in Los Angeles in 1999, he has become a familiar face in the creative improvised music scene, performing frequently with area experimental musicians such as Vinny Golia, Steuart Liebig, Nels and Alex Cline, and Jeff Gauthier. His most recent project is an improvised duo with trumpeter Jeff Kaiser called the Choirboys; their self- titled first album was released by pfMENTUM records in 2005.

In addition to his work as an artist and performer, Andrew is also employed by Cycling '74, the company that publishes and supports Max/MSP, and he is an expert Max programmer himself. In the last several years, he has developed a highly sophisticated generative sound-processing rig for modifying the sound of his acoustic instruments when he plays live, a setup he calls *Live Control*. Andrew's system is an excellent example of the kind of unique performance possibilities offered by Max/MSP, and he continually stretches the possibilities of human-computer interaction in his frequent improvised performances.

Live Control Hardware

In Andrew's Live Control system, he basically uses Max/MSP as a highly sophisticated effects processor for his saxophone, clarinet, and other woodwind instruments.

Andrew's system is more than just a Max patch, however; it is an integrated hardware-software setup that he continues to evolve and develop as he comes up with new ideas about

Figure 14.3 Andrew Pask. (left) performing with the Choirboys.

how to use it. He has been through at least five complete rewrites of his software interface so far, and is already working on the next version.

The hardware components of Andrew's setup include the following:

- A Macintosh PowerBook G4 with an 867MHz CPU and 768MB of RAM
- A Doepfer Pocket Fader MIDI controller

- A clip-on sax mic
- An RME Fireface audio interface
- An Eventide Eclipse rackmount effects unit
- An Eventide H8000 Ultraharmonizer rackmount multi-effects processor
- Four Doepfer FP5 foot controller pedals
- A Teabox from Electrotap L.L.C. (http://www.electrotap.com)
- A four-button custom-made MIDI controller switch worn around the neck

Signal Routing

Here's how it all works.

Andrew plays the sax or clarinet live and uses the computer and external effects equipment together as one highly sophisticated effects processor. After his signal goes through the processing system, one dry (uneffected) mono signal as well as one wet (with effects) stereo pair are output at the end, through the RME Fireface, and then connected to the PA system. This enables the live sound engineer to adjust the balance of wet and dry signal on the board.

The signal routing that enables Andrew to do all this is rather complex, but it is more or less like this:

First his live instrument signal is picked up by his clip-on mic.

This runs into the built-in preamps of the Fireface to boost the signal to a usable level, and then passes out directly to the Eventide Eclipse, which Andrew has set to provide gating and a bit of reverb on both the dry and wet audio outputs. (He has found the gating function in particular to be indispensable when playing an acoustic instrument in electronic contexts, as the noise of the other instruments around him or the sound from the main PA may otherwise cause feedback through his mic when he is not playing.)

Then the signal runs out of the Eclipse and back into the RME Fireface. Then he has routed it so that one dry mono output runs directly to the board, while three identical stereo feeds are passed to the PowerBook and the two separate effects engines of the H8000.

Max/MSP in Control

At this point, as the signal is split into three separate effects signal chains, Andrew uses Max/MSP running on his PowerBook to control everything that happens, using his custom Max patch. The main interface through which he controls everything looks like this (see Figure 14.4).

(Note that in classic Cycling '74 style, Andrew has wasted no time on designing a fancy graphical user interface for his Max patch, but has concentrated strictly on maximum functionality!)

In this image, there are three separate vertical volume indicators, showing the volume levels for the three distinct effects signal chains that Andrew has available.

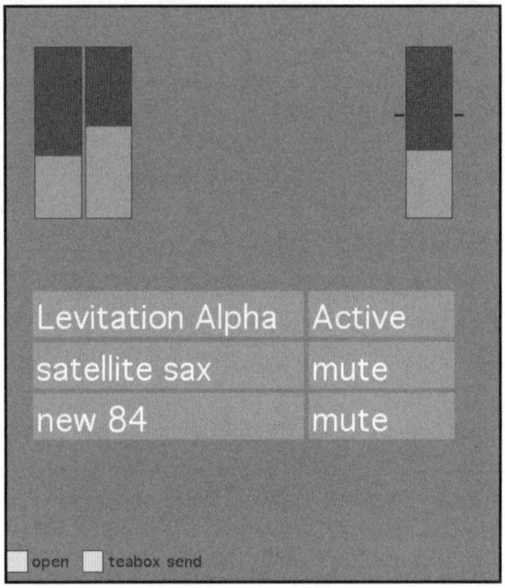

Figure 14.4 The main interface of Live Control.

Below this, there are three rows indicating which effects, if any, are active on each signal chain, as well as the currently selected status of each. Andrew can control the effects patch active on the Macintosh as well as all the effect and parameter settings of the Eventide H8000. In this configuration, the effects are configured and controlled completely from within the Max/MSP environment, but the actual audio processing is performed by the DSP hardware of the Eventide units, which is superior in quality to what can be done by effects running in software on the Mac. (This is why the Eventide units are so expensive and have such a legendary reputation for quality in the industry.)

The first row shows the selected patch name of the first effects chain running through the Eventide H8000, as well as the status of the effect indicated as active or inactive. Andrew has set up this signal feed exclusively for looping, and uses buttons on his MIDI neck controller to switch the looper functions on and off. Any loops set here will automatically sync to an incoming MIDI clock signal if one is present.

The second row shows the patch name of the stereo chain running through the second effects engines in the Eventide H8000 as well as a status expressed as mute, hold, or modulate (see below for further explanation of this).

Finally, the third row in the main interface here shows the name of the effects patch currently selected within the Max/MSP environment itself, primarily VST plug-ins hosted in Max. There is a status field for this row as well, also expressed as mute, hold, or modulate.

By using these controls, Andrew is able to change the effects patch setting and status of each of his three signal paths independently. He can use the sound output of only one of them at a time, or mix two or more of them together to get even more complex sounds.

Figure 14.5, part of Andrew's Max/MSP patch, shows how the signal is routed within Max as it goes through one of the VST effects:

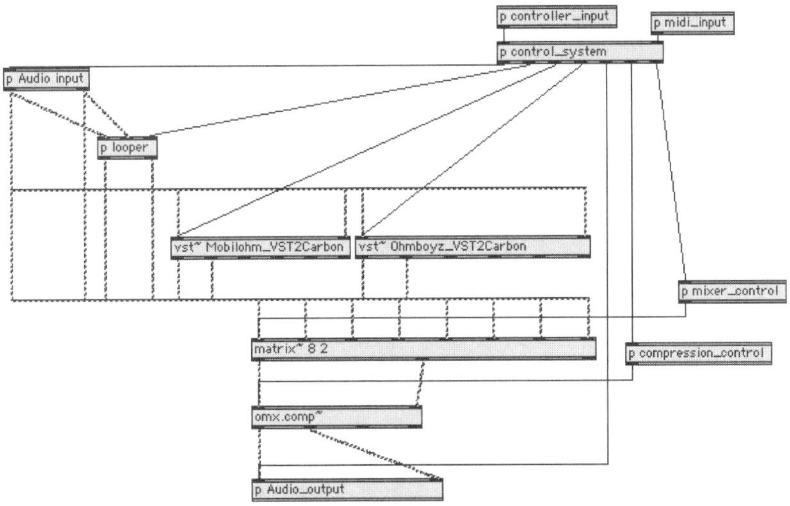

Figure 14.5 Audio routed through a VST effect in Andrew's Max patch.

The mute, hold, or modulate settings for the second and third channels are settings that Andrew has defined himself for use with the Doepfer FP5 footpedal controllers he uses.

As mentioned in the equipment list above, Andrew uses four of these footpedal controllers to manipulate the controls of his Live Control software when he plays. (He uses footpedals because his hands are usually engaged playing the saxophone when he performs live.) Here's how they are configured with his software:

- Pedal 1 controls the output volume of the dry (unaffected) mono output to the PA
- Pedal 2 controls the volume of the wet (effected) stereo output to the PA
- Pedal 3 controls the status of the second Eventide signal chain
- Pedal 4 control the status of the VST effects chain hosted in Max/MSP

The functions of the first two pedals are obvious, controlling the volumes of the dry and wet outputs respectively. Pedals three and four are routed to control the status of the second Eventide signal chain as well as the VST effects chain running through Max.

Andrew has set up these latter two effects chain with three possible states, reported in their respective status fields in the main interface: Mute, hold, and modulate. These work with the pedal controllers like this:

When the pedal is all the way back, in heel position, the channel is muted completely. In this case, no sound comes through the channel at all.

When the pedal is in an intermediate position between minimum and maximum, the channel will be put in modulate mode. In this case, it will semi-randomly cycle between effects settings, according to an algorithm Andrew has specified. He has also specified the set of effects settings among which the Max patch can randomly choose. The speed at which the changes between effects settings happen is controlled by the exact position of the footpedal.

When the pedal is all the way to the front, in toe position, the channel is in hold mode. This means that the effects settings are locked in and the channel will continue to hold the current settings until Andrew moves the pedal back again.

The Teabox interface is used to connect the pedals to the computer. It uses a S/PDIF connection to transmit MIDI data and is much more reliable when transmitting large amounts of MIDI information than a traditional DIN-style MIDI cable.

Random Inspiration

Having the effects cycle through different patches semi-randomly may seem crazy to some readers, but this is all part of Andrew's improvisational, freestyle approach to live music-making. He likes having the effects settings change while he is playing because it may suggest new musical directions to him. As he put it when I interviewed him, his effects rig becomes almost like a partner in the improvisation, and he can always count on his rig to come up with some surprising new ideas during the course of a performance.

In addition, the selection of effects is not *completely* random. Andrew has grouped them into families of similar types of effects, or effects that he feels "go together" in some sense. When a random change is triggered, Live Control will pick a new plug-in from the same group, so there will always tend to be some degree of coherence in the settings that are chosen.

When discussing his live rig, I asked him:

Q: But what is the point of all this, Andrew?

A: The point of it is that I am interested in the sound design possibilities of using DSP technology on the sound of my horn and using the resulting sounds in an interactive and dynamic way in a live situation.

Q: How do you see the use of computers in live music developing in the future?

A: I hope to see a stage where more musicians emerge that have a strong grasp of both music tech and music itself, instead of just being a geek or a musician. Also, processing power and other limitations will cease to be an important restriction [as computers continue to become cheaper and more powerful].

Take Me to the Limit One More Time

Andrew Pask's Max/MSP-based live performance is unique, and he has constructed it this way to suit a certain style of improvisation that he has been pursuing for many years. I include this description of his live setup here as an example of how far you can go in creating your own custom hardware-software system for performing your music live.

More on Andrew Pask and his music can be found at http://www.trippyhorns.com.

Alternatives to Max

edIT and Andrew's Max/MSP setups well illustrate the incredible power and flexibility of this multimedia software programming language. However, for some people just starting to explore this direction, Max/MSP may be too expensive (it is currently sold for $495 from the Cycling '74 Web site), especially if they aren't sure whether or not it will be a useful tool for them.

> **TRYING MAX/MSP**
>
> If you want to try Max/MSP out for a bit before paying $495 for a license, just download and install the full version from the Cycling '74 site. You can use it as a demo for thirty days without registration or payment.
>
> The Max/MSP download page on the Cycling '74 Web site is at http://www.cycling74.com/products/dlmaxmspmac.html.
>
> Also on the same page, you can download the Max/MSP Runtime instead of the full version of Max. The Runtime version is free, and it will allow you to download and make use of applications written in Max by other users. The main limitation is that you cannot create your own applications with the Runtime version.

In this case, there are a number of inexpensive or free alternatives if you are determined to create your own custom software application for live performance.

Some of the most commonly encountered alternatives to Max/MSP include Pd, jMAX, SuperCollider, and AudioMulch.

Pd (Pure Data)

Pure Data is a free, open-source version of Max/MSP, available for Mac OS X, Windows and Linux. Interestingly, Pure Data originated as a project of music technology researcher Miller Puckette, who was also one of the original authors of Max.

Pure Data is available for download from Puckette's Web site at http://www-crca.ucsd.edu/~msp/software.html, along with a number of his other software applications and publications about electronic music. According to Puckette's online biography, "He is currently working on a new real-time software system for live musical and multimedia performances called Pure Data ('Pd'), in collaboration with many other artists/researchers/programmers worldwide."

jMax

jMax is a free Java-based version of the Max environment developed at IRCAM.

You can install jMax on any of the major OSes; download the source code and check the installation instructions available on the IRCAM site at http://freesoftware.ircam.fr/rubrique.php3?id_rubrique=14.

SuperCollider

SuperCollider is another free alternative to Max/MSP, another programming environment that gives you the tools you need to create your own custom applications (see Figure 14.6).

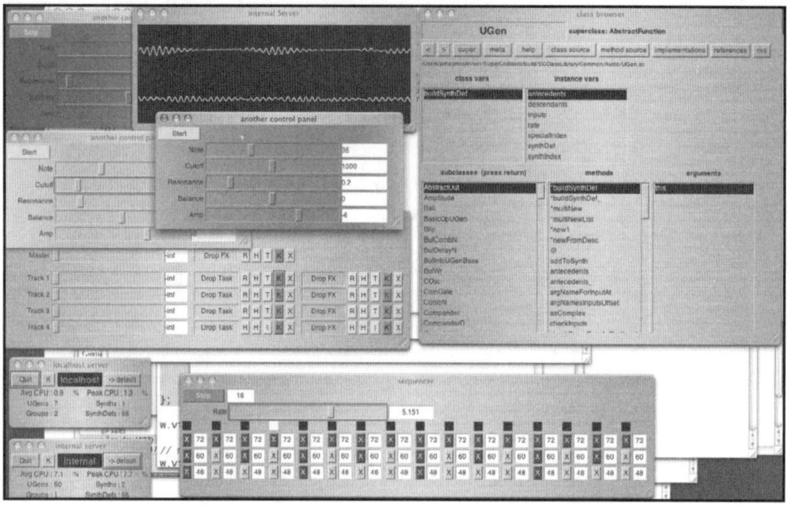

Figure 14.6 SuperCollider.

According to the SuperCollider Web site, "SuperCollider is an environment and programming language for real time audio synthesis. You can write programs to generate or process sound in real time or non-real time. SuperCollider can be controlled by MIDI, the mouse, a Wacom graphics tablet, and over a network via Open Sound Control."

SuperCollider is available for download from http://www.audiosynth.com. Only Mac OS X and Linux versions are currently available.

AudioMulch

AudioMulch, mentioned earlier in this book, is an audio software environment for Microsoft Windows. Software setups in AudioMulch are modular as in Max/MSP, and resemble a number of modules connected by virtual patch cords.

In comparison to Max/MSP, AudioMulch doesn't provide so much "under-the-hood" control of the actual programming, but rather gives the user an extensive set of pre-built objects that can then be assembled into far more complex setups.

Audio software objects included in the AudioMulch set include a test tone/noise generator, a drum machine, a bassline synthesizer, an additive synthesizer, a stored sample granulator, a loop player, a Shepard/Risset tone generator, and an arpeggiator.

Available effects include a reverb, a flanger, a phaser, a delay line granulator, ring/amplitude modulation, stereo delays, a dynamic stereo spatializer, a waveshaper /distortion function, a digital grunge inducer, and a pulsar comb filter. In addition, there are parametric EQ functions, a resonant comb filter bank, a Shepard/Risset filter bank, and granular filtering.

AudioMulch is available as a free time-limited beta from the author's Web site at http://www.audiomulch.com. Registering the beta through the Web site for $50 removes all time restrictions.

Having come to the end of this chapter about designing your own applications to play live, I will now turn to some more general speculations about where all this computer music craziness is leading us.

(Note that I have also written further about AudioMulch in Chapter 15, focusing more on the implications of the way it is being distributed, so read on...)

15 Conclusions and Speculations

In the preceding pages, we have covered a wealth of practical information about live computer music, looking at the hardware and software involved and how to use it. We have also heard directly from a number of today's electronic music performers about how they use these incredible live performance tools.

As we near the end of this book, however, I would like to take a few pages and take a step back from this close focus on technological details. As music technology continues to develop and progress at a mind-blowing pace here in the early years of the 21st century, it is easy to get lost in the whirl of details and not notice the huge changes taking place on a larger scale.

The global music industry, as well as our society's overall relationship with music itself, is being radically changed and reshaped by the impact of cheap digital music technologies. In this last chapter, I have included some speculations about how things are changing, the direction it is leading, and what it might all mean.

Changing the Means of Production Changes What Is Produced

Although many of us tend to take it for granted at this point, computer audio recording programs have brought fundamental changes to the process of creating, recording, and (more recently) performing music, changes that we don't often consciously reflect on. For example, when recording live instrument parts on analog multi-track tape instead of a computer hard drive, you usually want to get complete takes if you can, and performers will try their best to avoid mistakes or errors along the way. In this situation, while it is possible to correct some mistakes with punch-ins, it is generally considerably more difficult to work with tape-based recording.

However, recording digitally to a hard drive is an entirely different creative process. For example, I was originally a professional bassist before getting into computer music, and I still like to play my own basslines even in my electronic compositions. However, the way I track and record my bass guitar is completely different now than how I recorded when I was working as a studio bassist in Hong Kong.

Instead of trying to achieve one perfect take, and then at most patching up a few mistakes here and there by punching in, I will simply let the software record everything I play while I am jamming along with a track. Then, when I feel like I've laid down some usable grooves, I will go back through with my audio editing software and listen for those little bits and pieces that sound the best, where I really nailed the line I was trying to play. The best of these small choice bits will then become the riffs that anchor the entire track.

This is the way many computer-based music producers work: The whole emerges from the fragments. Every note they play can be cut and pasted just like the words in this book. Many different arrangements of mixes of the same song can be saved separately on the computer's hard drive, making possible an infinite number of different versions of the same track.

JON GUTWILLIG (Disco Biscuits, Philadelphia)

"We recorded 10,000 seven-second audio bites over dub beats. Then we started putting those bites together, and, in three cases, figuring out what the song was going to be afterwards. We'd take stuff originally meant for one song, shift the tempo, and put it in another."
(Quote from http://www.wired.com/news/mp3/0,1285,44074,00.html.)

Of course, on one level, this kind of remixology is nothing new; remixers have been making new tracks out of pre-recorded material at least since groundbreaking Jamaican dub producers such as Lee Perry, King Tubby, and Scientist were making their alternate "versions" of reggae tracks in the mid-1970s. Early European electronic composers such as Varèse, Stockhausen, and *musique concrète* pioneer Pierre Schaeffer explored such approaches to tape-based composition even earlier, as far back as the 1950s.

What has changed in recent years is the pervasiveness and ease of use of the new technology, as well as the fine degree of control it gives its users over the sonic material of their compositions.

The Aesthetics of Failure and the Influence of the Net

Writer and computer musician Kim Cascone discussed some of these ideas in connection with a new musical genre developing on the Internet in an influential 2001 article in *Computer Music Journal*. (The article is available online at http://www.fylkingen.se/hz/n3/cascone.html.)

"Over the past decade, the Internet has helped spawn a new movement in digital music. It is not academically based, and for the most part the composers involved are self-taught. Music journalists occupy themselves inventing names for it, and some have already taken hold: *glitch*, *microwave*, *DSP*, *sinecore*, and *microscopic music*. These names evolved through a collection of deconstructive audio and visual techniques that allow artists to work beneath the previously impenetrable veil of digital media" (Cascone, *Computer Music Journal*, Winter 2000 p. 12–18).

This new music is also commonly known as "microsound" music, after the Internet mailing list of the same name hosted at http://www.microsound.org, where many of its practitioners gather online to exchange ideas and discuss the latest developments in the field.

When Cascone speaks of artists working "beneath the previously impenetrable veil of digital media," he is talking about software tools that give electronic producers and composers an unprecedented level of control over their sonic materials. Sounds can be stretched, filtered, inverted, magnified, shrunk, twisted, distorted, and so on by means of advanced software tools such as SuperCollider and MAX/MSP, and these operations have become the main focus of musical attention among microsound producers. The microsound movement is especially concerned with the "aesthetics of failure," an artistic focus on the imperfections of digital audio technologies. As Cascone puts it, "...glitches, bugs, application errors, system crashes, clipping, aliasing, distortion, quantization noise, and even the noise floor of computer sound cards are the raw materials composers seek to incorporate into their music." He further explains that this new genre has developed in large part because of the digital exchange of tools and ideas enabled by the Internet:

"The Internet was originally created to accelerate the exchange of ideas and development of research between academic centers, so it is perhaps no surprise that it is responsible for helping give birth to new trends in computer music outside the confines of academic think tanks. A non-academic composer can search the Internet for tutorials and papers on any given aspect of computer music and obtain a good, basic understanding of it. University computer centers breed developers whose tools are shuttled around the Internet and used to develop new music outside the university."

In another words, the inmates are taking over the asylum...so to speak...!

Citing German electronic music artist Markus Popp (more commonly known as Oval) as one of the early innovators of the genre, Cascone points out that although this music based on digital breakdown is of recent origin, the use of "failure" as a creative resource is a direction many other musicians and composers had explored before, with John Cage probably the best-known example. What is new, he says, is that "ideas now travel at the speed of light and can spawn entire musical genres in a relatively short period of time."

The development of the microsound aesthetic is a fascinating example of how the widespread use of digital audio technologies and the Internet is affecting the development of music. Although many listeners might consider microsound music to be difficult or obscure, this Internet-spawned experimental aesthetic has already had considerable impact on more popular forms of electronic music, dance music, and pop. The resulting stylistic collisions have given us subgenres like microhouse (Luomo, Akufen, Farben), glitch hop (Prefuse 73, Dabrye), and microcrunk (edIT), and these "glitch" or "digital breakdown" sounds have become quite prevalent in the computer music underground. Certain software tools have become popular in the computer underground because they can easily be used to produce these kinds of sounds, such as the Buffer Override plug-in from DestroyFX and the Pluggo package of audio effects made by Cycling '74. The pitch-shifting and time-stretching functions of various audio recording software applications are also popular for creating these kinds of sounds, such as the Warping feature found in Ableton Live.

The Internet Provides the Means of Production

Another interesting aspect of the new electronic underground music scene is to extent to which this music is being produced with free software downloaded from the Internet. While the overwhelming majority of today's computer musicians do use at least some commercial software to produce their music, particularly for their master recording application, many also make use of some software found online. There are numerous online sites where you can find innovative new audio software, often made available for free or for a small charge directly from their creators. Using fresh new underground music software like this makes it possible to create sounds no one has ever heard before, staying ahead of the latest trends in production and performance.

There are even a few sites that serve as indexes to downloadable audio software and offer helpful information about them. If you are interested in this topic, I would recommend investigating the Shareware Music Machine (http://www.hitsquad.com/smm) as well as KVR Audio (http://www.kvraudio.com).

SoundRaider

One of my favorite examples of this kind of free software is SoundRaider (see Figure 15.1), available for download from the author, Andy Wilson, at http://www.andyw.com/ow.asp?SoundRaider.

Figure 15.1 SoundRaider.

As Wilson explains on his Web site, "SoundRaider is a music creation tool that works by scanning your hard drive for WAV format sounds and uses them to create industrial-ambient sound. Leave SoundRaider running on the desktop and listen to your hard drive muttering to itself."

When SoundRaider is run, it scans the hard drive of your Windows-based PC (unfortunately, there is no Mac version) and finds every WAV-format digital audio file you have stored there. It then uses an unexplained variety of stretching and pitching algorithms to make new loops out of your saved audio material, looping up to five different audio sources together at once to create unusual polyrhythms and sonic textures.

The random mix-and-match procedures of SoundRaider are very appealing in a Cageian way, and I have used it to create the seeds of numerous electronic compositions. As far as I know, there is no commercial software product on the market that can create the kinds of sounds output by SoundRaider, which have become an important part of my music. SoundRaider is an excellent example of how the Internet provides modern musicians with a constant stream of creative inspiration, freely available online. Many of today's most innovative computer musicians spend hours trawling the Internet in search of new software that will give them an edge as the pace of musical innovation in the underground scene continues to accelerate.

KIERAN HEBDEN a.k.a. FOUR TET (UK)

Kieran Hebden first became well known in the music world as the guitarist for British post-rock trio Fridge. In 1999, he began doing computer/electronic music under the name Four Tet and quickly became excited about the unexplored artistic frontiers opened up by new computer audio software.

"...getting involved in something that was developing and changing at such a rate that there was so much territory that hadn't been covered. To suddenly be in a world where you actually have a reasonable chance of managing to do something new...the range of possibilities is enormous. The computer can reproduce pretty much any sound a human can hear."

(Quote from Grooves magazine, issue 17, 2005.)

AudioMulch

Another example of the fascinating free software available online is an application called AudioMulch, which I have mentioned more than once in the preceding chapters. In addition to its musical/sonic possibilities, this application is also interesting for the way it is being produced and sold by its creator.

AudioMulch is a powerful compositional tool that provides capabilities not found in any other electronic music equipment or software, and it is only available via download from its creator's Web site. A free version is available which will expire after a trial period, after which it must be downloaded again, or one can register the software online for $50. (After registering, the software can be used indefinitely.)

As mentioned in the previous chapter, AudioMulch is a modular environment that allows you to create your own customizable setups in software. Many different approaches to composition and performance are possible with this program.

AUDIOMULCH

"AudioMulch is an interactive musician's environment for computers running Microsoft Windows. Bringing together the popular with what has up to now been considered experimental, AudioMulch merges the worlds of mainstream electronica and electroacoustic sound composition to create a fluid sonic environment only limited by the artist's imagination."

"While many of the processes featured within AudioMulch are not new to computer music programs, it is the software's ability to carry out these traditionally 'studio' or 'non-real-time' signal processing techniques in real-time that emerges as its major asset. With AudioMulch, music that has for so long been limited to the pre & post-production practices of a studio can emerge in a new LIVE and interactive context."

"Through the essentially unlimited (only by the power of the computer) combination of a network of synthesis and processing contraptions, AudioMulch allows the user to extend their current audio processing capabilities or create new music within their computer without additional expensive software or hardware systems."

(Quotes from the AudioMulch info page at http://www.audiomulch.com/info.htm.)

Because of this program's unique capabilities, a large community of AudioMulch users has grown up around the world, with the "mulch-discuss" mailing list (hosted by the program's creator) serving as a virtual meeting place for users to discuss new ideas for using the software live or in the studio. According to the author, Australian electroacoustic composer Ross Bencina, many tens of thousands of copies of AudioMulch have been downloaded from his Web site by users throughout the world.

Again, AudioMulch is only one example of the rapidly proliferating compositional tools that are being distributed over the Internet. Web sites such as Shareware Music Machine (http://www.hitsquad.com/smm), Harmony Central (http://www.harmony-central.com), and MP3 Machine (http://www.mp3machine.com) offer aspiring producers access to a wealth of inexpensive or free tools that in many cases are only available on the Net. It is too early to say what impact this may have on the development of music in the long term, but at the very least, the rapidly expanding array of compositional software available should ensure that would-be electronic composers have a wide range of different working environments to choose from, each with its own unique potentials and limitations. I expect to see more and more mutation, diversity, and change in musical genres and approaches as new software tools are continually developed.

Mining Raw Musical Materials Online

In my own work as a composer and performer, I have made extensive use of "found sounds" from the Internet (including, for example, the sounds of a Japanese train station at rush hour or of electromagnetic activity in the earth's upper atmosphere). I find the vast diversity of sounds available online to be an endless source of inspiration and creativity.

Many of today's postdigital audio artists obtain sounds and samples from online sound archives or file-sharing systems. The prevalence of such massive archives and exchange networks suggests a way of understanding the Internet as a kind of global memory bank of sounds, images, and ideas that are available to digital artists to be recombined into their own electronic mosaics.

Of course, when sampling sounds found online for commercial use or an album release, you always have to be careful about copyright issues. However, it has always been a common practice among electronic and hiphop artists alike to disguise the source of a sample by using effects and digital signal processing to transform the original sound beyond recognition.

Falling Costs of Digital Music Technology

While MP3 players and online music downloading (both legal and illegal) have significantly changed the way people learn about and listen to music in recent years, the widespread use of computers and audio software is at the same time revolutionizing the way music is created and performed. As music production has transitioned from hardware to software, the price of a pro- or near-pro-quality computer audio recording and editing system has come down to a fraction of what it was even just a few years ago, and much of the production work that used to be billed by the hour in an expensive studio now happens in basements or bedrooms instead.

These new digital technologies of music creation are bringing ever more sophisticated recording technologies to more and more aspiring artists and creators at ever-lower prices. It is amazing to reflect on how much prices have actually fallen for the audio technologies we take for granted today and how much these technologies have progressed.

My home studio, which is almost completely software-based except for my bass guitars, runs on a Pentium 4 PC computer running Windows XP that I built myself. This system gives me more precise control over the sounds I am working with than the most powerful professional studios ten or fifteen years ago, and for only a small fraction of the cost. For example, one of the earliest hard-disk based recording and editing systems was the New England Digital PostPro system. The NED PostPro, one of the most advanced recording systems of its time, was far less powerful and versatile than my current PC-based studio, yet it sold for more than $200,000. In contrast, I put together my current computer audio production system for less than $3,000.

Although the capabilities of the NED PostPro now seem primitive compared to what I am able to do with my PC, even early hard-disk recording systems were a considerable advance over earlier tape-based technologies in terms of the power and control over sound they provided. New approaches to composition and editing were made possible by the powerful capabilities of these systems, yet their use was limited to those who were able to pay: Film and television production companies, wealthy pop music artists, and major record labels.

The Folk Music of the Future

Right now, cheap computer audio technologies (the technologies I'm writing about in this book) have changed everything. Sean Booth, one-half of the influential British experimental electronic music group Autechre, imagined computer music as the folk music of the future in an online interview with German music webzine *de:bug_texte* several years ago:

"Folk has always been economically defined. [Consider] indie [guitar band] music, the cheapest thing to buy in the 80s was probably a guitar and a little fuzzbox, so they made guitar and fuzzbox music...there is very little independent music that uses guitars anymore cause it just costs more then computers, end of story. Computers are just the cheapest way for people to make music now... The next few years there is going to be a really major upsurge cause now it is not only kids that are into electronic music or dance music that are using computers, it's everyone. Anyone who is into music is getting one." (From German ezine *de:bug_texte* at http://debug.tool42.com/cgi-bin/debug.pl?what=show &part=texte& ID=1825).

Booth's last point here, that people are using computers to create all kinds of music and not just "electronic" or "dance" music, is a clue to the larger significance of cheap digital recording technologies and Internet transmission for music. A computer-based recording studio provides any kind of aspiring artist with the tools to record, edit, mix, and arrange any kind of music and create a salable recording. With the addition of a few well-placed microphones, my PC system could be used to create, edit, mix, and distribute recordings of Appalachian bluegrass or garage rock, as well as electronic dance tracks. We are seeing the results of these developments today in terms of the huge explosion of amateur or semi-professional CDs of all genres being produced in home studios and sold both locally and through Web sites like CDBaby (http://www.cdbaby.com).

This is not happening just within the US—it is a global phenomenon. A survey of the underground music scene in Lebanon in the October 2001 issue of *The Wire* magazine described how dropping prices have made computer music production accessible even for more and more musicians in developing countries: "Faced with a lack of rehearsal spaces, rejection from record companies, and a very limited number of venues to perform in, certain aspiring musicians have instead embraced DIY computer music... Music geeks and freaks have thus been making their own blend of Lebanese bedroom electronica, available on privately pressed CD-Rs, in tiny editions that pass within circles of friends and artists."

Already today we can this see the folk music of the future on display in the computer music house parties and underground multimedia events here in Los Angeles that I have mentioned throughout this book, and similar scenes exist here and there in cities around the world. The technologies of computer music production and performance have become so inexpensive and portable that a whole new kind of high-tech jam session has become common. A group of musicians will bring their computers to a club or private home to play their music for each other and talk about the latest releases from their favorite computer artists, bringing to mind the kind of private jam sessions that were so important throughout the development of American jazz.

This so-called "bedroom electronica" scene has had little mainstream cultural impact so far, but it has already produced at least one genuine chart-busting artist, the Postal Service. Their music has even been labeled "lap-pop" by some critics because they rely heavily on laptop computers for production and performance. (Jimmy Tamborello, one-half of the band Postal Service, springs from the underground electronic music scene in Los Angeles and also releases and performs his own music under the name Dntel.)

Getting Easier

One of the main potential factors holding back the future growth of computer-based music as the folk music of the future is the complexity of creating music on a computer. It is a major task to learn one of today's massive DAWs like Digidesign's Pro Tools or Apple's Logic in any detail, requiring considerable time and effort. However, some of today's software tools for creating and performing music with computers have been made easier to use than ever before. Kim Cascone observes that many audio software interfaces have become simple enough to be played as "virtual instruments" that require little or no special technical training to use:

"Because the tools...embody advanced concepts of digital signal processing, their usage... tends to be based on experimentation rather than empirical investigation. It has been said that one does not need advanced training to use digital signal processing programs—just 'mess around' until you obtain the desired result." (Cascone, *ibid.*)

Of course, Cascone is assuming that the would-be computer musician is already at least computer-literate, but still it is true that creating music with a computer is already much easier than it has been in the past, and entry-level audio recording software packages like Apple's GarageBand are making it easier and easier for musicians to produce their own music with a computer.

Fight the Power

Many new Web sites related to digital music have sprung up to provide computer music artists with the knowledge and the software tools they need to create music and prepare it for online distribution. The creators of at least some of the Web sites devoted to distributing these new means of musical production consciously see themselves as aiding and abetting a revolutionary change in music's infrastructure—rebels fighting to free music from the capitalist grid in which it has so long been embedded. For example, the following manifesto from the "Digital Sampling and Shareware Resource" site refers to Jacques Attali's prediction that music would soon enter a new age of economic organization.

THE DIGITAL SAMPLING AND SHAREWARE RESOURCE

"Supplying a free tools and free samples resource for the computer user via the Internet is revolutionary in that for the first time in history anyone with access to a PC and a modem can equip themselves with the tools to create any and every sound imaginable, to compose professional quality electronic music, which can then be distributed to communities worldwide...

"The World Wide Web may be becoming more commercialized by the second, but the anti-capitalist ideals that are the Web's foundation, too, are growing, and are in fact presenting the commercial interests a most formidable challenge in that they (we) no longer have to solely rely on commercial entities for materials for production or distribution. The Digital Sampling and Shareware Resource (D.S.S.R.) Web site is one of an increasingly growing number of free resource sites whose sole purpose is for the free distribution of tools allowing people to create the conditions for taking pleasure in the act of composing. According to the theories put forth by Attali, then, the revolutionary age of Composition is now upon us."

(Vincent Baker writing on the Digital Sampling and Shareware Resource Web site at. Unfortunately, this particular site is no longer online but there are many other sites carrying on its mission of redistributing free software to music creators.)

This kind of anti-capitalist, anti-corporate music rhetoric is quite common in the MP3 scene and can be seen as a specific manifestation of the general "information wants to be free" ethos that continues to permeate many areas of Internet culture.

Postdigital Music as Social Prophecy

The software-fueled Internet-based computer music scene is providing opportunities for artists who might have been marginalized in the past, it is increasing opportunities for collaboration as well as accelerating the diffusion of musical ideas, and it is providing would-be composers with new tools for creating their music as well as distributing it.

Of course, these phenomena are still in their early stages, and admittedly we cannot know exactly how these trends will develop in the future. In my own work as a computer DJ, however, I often find myself weaving together DJ sets out of music I have obtained directly from musical creators around the world and thinking about how much the music world has changed already, and what direction these changes will take in the future. Beyond the effects I have cited above, for example, I am also beginning to feel that there is a certain quality of authenticity and a willingness to experiment reflected in much of today's "laptop electronica." The relatively low cost of the equipment necessary to produce this music has brought us to a position of enviable artistic autonomy for many of today's artists, who can afford not to "sell out" because they don't require much money to continue producing their music.

JACQUES ATTALI (Musicologist and Economist, France)

"Music is prophecy... It makes audible the new world that will gradually become visible, that will impose itself and regulate the order of things; it is not only the image of things, but the transcending of the everyday, the herald of the future."
(Attali, *Noise: the political economy of music*, English translation by Brian Massumi, page 11.)

In recent years we have witnessed the beginning of the transition to a new kind of music world made up of complex networks of relationships between producers and consumers, artists and audiences, composers and their sonic materials. An understanding of these complex musical networks may in turn serve us well as a potential guide to the directions in which our newly wired global society as a whole is evolving.

Changing Models of Consumption and Production: Getting into the Act

In *Any sound you can imagine*, author Paul Théberge argues that contemporary musicians are increasingly becoming consumers of music and technology as well as producers. Théberge's book is an insightful study of the relationship between the rapid advances in music technology over the past few decades and the accompanying changes that have occurred in contemporary musical practice. One of his main points is that the consumption of new musical technologies by musicians and composers has become a fundamental part of their approach to musical creation:

"In effect, musical production has become closely allied to a form of consumer practice, where the process of selecting the "right" pre-fabricated sounds and effects for a given musical context has become as important as "making" music in the first place. Musicians are not simply consumers of new technologies, rather their entire approach to music-making has been transformed so that consumption—the exercise of taste and choice—has become implicated in their musical practices at the most fundamental level."

"...the kind of consumer practice within musical production that I have described appears to have been complemented by a new kind of engagement with recorded material on the part of consumers, thus constituting a kind of production practice within consumption."

(From *Any sound you can imagine* by Paul Théberge, pages 200 and 251.)

Musicologist Timothy D. Taylor of Columbia University has made some similar points in his writing, arguing that we are on the threshold of a fundamental change in the relationship between modern audiences and the music they listen to:

"Until recently, music was pretty much used as manufactured—companies made recordings, consumers played them back... But, whereas in the past only someone with a studio could alter recorded music—with the main, and important, exception of hip hop musicians scratching their LPs—with digitally-recorded music, and with inexpensive software or even free Internet Web sites, it is now possible for music fans to remake and remix somebody else's music. With an MP3, one can play the music, or one can play with it, using any one of a number of available software packages; the listener can be a DJ, a remixer, a soundscape artist, and engineer. And much of the software that makes this possible is free or cheap..."

(Quote from an unpublished research paper by Timothy D. Taylor, "Digital Technology and New Modes of Music Consumption," page 4.)

The changes in the listener's relationship to music that are implied here (and that I have been pointing to at least obliquely throughout this book) may ultimately go some way towards reversing the separation between producers and consumers of music in Western societies. In many premodern societies, the communal practice of music and dance is something that everyone participates in, with religious and social significance that draws the community together. However, in modern Western societies, we have long made a powerful division between performers and listeners.

In the future, predicts cyber critic Arthur Kroker, "everybody will be a media hacker, recoding the electronic frontier at will" (Kroker, *Data Trash*, page 15) and we can see a glimpse of this future now in the new technologies available for listeners to interact with music rather than passively consume it.

> **ELIOT VAN BUSKIRK (Online Columnist for the CNET Music Center)**
>
> "...what had drawn me to the festival in the first place was the idea that fans would be tinkering with their favorite songs, so I started checking out the Beatnik Mixman DM2 Digital Music Mixer zone. Watching people use this device was fascinating. They'd start out just sort of poking buttons randomly to bring loops and samples into the mix. But soon enough, they'd find themselves entranced by their own mix, heads would start bobbing, and their faces would take on the focused look of a professional at work. You could almost see the moment when something clicked and listener became performer."
> (From van Buskirk's online column CNET MP3 Insider Dispatch 3 Aug 2001, "On watching fans create.")

Future of Electronic Music in the US?

After a boom in the mid-late 1990s, sales of so-called "electronica" are way down in the US. The American rave and club scene is far smaller than at its late-90s peak, and many trendy American college students listen to indie rock or hiphop rather than electronic music. This is a subject that often comes up when discussing computer music performance these days: Sure you can use the computer to perform, but do Americans really care about electronic music any more?

Although many industry observers might laugh at the idea that electronic music is still a significant force on the current American music scene, this perspective ignores the fundamental reality that virtually *all* popular music these days is electronic at some level. Few of today's studios record on tape any longer, and even country music albums are routinely recorded using an all-digital Pro Tools system or other hard disk recording-based setup. Most of the mixing, effects, editing, mastering, and other stages in the production process are all conducted in the digital realm, inside a computer.

Further, some of the most popular genres of American pop music have been almost completely transformed into electronic music without anyone quite noticing the fact. Much of today's chart-topping vocal pop music, as well as most R&B and hiphop tracks, are made at least in part with computers and software, and electronically-produced music can be heard all day long in any American city on most of the major FM radio stations. Today's top producers, such as the Neptunes or Timbaland, are just as reliant on the latest music technology as any of today's "electronic" artists. Top hiphop producers use many of the same hardware and software tools to make their music as do cutting-edge IDM artists like Richard Devine.

Looking at things this way, we can see that in fact, electronic music is one of the most popular types of music in the United States and has been for a long time. The distinction here is that different styles of electronic music have become dominant in the US than has been the case in Europe or Asia for the most part. In the words of industry observer Susan Mainzer, "dance music, in America especially, is all about hip hop beats," and I would agree to a large extent. Electronic music in America has recombined with the unique heritage of African-American music to create new forms and hybrids quite different from the electronic music popular in Germany or England, for example.

Many readers of this book may be primarily interested in using the computer to perform electronic dance and postdance styles like techno, breakbeat, or IDM. However, it is important to bear in mind that the computer can be a very powerful performance tool for other popular genres of music as well, and I have tried to emphasize this throughout. As seen in the chapter on digital DJing, even hiphop DJs and performers, long reluctant to give up their vinyl records, are now turning to computer-based performance via DJ programs like Serato Scratch that allow the use of turntables to control the playback of tracks from the computer. In many cases, the audience may not even be aware that a computer is being used in the performance, and this is not important. As always, it is the end musical result that counts, not the means used to achieve it.

EPILOGUE

Return from Kuala Lumpur

As I write the last pages of this book, I am on a Singapore Airlines flight from Southeast Asia back to California, where I have just finished playing laptop computer and bass guitar at clubs in Malaysia and Singapore with my band Digital Cutup Lounge. As our plane hurtles through the air high above the Pacific Ocean, I am reflecting on how much the music world has changed in recent years and how widely accepted using computers in performance has become.

When I first started using computer live in the late 1990s, it still seemed somewhat unlikely to me that live computer music would ever draw much of a popular audience. Even when I started my first laptop band and began doing live gigs in 1999, performing with a computer was still just a sideline to my work as a bassist, and I didn't think it would ever become an important part of my professional career. In fact, my partner Stephen and I treated the whole thing as something of a joke at first, often commenting to each other that in all likelihood only fellow computer geeks would be interested in seeing us play out live with our computers in a nightclub or concert setting.

Once, this prediction literally came true. After we did an interview with the technology writer from a local newspaper, the *Hong Kong Mail*, our next gig at the Jazz Club was packed with local computer programmers and technology freaks instead of the usual music fans and night-club enthusiasts.

However, as time went on and we did more and more gigs together as Digital Cutup Lounge, it quickly became clear to us that the computer was indeed a viable live performance tool. We began drawing more and more people to our live sets in Hong Kong clubs and DJ bars, which usually involved us DJing and mixing together electronic beats and sounds in combination with one or more jazz musicians who improvised along with our live mix.

At first it seemed that our use of computers for DJing and performing was perceived more as a novelty than anything else, and we got a lot of local publicity along the lines of "Wow! These guys are using computers *on stage!*" As time went on, though, computers in live music quickly became more or less accepted as normal and the novelty factor has receded, at least in some circles.

Our recent gigs in Asia re-emphasized this to me as I watched the reaction of the audiences in Malaysia and Singapore to our live computer band. No longer do the computers seem to bring a surprise from anyone watching us; rather, the use of computers seemed to have become taken for granted already, just as DJs playing records on turntables were earlier accepted as performers on nontraditional "instruments." Our recent audiences seemed more interested in the music we were playing rather than how we were playing it, which is just as it should be. No matter which of the technologies covered in this book you eventually end up using in your own live computer music performances, ultimately the most important thing is the musical result, the actual sound that people will hear at the end of your digital signal chain.

As an interesting side note, I used the same laptop to play these gigs that I have used to write this book, my trusty iBook G4 (see Figure 16.1).

Figure 16.1 Showdown in Kuala Lumpur: The author facing off with partner Stephen Ives in classic laptop battle action.

Fortunately, we didn't suffer any power surges or other electrical anomalies while we were playing or I would have lost all the work I did on the plane on the way over there...!

Index

A

D

E

H

I

J

K

S

T

X

Y

Z